D1308959

Database Design

Ryan K. Stephens
Ronald R. Plew

201 West 103rd St., Indianapolis, Indiana, 46290 USA

Database Design

Copyright © 2001 by Sams Publishing

All rights reserved. No part of this book shall be reproduced, stored in a retrieval system, or transmitted by any means, electronic, mechanical, photocopying, recording, or otherwise, without written permission from the publisher. No patent liability is assumed with respect to the use of the information contained herein. Although every precaution has been taken in the preparation of this book, the publisher and author assume no responsibility for errors or omissions. Nor is any liability assumed for damages resulting from the use of the information contained herein.

International Standard Book Number: 0-672-31758-3

Library of Congress Catalog Card Number: 99-63863

Printed in the United States of America

First Printing: November 2000

03   02   01   4   3   2

Trademarks

All terms mentioned in this book that are known to be trademarks or service marks have been appropriately capitalized. Sams cannot attest to the accuracy of this information. Use of a term in this book should not be regarded as affecting the validity of any trademark or service mark.

Warning and Disclaimer

Every effort has been made to make this book as complete and as accurate as possible, but no warranty or fitness is implied. The information provided is on an "as is" basis. The author and the publisher shall have neither liability nor responsibility to any person or entity with respect to any loss or damages arising from the information contained in this book.

ASSOCIATE PUBLISHER
Bradley L. Jones

EXECUTIVE EDITOR
Rosemarie Graham

ACQUISITIONS EDITOR
Geoff Mukhtar

DEVELOPMENT EDITOR
Songlin Qiu

MANAGING EDITOR
Charlotte Clapp

PROJECT EDITOR
Carol Bowers

COPY EDITORS
Rhonda Tinch-Mize
Bart Reed
Mary Ellen Stephenson

INDEXER
Bill Meyers

PROOFREADER
Katherin Bidwell

TECHNICAL EDITORS
James Drover
Beth Boal
Kai Soder

TECHNICAL REVIEWERS
Baya Pavliashvili
Rafe Colburn

MEDIA DEVELOPER
J.G. Moore

INTERIOR DESIGNER
Anne Jones

COVER DESIGNER
Anne Jones

PRODUCTION
Gloria Schurick

Overview

Contents

PART II Analyzing and Modeling Business Requirements 111

5 Gathering Business and System Requirements 113

About the Authors

Ryan K. Stephens is president and CEO of Perpetual Technologies, Inc. of Indianapolis, IN, a company specializing in Oracle consulting and training. Mr. Stephens teaches Oracle classes for Indiana University-Purdue University in Indianapolis, the Department of Defense, and companies in the commercial sector in the Central Indiana area. Mr. Stephens is a seasoned Oracle DBA, possessing more than 10 years' experience in Oracle database administration and development. Mr. Stephens has taken part in many other Sams' titles, including the lead on *Sams Teach Yourself SQL in 21 Days* (2nd and 3rd editions) and *Sams Teach Yourself SQL in 24 Hours* (1st and 2nd editions), and chapter contributions for some of the *Oracle Unleashed* titles. Mr. Stephens is also a programmer/analyst for the Indiana Army National Guard. Mr. Stephens resides in Indianapolis with his wife, Tina, and son Daniel, and is waiting on his second child who is only months away.

Ronald R. Plew is vice president and CIO of Perpetual Technologies, Inc. Mr. Plew performs several duties including teaching Oracle for Indiana University-Purdue University in Indianapolis and performing Oracle DBA support and consulting for the Department of Defense. He is a graduate of the Indiana Institute of Technology out of Fort Wayne. Mr. Plew is a member of the Indiana Army National Guard, where he is a programmer/analyst. He has been working with Oracle for more than 15 years in various capacities. Mr. Plew is the co-author of *Sams Teach Yourself SQL in 21 Days* (2nd and 3rd editions) and *Sams Teach Yourself SQL in 24 Hours* (1st and 2nd editions). Mr. Plew resides in Indianapolis with his wife, Linda.

Contributing Authors

Charles Mesecher is a 1976 graduate of Western Illinois University with a BS in Psychology and Education and an MBA from Webster University. He is currently employed by the U.S. Department of Defense as an Oracle DBA working on the Defense Finance and Accounting Service corporate database and corporate warehouse projects. Mr. Mesecher is also an associate professor in information systems at the University of Indianapolis, provides Oracle training for Indiana University-Purdue University in Indianapolis, and is a lead instructor for Perpetual Technologies, Inc.

Christopher Zeis is the Technical Manager for Perpetual Technologies, Inc. He also functions as an Oracle DBA, specializing in consulting, database configuration, and performance tuning. He is also an Oracle instructor for Indiana University-Purdue University in Indianapolis. Mr. Zeis is also an Oracle DBA for the Indiana Army National Guard. He resides in Indianapolis with his wife, Shannon.

John Newport received a Ph.D. in theoretical physics from Purdue University. Following graduate school, he worked 11 years as an avionics software consultant for the U.S. Navy. He is the founder of Newport Systems Incorporated, a consulting group specializing in software requirements and design. Dr. Newport is a member of the Institute of Electrical and Electronics Engineers. He is also a commercial pilot with instrument and multi-engine ratings. His wife, Nancy, is manager of an online database system.

About the Technical Editors and Reviewer

James Drover is a Solutions Consultant for Compaq's eBusiness Solutions Center. He provides end-user customers enterprise solutions that focus on high availability clusters and databases solutions. He had 10 years of production IT experience before joining Compaq in 1996 in the Canadian Benchmark Center focusing on database benchmarks and most recently eBusiness technologies.

Beth Boal has worked in the field of Information Technology since the early 80s, specializing in data skills, particularly logical and physical data modeling and relational database design. She has been a speaker at industry conferences on strategic planning and model management. She is currently President of The Knowledge Exchange Co., a training and consulting company that specializes in data and process modeling, teaching effective analysis skills and project management.

Baya Pavliashvili is a software consultant with G.A. Sullivan specializing in database design, development, and administration. Baya received his Bachelors degree in Computer Information Systems from Western Kentucky University. He is an MCSE, MCSD, and MCDBA.

Dedication

This book is dedicated to my birth mother, Rosemary Ooley, and to her daughter and my new sister, Christina Todd. Our paths crossed for the first time this year, making dreams come true for each of us.

Love you both,

—Ryan

Acknowledgments

There are many individuals to whom I owe a great deal of thanks and recognition for the successful completion of this book. First, I would like to extend my appreciation to my family, mainly to my wife and son Daniel, for their patience during the length of this project. Those of you out there who have also written books or other lengthy manuscripts know what it's like to sacrifice time away from your family. I also extend my appreciation to the editorial staff at Sams—these guys really care about the quality of the book, are thorough in the work they do, and seem to enjoy it. Thanks also to Jim Abbott for some of the diagrams generated and used in this book, and to Nancy Kidd for her contribution. The timely completion of this book would not have been possible without the aid of my coauthor Ron and the contributing authors Chuck Mesecher, Chris Zeis, and John Newport. It is a pleasure to work with each of you. With sincerity, thanks again to everyone.

—Ryan

I want to thank and tell my family how much I love them: my wife, Linda; my mother, Betty; my children Leslie, Nancy, Angela, and Wendy; my grandchildren Andy, Ryan, Holly, Morgan, Schyler, Heather, Gavin, Regan, Cameron, and Caleigh; my sister Arleen; my brothers Mark and Dennis; my sons-in-law Jason and Dallas. Love all of you!!

—Poppy

Tell Us What You Think!

As the reader of this book, *you* are our most important critic and commentator. We value your opinion and want to know what we're doing right, what we could do better, what areas you'd like to see us publish in, and any other words of wisdom you're willing to pass our way.

As an Executive Editor for Sams, I welcome your comments. You can fax, email, or write me directly to let me know what you did or didn't like about this book—as well as what we can do to make our books stronger.

Please note that I cannot help you with technical problems related to the topic of this book, and that due to the high volume of mail I receive, I might not be able to reply to every message.

When you write, please be sure to include this book's title and author as well as your name and phone or fax number. I will carefully review your comments and share them with the author and editors who worked on the book.

Fax:	317-581-4770
Email:	Rosemarie.Graham@samspublishing.com
Mail:	Rosemarie Graham
	Executive Editor
	Sams Publishing
	201 West 103rd Street
	Indianapolis, IN 46290 USA

Introduction

Designing a database is much like designing anything else: a building, a car, a roadway through a city, or a book such as this. Much care must be taken to plan a design. If time is not taken to carefully plan the design of an object, the quality of the end product will suffer. Many approaches can be taken to explain database design. It can be debated indefinitely what to include, what not to include, and in what order to present the material. This book takes an approach to database design that focuses mainly on the logical methods involved in deriving a database structure. We explain the thought process involved in converting an organization's data storage needs into a relational database. This book is for any level of user, from beginner to expert, who is interested in designing a relational database management system.

Another approach we have taken in this book is the extensive use of figures in many of the chapters. It is a given fact that people tend to learn better by visualizing the material being discussed. Many books that we have seen on the market lack adequate visual presentation. The authors of this book are either current or former university-level instructors. Our experience is that a hands-on and visual approach aids the students tremendously in their understanding of the material. Although this is not a hands-on book, the readers can easily practice the material discussed in this book by expanding on the examples we show and conjuring further examples of their own.

Who Should Read This Book?

This book is for any individual who wants to learn how to design a relational database from the ground up. The concepts covered in this book are beneficial to a wide variety of individuals in the business community, as all types of individuals are involved in most database design efforts.

Some of the individuals who will get the most out of this book include

- Database administrators who desire to increase their understanding of modeling and design concepts to increase their effectiveness of administering a relational database management system, as well as increasing their ability to provide valuable guidance and assistance to developers.
- Developers who desire to learn how to mold a relational database based on the business needs of an organization.
- Developers and other technical team members (such as database administrators) who are involved in the modernization of an organization's old database using the relational model.

- Business owners and management who possess a dire need to provide their organization with a database with which to effectively manage the organization's data to increase overall productivity.

- Anybody else interested in learning to design a relational database, including those interested in an information technology career, or those trying to get their foot in the door with an organization that uses, or plans to use, a relational database management system.

What Makes This Book Different?

Many books have been written about database design, so why this book? As various good books exist on this topic, many have fallen behind in technology, whereas others have left out many concepts related to database design which we feel are key. For example, many database design books fail to adequately cover normalization, which happens to be an integral part of database design. Some design books discuss databases in general, and some focus on specific database models such as relational or object-oriented. For many reasons, which will become evident as you read this book, the relational database is the best choice for most situations in today's business world. For this reason, we feel there is a need for an updated book on relational design, which will include previously neglected features, as well as include features that have evolved since the inception of the relational database years ago.

Some of the key features covered in this book that increases value over other related titles on the market are

- A strong focus on logical modeling and the thought process behind designing a usable database for an organization.

- A detailed discussion of normalization, with many practical examples to ease the complexity of the subject.

- A detailed discussion of change control, also referred to by some organizations as change management or configuration management.

- The extensive use of figures and examples to illustrate important design concepts.

- Discussions of the use of automated design tools during the design process.

- Thorough discussions of data and process modeling techniques to ensure all requirements have been gathered to design a database that will assist an organization with reaching its goals.

- The practical application of design concepts to a sample computer training company we created for this book, called TrainTech.

- A practical case study.

Relational databases have been around for many years, and will be around for many years to come because of their capability to manage large amounts of data, their performance, and reliability. There are various modern databases to choose from as alternates to the relational database. However, the relational database is the clearest choice in most situations if the organization does not want to gamble with the integrity of its data.

This book does not cover Object-Oriented (OO) and Object-Relational (OR) databases significantly enough to fully understand their concepts. We do, however, provide broad comparisons between these database models in order to clarify the reader's understanding of the relational database's architecture, its current place in information technology, and its possible future. The comparisons between different database models also help to identify the advantages of the relational model.

Structured Query Language (SQL) is the standard language used to communicate with any relational database. SQL is referenced in many places throughout this book. However, in no way does this book intend to teach the reader how to write SQL code. A good knowledge of SQL is assumed for an individual wishing to design a relational database. Other books can be purchased, in addition to this one, to supplement the knowledge presented here. It is logical to have at least some experience with a relational database and understand some level of SQL before learning about database design—although SQL can be learned after database design is understood. The important thing is that the designer has a good understanding of both SQL and the concepts of relational database design before attempting to begin a design project.

Many Relational Database Management System vendors provide products in today's market. Some of the most popular RDBMS products include Oracle, Microsoft SQL Server, Sybase, Informix, DB2, and Microsoft Access. Oracle is the current leader in the market by far. Because of our knowledge of and experience with Oracle, some examples in this book that require SQL code are shown using Oracle's implementation. SQL, though a standard language, might vary in exact syntax from vendor to vendor. All concepts in this book that are represented by vendor-specific examples are applicable to any RDBMS.

Computer Aided Systems Engineering (CASE), also called *Computer Aided Software Engineering*, is the use of an automated tool to design a database or application software using a given methodology. CASE is a traditional name that many software development vendors are trying to avoid; it has obtained a bad name because of misperceptions of the various tools' capabilities. In this book, we use the term *Automated Design (AD)* tool to describe various tools that help automate the task of designing a database. A tool is exactly that—a tool; to be used to assist the database designer, who should already be knowledgeable of a particular database design methodology.

NOTE

One topic included in this book that might be controversial to some individuals is business process modeling. Although business process modeling relates more to the development of an end-user application versus a database, process models can be used to cross-check data elements that have been defined for an organization. We feel that the inclusion of process modeling concepts are important as related to the ensurance of complete data definition for an organization.

Table Conventions Used in This Book

Two types of tables have been used in this book to provide the reader with various examples: numbered and unnumbered tables.

- Numbered tables—for example, Table 3.1 for Figure 3.1 of Chapter 3—are used to structure certain examples in a format that is most readable. These tables are used to list items and their descriptions or components, or to show data that resides in a database table.

    An example of a numbered table follows.

Table I.1   PEOPLE

NAME	ADDRESS	CITY	STATE	ZIP
STEVE SMITH	123 BROADWAY	INDIANAPOLIS	IN	46227
MARK JONES	456 MAIN ST	INDIANAPOLIS	IN	46238

- Unnumbered tables are primarily used to illustrate database tables, with or without data. The term *table* is one of the most important terms when discussing relational databases. Note the difference between database tables and numbered tables embedded in the chapter text.

    An example of an unnumbered table follows.

INSTRUCTOR	COURSES_TAUGHT	DEPARTMENT
#instructor_id	#course	#department _id
fname	#department_id	department_name
mi	#section	department_address
lname	#semester	
	#year	
	instructor_id	

How This Book Is Organized

This book is arranged into four sections, logically divided for a clearer understanding to the reader. Each section in the book begins with a brief overview of the coverage in the section. These sections are briefly described in Table I.2.

Table I.2 Book Content Overview

Book Section	Brief Description of Content
Part I	Part I provides an overview of database design, beginning with basic database fundamentals, covering different database models that can be used, discussing the process of planning a design effort, and ending by discussing the phases of design according to the methodology selected.
Part II	Part II is the largest section of the book, focusing on the analysis and modeling of business requirements, from initial interviews to the creation of the logical model in the form of *Entity Relationship Diagrams (ERD)* and process models. This section represents the most significant steps involved in database design.
Part III	Part III discusses the physical design of the database. This section discusses the conversion of the logical model covered in the last section into tables, columns, constraints, and views. This section ends with a case study showing a rapid design of a practical database.
Part IV	Believe it or not, there is life after design. This section covers topics such as the implementation of database security, managing changes to a database throughout its life, and the thought process involved in considering redesign for a legacy database.
Appendixes	We have included useful appendixes to supplement the content of the book, to include an example of a physical relational database implementation and diagrams of some common database designs with which most readers can relate.
Glossary	A glossary is included as a quick reference of definitions for your convenience.

Many hands were involved in the collaboration of effort to accomplish the writing of this book. Much planning and revision took place to the table of contents in order to most logically present the material to you as the reader for better understanding. We hope that you enjoy learning from this book as much as we enjoyed writing it. There is much to be learned. This book should establish a fundamental foundation on which you can build in order to thoroughly understand the concepts of relational database design, at the same time venturing into future technology, as it is constantly being adapted to satisfy the needs of modern organizations.

What's on the Web Site?

As a supplement to the book, we have provided additional material to assist you on Macmillan's Web site. The URL of the book's Web site is www.mcp.com. After entering this book's ISBN and pressing the Search button, you will be presented with the book's page where you can download the Web contents for this book by following the instructions.

The information found on the Web site includes the following:

- A link to the authors' Web site
- Web links for more information on database models
- A sample change control form as shown in Chapter 16, "Change Control"
- A sample detailed ERD that has been expanded upon from Chapter 14, "Applying Database Design Concepts"
- Links to third-party vendors for automated design software
- A database design self test

Note that the Web contents for this book are presented in a .pdf file format (an Adobe Acrobat document). You must install the Acrobat Reader 4.0 on your computer in order to read the Web contents in the .pdf format. If you are not familiar with the Adobe Acrobat Reader and its features, simply open the Acrobat Reader and select the Reader Online Guide item from the Help menu. It will tell you how to navigate an Acrobat document and how to use the icons on the menu bar of the Acrobat Reader screen. Adobe Acrobat Reader 4.0 can be downloaded at Adobe's Web site: www.adobe.com.

Overview of Database Design

IN THIS PART

Chapter 1, "Understanding Database Fundamentals," begins by defining a database and explaining database-related concepts. Terminology is briefly covered in this chapter that will be used throughout the remainder of the book. This chapter also discusses the trademarks of a well-designed database.

Chapter 2, "Exploration of Database Models," discusses the main types of database models that have been used to store organizations' data. The different types of models are compared to one another, with focus on the relational database model. This chapter also discusses the selection of a particular database model, as well as the selection of database software.

Chapter 3, "Database Design Planning," defines database design and explains the importance of design. At this point, the reader understands the basic fundamentals of databases and is ready to begin thinking about design. This chapter discusses the thought process in preparing for a design project, as far as devising a work plan, designating a design team, assigning tasks, selecting a design methodology, and using an Automated Design (AD) tool.

Chapter 4, "The Database Design Life Cycle," discusses common database methodologies in detail, such as the traditional and Barker methods. This chapter also covers key processes involved in the design of a database such as data definition, process definition, and business rule definition. Finally, this chapter covers the basic life cycle of a database, referring to change management that is covered in more detail later in the book.

Understanding Database Fundamentals

IN THIS CHAPTER

Before designing a database, it is important to understand the basic fundamentals of databases and how they are used. Everyone uses databases on a regular basis, some manual and others automated. The reasons databases are used are important, as these reasons help determine how to begin designing a database for a particular business.

Database environments are also important to understand from a broad perspective when designing a database. A database environment consists of the hardware and operating system platform on which the database resides. A database environment also includes a means through which the user can access the database, such as a network. The database environment can help determine what type of database model should be used, and how the database will be implemented and managed.

Some basic fundamentals exist that a database designer must understand before plunging into the seemingly bottomless pit of a major corporate database design effort. This chapter covers those basic concepts and will, if understood, forge a path toward the successful design of a database. Some key concepts discussed in this chapter are

- Business elements used to define a database
- Basic database elements
- Data integrity
- Design concepts

Business modeling deals with capturing the needs of a business from a business perspective. The first section deals with processes, business rules, and categorizations of business data. Until they are involved in a design effort, many people fail to realize the importance of understanding the intricacies of a business. What makes the business tick? What kind of data does the business maintain? Is the data static, or does it change often? What business rules affect how the data is stored and accessed? All these questions must be answered before proceeding with any design effort. Basic database terminology involves the concepts required to understand most modern database structures. Design terminology involves terms that are relevant to the process of evaluating and converting a business model into a database model. Here, we discuss design methodology. It is important that you select the most appropriate methodology for your particular situation. What tools will be used during the design effort? We also discuss the difference between database design and application design.

Before getting into design, it is also important to understand the hallmarks of a good database. The following points are commonly used to determine the quality of a database: the database's storage ability, data protection and security, data accuracy, database performance, and data redundancy.

What Is a Database?

A *database* is a mechanism that is used to store information, or data. Information is something that we all use on a daily basis for a variety of reasons. With a database, users should be able to store data in an organized manner. Once the data is stored, it should be easy to retrieve information. Criteria can be used to retrieve information. The way the data is stored in the database determines how easy it is to search for information based on multiple criteria. Data should also be easy to add to the database, modify, and remove.

A *legacy database* is simply a database that is currently in use by a company. The term legacy implies that the database has been around for several years. The term legacy can also imply that the existing database is not up to date with current technology. When a company has determined to design a new database, the existing database is considered the legacy database.

Examples of databases with which we are all familiar include

- Personal address books
- Telephone books
- Card catalogs at libraries
- Online bookstores
- Personal finance software
- Road maps

Some of these databases are static, whereas others are dynamic.

For example, a road map is a static database (in an abstract sense) that contains information such as states, cities, roadways, directions, distance, and so forth. By looking at a map, you can quickly establish your destination as related to your current location. Once the road map is printed, it is distributed and used by travelers to navigate between destinations. The information does not change on a map. There is no way to change the information on a map without printing new maps and redistributing them. A telephone book is also a static database because residential and commercial information is listed for a particular year. As with a road map, telephone book entries cannot be changed once the book is printed (unless they are changed by hand).

A personal address book is a good example of a dynamic database that many of us use on a daily basis. The address book is dynamic in the sense that entries are changed in the book as friends and family move or change telephone numbers. New friends can be added and old friends can be removed, although this can be done by hand. An online bookstore is also a dynamic database because orders are constantly being placed for books. On a regular basis, new authors and titles are added, titles are removed, inventory is updated, and so forth.

What Are the Uses of a Database?

One of the most traditional manual processes with which most of us are familiar is the management of information in a file cabinet. Normally, folders are sorted and stored within drawers in a file cabinet. Information is stored in individual folders in each drawer. There might even be a sequence of file cabinets, or several rooms full of file cabinets. In order to find a record on an individual, you might have to go to the right room, and then to the right cabinet, to the right drawer, then to the right folder. Whether a manual process or a database is utilized, organization is the key to managing information.

Other examples of manual processes might include

- Working with customers over the phone
- Taking orders from a customer
- Shipping a product to a customer
- Interviewing an employee
- Searching for a particular resumé in a file cabinet
- Balancing a checkbook
- Filling out and submitting a deposit slip
- Counting today's profits
- Comparing accounts payable and accounts receivable
- Managing time sheets

As you can probably deduct on your own, many of the manual processes mentioned can be fully automated. Some manual processes will always require manual intervention. A database is useful in automating as much work as possible to enhance manual processes.

Some of the most common uses for a database include

- Tracking of long-term statistics and trends
- Automating manual processes to eliminate paper shuffling
- Managing different types of transactions performed by an individual or business
- Maintaining historic information

An example of long-term statistics and trends can be seen with a product ordering system. Take a televised product advertising and ordering program, such as QVC. Statistics might need to be gathered concerning the sales for each month during the year for several years, the products sold the most during certain time periods, the products sold the most overall, the frequency of orders for a particular product, and so on. Trends might involve the products that are the hottest, when the products are most popular, and what types of individuals tend to order certain types of products. Statistics and trends might help determine the type of products to offer, when to offer the products, what type of discount to offer, and the time of day or night each product is advertised.

A database might exist to minimize or eliminate the amount of paper shuffling. For instance, imagine that you work in the human resources department for a company and that you are responsible for hundreds of resumés. The traditional method for storing resumés is in a file cabinet. The resumés are probably alphabetized by the individual's last name, which makes a resumé easy to find if you are searching by name. What if you wanted to find all resumés for individuals who had a certain skill? With a manual filing system, you would find yourself reading every resumé looking for the desired skill, which might take hours. If resumé information was stored in a database, you could quickly search for individuals with a particular skill, which might only take seconds.

There are two types of relational databases, each of which is associated with particular uses. A particular relational database type is used based on the required uses of the data. These two types are the Online Transactional Processing Database and the Online Analytical Processing database.

A *transactional*, or *Online Transactional Processing (OLTP)*, database is one that is used to process data on a regular basis. A good example of a transactional database is one for class scheduling and student registrations. Say that a university offers a couple hundred classes. Each class has at least 1 professor and can have anywhere between 10 and 300 students. Students are continually registering and dropping classes. Classes are added, removed, modified, and scheduled. All of this data is dynamic and requires a great deal of input from the end user. Imagine the paperwork involved and the staff required in this situation without the use of a database.

An *Online Analytical Processing* (OLAP) database is one whose main purpose is to supply end-users with data in response to queries that are submitted. Typically, the only transactional activity that occurs in an OLAP database concerns bulk data loads. OLAP data is used to make intelligent business decisions based on summarized data, company performance data, and trends. The two main types of OLAP databases are Decision Support Systems (DSS) and Data Warehouses. Both types of databases are normally fed from one or more OLTP databases, and are used to make decisions about the operations of an organization. A data warehouse differs from a DSS in that it contains massive volumes of data collected from all parts of an organization; hence the name warehouse. Data warehouses must be specially designed to accommodate the large amounts of data storage required and enable acceptable performance during data retrievals.

Historic information can be maintained. *Historic* data is usually related to and often a part of a transactional database. Historic data may also be a significant part of an OLAP database. For companies that desire to keep data for years, it is usually not necessary to store all data online. Doing so will increase the overall amount of data, which means that more information will have to be read when retrieving and modifying information. Historic information is typically stored offline, perhaps on a dedicated server, disk drive, or tape device. For example, in the infrequent event that a user needs to access corporate data from three years ago, the data can be restored from tape long enough for the appropriate data to be retrieved and used. The question is, how long should data be stored online? This question can only be answered by the customer.

Who Uses a Database?

Database users exist for just about any organization that you can imagine. Think of individuals such as bankers, lawyers, accountants, customer service representatives, and data entry clerks. Now try to imagine how each of these individuals might use a database. For example, a banker would use a database to keep track of different individual and business accounts, lines of credit, personal loans, business loans, and so forth. If a customer wants to close his account, which is worth, say, 10,000 dollars, it would be nice for the banker to verify the individual's personal information.

We all use databases, often unknowingly. When you use your ATM card to withdraw money from a bank, a database is accessed by you indirectly. As money is withdrawn, the dollar amount of your funds must be adjusted. For example, if money is withdrawn from the checking account, the given amount is deducted from the checking account. If money is transferred from the savings to checking account to cover a bad check, a given amount is credited to the checking account and deducted from the savings account.

Database Environments

A *database environment* is a habitat, if you will, in which the database for a business resides. Within this database environment, users have means for accessing the data. Users might come from within the database environment, or might originate from outside the environment. Users perform all different types of tasks, and their needs vary as they are mining for data, modifying data, or attempting to create new data. Also within the environment, certain users might be either physically or logically restrained from accessing the data.

Various possible environments exist for a database. In the following subsections, we provide an overview of the three most common database environments:

- The mainframe environment
- The client/server environment
- The internet computing environment

Mainframe Environment

The traditional environment for earlier database systems was the mainframe environment. The *mainframe environment* consisted mainly of a powerful mainframe computer that allowed multiple user connections. Multiple dumb terminals are networked to the mainframe computer, allowing the user to communicate with the mainframe. The terminals are basically extensions of the mainframe, they are not independent computers. The term *dumb terminal* implies that these terminals do no thinking of their own. They rely on the mainframe computer to perform all processing.

One of the main problems in the mainframe environment is the limitations that are placed on the user. For example, the dumb terminal can only communicate with the main computer. Other tasks might include manual processes, the use of a word processor, or a personal computer that does not interface with the main computer. Most companies today have migrated their systems to the client/server environment for reasons that are discussed in the next section. Figure 1.1 illustrates the mainframe environment.

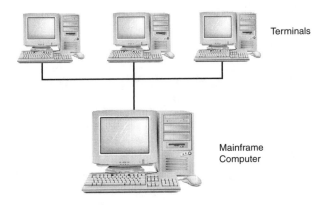

Terminals

Mainframe
Computer

FIGURE 1.1
Terminal connections to a mainframe computer.

Client/Server Environment

A number of problems that existed in the mainframe environment were solved with client/server technology. The *client/server environment* involves a main computer, called a server, and one or more personal computers that are networked to the server. The database resides on the server, a separate entity from the personal computer. Each user who requires access to the database on the server should have her own PC.

Because the PC is a separate computer system, an application is developed and installed on the PC through which the user can access the database on the server. The application on the client passes requests for data or transactions over the network directly to the database on the host server. Information is passed over the network to the database using open database connectivity (ODBC) or other vendor specific networking software. One of the problems in the client/server environment is that when a new version of the application is developed, the application must be reinstalled and reconfigured on each client machine, which can be quite tedious and very time-consuming.

Although additional costs are incurred by establishing and maintaining an application on the PC, there are also many benefits. The main benefit is that the PC, because it has its own resources (CPU, memory, disk storage), can be involved in some of the application processing, thereby taking some of the overall load from the server and distributing work to all of the clients. Because PCs can "think" on their own and run other applications, users can be more productive. For example, a user can be connected to the database on the server while simultaneously working with a document and checking email. Figure 1.2 illustrates the client/server environment.

NOTE

The client/server environment is probably the most widely implemented database environment today.

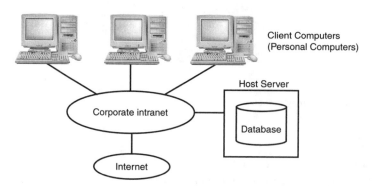

FIGURE 1.2

Database accessibility in a client/server environment.

Internet Computing Environment

Internet computing is very similar to client/server computing. As with the client/server environment, a server, a network, and one or more PCs are involved. Internet computing is unique because of its reliance on the Internet. In a client/server environment, a user might be restricted to access systems that are within the corporate intranet. In many cases, client machines can still access databases outside of the corporate intranet, but additional customized software might be involved.

One aspect of Internet computing that makes it so powerful is the transparency of the application to the end user. In the Internet computing environment, the application need only be installed on one server, called a *Web server*. A user must have an Internet connection and a supported Web browser installed on the PC. The Web browser is used to connect to the destination URL of the Web server. The Web server, in turn, accesses the database in a fashion supported by the application, and returns the requested information to the user's Web browser. The results are displayed on the user's PC by the Web browser. End-user application setup and maintenance is simplified in the Internet computing environment because there is nothing to install, configure, or maintain on the user's PC. The application need only be installed, configured, and modified on the Web server, reducing the risk of inconsistent configurations and incompatible versions of software between client and server machines. When changes are made to the application, changes are made in one location; for example, on the Web server.

Figure 1.3 illustrates a sample Internet computing environment.

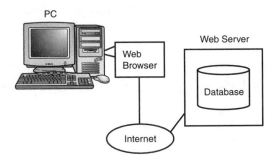

FIGURE 1.3
Database accessibility in an internet computing environment.

NOTE

More companies are making their databases available to the Internet. Because anyone with a computer and an Internet connection can access the Internet, strict security measures must be taken to ensure that unauthorized users are not allowed access to sensitive data. Features such as firewalls and database security mechanisms must be implemented to protect data from hackers and other users with malicious intentions. Database security will be discussed in Chapter 15, "Implementing Database Security."

In the Internet computing environment, many organizations are integrating the concept of the N-Tier architecture. The N-Tier architecture is a concept similar to a middle tier or three tier computer architecture. In a three tier architecture, there is a client layer, an application layer, and a server or database layer. The "N" in N-Tier stands for any number of tiers to complete the transaction or request.

From Where Does a Database Originate?

Business modeling is the process of evaluating and capturing the daily tasks performed by a business, and the origination of any database. The foremost task in business modeling is taking time to talk to the individuals in the company who make decisions, those who work face to face with the data, and others who perform tasks that might or might not be related to the storage requirements of the database. When designing a database, the designers must understand the business as well as the users of the proposed database. Failure to fully understand the business usually yields an incomplete or inaccurate data model, or both. All businesses have a need to maintain data in some form, and it is the responsibility of the designer to extract a company's needs and formulate those needs into a working model, which will eventually become a functional database with an easy-to-use application for the end user.

The following subsections explain some basic concepts involved in business modeling. These concepts include business rules, business processes, data, analysis, entities, attributes, and re-engineering.

Business Rules

Businesses have rules. These rules affect how the business operates in many different ways. From the perspective of designing a database, business rules are important because they tell us how data is created, modified, and deleted within an organization. Rules place restrictions and limitations on data, and ultimately help determine the structure of the database, as well as the application used to access the database. Every company has its own rules. Different companies have different needs when storing data; there is no standard set of business rules.

Two broad categories of business rules associated with the design of a database system are as follows:

- Database-oriented
- Application-oriented

Database-oriented rules are those that affect the logical design of the database. These rules affect how the data is grouped and how tables within the database are related to one another. These rules also affect the range of valid values for data, such as constraints placed on columns.

Application-oriented rules deal with the operation of an application through which a user interfaces with the database. Data edits can be built into the application interface as a check and balance against the constraints that reside in the database. Application-oriented rules are more directly related to how processes are conducted and what methods are used to access data in the database.

Business Processes

Business processes deal with the daily activities that take place. Business processes are conducted either manually, by individuals within the organization, or they are automated. Businesses function through business processes. Data is entered into the database through some business process. Business rules affect how the data can be entered. For example, when a customer orders a book from an online bookstore, several business processes are invoked. Some of the business processes involved in this scenario might include

1. An order is received from a customer.
2. The inventory is checked for product availability.
3. The customer's order is confirmed.
4. The warehouse is contacted.
5. The product and invoice are shipped to the customer.

Some of these processes directly affect the data, whereas other processes might not be directly associated with the data. For example, an entry might or might not be made to the database every time the warehouse is contacted. However, each one of these rules help determine the requirements for the database and the application interface.

Information and Data

Information is defined as the knowledge of something; particularly, an event, situation, or knowledge derived based on research or experience. *Data* is any information related to an organization that should be stored for any purpose according to the requirements of an organization. For example, an online bookstore must keep track of book titles, authors, customers, orders, book reviews, book editions, shipping, and much more information. The data that each organization uses and stores is obviously different for each individual company. Data stored is used to make business decisions, allowing an organization to simply function, or function more effectively.

There are basically two types of date that reside in any database:

- Static, or historic
- Dynamic, or transactional

Static, or *historic* data is seldom or never modified once stored in the database. For example, historic data for a company can be stored offline and accessed only when needed. Historic data never changes. Certain historic data can be used to track trends or business statistics, and can be used later to make business decisions. *Dynamic*, or *transactional* data, is data that is frequently modified once stored in the database. At a minimum, most companies have dynamic data. Most companies have a combination of both dynamic and static data. For example, an online bookstore has mostly transactional data because customer orders are constantly being processed. An online bookstore, however, might also need to track statistics, such as the book categories that have had the highest sales in the Midwest over the past five years.

Requirements Analysis

Requirements analysis is the process of analyzing the needs of a business and gathering system requirements from the end user that will eventually become the building blocks for the new database. During requirements analysis, business rules and processes are taken into consideration. Interviews are conducted with the end user, as well as other individuals who have a knowledge of the system or business rules. Information is gathered from the legacy system if it exists, as well as individuals who participate in the daily business processes. This information will all be integrated into the proposed system.

As discussed later in this book, each phase of the system development process will involve deliverables. In the analysis phase of a system, a requirements document should be established that outlines the following basic information:

- Objectives and goals of the business as it pertains to the proposed system
- A list of proposed requirements for the system
- A list of business processes and rules
- Documentation for current business processes, or documentation from the legacy system

After this document is established, it will be used to drive the design effort. The document will probably need to be revised throughout the design of the system. Chapter 5, "Gathering Business and System Requirements," provides a more detailed discussion of necessary documentation.

NOTE

Documentation is important for any system. What better time to start than during the initial analysis of the business? Documentation should be strictly maintained and revised as needed during the life of any system, although most companies seem to have serious shortcomings in this area. The more research and documentation performed up front will make the entire design effort, as well as subsequent design or redesign efforts, go more smoothly.

Entities

An *entity* is a business object that represents a group, or category of data. For example, a category of information associated with an online bookstore is book titles. Another category is authors because an author might have written many books. Entities are objects that are used to logically separate data. In Chapter 10, "Modeling Business Processes," entity modeling is discussed in detail.

Attributes

An *attribute* is a sub-group of information within an entity. For example, suppose you have an entity for book titles. Within the book titles' entity, several attributes are found, such as the actual title of the book, the publisher of the book, the author, the date the book was published, and so on. Attributes are used to organize specific data within an entity.

Business Process Re-engineering

Business process re-engineering (BPR) is the task of reworking business processes in order to streamline the operations of an organization. BPR may involve redesigning an existing system in order to improve methods for storing and accessing the data in conjunction with the business processes that have been refined. If an existing system is re-engineered, it is important to understand how the existing system works, and to understand the deficiencies of the current system. What will the company gain by creating a new system based on the refinements of processes? Will the company's goals be met with the new system? What costs will be involved during the re-engineering process? A company must decide whether the costs and efforts required to design a new system will be offset by the benefits gained. These concepts are explored further in Chapter 17, "Analyzing Legacy Databases for Redesign."

What Elements Comprise a Database?

This section deals mainly with the objects that comprise a database. Several concepts are worthy of coverage within the scope of the database as it relates to database design. As you progress through the book, you will see how the origination of business information and databases, which was discussed in the last section, is formulated into database elements. The intent here is to provide a brief coverage of basic database elements to provide you with a basic understanding of the elements found in a database. Each of these elements are explained thoroughly throughout the book, eventually clarifying the processing of designing a database.

Several topics are discussed in the following sections. These topics include:

- The database schema
- Schema objects
- Tables
- Fields and columns
- Records and rows
- Keys
- Relationships
- Data types

> **NOTE**
>
> Many of the concepts in the following sections relate to all databases, whereas others are specific to modern databases, which are discussed in detail in Chapter 2, "Exploration of Database Models."

Database Schema

A *schema* is quite simply a group of related objects in a database. Within a schema, objects that are related have relationships to one another, as discussed earlier. There is one owner of a schema, who has access to manipulate the structure of any object in the schema. A schema does not represent a person, although the schema is associated with a user account that resides in the database.

The three models associated with a schema are as follows:

- The *conceptual* model, also called the *logical model*, is the basic database model, which deals with organizational structures that are used to define database structures such as tables and constraints.

- The *internal* model, also called the *physical model*, deals with the physical storage of the database, as well as access to the data, such as through data storage in tables and the use of indexes to expedite data access. The internal model separates the physical requirements of the hardware and the operating system from the data model.

- The *external* model, or *application interface*, deals with methods through which users may access the schema, such as through the use of a data input form. The external model allows relationships to be created between the user application and the data model. Figure 1.4 depicts a schema in a relational database.

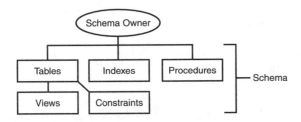

FIGURE 1.4
Collection of objects that comprise a database schema.

NOTE

A schema object is an object that resides within a schema. The most typical object found in a database is a table. Other types of objects can reside in a schema, such as indexes, constraints, views, and procedures.

The table is the most fundamental element found in a database schema. Columns and rows are associated with tables. Tables, columns, and rows are discussed in the following subsections.

Table

A *table* is the primary unit of physical storage for data in a database. When a user accesses the database, a table is usually referenced for the desired data. Multiple tables might comprise a database, therefore a relationship might exist between tables. Because tables store data, a table requires physical storage on the host computer for the database.

Figure 1.5 illustrates tables in a schema. Each table in the figure is related to at least one other table. Some tables are related to multiple tables.

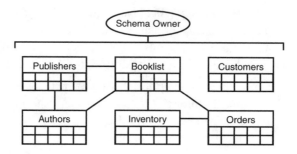

FIGURE 1.5
Database tables and their relationships.

Four types of tables are discussed in this book, each of which are more thoroughly detailed in Chapter 11, "Designing Tables:"

- Data tables store most of the data found in a database.
- Join tables are tables used to create a relationship between two tables that would otherwise be unrelated.
- Subset tables contain a subset of data from a data table.
- Validation tables, often referred to as *code* tables, are used to validate data entered into other database tables.

Tables are used to store the data that the user needs to access. Tables might also have constraints attached to them, which control the data allowed to be entered into the table. An entity from the business model is eventually converted into a database table.

Columns

A *column*, or *field*, is a specific category of information that exists in a table. A column is to a table what an attribute is to an entity. In other words, when a business model is converted into a database model, entities become tables and attributes become columns. A column represents one related part of a table and is the smallest logical structure of storage in a database. Each column in a table is assigned a data type. The assigned data type determines what type of values that can populate a column. When visualizing a table, a column is a vertical structure in the table that contains values for every row of data associated with a particular column.

In Figure 1.6, columns within the Customers table are shown. Each column is a specific category of information. All of the data in a table associated with a field is called a column.

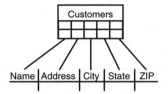

FIGURE 1.6
Columns in a database table.

Rows

A *row* of data is the collection of all the columns in a table associated with a single occurrence. Simply speaking, a row of data is a single record in a table. For example, if there are 25,000 book titles with which a bookstore deals, there will be 25,000 records, or rows of data, in the book titles table once the table is populated. The number of rows within the table will obviously change as books' titles are added and removed. See Figure 1.7 for an illustration of a row of data in a table.

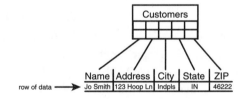

FIGURE 1.7
Row of data in a database table.

Data Types

A *data type* determines the type of data that can be stored in a database column.

Although many data types are available, three of the most commonly used data types are

- Alphanumeric
- Numeric
- Date and time

Alphanumeric data types are used to store characters, numbers, special characters, or nearly any combination. If a numeric value is stored in an alphanumeric field, the value is treated as a character, not a number. In other words, you should not attempt to perform arithmetic functions on numeric values stored in alphanumeric fields. Design techniques such as this will be discussed in more detail throughout the book. *Numeric* data types are used to store only numeric values. *Date and time* data types are used to store date and time values, which widely vary depending on the relational database management system (RDBMS) being used.

Does the Database Have Integrity?

Data integrity is the insurance of accurate data in the database. Within the scope of the database, data integrity is controlled mostly by column constraints. *Constraints* validate the values of the data placed in the database. Constraints can be implemented at both the column level and the table level. Constraints can be used to ensure that duplicate data is not entered into the database. Constraints are also typically used to ensure that new or modified table data adhere to the business rules defined. The use of constraints to enforce business rules is discussed in more detail in Chapter 12, "Integrating Business Rules and Data Integrity."

Referential integrity is the process of ensuring that data is consistent between related tables. Referential integrity is a concept that deals with parent/child relationships in the database. Referential integrity constraints are created in order to ensure that data entered into one table is synchronized with other related tables. Values from one column are dependent on the values from another column in another table.

Referential integrity is controlled by keys. A *key* is a column value in a table that is used to either uniquely identify a row of data in a table, or establish a relationship with another table. A key is normally correlated with one column in table, although it might be associated with multiple columns. There are two types of keys: primary and foreign.

Primary Keys

A *primary* key is the combination of one or more column values in a table that make a row of data unique within the table. Primary keys are typically used to join related tables. Even if a table has no child table, a primary key can be used to disallow the entry of duplicate records into a table. For example, an employee's social security number is sometimes considered a primary key candidate because all SSNs are unique.

Foreign Keys

A *foreign* key is the combination of one or more column values in a table that reference a primary key in another table. Foreign keys are defined in child tables. A foreign key ensures that a parent record has been created before a child record. Conversely, a foreign key also ensures that the child record is deleted before the parent record.

Figure 1.8 illustrates how a foreign key constraint is related to a primary key constraint. The Auth_id column in the Booklist table references the Auth_id in the Authors table. Authors is the parent table and Booklist is the child table. If a record for Auth_id=3 needs to be created, the record must be inserted into the Authors table first. If an author needs to be removed from the database, all references to the author must first be deleted in Booklist, the child table.

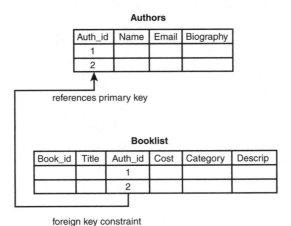

FIGURE 1.8

Referential integrity, or parent/child relationships.

NOTE

Referential integrity should be established from the beginning, and implemented before any data is allowed into the finished database. The implementation of referential integrity should never be put off to allow the existence of inconsistent or unrelated data, such as orphan child records, which are child records with no related parent records.

Relationships

Most databases are divided into many tables, most of which are related to one another. In most modern databases, such as the relational database, relationships are established through the use of primary and foreign keys. The purpose of separating data into tables and establishing table relationships is to reduce data redundancy. The process of reducing data redundancy in a relational database is called *normalization*, and is discussed in detail in Chapter 8, "Normalization: Eliminating Redundant Data."

Three types of table relationships that can be derived are as follows:

- One-to-one—One record in a table is related to only one record in another table.
- One-to-many—One record in a table can be related to many records in another table.
- Many-to-many—One record in a table can be related to one or more records in another table, and one or more records in the second table can be related to one or more records in the first table.

Figure 1.9 briefly illustrates table relationships in a relational database. A relational database allows parent tables to have many child tables, and child tables to have many parent tables. The figure shows two tables. Table 1 has an ID column (primary key) and Table 2 has an FK column (foreign key). In the one-to-one relationship example, notice that for every ID in Table 1, there is only one ID in Table 2. In the one-to-many relationships example, notice that the ID of 1 has many occurrences in Table 2. In the many-to-many relationship example, notice that the ID in Table 1 might occur multiple times in Table 2 as a foreign key, and the ID in Table 2 might occur multiple times in Table 1.

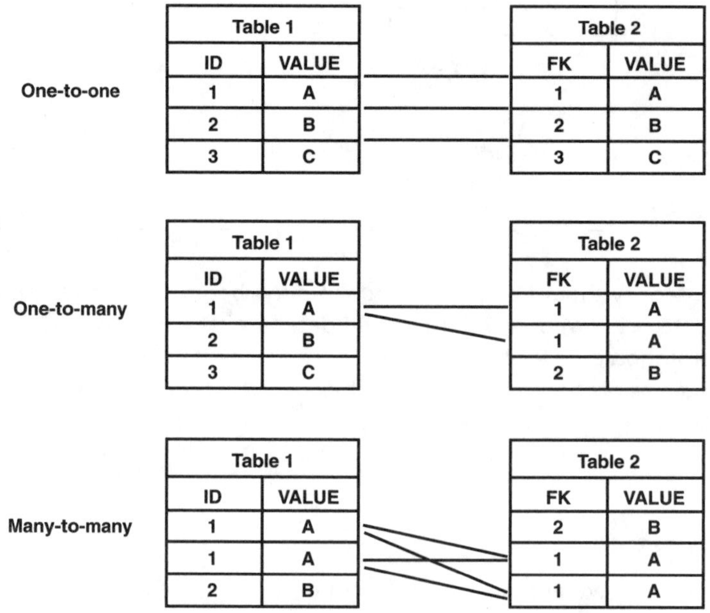

One-to-one

Table 1			Table 2	
ID	VALUE		FK	VALUE
1	A		1	A
2	B		2	B
3	C		3	C

One-to-many

Table 1			Table 2	
ID	VALUE		FK	VALUE
1	A		1	A
2	B		1	A
3	C		2	B

Many-to-many

Table 1			Table 2	
ID	VALUE		FK	VALUE
1	A		2	B
1	A		1	A
2	B		1	A

FIGURE 1.9

Available table relationships in the relational model.

Key Database Design Concepts

This section focuses on some basic concepts associated with the database design process. Before a design effort can proceed full speed ahead, the designer must first take time to understand the business. Understanding the business involves understanding the entities, data, and rules within an organization, and then converting these attributes of the business into a business model. Then, the designer must have a solid comprehension of the proposed database model. Finally, the designer will convert the business model into a database model, using a design methodology, whether automated or a manual process.

The following subsections in this chapter briefly describe these topics: design methodology, converting the business model to design, and application design.

Design Methodology

A design methodology is the approach taken toward the design of a database. It is the process of designing a database with a sound plan from the beginning. For individuals lacking the proper knowledge and experience, designing a database probably involves a great deal of trial and error. If an individual understands database fundamentals and design concepts, the basic steps of the database design process, and has a structured plan (has selected a design methodology), the design process should produce a quality product to the customer.

Some of the advantages of using a design methodology include

- It provides a step by step guide toward database design.
- Little or no trial and error is involved.
- It is easy to document the database and application with the availability of design plans, drawings depicting the organization's needs, and other deliverables specified.
- It is easy to modify the database in the future as organization and planning eases the tasks of managing changes.

Converting the Business Model to Design

Database design is the process of converting business objects into tables and views. It is the process of actually designing a database based on a business model. Business model components such as entities and attributes are converted into tables and columns. Constraints are added to columns where necessary in order to enforce data and referential integrity. Views of tables might be created in order to filter the data that a user sees, or to simplify the query process.

After the design of a database is complete, the entire business model (business processes, rules, and entities) will have been converted into a functional database in which corporate data can be stored, modified, and easily retrieved. Figure 1.10 illustrates the conversion process from the business model to the database model.

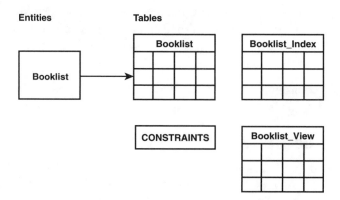

FIGURE 1.10
Conversion of business model to the database model.

Application Design

Application design is the process of creating an interface for the end user through which the database can be accessed. It is the process of transforming business processes that have been defined into a usable application through which the end user can easily access information in the database. A typical application might consist of a set of forms that allow the end user to create new records in the database, update or delete existing records, or perform queries. The application might also include canned queries and reports. Common tools used to develop an application include Oracle Designer, Oracle Developer/2000, Visual Basic, C++, and PowerBuilder. Application design, although an essential part of the overall design process, is out of the scope of this book. This book focuses on the database design process versus application design—although the design of an application is an integral supplement to the database itself. Figure 1.11 illustrates the conversion from the business model to the application generation.

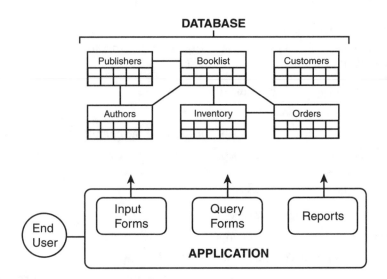

FIGURE 1.11

The application interface to the database.

What Makes a Good Database?

The definition of a good database is relative to the requirements of each customer because every situation is different. A good database is determined as seen through the eyes of the customer, the end user, the database administration team, and management. If all parties are happy with the database, the allocation of resources to design a new database might be unnecessary. On the other hand, if some of the parties involved are unhappy about a few things, it might be worthwhile to begin designing a new database. Keep in mind that there might not be an existing database in place. If a database is not currently in use, it is still important to understand the key principles of a "good" database before thinking about designing one.

There are many hallmarks of a good database, the most common of which are discussed in the following subsections and consist of

- Data storage needs having been met
- Data is readily available to the end-user
- Data being protected through database security
- Data being accurate and easy to manage
- Overall database performance being acceptable
- Having a minimized amount of redundant data stored

Storage Needs Met

The foremost objective of a database is to store data. In order to determine if data storage is adequate, the following questions might be of use:

- Have all storage needs been met for the database?
- Has all data been stored effectively?
- Is the database model used capable of handling the complexity of business relationships?
- Is the database model used capable of handling the estimated volume of data for the proposed database?
- Is the hardware adequate for storage needs?
- Does the database software meet the storage needs?
- What data is stored offline as opposed to online storage?
- How easy is it to access offline data storage?
- Has all unnecessary online data been purged or archived into an offline storage device?

Some of the factors that affect data storage include the design of the database, the database software, the hardware and operating system on which the database runs, and the types of data stored. As you will learn throughout the book, it is imperative to carefully plan the design of the database so that all storage needs are met. A database software program must be used to implement a database that has been designed. Some vendors provide features that others do not with their database software. Although the hardware and disk space on which the database runs may have been adequate initially, the database may have grown beyond the physical limits of the hardware. Finally, the type of data stored must be considered. Online data is data that is readily available to the end user and is stored in the database. Offline data is data that is archived and not stored in the database. If no data is ever archived, it can appear that storage needs are not being met.

Data Is Available

What good is a database if data is not readily available to the end-user? Data must be available as requested by the end-user, during all hours of business operation. Many organizations are referred to as 24X7 shops. This means that data must be available twenty-four hours a day, seven days a week, to satisfy the needs of many groups of users that have a need to potentially access the database from many sites in different time zones around the world. Database down time is often necessary, but must be scheduled around hours of peak user activity. Database down time should not occur if it has not been scheduled. However, down time sometimes occurs from time to time based on factors that are related to the design of the database. If data is not available when expected, then the database is not fulfilling its purpose.

Data availability is also related to the user's expected and perceived performance of the database. Consider this: A user starts an application and performs some function that requests data.

Depending on the nature of the request, it may take several minutes or seconds for data to become available, or it might appear instantly on the screen. In the production environment, perception is reality, and if a user feels an application or database is slow, it will create the perception of poor performance. A database environment may be simply stellar in its design and implementation, but expectations might overtake the possible realistic performance of the database and application. In some cases, small changes to the application may help, assuming the database itself has been well-designed. For example, an OLE database call into a Visual Basic record set object may take several seconds. When the screen is painted, an additional few seconds is required. Suppose the screen is painted while the record set is being retrieved from the database. The few seconds it takes to paint the screen so that the screen from the application and the data from the database pop together may be worth it. In this example, the users perceived the database to be slow. A simple change in perception solved the issue.

Data Protected

After the data is stored in the database, it is important to ensure that the data is well protected. Database security should be established to protect the data from unauthorized users. Some questions that might be asked to determine how well the data is protected include the following:

- Does security exist in the database?
- Is the data protected from outside users?
- Is the data protected from internal users?
- How easy is it for unauthorized users to access the data?
- Have there been any security breaches since the database implementation?
- How easy is it to limit the access to various groups of users within the scope of the database?
- How easy is it to grant and revoke data access to various groups of users?

Without database security, the database can easily become corrupted, whether intentional or not. It is important to restrict access to the database from individuals not requiring access. As a general rule, you should be able to limit the access to the data at a very low level. Many databases are designed with little or no security. Although a lack of security does not justify the complete redesign of a database, it is a definite setback and can cause problems that leave decision makers with the impression that they have a poor database.

Data Is Accurate

Suppose that storage is sufficient and security is established. Security will stop unauthorized users from entering the database, but what is there to protect the data from users with access? Mainly, constraints should be used to control the allowed data. Constraints are normally applied at the column level, verifying data entered for a particular column. Constraints, however, cannot completely eliminate the chance for inaccurate data. It is the main responsibility of the end user to properly manage the data that is entered.

The following questions will help determine if precautions have been taken to ensure that data is as accurate as possible:

- Has referential integrity been applied (primary key and foreign key constraints)?
- What other constraints have been established to check the uniqueness or validity of data?
- Are data relationships easily maintained within the database?
- How easy is it for the end user to enter invalid data into the database?
- Are there edits and constraints in the application interface that supplement those in the database?
- Have code tables been established for common data?

Is data consistent within the database? Consistency is related, but not the same as accurate data. Users should be forced to enter data in a consistent manner. A database becomes corrupted if the end user is allowed to enter data in a fashion that is inconsistent with the way other users are entering data. This affects the integrity of the data.

Acceptable Performance

Performance is a major issue for any database. All parties are worried about performance, from the end user to the database administrator to management. If the end user is not happy, the customer is not happy because the job is not getting done. If the customer is not happy, management is not happy. When management is not happy, nobody is happy—sort of like "when Mom isn't happy, nobody's happy." The following questions can be raised to determine whether database performance is acceptable:

- What is the expected response time for transactions and small queries?
- How does the database perform overall according to the end user?
- How does the database perform during high peak times of transactional activity?
- How does the database perform during batch operations, such as massive data loads and queries against large amounts of data?
- If performance problems exist, are these problems related to the design of the database, the application interface, network problems, or hardware?

There is often a grand difference between performance as expected by the end user versus realistic performance. Users often expect instantaneous response time. Usually, an acceptable response time to retrieve a record from the database or to perform a relatively small transaction is somewhere between one and five seconds. This type of response time is often obtainable, depending on factors such as the design of the database, the design of the application, the speed of the hardware, and the speed of the network. If performance is not acceptable to the customer and end user, it is important to evaluate performance carefully to identify the point of degradation. Also, keep in mind that more time must be allowed for batch loads or queries against large amounts of data because more data is being processed.

Redundant Data Is Minimized

One of the main goals when storing data in a database is to reduce or eliminate redundant information. Data should be stored one time in the database if possible. If an occurrence of data is stored multiple times in the database, the data must be updated in many places when changes are required. Likewise, the data might have to be added or removed in multiple places. Redundant data can lead to both inconsistent and inaccurate data. Inaccurate data is caused in the sense that the data might be wrong altogether when entered in a duplicate location. Inconsistent data might be derived in the sense that the data might be entered in different ways in different locations.

For example, if an address is stored in multiple locations, the chances increase for an end user to enter data inconsistently according to other data stored in the database.

| Location #1 | address entered as "123 Elm Street" |
| Location #2 | address entered as "123 ELM ST." |

There are two things to consider in this example. First, street was abbreviated in the second location. Second, the entire address was entered in uppercase in the second location, where it was entered in mixed case in the first location. With these two simple inconsistencies, it would be more difficult to compare the two values than if the address was stored only one time in the database. Data inconsistency because of redundant data can cause great confusion to the end user when retrieving and modifying data; thus, a major concern when designing a database. Redundant data is minimized through a process called *normalization*. Chapter 8, "Normalization," involves a detailed discussion.

Summary

A database is an automated mechanism used to store information that is required for a business to function. Databases can also be used by individuals. There are simple databases that we all use everyday such as a telephone directory, and complex databases, such as those used to process mail orders over the Internet. Databases can contain static or dynamic data, or both. Static data does not change. Dynamic data changes regularly.

The three most basic environments for a database include the mainframe, client/server, and Internet computing environments. The mainframe environment involves one main supercomputer that performs all the processing. The mainframe computer has dumb terminals attached that allow the user to communicate with it. In the mainframe environment, the application and database both reside on the mainframe computer. The client/server environment involves a host computer (server), one or more personal computers, and some form of a network through which the host computer is made available to the personal computers (clients). In a client/server environment, much of the load is taken away from the server as the PCs (clients) are able to perform some of the processing on their own. In a client/server environment, the database resides on the host server, whereas the application resides on each individual PC. In the Internet computing environment, PCs are connected to a corporate intranet or to the Internet. A host computer (Web server) is also connected to the intranet or Internet. The target database might reside on the Web server, or some other computer that might be within the corporate firewall. The user implements a Web browser on the PC to access the Web server, which accesses the database for the requested information. The information, once retrieved from the database, is passed back to the Web browser on the user's PC. In the Internet computing environment, the application resides only on the Web server, which simplifies the process of installing, configuring, and making modifications to the application. Most companies today seem to have implemented the client/server environment, although many companies are now progressing toward internet computing, or the combination of internet and client/server computing.

Business modeling involves the evaluation of the business. From the database design perspective, this involves the definition of business processes, rules, and data. Business processes are tasks performed by individuals within the business. Business rules determine how the business model is structured, what categories of data are needed, and how the data can be modified and accessed. It is important to conduct interviews with key players in the business as well as end users to grasp a good understanding of the overall system requirements for the business. The business model is complete when all requirements are captured, and these requirements are modeled into business objects such as entities and attributes. Entities are categorized groups of data, and attributes are specific data within entities.

Within a database, one or more schemas exist. A schema is a collection of objects that are related to one another. Normally, each database system is associated with a single schema. The owner of a schema is called the schema owner, which is associated with a user account in the database. Objects such as tables and views are found in a schema. The table is the primary unit of storage for data in a relational database.

Database design deals with the conversion of the business model into an optimally structured database model. Database tables are designed from entities, which categorize a business's data. Attributes that were defined in the business model become columns in tables. The database design phase of system development is when the designer gets serious about creating views of tables, specifying constraints, ensuring that data integrity is complete, and creating other objects such as indexes. After the database itself is designed, an application for the end user must be designed because the user cannot be expected to fully understand the structure of the database. With a basic understanding of databases and the different types of database environments, you are well on your way to deciding on a database model that is best for your organization.

Exploration of Database Models

IN THIS CHAPTER

When designing a database, it is useful to understand a bit about the history of databases and the different types of databases. With a general understanding of the different types of databases and database environments, the database designer can draw more intelligent conclusions about how to proceed with any database system design effort. Database technology has taken great strides ever since database systems were first developed and used. From basic file storage, or flat-file systems, data can now be stored such that its physical storage is transparent to the user. With today's database technologies, the user need only understand the business and the data within the business. This chapter will discuss the most common database models in use today.

As the purpose of this book is to explain database design from the standpoint of the relational model, it is imperative to understand the conversion that takes place from a business model into a working database. To understand this conversion process, you must have a good understanding of the database model to be used, most likely the relational model. With a good plan, a good understanding of the business, and a good understanding of the relational model, business objects can easily be represented in a database. The relational model is a stable environment in which a company can most effectively control its data and applications.

> **NOTE**
>
> The most commonly implemented database in the modern world is called the relational database. For this reason, this book is structured around designing a database using the relational model. You will soon find that with the relational model, it is easy to structure your database such that data integrity is most effectively implemented.

Types of Databases

Every company needs a database. Companies and individuals alike use databases every day, some unknowingly. Many different types of databases exist, some simple, others very complex. When you search for a company in the Yellow Pages to pave your driveway, you are referencing a database. When you order a book from an online bookstore on the Internet, you are accessing a database. One of the simplest forms of a database with which each one of us are familiar is a filing cabinet. Information is stored in cabinet drawers, in folders, and even subfolders. Many companies still shuffle paperwork on a day-to-day basis instead of storing their information in a computer. Although the complete elimination of paperwork is virtually impossible for any company, the benefits of storing data in a database on a host computer system outweigh the costs of learning to use a data management program.

The basic steps involved in the design of any database is the company's decision to allocate resources to learn about databases, to design the structure for their database, and to implement and manage the database. After the database has been designed and an application has been developed or purchased through which to access the database, overall management of the database should be simple for an experienced database administrator. After a company has committed to the design effort for a database system, the database model to be used must be established.

The following database models (types) are discussed in this section:

- Flat-file database model
- Hierarchical database model
- Network database model
- Relational database model
- Object-oriented (OO) database model
- Object-relational (OR) database model

A *database management system (DBMS)* is a software product that is used to store data. Vendors design DBMSs based on a particular database model. A DBMS should have the following characteristics:

- Data is stored on some hardware device and should persist after being accessed. Access methods include the creation of new data, modification of existing data, and deletion of data. This is referred to as *data persistence*.
- Multiple users should be allowed to access data simultaneously, called *concurrency*.
- Transactions are managed, allowing for the manipulation of data, and the ability to save a group of work.
- A query language should be available to retrieve data based on criteria supplied by the user.
- Data should be recoverable from a failure. If data is lost, the DBMS should have the capability to recover the data to any given state.

The following sections briefly describe each database model, as well as the benefits and drawbacks of each model. It is important to understand the basic concepts of each database model in order to make an intelligent decision on which model to implement.

Flat-File Database Model

Before vendors such as Oracle and Microsoft started developing database management systems that run on a computer, many companies that were using computers stored their data in flat files on a host computer. The use of flat files to store data was predominant in the mainframe era. A flat-file database consists of one or more readable files, normally stored in a text format. Information in these files is stored as fields, the fields having either a constant length or a variable length separated by some character (delimiter).

Following is an example of a flat file with constant length fields:

```
1234     Ernest Hemingway     For Whom the Bell Tolls
5678     Charles Dickens      Great Expectations
4321     Ernest Hemingway     A Farewell to Arms
8765     Jack London          White Fang
4523     Jack London          Call of the Wild
3456     Mark Twain           Adventures of Huckleberry Finn
```

In this example, there are obviously three fields: an identification number, the author name, and the title of the book. Each field has a constant length because the identification number always starts in column #1 and ends in column #4, the author name starts in column #6 and ends in column #25, and so on.

Following is an example of a flat file, with variable length fields separated by a given delimiter:

```
1234:Ernest Hemingway:For Whom the Bell Tolls
5678:Charles Dickens:Great Expectations
4321:Ernest Hemingway:A Farewell to Arms
8765:Jack London:White Fang
4523:Jack London:Call of the Wild
3456:Mark Twain:Adventures of Huckleberry Finn
```

There are also three fields in this example. Each field is separated by a colon. The fields are not a constant length in the example. When using field separators, you should make sure that the field separator is not a character that can be found in the data.

> **NOTE**
>
> Sometimes flat files are created and used to migrate data from one database implementation to another, particularly with relational databases.

Every flat-file database system is different because companies store different data and companies have different needs. After a flat-file system has been created and the data has been stored in these files, a method must be devised in order to retrieve the data, create new records, update records, or delete records. For instance, if you wanted to get a list of each one of the titles authored by Jack London, you would have to find every record that had an occurrence of

`"Jack London"`. In addition to finding each record with the string `"Jack London"` in the second field, you would want to filter the data so that only the title of the book, which is the third field, is retrieved.

The problem of accessing the data requires a collection of programs to be written that access the information stored in the flat files—unless you expect the user or customer to search the flat files themselves in order to access the data, which would be quite unacceptable. One of the main problems with a flat-file database system is that not only do you have to understand the structure of the files, but also you must know exactly where data is physically stored. Additionally, your database will probably require numerous flat files, which might have data related to other data stored in some other file. Managing data relationships is a difficult task in the flat-file database environment.

Following is an overview of the drawbacks of a flat-file database:

- Flat files do not promote a structure in which data can easily be related.
- It is difficult to manage data effectively and to ensure accuracy.
- It is usually necessary to store redundant data, which causes more work to accurately maintain the data.
- The physical location of the data field within the file must be known.
- A program must be developed to manage the data.

Hierarchical Database Model

A hierarchical database is a step above that of a flat-file database, mainly because of the ability to establish and maintain relationships between groups of data. The architecture of a hierarchical database is based on the concept of parent/child relationships. In a hierarchical database, a root table, or parent table, resides at the top of the structure, which points to child tables containing related data. The structure of a hierarchical database model appears as an inverted tree, as shown in Figure 2.1.

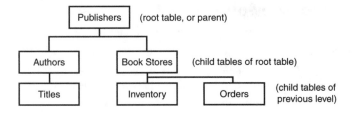

FIGURE 2.1

The Hierarchical Database Model.

In Figure 2.1, Publishers is the root table. Publishers has two child tables: Authors and Bookstores. A publisher has many authors to whom it contracts, as well as many bookstores to which it supplies books. Authors is a parent table to the Titles table, as Bookstores is to Inventory. Titles is a child table of Authors, as Inventory and Orders are child tables of Bookstores. One of the problems with this hierarchical layout is that redundant book title information would have to be stored in the Inventory table because there is no direct association between Authors and Bookstores.

> **NOTE**
>
> As previously mentioned, it is a good practice to store as little redundant data in a database as possible. One of the implications of having redundant data is that data will have to be modified multiple times, depending on the level of redundancy. Processes must be in place to ensure that all appropriate data is updated when necessary to avoid inconsistent data in the database.

A parent table can have many child tables, but a child table can have only one parent table. To get to a child table, the parent table must first be accessed. Related tables within the hierarchical structure are linked by a pointer, which points to the physical location of a child record.

Benefits of the hierarchical model over the flat-file model:

- Data can be quickly retrieved.
- Data integrity is easier to manage.

Drawbacks of the hierarchical model:

- Users must be very familiar with the database structure.
- Redundant data is stored.

Network Database Model

Improvements were made to the hierarchical database model in order to derive the network model. As in the hierarchical model, tables are related to one another. One of the main advantages of the network model is the capability of parent tables to share relationships with child tables. This means that a child table can have multiple parent tables. Additionally, a user can access data by starting with any table in the structure, navigating either up or down in the tree. The user is not required to access a root table first to get to child tables.

The relationship between tables in the network model is called a set structure, where one table is the owner and another table is a member. This is the same basic concept as the parent/child relationship discussed earlier. Set structures can represent a one-to-many relationship between tables. Application programs that access the network database use set structures to navigate to different parts of the database; therefore if a set structure is modified, application programs that access the database must also be modified. Figure 2.2 illustrates set structures.

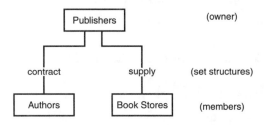

FIGURE 2.2
The Network Model.

In Figure 2.2, the Publisher table owns two tables: Authors and Bookstores. Authors and Bookstores are each members of the Publisher table. Publishers contract work to authors and supply finished books to bookstores. The set structure between Authors and Publishers is called Contract.

Figure 2.3 illustrates how child tables, or members, can be shared by parent tables. In this figure, the Titles table is owned by both Authors and Bookstores. Both Authors and Bookstores require a relationship with Titles. Although two set structures can be used to access the Titles table, book title information is only stored in one table, thus reducing data redundancy.

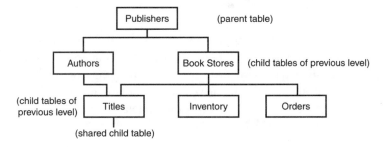

FIGURE 2.3
A Shared Child Table.

The benefits of the network database model are as follows:

- Data is accessed very quickly.
- Users can access data starting with any table.

- It is easier to model more complex databases.
- It is easier to develop complex queries to retrieve data.

The drawbacks of the network database model are as follows:

- The structure of the database is not easily modified.
- Changes to the database structure definitely affect application programs that access the database.
- The user has to understand the structure of the database.

Relational Database Model

The relational database model is the most popular database model used today. Many improvements have been made to prior database models that simplify data management, data retrieval, and change propagation management. Data is easier to manage, mainly through the use of integrity constraints. The retrieval of data is also a refined process, allowing the user to visualize the database through relational table structures and to ask for specific data without a detailed knowledge of the database layout. Changes are also easier to propagate, thanks to features such as integrity constraints and the benefits that normalization (reduction of data redundancy) provides.

The primary unit of storage in a database is a table, or group of related data. A table consists of rows and columns, as defined in Chapter 1, "Understanding Database Fundamentals." In review, a row is associated with an individual record in the table, and a column contains values for all rows associated with a particular field. Tables can be related to one another through common column values, called keys.

Three different types of table relationships are allowed: one-to-one, one-to-many, and many-to-many. Different relationships should be allowed to exist between tables in a database. For example, one table might be required to have a record based on the existence of a record in another table. Some tables might optionally have one or more existing records that correspond to records in another table. A detailed discussion of these relationships is found in Chapter 7, "Understanding Entities and Relationships."

Table relationships are defined by referential integrity, which suggests the use of primary key and foreign key constraints. Referential integrity is the use of these constraints to validate data entered into a table and manage the relationship between parent and child tables. Other types of constraints can also be created to control the permissible data in particular table columns and to establish relationships between tables.

Figure 2.4 illustrates a basic relational database model. In the relational model, there is no root table, although parent and child relationships of tables are allowed. A parent table can have multiple child tables, as a child table can have multiple parent tables (bi-directional relationships).

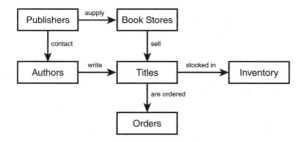

FIGURE 2.4
The Relational Model.

Benefits of the relational model are as follows:

- Data is accessed very quickly.
- The database structure is easy to change.
- The data is represented logically, therefore users need not understand how the data is stored.
- It is easy to develop complex queries to retrieve data.
- It is easy to implement data integrity.
- Data is generally more accurate.
- It is easy to develop and modify application programs.
- A standard language (SQL) has been developed.

Drawbacks of the relational database model are as follows:

- Different groups of information, or tables, must be joined in many cases to retrieve data.
- Users must be familiar with the relationships between tables.
- Users must learn SQL.

NOTE

The relational database is discussed in more detail later in this chapter and throughout the remainder of the book because the relational database model is the most popular and stable model being implemented today.

Object-Oriented (OO) Database Model

During the last few years, object-oriented programming has become popular with languages such as C++, Visual Basic, and Java. An OO programming language allows the programmer to work with objects to define an application that interacts with a relational database (since most companies now use the relational database model). For example, elements within a program or database application are visually represented as objects. These objects have assigned properties, which can be modified, and can also be inherited from other objects. Related types of objects are assigned various properties that can be adjusted to define the particular object and determine how the object will act. With these OO programming tools, applications are now easier to develop and maintain. Many mundane programming tasks can be automated by an OO programming tool, thus reducing the amount of time it takes to develop an application, increasing overall productivity.

A problem with the relational database as OO programming technology advances is that developers must understand both the relational database language (SQL) as well as the OO programming language (Java, for example) that is to be used to design the application. It is important for developers to understand relational database concepts in order for the application to access the data. It can be confusing for the developer to switch modes of thinking between relational and OO.

An object-oriented database is a database in which data can be defined, stored, and accessed using an OO programming approach. For an OO database, a select OO programming language is used to define the structure of the database as well as create an application through which to interact with the database.

NOTE

The object query language is used to manage data in an OO database. The object query language, OQL, is based on the standard relational language SQL, but has additional features that allow data to be stored and accessed as objects with properties.

Figure 2.5 illustrates an example of an OO database and its implementation. The figure shows that the OO database is defined using an OO programming language such as Java. The end-user application is also created using the OO language. The OO code is compiled, and a compatible database and application are produced. An object database management system is used to link the database and the application.

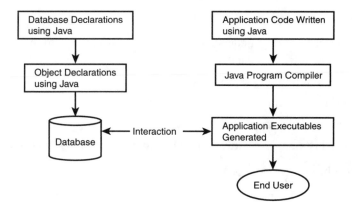

FIGURE 2.5

The Object-oriented Database.

The two basic structures in an OO database are as follows:

- Objects
- Literals

Objects are structures that have identifiers through which an object can be associated with other objects. Literals are values associated with objects, and have no identifiers. Objects and literals are organized by types, where all elements of a given type have the same set of properties, which can be modified for each individual object. A class is the equivalent of a table in a relational database. Operations are used to retrieve values from other classes, to add values, and to remove values. Figure 2.6 illustrates how data is related in an OO database.

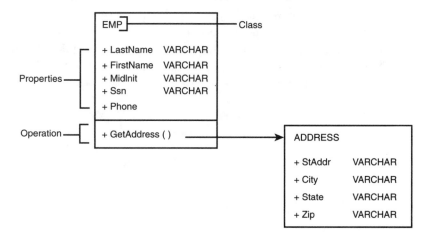

FIGURE 2.6

The Object-oriented Data Model.

Benefits of the object-oriented model are as follows:

- The programmer need only understand OO concepts as opposed to the combination of OO concepts and relational database storage.
- Objects can inherit property settings from other objects.
- Much of the application program process is automated.
- It is theoretically easier to manage objects.
- OO data model is more compatible with OO programming tools.

Drawbacks of the object-oriented model are as follows:

- Users must learn OO concepts because the OO database does not work with traditional programming methods.
- Standards have not been completely established for the evolving database model.
- Stability is a concern because OO databases have not been around for long.

Object-Relational (OR) Database Model

Although some rough seams exist between the object-oriented and relational models, the object-relational model was developed with the objective of combining the concepts of the relational database model with object-oriented programming style. The OR model is supposed to represent the best of both worlds (relational and OO), although the OR model is still early in development. As we speak, vendors are implementing OR concepts into their relational databases, as the International Standards Organization (ISO) has integrated OR concepts into the new SQL standard, referred to as SQL3. SQL3 is also referred to as SQL99.

Figure 2.7 illustrates an example OR implementation in the Oracle8 relational database management system (RDBMS). Two user-defined types have been created: PERSON and ADDRESS. Each type has columns that define specific data for a column in the base table, providing a 3D effect for the data. For example, the EMP_INFO column in the EMP table has a type of PERSON. PERSON is broken down into the specific categories LAST_NAME, FIRST_NAME, MID_INIT, and SSN.

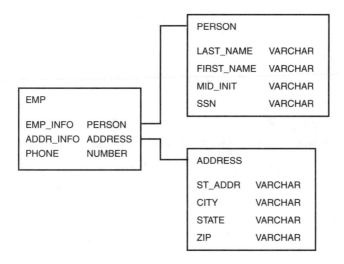

FIGURE 2.7

The object-relational database.

Benefits of the object-relational model are as follows:

- The relational database has more of a 3D architecture.
- User-defined types can be created.

Drawbacks of the object-relational model are as follows:

- The user must understand both object-oriented and relational concepts.
- Some vendors that have implemented OR concepts do not support object inheritance.

The Modern Database of Choice

This book discusses database design from the standpoint of the relational database model. Why the relational database? For several reasons, the relational database model has proven to be the choice database for most organizations in the modern world. The relational database has been around for three decades, but the technology is still new for some companies who rely solely on manual processes. For companies that have employed databases that have been around for years, the relational database is still preferred for most redesign efforts.

So why is the relational model so attractive?

- It is the most stable.
- RDB standards are well established by organizations such as the International Standards Organization (ISO) and the American National Standards Institute (ANSI).

- There are many RDB vendors to choose from, including Oracle, Microsoft, Informix, IBM, and Sybase.
- It is easy to convert between different relational database implementations.
- It is easy to define and maintain data with SQL.
- It is easy to manipulate data with SQL.
- The ad hoc query process is simple.
- Data is well-protected through referential integrity and other constraints.

The following subsections discuss the relational dastabase in a bit more detail that will assist in your overall understanding for designing a relational database. First, the characteristics of a relational database are discussed as outlined by the creator of the relational model. Then, the various objects that are most commonly found in a relational database are outlined. Finally, the standard language used to communicate with a relational database, SQL, is discussed briefly.

Relational Database Characteristics

The relational model was designed by the IBM research scientist and mathematician, Dr. E.F. Codd. Two of Dr. Codd's main focal points when designing the relational model were to further reduce data redundancy and to improve data integrity within database systems. The relational model originated from a paper authored by Dr. Codd entitled, "A Relational Model of Data for Large Shared Data Banks," written in 1970. This paper included the following concepts that apply to database management systems for relational databases:

- A relational database management system (DBMS) must be able to manage databases entirely through its relational capabilities.
- All information in a relational database (including table and column names) is represented explicitly as a value in tabular format.
- Every value in a relational database is guaranteed to be accessible by using a combination of the table name, primary key value, and column name. This means that you need not know the physical location of the data, and that you can directly access any row of data in a database table independently.
- The DBMS should provide support for the treatment of null values (unknown or inapplicable data), which are distinct from default values, and independent of any domain.
- The description of the database and its contents is represented at the logical level in tabular format and can therefore be queried using the database language. This refers to metadata that is stored in the data in regards to the database itself. Metadata is data about other data.

- At least one supported language must have a well-defined syntax and be comprehensive. It must support data definition, manipulation, integrity rules, authorization, and transactions.

- All views that are theoretically updateable can be updated through the system.

- The DBMS supports set-level retrievals, inserts, updates, and deletes.

- Application programs and ad hoc queries are logically unaffected when physical access methods or storage structures are altered.

- Application programs and ad hoc queries are logically affected as little as possible when changes are made to the table structures. Although, if a table is split into two tables, the application will have to be changed so that the appropriate columns are accessed from both tables.

- The database language must be capable of defining integrity rules to protect the data. These rules must be stored in the online catalog, and cannot be bypassed when data is modified.

- Application programs and ad hoc queries are logically unaffected when data is first distributed or when it is redistributed. Distribution refers to how data is stored on hardware devices.

- It must be possible to bypass the integrity rules defined through the database language by using lower-level languages.

Relational Database Objects

Various types of objects can be found in a relational database. Some of the most common objects found in a relational database include

- Table—A table is the primary object used to store data in a relational database. When data is queried and accessed for modification, it is usually found in a table. A table is defined by columns. One occurrence of all columns in a table is called a row of data.

- View—A view is a virtual table, in that it looks like and acts like a table. A view is defined based on the structure and data of a table. A view can be queried and sometimes updated.

- Constraint—A constraint is an object used to place rules on data. Constraints are used to control the allowed data in a column. Constraints are created at the column level and are also used to enforce referential integrity (parent and child table relationships).

- Index—An index is an object that is used to speed the process of data retrieval on a table. For example, an index might be created on a customer's name if users tend to search for customers by name. The customer names would be stored alphabetically in the index. The rows in the index would point to the corresponding rows in the table, much like an index in a book points to a particular page.

- Trigger—A trigger is a stored unit of programming code in the database that is fired based on an event that occurs in the database. When a trigger is fired, data might be modified based on other data that is accessed or modified. Triggers are useful for maintaining redundant data.

- Procedure—A procedure is a program that is stored in the database. A procedure is executed at the database level. Procedures are typically used to manage data and for batch processing.

The first four objects deal with the definition of the database, whereas the last two objects deal with methods for accessing database objects. Objects in a relational database provide users with a logical representation of data, such that the physical location of the data is immaterial to the user.

SQL: The Relational Database Language

Structured Query Language, more commonly referred to as SQL, is the standard language used to issue commands to and communicate with a relational database. With SQL, you can easily enter data into the database, modify data, delete data, and retrieve data. SQL is a nonprocedural language, which means that you tell the database server what data to access, not necessarily what methods should be used to access the data. SQL contains the following three sub-languages that allow you to perform nearly any operation desirable within a relational database:

- Data Definition Language (DDL)
- Data Manipulation Language (DML)
- Data Query Language (DQL)

DDL is used to define the structure of the database, to include creating tables, dropping tables, defining views, indexes, and constraints, and so on. DML allows you to modify data within the database. DQL allows you to retrieve information from the database with ease.

Because SQL is the standard language used for databases created using the relational model, relational databases are made portable to many different environments. After a user has learned SQL, he can work with any relational database with minor adaptations.

Following is a simple example of a SQL command that is used to create a database table:

```
CREATE TABLE PRODUCTS
(PROD_ID    NUMBER(4)       NOT NULL,
 NAME     VARCHAR2(30)    NOT NULL,
 COST     NUMBER(6,2)     NOT NULL,
 DESCRIP    VARCHAR2(200)     NULL);
```

The table name is PRODUCTS. The column names are PROD_ID, NAME, COST, and DESCRIP. Each column is assigned a data type, which is used to control the data that can be inserted into a column. Columns might or might not contain NULL, or missing, values. The DESCRIP column is the only column that may contain NULL values based on the definition of this table. A row of data would consist of only one occurrence of each of the columns in the table.

For example, a row of data in the PRODUCTS table might appear as follows:

P01	CALENDAR	11.99	SPIRAL BOUND

The following SQL command is used to insert data into a table:

```
INSERT INTO PRODUCTS
VALUES (1, 'Y2K CALENDAR', 12.99, 'OUR LATEST CALENDAR');
```

The INSERT command deals with one row of data. Values are specified to be inserted into the table, which correspond to the order in which columns are defined by the table definition.

The following SQL command is used to retrieve data from a table:

```
SELECT NAME, COST
FROM PRODUCTS
WHERE COST < 20;
```

The SELECT statement is the query command in SQL. The output of this statement shows the name and cost of all products that have a cost less than 20.

Web Links for More Information on Database Models

The following Web links contain additional information for the reader interested in the pursuit of concepts associated with other database models, mainly object-oriented and object-relational.

- http://www.dwinfocenter.org

  Provides information on tools and techniques to design, build, maintain, and retrieve information from a data warehouse.

- http://www.intelligententerprise.com

  Intelligent Enterprise's Database Programming and Design online with outstanding articles for database design and development.

- http://www.dacs.dtic.mil/techs/oodbms2/oodbms-toc.shtml

  Standard information and concepts on Object-Oriented Database Management Systems.

- http://s2k-ftp.cs.berkeley.edu:8000/postgres/papers

  Database papers, most technical reports, and links to the most common database vendors and information.

- `http://www.cetus-links.org/oo_data_bases.html`

  A descriptive explanation of Object-Oriented Database Design.

- `http://www.oracle.com/database/index.html`

  An extensive explanation of Oracle's Internet Database8i that incorporates Java, Web-server, and file system abilities.

Making Your Selection

Before starting to design a database, two vital questions must first be answered:

- What database model will be used?
- What database software will be used?

The answer to the first question, concerning the database model of selection, is usually the relational database, and so is the focus of this book. If you are interested in implementing another model, such as the OO database model, this book will not be of much help to you other than with your understanding of relational objects (which would be necessary if converting a relational database to an OO database). Before deciding on a model, you should carefully study the benefits of each model as related to the basic requirements that the business has for a database. How long will the proposed database exist? How important will it be to stay current with technology?

NOTE

If you are concerned with staying current with technology, but want the reliability of a relational database, you might implement a form of an object-relational database. Many vendors today are supplying OR features in their relational database management systems.

Many choices exist when selecting a relational database management system (RDBMS). Many vendors are competing in the endless battle of providing software that is easier to use, providing the most features, and performing the best. You might find a major difference between the cost of various software, which might be why it is important to compare the features of the available software on the market with the needs of the company's proposed database. "What you pay for is what you get" is commonly stated when deciding on many products. Database software seems to be no different.

Summary

Several different types of database models exist from which the database designer has to choose. The first type, traditional to most companies involved with information technology, is the flat-file database. This database type required data to be stored in readable files on the host operating system. With the hierarchical model, information was stored in tables using parent/child relationships, but with many limitations compared to later models. The network model improved on the hierarchical model in the area of parent/child relationships. Relationships are easier to manage, and it is much easier to navigate to different tables within the database. Nearly all problems with previous data models were solved with the development of the relational model.

The relational model improved on parent and child table relationships and proved a way to reduce the amount of redundant data stored. The goal of the object-oriented model was to make data storage more compatible with object-oriented programming tools, which has yet to be refined. Finally, the object-relational model displayed an attempt to combine the concepts of object-oriented programming with the relational database, which also needs much improvement. Although the different models have pros and cons, the obvious choice for most situations is the relational model. Most companies today have implemented the relational database model for its ease of use and reliability over the other models mentioned. One thing that is certain is the fact that technology does not wait around for anyone. It is constantly moving in a forward motion and at a fast pace. Having an understanding of the progression of the different database models and database environments will prepare you for future design efforts and implementations.

Database Design Planning

IN THIS CHAPTER

When designing a database, the goals must be clearly defined in order to ensure that the development process runs smooth from phase to phase, that the effort is cost-effective, and that a complete and accurate model is derived. The primary goal of the end product, the completed database, must be a database that meets the data storage needs of the customer. It is important to identify the short-term and long-term goals, the services or products provided, the different types of business processes, the types of users who perform these processes, the expectancy of the new database, and the customer's perception of the database. How will the new database benefit the end user? How will the new database evolve in both the near future and distant future? Are there manual processes that can be automated? What existing automated processes can be refined? These are just a few considerations that should be taken when defining design goals for a new database.

The following topics are discussed as related to the goals that should be taken into consideration before designing a database:

- What is database design?
- Importance of database design
- Planning database design
- Trademarks of a solid database design
- Design methodologies
- Logical versus physical modeling
- Using automated design tools

What Is a Database Design?

Webster's dictionary uses the following phrases to define the term design:

- "To prepare the preliminary plans or sketch for"
- "To intend for a definite purpose"
- "The combination of details or features of something constructed"
- "To plan and fashion artistically or skillfully"
- "Adaptation of means to a preconceived end"

Each of Webster's definitions can be used to explain the purpose of database design and the events that should take place during database design.

"To prepare the preliminary plans or sketch for" implies that there is more work in database design than what is obvious on the surface. Before the actual design of the database occurs, there is much planning involved. Before any design effort commences, the "definite purpose" of the database should be clearly defined. The problems of the legacy database or manual processes should be addressed, and solutions are proposed. There should not be any questions as to the purpose of the proposed database.

Many "details and features" are involved during the design of any database. Once the purpose of the database has been established, the design team should study all of the details and features that comprise the business. These details and features, once gathered and often "sketched," are eventually formatted into a database structure using a predetermined database model. During the actual design of the database, these details and features are "fashioned artistically and skillfully" into a database model, which will most likely be modified numerous times before the design process is complete.

"Adaptation of means to a preconceived end" is an excellent phrase used to describe the activities of database designers in many situations. The designers must be able to adapt the phases and tasks in database design to roll with the changes and meet the customer's needs. Often, the designers find that the customer's needs for a database are refined throughout the design process, or even changed drastically. The designers should be able to receive further requests that affect the functionality of the database, and be able to adapt the steps taken during the different phases of design if necessary to integrate any changes proposed.

Three very basic phases of database design exist, all of which will be discussed in great detail throughout this book:

- Requirements gathering—Is the process of conducting meetings and/or interviews with customers, end users, and other individuals in the company to establish the requirements for the proposed database. Requirements involve, but are not limited to, the following information:

    How the business does business

    Business rules and processes

    Information about the current database being used

    Future needs of the business as related to the database

- Data modeling—Is the process of visually representing the data for a business, and then eventually converting the business model into a data model. The data model generated is used to ultimately create the tables, views, and other objects that comprise the database.

- Database design and normalization—Is a phase in which the business model (logical model) is converted into a physical model (tables). Also part of design is normalization, or the reduction or elimination of data redundancy.

Usually, the lines between these three phases are foggy, and might not seem clearly defined because the requirements of every business and the skill sets of individuals within every company, vary.

3

DATABASE DESIGN PLANNING

Importance of Database Design

Now that the concept of database design has been thoroughly defined, it is imperative to understand the importance of the design process. Although the importance of design might seem obvious, just remember that design seems obvious to most people until they are submersed into a major project with intense deadlines and little direction. Before starting, the design team must step back, take a deep breath, and plan the steps of the design process carefully before lunging foreword uncontrollably. It is important that the database design project gets off to a good, clean start with a solid plan.

The main reason good database design is so important is that organization is promoted. The designers have more control over the design, implementation, and management of any project if the project is well thought out. Because the database design's goal is to completely capture all a business' data storage needs, its product should be an accurate and easy-to-use database that performs well.

Suppose that the design of a database has been well thought out, and the final database is complete in that it entails all business processes, rules, and has an application interface that is easy for the customer to use. In a database such as this, data is easily retrieved and modified. Also from the user perspective, the actual design of the database is transparent as the end user works with the application. From the database administration standpoint, maintenance on the database is simplified and easy to perform. The database itself will ensure data integrity and adherence to business rules.

Now, consider a database that has been thrown together fiercely with little thought during initial design. All business rules might not have been captured. Data integrity might not be fully implemented because all rules have not been captured. Why are business rules and processes missing? There are missing elements because there was not clear direction on how to proceed with the design phase. Without a well-thought out design plan, customers and users were not interviewed thoroughly enough, and feedback sessions might not have been conducted with the end user and customer to ensure that all business elements were completely captured. Now, the company is stuck with a database that isn't fully functional and might involve additional manual processes to ensure data accuracy and consistency, which defeats the purpose of database planning and design. A situation such as this is frustrating for management, the technical team, and especially the customer.

Planning Database Design

The only true chance the design team has to get a handle on the design of a database takes place before the design process actually begins. Before any significant action should be taken toward gathering requirements, business modeling, or database design, a solid plan must be devised. It is important to carefully plan the flow of the project to ensure that the objectives of design of the proposed database have been defined and that all steps in the design process have been outlined. After all the design steps have been outlined, the overall process should go smoothly, and each phase within the database design should seamlessly blend into each subsequent phase with minimal bumps in the road.

After the design steps for the proposed database have been clearly defined, all parties involved in the design should understand basic goals of the database, the milestones and deliverables set forth, and the importance of meeting the established deadlines. A design team will be formed and tasks will be assigned.

The following subsections discuss the design planning process, which has been divided into these categories:

- Defining the mission statement
- Defining design objectives
- Devising a work plan
- Setting milestones and deliverables
- Establishing project deadlines
- Assigning tasks

The Mission Statement

The mission statement is a summation of the overall purpose of the proposed database. Typically, management is the main force involved in determining the mission statement. Management, developers, and end users are all involved in determining the mission objectives, or the detailed goals set forth for the database. Mission objectives will be used to devise the design plan and to establish milestones that mark the progression of the development project. The mission statement should be further refined by answering the following questions:

- What is the purpose of the database?
- Who will use the database?
- What type of database will this be?
- What models and methodologies will be used?
- Is this a new database?
- Will this database be molded after a legacy database?
- Will the database need to be modified in the near future?
- Will there be multiple databases?
- How will the customer access the database?

It is important to determine who the users of the proposed database will be. Who will be accessing the database, and how will the database enhance the end users' performance on the job? The database should be user friendly and practical, with a relatively low learning curve for the end user. The development team should understand the different types of users, and the scope of each user's job functions. The number of concurrent users can affect design proactive measures such as database performance. Because the user is the reason any database exists, the development team's interpretations of the business and the purpose of the proposed database should be inline with that of the end user.

If a new database is being designed, the design team will not have much material to use for comparison with the new database. If there is no legacy database, most processes are probably manual. The users might not know exactly what to ask for, or they might ask for too much. Sometimes the demands of the end user can seem unreasonable because they sometimes view the design of a database as some magical resolution orchestrated by the development team. The development team must not only understand the business of the end user, but must convey the possibilities as well as the limitations of the new database.

The design of a database should have the end-user application in mind. The database is one of a two-part solution for the end user and the business. The features of the database should facilitate the needs of the business and the end user such that all elements of the back-end database and the front-end application are knitted closely together—with the goal of an application that renders the actual design and structure of the database as transparent to the end user as possible.

Case Study—TrainTech

Throughout the course of this book, we will be designing a database using the relational model. The business for which the database is needed is a student registration database for a small training company. Let's call this training company TrainTech. The basic information to be maintained in this database includes

- Class information
- Instructor information
- Student/customer information
- Class schedules
- Class materials
- Accounts payable
- Accounts receivable

As we progress through the book, more details will be added to this basic information where appropriate, and will be used to show how a business model is derived, and eventually transformed into a database model. By the end of the book, we will provide examples of models and physical designs based on TrainTech. The mission statement for TrainTech follows.

Mission Statement and Objectives for Our Model Company, TrainTech

Mission statement—An automated business system is needed to manage and track student class registrations, class schedules, instructors, and instructor availability.

Mission objectives:

- The manual process of managing the training program will be automated.
- Internal users will be accessing the database.
- The relational model will be used.
- An automated design (AD) tool will be used to design the database.
- Currently no database is in place to meet the present needs (no legacy database).
- The database might need to be modified as the training company grows and more data storage requirements are established.
- This will be a single database that will reside in one location.
- The users will implement a form interface to query and make changes to data in the database.
- Instructors should be able to query the database and check the status of classes they teach.
- In the future, a portion of the database can be made available online so that students can query the status of classes or programs for which they are scheduled.

Devising a Work Plan

After the mission statement and design objectives have been defined, it is time to devise a work plan that will be used as a guide for the design of the database. A work plan is an outline that breaks down the steps involved.

Following are preliminary considerations for devising a work plan:

- Location of the work to be conducted.
- A design team must be established.
- Business rules.
- Hardware to be used.
- Software to be used.
- Tools for development.
- Tools for the end users.
- Backup plan for development work done.
- Database environments used for development.

- Basic standards and naming conventions.
- Database environment for production.

The work plan is discussed in more detail, and an example is fully developed in Chapter 5, "Gathering Business and System Requirements."

Setting Milestones and Making Deadlines

A *milestone* is a significant point in the database design process. The most common events in the design process that are associated with milestones are the completion of the different design phases. Following are common milestones:

- All business requirements are gathered.
- A work plan is devised.
- Entities and attributes are established.
- The logical design of the database is complete.
- The physical design of the database is complete.
- The database is tested.
- The database is implemented into production.

Project timeframes should be determined for each milestone established. Deadline dates are established and associated with each milestone. Deadlines are typically set by management and project leads of the development team. Often, the drop-dead date is first established for the final product. Then, the design team might work backwards in order to establish deadline dates for each phase of development. With this type of mindset, it is easy to fall into the trap of not allowing enough time in the beginning to plan the design process and completely gather all the facts necessary to start the design. If the drop-dead date is unreasonable—which in most cases it is—different parts of the phases throughout database design can be rushed, and the final design might not be as good as it could have been. Therefore, reasonable deadlines should be set for milestones, while also realizing the pressure at hand to quickly crank out a working database and application. Whatever the circumstance, deadlines must be set to ensure the forward motion of the project. As with most aspects of life, if a goal or deadline is not set, nothing will be accomplished.

Caution

Not allowing enough time when planning design and gathering business requirements will inevitably cause more work and time in the long run. The final database model might be incomplete (not accurately representing all data), and effort will have to be dispensed in order to rectify the problems encountered via a poor design.

Establishing the Design Team and Assigning Tasks

After a work plan has been established and milestones with deadlines are set, a design (development) team is established if one does not already exist. The design team might consist of one or many individuals. The responsibility to design a database might fall into the hands of only one individual for smaller companies. In fact, this one individual might comprise the entire IT department. For larger companies with larger projects, many individuals will most likely be involved.

Figure 3.1 illustrates a typical design team for a relatively large project. The project lead is the central point of contact for all members of the design team. As you can see, each type of member in the design team has his own responsibilities. The database administrator (DBA) and end users are somewhat detached from the actual design process. The database administrator is involved primarily in establishing a development environment and enforcing security. The end users are interviewed by members of the design team while gathering business and system requirements. Later, the DBA will help implement the finished product while the end user waits to use the finished product.

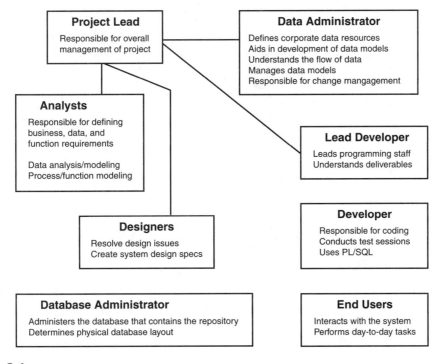

FIGURE 3.1

A typical design team.

Different tasks within the work plan are distributed to various members, or small groups, within the design team by the project manager. The distribution of work to multiple members of the design team allows concurrent work on the project to take place, expediting the overall process tremendously. When tasks are assigned, individual designers or small groups work toward small-scale goals for each task as outlined in the work plan. Deliverables, which usually include a status report, are made to the project manager by individuals on the design team. Each task assigned to an individual designer should have a deadline with the timeline of the entire project in mind.

Figure 3.2 illustrates how tasks are assigned to members of a design team. The project lead will distribute work to the team leaders, who assign individual tasks to the members of the team. After the individual members have completed their assigned tasks, a deliverable is provided to the team leader. The team leader might determine that more work needs to be done before the deliverable is sent back to the project lead. When the project lead receives deliverables from the team leaders, the project lead might also determine that more work needs to be done. If more work is required, the task is reassigned to the appropriate team or individuals.

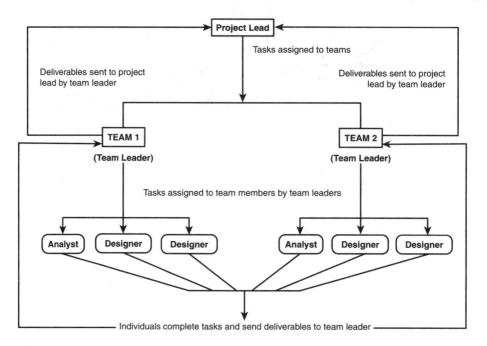

FIGURE 3.2

Task assignment and deliverables in a design team.

Trademarks of a Solid Database Design

If the design of a database has been well-planned, a valuable database will be derived for the customer. The key to a design with little friction is having a workable design plan. The design plan is dependent on the work involved in establishing the goals of the proposed database, as paralleled to the needs of the business itself. Although the design plan represents a small portion of the work involved during a design effort, a successful design effort cannot take place without a good plan.

Trademarks of a good database design include

- A functional database is generated.
- The database accurately represents the business's data.
- The database will be easy to use and maintain.
- Acceptable response time exists for the end users.
- Modifications are easily made to the structure.
- Data can be retrieved and modified easily.
- Down time because of poor design is minimized.
- Very little maintenance is needed.
- Data is kept safe by planning for security.
- Redundant data is minimized or nonexistent.
- Data can be easily backed up or recovered.
- The actual structure of the database will be virtually transparent to the end user.

Overview of Design Methodologies

Design methodologies deal with how a company goes about designing a database. What phases will be involved during the design process? A methodology represents the thought process used by the design team in order to develop a database model. Some of the questions that should be raised when selecting a design methodology are

- What tools are available to aid in design?
- How critical is development time?
- What are the skills of the developers?
- Will the project require outsourcing?
- What resources are available for the project?

The most predominant factor when selecting a design methodology is the technology or tools available at the time design begins. Software products can be used to perform most tasks associated with database design. However, tools should be used only to enhance, not drive the design process. Developers should never rely on a tool to do all the work. Tools rely heavily on the experience of the developer in order to guarantee a database model that will yield an acceptable design and a well-performing database.

The time allotted to design and implement a database might not allow for a lengthy, drawn-out design. Although rushing through design might jeopardize the quality of the end product, some situations might require that the phases of the design methodology chosen be condensed. Rapid development might occur for a database, but phases of design must be clearly marked, and the design process must be documented such that changes can be easily made to the database. If rapid development is required, modifications will inevitably need to be made, which makes version control of databases and applications very important.

If individuals in the company do not have expertise to design a database, outsourcing work might be involved. If outsourcing occurs, the company might have less control over the methodology or tools used to design the database. Also, if work is outsourced, the total cost of design can be much higher. The tradeoff, however, is that the end user will hopefully have a database of higher quality on a more timely basis. Individuals can then study the design performed so that training needs can be assessed and an attempt can be made to design subsequent databases. If outsourcing occurs, documentation must be released by the outsourcing agency so that developers in the company can more easily understand the structure of the database model. The corporate budget might not allow for a consulting agency to visit again.

Design methodology traditionally involves the following three phases:

1. Requirements analysis
2. Data modeling
3. Design and Normalization

Requirements analysis involves capturing the needs of the business, and converting those needs into the requirements for a business system. Information is gathered in order to begin modeling the database in the data modeling phase. During data modeling, business processes, rules, entities, and organizational units are visually represented in order to provide the design team with a good understanding of the business system's needs. Finally, objects in the data model are designed into tables and normalized to reduce the amount of redundant data stored in the database. Most methodologies follow these three steps.

In Chapter 4, "The Database Design Life Cycle," specific design methodologies are discussed in greater detail.

If a design methodology is used, the design effort will be more organized. When using a design methodology, the design team will have a step-by-step plan for designing the proposed database at hand. After a design plan has been formulated, it will be easier to assess the skills of developers to determine if training is needed before proceeding with the project. The result of using a methodology and following it step by step will be a complete and accurate data model, and eventually an improved end product. Using a methodology might involve more time up front when planning the design effort, but much time will be saved in the long run. There will be much fewer times that a redesign will need to occur for a particular business process or entity. If mistakes are made, you will have the knowledge to correct these mistakes before it is too late or before much time is invested.

Logical Versus Physical Modeling

After all business requirements have been gathered for the proposed database, these requirements must be modeled. Models are created to visually represent the proposed database so that business requirements can easily be associated with database objects to ensure that all requirements have been completely and accurately gathered. Different types of diagrams are typically produced to illustrate the business processes, rules, entities, and organizational units that have been identified. These diagrams often include entity relationship diagrams, process flow diagrams, and server model diagrams. An entity relationship diagram (ERD) represents the entities, or groups of information, and their relationships maintained for a business. Process flow diagrams represent business processes and the flow of data between different processes and entities that have been defined. Server model diagrams represent a detailed picture of the database as being transformed from the business model into a relational database with tables, columns, and constraints. Basically, data modeling serves as a link between business needs and system requirements.

Two types of data modeling are as follows:

- Logical modeling
- Physical modeling

It is important to understand the difference between logical and physical modeling, and how they relate to one another. Logical and physical modeling are described in more detail in the following subsections.

Logical Modeling

Logical modeling deals with gathering business requirements and converting those requirements into a model. The logical model revolves around the needs of the business, not the database, although the needs of the business are used to establish the needs of the database.

Logical modeling involves gathering information about business processes, business entities (categories of data), and organizational units. After this information is gathered, diagrams and reports are produced including entity relationship diagrams, business process diagrams, and eventually process flow diagrams. The diagrams produced should show the processes and data that exists, as well as the relationships between business processes and data. Logical modeling should accurately render a visual representation of the activities and data relevant to a particular business.

> **NOTE**
>
> Logical modeling affects not only the direction of database design, but also indirectly affects the performance and administration of an implemented database. When time is invested performing logical modeling, more options become available for planning the design of the physical database.

The diagrams and documentation generated during logical modeling is used to determine whether the requirements of the business have been completely gathered. Management, developers, and end users alike review these diagrams and documentation to determine if more work is required before physical modeling commences.

Typical deliverables of logical modeling include

- Entity relationship diagrams
- Business process diagrams
- User feedback documentation

Each of these deliverables are covered in subsequent chapters.

Typical design phases that apply to logical modeling:

- Gathering requirements
- Requirements analysis

Physical Modeling

Physical modeling involves the actual design of a database according to the requirements that were established during logical modeling. Logical modeling mainly involves gathering the requirements of the business, with the latter part of logical modeling directed toward the goals and requirements of the database. Physical modeling deals with the conversion of the logical, or business model, into a relational database model. When physical modeling occurs, objects are being defined at the schema level. As stated in Chapter 1, "Understanding Database Fundamentals," a schema is a group of related objects in a database. A database design effort is normally associated with one schema.

During physical modeling, objects such as tables and columns are created based on entities and attributes that were defined during logical modeling. Constraints are also defined, including primary keys, foreign keys, other unique keys, and check constraints. Views can be created from database tables to summarize data or to simply provide the user with another perspective of certain data. Other objects such as indexes and snapshots can also be defined during physical modeling. Physical modeling is when all the pieces come together to complete the process of defining a database for a business.

Physical modeling is database software specific, meaning that the objects defined during physical modeling can vary depending on the relational database software being used. For example, most relational database systems have variations with the way data types are represented and the way data is stored, although basic data types are conceptually the same among different implementations. Additionally, some database systems have objects that are not available in other database systems.

Implementation of the Physical Model

The implementation of the physical model is dependent on the hardware and software being used by the company. The hardware can determine what type of software can be used because software is normally developed according to common hardware and operating system platforms. Some database software might only be available for Windows NT systems, whereas other software products such as Oracle are available on a wider range of operating system platforms, such as UNIX. The available hardware is also important during the implementation of the physical model because data is physically distributed onto one or more physical disk drives. Normally, the more physical drives available, the better the performance of the database after the implementation. Some software products now are Java-based and can run on virtually any platform. Typically, the decisions to use particular hardware, operating system platforms, and database software are made in conjunction with one another.

Typical deliverables of physical modeling include the following:

- Server model diagrams
- User feedback documentation
- Database design documentation

Typical development phases that apply to physical modeling:

- Design
- Implementation
- Maintenance

Automated Design Tools

Automated design tools (formerly known as CASE tools) are graphical user interface (GUI) applications that are used to aid in the design of a database or database application. Automated design tools are used to automate and expedite the task of designing a business system. These automated tools store information about business requirements and assist in the overall design and generation of a business system.

Automated design (AD) tools are vendor-specific. Countless AD tools are available today with a variety of features. All AD tools have one goal in common—to assist the developer in assuring that a complete database model or database application is designed in a timely fashion.

Some of the most robust features of many AD tools include the following:

- The capability to capture business and user needs
- The capability to model business processes
- The capability to model the flow of data in an organization
- The capability to model entities and their relationships
- The capability to generate DDL to create database objects
- Full life cycle database support
- Business process reengineering/reverse engineering
- Database and application version control
- Generation of reports for documentation and user-feedback sessions

The features, benefits, and drawbacks of using an Automated Design (AD) tool are discussed in more detail in the following subsections.

Oracle Designer

Oracle Designer (formerly called Oracle Designer/2000) is one of the most powerful CASE tools on the market because of its capability to store information in a single repository. The repository is basically a schema in a database that contains metadata (data about other data). System and application design information is stored in this central repository so that data can be shared among a team of developers. Unfortunately, this capability makes Oracle Designer a resource-intensive application for the client/server computing environment, which might require a more powerful server with more memory, depending on the number of concurrent users. However, the benefits of using Designer normally outweigh the costs involved for the software licensing and additional hardware for most medium- to large-sized companies.

Over the past decade, Oracle Corporation has grown tremendously and has made its presence known in most large companies and government agencies, particularly those that have chosen to use the relational database model. Many government agencies have designated the Oracle RDBMS (relational database management system) as their standard software. Many agencies have also mandated that system design and development is performed using Oracle Designer and Developer/2000.

Some of the features of Oracle Designer include

- Business processes are easily modeled.
- Data flows are easily modeled.
- Entity relationship diagrams can be created.
- Existing databases can be reverse engineered.
- It is easy to convert the business model into a data model.
- A central repository allows information to be shared among developers.
- DDL is easily generated.
- Application code and forms can be generated.

3

Why Use an Automated Design Tool?

So, why use an automated design tool? Sure, there is the obvious reason—more of the design process is automated and as much of the mundane tasks are performed by the application. But what are the real benefits to the development team, the company, and the customer?

First of all, overall productivity is increased because many of the traditionally manual tasks are automated. Less time is spent performing tedious tasks, and more time is spent thinking about the actual design of the database. Because an AD tool automates much of the design process, the time taken to design a database is reduced. Because time involved is reduced, more time is available to interview the customer, conduct user feedback sessions, and pay closer attention to the details of the business. Unfortunately, because management probably realizes that an AD tool is supposed to increase productivity, demands might be placed on the development team to produce a database and a working application in a time frame more unreasonable than ever before. The development team might not be any happier, but the company is happier because the database can be designed with lower costs because of the reduction in time involved.

Fine, you might be in the same time crunch as you were before an AD tool was used. Another great benefit of using an AD tool is the improved quality of the end product. Regardless of most situations, the customer wants the database yesterday, and management often follows suit. One thing you can be sure of is that if the AD tool is properly used, it will be easier to ensure that all business processes, entities, and rules have been captured. Features such as process models and entity relationship diagrams help the designer visualize the database, making the business easier to understand and making it easier to correlate the business with a data model. Diagrams are easy to draw and easy to read in most cases. Reports can be produced to show the business elements that have been captured. Oracle Designer, for instance, allows a matrix diagram to be generated, which can be used to show the completeness of usage between elements such as business processes and entities.

Some AD tools can be used to manage changes that occur to a database system or an application. Changes are first made to the data model using the AD tool; then DDL is generated, the changes are propagated to test, and finally the system is moved to production. Many AD tools support the full life cycle of a database or application, as well as full support of the basic phases of database design (analysis, data modeling, normalization).

An AD tool should promote better organization during the development process. You can clearly see the work that has been performed using an AD tool if the AD tool has been used properly. Some AD tools allow work performed by designers to be shared. By sharing data, design team members can see the work performed by other members of the team and can access the same objects; thus duplicate effort is minimized. However, communication between team members is often a problem, even when using an AD tool.

Without the use of an AD tool, business systems are designed manually, allowing for the following problems:

- Manual intervention means more time, which equates to higher costs.
- Manual intervention also means greater possibilities for errors exist.
- Less structured design and development process.
- Communication is less consistent.
- Business requirements might not have been completely captured.

Advantages of an Automated Design Tool

Following is a summarization of the benefits associated with using an AD tool for system design or application development:

- The designer can easily generate readable diagrams to help the development team, management, and customer visualize the business and proposed database.
- Chances for errors because a lot of manual work is reduced.

- Mundane tasks are automated.
- The development process is expedited.
- The development process can cost less because less time is spent.
- The amount of code to be written is reduced.
- Easy to convert the business model to a working database model.
- Easy to ensure that all business requirements have been captured for the proposed database.
- A higher quality, more accurate product is produced.

> **NOTE**
>
> One of the most common pitfalls of using an AD tool is that management expects too much of the AD tool. Also, developers often think that an AD tool will do the thinking for them. On the contrary, the developer must understand how to design a database. Remember that the purpose of an AD tool is to enhance the tasks of an experienced developer. Contrary to popular belief, an AD tool will not make your coffee, read your junk mail, or answer the phone. However, it walks the developer through the design process so that he can determine whether all necessary steps have been followed toward a functional database.

3

DATABASE DESIGN
PLANNING

Disadvantages of an Automated Design Tool

We discussed many of the advantages of using an AD tool. Now, we will make you aware of some of the disadvantages. Following is a summarization of these disadvantages as related to the design of a database or an application:

- More expenses involved for the tool itself.
- Additional hardware costs might be incurred to support the tool selected.
- Developers might require special training to use the tool, which can cost the company significantly.
- An AD tool might not meet the expectations of management or the design team.
- High learning curve involved to learn how to use the tool.
- The developer must completely understand the design process.
- Many developers end up using the AD tool as a crutch.

Understanding the Capabilities of an Automated Design Tool

In the modern IT department, an AD tool will most likely be used to develop a database system or an application. Before an AD tool can (or should) be used, all parties involved must understand the capabilities and limitations of the tool.

Following are some dependencies of a successful database implementation using an AD tool:

- Management must understand the capabilities of the tool.
- Management must understand the limitations of the AD tool.
- Developers must take advantage of all capabilities of the tool.
- Designers and developers should be trained to use the AD tool.
- Might require initial consulting support for new projects.
- Although an AD tool simplifies many tasks, avoid short cuts throughout the design process.
- Define naming conventions and standards to be used before using the tool.
- Make sure that the tool is compatible with the database software.
- Ensure that developers have sufficient knowledge and experience to use the tool.

Before selecting a tool, try to research the history of the tool and other individuals' experiences with the tool. Although it is normally best to get the latest version of a tool, you might want to hold off on new versions with dramatic changes until other users have had a chance to find all the bugs.

Summary

Database design is a premeditated effort to gather the requirements of a business and formulate those requirements into a data model. Database design is a meticulous process that requires close attention to detail, involving deep planning, user/customer interaction, and drawing diagrams that provide a visual representation of business functions and data.

Database design requires much planning. The more time spent identifying the goals of a business system and planning the actual design process, the less time and frustration will be expended in the long run trying to resolve a poor design. The objectives of the proposed database must be clearly defined in order for the development team to properly gather the requirements. A work plan should be devised to provide guidelines for developers on how the flow of the design project will progress. Milestones should be set, which mark major events throughout the design process. Each milestone should be assigned a projected due date. Before design begins, a design team is formed and tasks are assigned to groups or individuals on the team.

Individuals on the design team submit deliverables to the team leader (the design team can be broken into smaller teams in order to distribute work more efficiently). The customer and management might also require deliverables, such as reports and diagrams used during user-feedback sessions.

Many aspects of a good database design will only be seen if adequate time is spent planning the design, and the specific steps of the design methodology used are closely followed. Therefore, a database will be produced that meets the users' needs. Data stored in a well-designed database will be accurate and easy to maintain. From the administrative perspective, the database will be easy to maintain. Data integrity will be implemented and the constraints that are defined based on the data model will ensure data consistency. Finally, there should be a balance between minimizing redundant data and optimizing database performance.

There are two basic types of modeling: logical and physical. Logical modeling is the process of modeling the activities of a business, and how those activities relate to the business data. Logical modeling usually involves the generation of business process models and entity relationship diagrams. Physical modeling is the process of converting the logical model, or business model, into a database model. The entities that exist in the logical model become database tables in the physical modeling. During physical model, also called database design, views and indexes are also defined based on tables that have been defined. The physical model is associated with the physical schema that actually comprises the database objects that the end user will eventually access.

Using automated design tools is the process of using a GUI tool to assist in the design of a database or database application. Many vendors provide a wide variety of AD tools, although the goal of all AD tools is basically the same: to assist the developer during the database and application design to produce a more complete model and reduce the chance for errors during implementation. Many features are common to most AD tools. AD tools typically allow the developer to easily generate diagrams such as process models and entity relationship diagrams. One of the greatest assets of using an AD tool is that the amount of manual coding to produce DDL or application code is minimized, or does not exist. For example, an AD application may generate all the code you need based on the information supplied to the tool during analysis and design.

Now that the database design has been defined and the goals of the design process have been discussed, it is important to understand the basics of using a particular methodology to design a database. The next chapter discusses design methodologies, the actual process of database design, and the life cycle of a database in detail.

3

DATABASE DESIGN PLANNING

The Database Design Life Cycle

IN THIS CHAPTER

Various methodologies might be used when designing a relational database. A design methodology is the thought-process and steps taken during the design of a database system. Methodologies that are used during database design are driven mainly by the knowledge and experience of developers, as well as automated design (AD) products that are available.

Presently, you should understand the basic definition and goals of the database design process. In this chapter, the database design process will be discussed in more detail as related to design methodology. The design process described in this book includes the steps of the Barker method, which is discussed later.

Business process re-engineering (BPR) is often a key process in the design of a system. Simply defined, BPR is the process of reworking an existing database or application to make things better. BPR also plays a significant role during the actual life of a database system that has been developed. As time passes, new business requirements might arise that require the system to be modified or re-engineered. The re-engineering of an existing system might consist of numerous minor changes to existing processes, or might involve a complete overhaul to the structural design of the database.

Finally, the life cycle of the database from implementation to its nonexistence is discussed. Once a database has been designed, it is implemented, or made available to the end user. Three vital environments exist for a database that has been designed.

1. Development environment
2. Test environment
3. Production environment

The objective of this chapter is to describe database design methodology, and to show briefly how to begin designing a relational database based on a methodology chosen. The process of design is woven together with the life of the database during and after implementation. It is important to understand and consider the use of the concepts discussed before starting the actual design process.

The System Development Process

By now, you should have a good understanding of database design and the typical goals and expectations of a database design effort. It is most important that ample time is reserved to plan the entire design process. The actual design of a database system, referred to here as the system development process, involves several steps. The steps involved will vary depending on the methodology used.

The following methodologies will be discussed in detail:

- The traditional design method

- The Barker method
- Adapted design methods

Most methodologies root from the traditional method. The Barker method for designing a database expands on the steps involved in the traditional method. These two basic methodologies will be used as the basis for the design process discussed in this book. Adapted design methods might also be used. In fact, some situations might require that a selected method be modified to meet the exact needs of a business.

Regardless of the methodology used, common sense dictates that system development consists of the following basic principles:

1. Determining the need for a system
2. Defining the goals for the system
3. Gathering business requirements
4. Converting business requirements to system requirements
5. Designing the database and application interface
6. Building, testing, and implementing the database and application

You will find that all these basic principles are considered regardless of the design methodology selected. Throughout the book, these principles are explained in great detail so that there is no confusion on how a relational database should be designed for optimal functionality and performance.

Traditional Method

Most methodologies used today stem from that of the traditional method. Three of the primary phases involved in the traditional method are as follows:

1. Requirements analysis
2. Data modeling
3. Normalization

Figure 4.1 illustrates the fundamental steps involved in the traditional method. During the requirement-analysis phase, research is conducted in order to capture all the business needs as related to the proposed database system. Interviews are conducted by the development team in order to gather the information that will be used to design the database system. The data modeling phase involves the creation of the logical data model that will be used to define the physical database structures, or the physical data model. After the system has been modeled and designed, the normalization process is used to eliminate (or reduce as much as possible) redundant data. The following subsections discuss these steps in more detail.

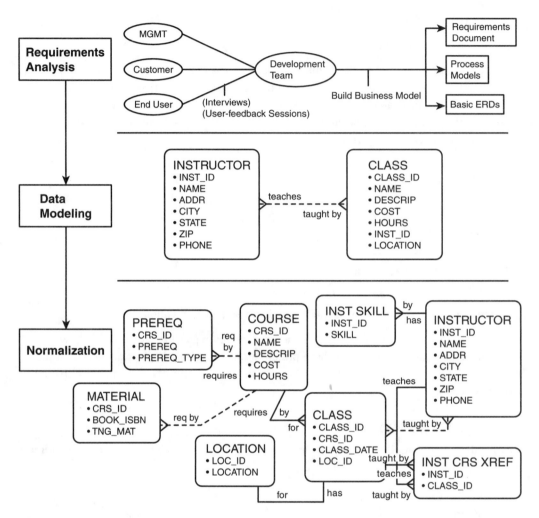

FIGURE 4.1

The traditional design method.

Requirements Analysis Phase

Regardless of the design methodology used, requirement-gathering is always (and obviously) the first step taken toward designing an information system. There is no way to intelligently commence a design effort without adequate knowledge of the business itself. Business requirements are the data, processes, and rules that comprise a business.

Different types of users play a major role during the requirements phase of the traditional design method. The two basic types of users are application users and system users.

Application users consist of the end user and the customer. This is the user who implements the application interface to access the database that has been designed. The system user consists of developers, database administrators, programmers, and other members of the system design team or information technology department. Each of the aforementioned users plays a significant role during the requirements phase. For example, the customer might be interviewed in order to gather the needs that the customer has for the proposed database system. The end user will be interviewed in order to identify the needs that she has as far as accessing the back-end database that has been developed. Often, the customer and end user is the same individual or group of individuals. The system users, which are comprised mainly of the database design team, use the database and software tools to design and maintain an information system. The database administrator might be required to establish a development environment for the design team. For example, the development environment might consist of a back-end database that is used to host a repository that stores design information used by an automated design tool.

After all appropriate parties have been interviewed, the development team is responsible for considering all the issues and requirements brought forward by the customer, the end user, and perhaps management in order to begin formulating a basic model of the actual processes involved in the daily operations of the business. The parties interviewed will help the development team determine the categories of data, business processes, rules, and other information important to begin modeling the system.

> **NOTE**
>
> The development team cannot capture the complete needs of the business without taking into consideration the issues raised during interviews and conducting frequent user feedback sessions. What is the purpose of the database? This is a question that must be answered before the design process actually begins. But this is also a question that should be raised throughout the design process in order to ensure that the original goals set forth for the system are being met.

In order to ensure that the requirements phase runs smoothly, and that all the needs of the business and the end-user community are completely gathered, an analysis plan should be devised in order to guide the development team. The developers are the primary users of the analysis plan. The analysis plan should include milestones for the development team throughout the course of the requirements phase. The analysis plan is basically an outline of the events that will occur during the requirements phase of the design process.

One of the most important products of the requirements phase is an entity relationship diagram that illustrates the business model. This diagram is also referred to as an analysis ERD. The point of this initial ERD is to provide the development team with a picture of the different categories of data for the business, as well as how these categories of data are related to one another. The analysis ERD might also be used during user feedback sessions to show the user, customer, or management work that has actually been performed so far. The ERD can also be used when compiling summarized documentation of what occurred during the requirements phase. Keep in mind that this ERD should be simple and focused on the business, not the actual system. Later, this analysis ERD will be used during the detail design of the database system.

Another product of the requirements phase is the process model. The process model is used to illustrate all the parent and child processes that are performed by individuals within a company. The process model gives the development team an idea of how data moves within the organization. Because process models illustrate the activities of individuals in the company, the process model can be used to determine how a database application interface is designed. Both the analysis ERD and the process models are included in the requirements document, which outlines all the needs for a system from the business perspective.

Other issues such as performance of the system might be taken into consideration for the requirements phase. The performance of the current system that the user employs might be unacceptable, or prohibit the user from maximizing the use of his time. If performance issues are raised and addressed up front, fewer changes will have to be made to the system after initial implementation into production. Performance issues should be major considerations when designing a database.

Good candidates for questions can be obtained by gathering the aforementioned requirements include the following: What are the future needs of the business? Will the database grow after a certain period of time? Is the business planning to merge with another business, extending the overall processes that will comprise the daily operations. How will the end user's needs change over the course of the next year or two in terms of accessing the data? A developer should never think that after a database has been designed, major modifications will never occur. Business needs are always changing; therefore a database should be designed with future needs in mind.

After preliminary questions have been raised to gather requirements, additional questions should be raised that are pertinent to database design. Are there any other needs the user has in terms of accessing the database? What tools will be used to access the database? Will in-house software be developed for the end user? Will a large number of concurrent users be accessing the database, and will large amounts of data be heavily accessed on a frequent basis? All these questions should be answered to determine exactly how a database will be modeled. The next section deals with the steps involved in modeling a database after all the business requirements have been captured.

Data Modeling Phase

Data modeling is the process of visually representing all the business requirements that were established during the requirements phase of the design process. During the first parts of the data modeling phase, processes and entities that were previously defined are now defined in more detail. The basic ERD is detailed to include attributes within each entity. Attributes might be assigned different properties that dictate the specific type of data to be stored. Process models are used to determine how processes access entities within the organization. During logical modeling, relationships that were established between entities are refined if necessary, and business rules are integrated into the model.

During the data modeling phase of the design process, the focus is now on the proposed system; whereas during the requirements phase, the focus was solely on the business. All the business needs that were gathered during the requirements phase and molded into a logical data model are now converted into a physical database model. In other words, the business model is converted into a data model, representing tables and columns. The logical data model is used to actually design the physical database structures that comprise a database schema. Logical modeling is actually the first step of database design.

> **NOTE**
>
> Business rules are used to determine the relationships that exist between entities and tables, and how data is handled by the end-user through processes. Business rules may be integrated at the back-end database level, the front-end application level, or at the middle tier level in n-tier applications. Two-tier may be how the database environment we describe here initially looks, but it is not how it is often built and implemented. The main focus of this book is on the design of the database itself; however, it is also important to study the integration of business rules at various levels to understand the big picture. Chapter 12 discusses the integration of business rules into the database design process, and also explains how business rules may be distributed among various levels in an n-tier database application.

4

THE DATABASE
DESIGN LIFE
CYCLE

Physical data modeling will either be a fairly simple process, or might result in a lot of aggravation depending on the work that has been accomplished during the requirements phase and logical data modeling. For example, if the requirements were not completely collected during the requirements phase, more work will have to be done during the logical modeling phase in order to derive an accurate logical data model. If the logical data model is not complete, incompleteness will be carried over into the physical model, which affects the finished product. In addition to the extra work that will inevitably occur during the data modeling phase, the development team might find it necessary to refocus on the initial phase in order to completely capture the needs of the business.

By now, all business units and entities should have been defined, and all detail should have been added to the process models in the ERDs. Although management is often eager to produce a finished product to present to the customer, the development team should never be too hasty to proceed to the next step of the design process. Again, failure to ensure that the data model is complete during the modeling phase might require more work during the next phase. In addition, inadequacies might exist in the finished system that require immediate attention and fixes.

Referring back to Figure 4.1, you can see that detail has now been added to the ERD. Two entities are shown: instructor and class. The instructor entity contains information about individual instructors who teach classes. The class and the instructor entity tracks information about classes that are taught by instructors. You can also see that a relationship has been defined between the two entities. The relationship shown here is a many-to-many relationship, which will be discussed in more detail in Chapter 7, "Understanding Entities and Relationships." We will also show how a cross-reference table can be used to avoid the occurrence of many-to-many table relationships. The data model you see here will be used to generate database tables and columns.

Normalization Phase

After the business model has been converted into the logical data model and the initial design of the physical database has occurred (physical data model), it might be necessary to normalize the contents of the database. Normalization is important because it reduces the amount of redundant data in the database. Depending on the level of normalization, redundant data might be completely eliminated. During the normalization process, large tables with many columns are divided, or split, into smaller tables with a smaller number of columns. The main benefit of normalization is to promote overall data consistency between tables and data accuracy through the reduction of redundant information that is stored. In essence, data only needs to be modified in one place if an occurrence of the data is only stored one time. The primary drawback of normalization, however, is the fact that performance might suffer drastically in a database that has been normalized. The further a database is normalized, the more performance will be affected. The level of database normalization will vary for each company in each situation. The level of normalization also depends on the type of database that is being designed. For example, a database that is being designed for a high-level of transactional activity will not be affected performance-wise nearly as much as a database receiving large queries, such as a data warehouse.

If a database has been normalized, it might be concluded that the trade-off of decreased performance is not acceptable for the customer. In this case, the development team might determine that it is necessary to normalize the database to a certain degree. Denormalization is the process of combining database structures to increase the amount of redundant data stored in the database, with the goal of improving performance for the end user. When a database has been designed, it is often difficult to determine exactly how all performance will be affected based on the design of the database. Other factors are involved in database performance, although the design of a database is by far the most important.

Referring back to Figure 4.1, you can see that in the normalization phase of database design, the existing database structures, such as the instructor and class entities, have been normalized, or broken down into multiple entities in order to reduce the amount of redundant data. For example, the instructor table has been broken down into an instructor entity and an instructor skill entity. Also, the class entity has been broken down into several additional entities. The main entity, which was class, is now course. Course represents a specific course that is taught by the training institution. The class entity represents each occurrence of a course, or each time a course is taught. The training institution might have several locations at which classes are taught. Therefore, it is unnecessary to store the name of the location for each class that is taught—only the ID for the location is necessary. The ID for the location is used to reference the location name that is found in the location entity. Additionally, a course might have prerequisites and materials, such as a background in science and a textbook and lab materials. Because a course might have many prerequisites and many materials, it is better to store the detailed information in separate entities. This is normalization.

The following normal forms are discussed in Chapter 8, "Normalization: Eliminating Redundant Data."

- First normal form
- Second normal form
- Third normal form
- Fourth normal form
- Fifth normal form
- Domain/key normal form

The Barker Method

The Barker method for relational database design uses the same principles as the traditional method. The Barker method was named after Richard Barker, a board director of Oracle Corporation. Richard Barker was responsible for the initial effort to design Oracle's automated design tool (formerly referred to as a CASE tool), which is now referred to as Oracle Designer. One of the foremost goals was to design an automated design tool that assisted the developer in all phases, during the full cycle of system development as well as in the design of a relational database. The Barker method is a real-time version of the traditional method, providing more steps in order to better organize a database design effort.

The Barker method involves the following seven phases:

1. Strategy
2. Analysis
3. Design
4. Build
5. Documentation
6. Transition
7. Production

Strategy involves planning the design effort. In the analysis phase, the development team interviews key employees to gather all the business requirements—which will be used as a model for the system. During the design phase, a physical model is designed based on the logical model that was designed in the analysis phase. After the design is complete, the database is built. The use of documentation is extremely beneficial, both for system users and application users. During the transition phase, data is prepared to be moved into the production environment. The end-user application is tested against the database with real data to ensure that all components of the application function properly and that the integrity of the data as stored in the database is consistent. Finally, the database is ported into a production environment, where it is available to the end user for daily use.

Figure 4.2 illustrates the phases of the Barker method. Each of these phases will be discussed in detail in the following subsections. Each subsection will refer back to this figure to explain the basic concepts of each phase. You might want to review the figure briefly before you continue.

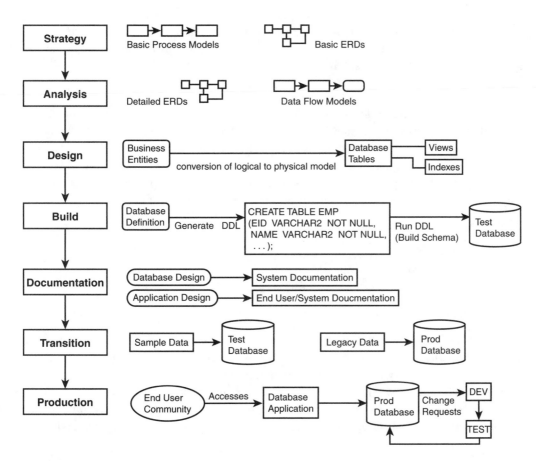

FIGURE 4.2

Database design using the Barker method.

Strategy Phase

As in the requirements phase of the traditional method, the strategy phase of the Barker method addresses the needs of the business. During the strategy phase, the needs of the system are not considered whatsoever. In this phase, a strategy document might be developed to guide the development team to the next phase, analysis. During the strategy phase, two different types of diagrams might be produced: a strategy ERD and process flow diagrams. The strategy ERD is used to break down the basic categories of information that the business stores into entities. The strategy ERD should be very simple, showing only the business entities and their relationships to one another. The process flow diagrams should also be fairly simple, showing the basic parent and child processes that are performed by individuals within the company.

Later, during the analysis phase, more detail can be added to these diagrams. These diagrams should be kept simple during the strategy phase in order to ensure that all the needs of the business are being completely captured by the business model.

Analysis Phase

During the analysis phase of the Barker method, the development team attempts to completely gather all requirements of the business that will be used to design the system. At this point, the focus is on the end users' needs and business requirements, not on the system itself. Now, it is very important to ensure that all details are gathered, such as attributes within entities, all process steps, relationships between entities, and data flows between processes and entities. An entity that is being accessed by a process is also referred to as a data store.

The main deliverables of the analysis phase are as follows:

- An analysis ERD
- A function hierarchy diagram
- Data flow diagrams
- Requirements document

The analysis ERD should outline all details of entities that the development team is aware of at this point. Primarily, all attributes of entities (which will eventually become columns in a table) should be defined. Primary keys might also be defined for entities. Data types might be set as well as constraints, if known. Remember, the more work that is done during the analysis phase, the less work that will have to be performed during the design phase. Additionally, if more time is spent during the analysis phase, chances are increased in having a more complete product.

When analysis is thought to be complete, an end-of-phase evaluation should occur. During analysis evaluation, it is important to verify that all deliverables of the analysis phase were met. It is also critical that all business processes and entities have been defined before proceeding to the design phase. Questions that might be raised during the analysis evaluation include the following:

- Are the business requirements complete?
- Have all rules been defined?
- Is the ERD complete?
- Have all business processes been completely defined?

Figure 4.2 shows how data flow models might be generated from the basic process models. In the data flow model shown, the second process step accesses an entity. This entity is also referred to as a data store. The arrow protruding from the second process step to the entity is called a data flow. Data flows are used to determine how and when entities are accessed.

Access to entities includes mainly data retrievals, updates to information, the insertion of new information, and deletion of information. If all processes, data flows, and entities are completely defined during the analysis phase, you should have a business model that illustrates how each entity is accessed.

Design Phase

The objective of the design phase in the Barker method is to physically design the schema that will be built based on the business model defined during the strategy and analysis phases. The work that takes place during the design phase is called a physical model. During design, logical process flows are converted into physical process flows and logical ERDs are converted into diagrams that represent a physical database.

The logical process flow diagrams are models of all the processes and functions that are performed by individuals within the organization. The physical process flows are based on logical flows, but include those processes which will be used to model the system. The physical process flows are generated during design, comprising the application part of the design process.

The logical database structure consists mainly of entities and attributes and the relationships between the entities. During the physical design of the database, business entities are converted into database tables. Entity attributes are converted into table columns. During the design phase, all data types and constraints must be completely defined for the database model. In design, all the finishing touches are applied to the proposed database that has been designed. Other work to be performed might include normalization or denormalization of tables. If using a CASE tool, the design phase is the last chance the developer has to make changes to the structure of the database before the DDL that is actually used to build the database in a database environment is generated.

In Figure 4.2, you can see that all business entities, comprising the logical model, are converted into database tables, or the physical model. Views might also be created based on database tables for many purposes, which will be discussed in Chapter 13, "Designing Views." One of the main purposes for creating views is to summarize data found in database tables. Also, indexes might be created on database tables in order to improve the performance of operations that access data in database tables.

Build Phase

After the database design phase is complete, it is time to build the database. Building the database involves the actual creation of the database that has been designed in the physical database environment. During the database build phase, the database is physically laid out in this environment that has been established by the database administrator. At this point, very little work is required as compared to the work involved during the previous phases of the design process.

During the build phase, the following aspects of database implementation should be considered:

- Sizing of tables
- Sizing of indexes
- Utilizing available hardware components
- Distributing database-related files on hardware
- Utilizing existing database environments that are available

Figure 4.2 shows how DDL is generated based on the database definitions that were established during the design phase. For example, a CREATE TABLE statement was generated for the employee table based on the definition of the employee table from the physical database model. After the DDL has been generated, the DDL is executed in a test database environment to build the initial schema. The database should never be implemented into the production environment without first being tested thoroughly.

Documentation Phase

It is critical that documentation is devised for all users of the database and database application. Figure 4.2 shows two types of documentation that should be devised for an information system: system documentation and end-user documentation. System documentation is based on the structure of the actual database. The audience for the system documentation includes developers, programmers, database administrators, and technical management. End-user/System documentation is based primarily on the design of the application. The audience for the end-user documentation is the end user and the customer.

Documentation should be revised when necessary. For example, as a database is redesigned, the system documentation should be modified to show the changes made to the structure of the database. When changes are made to the database application interface, modifications should be made to the end-user documentation. How many times has the end user had poor or, worse, no documentation for the application system. The application documentation is a valuable tool that is used in the training of the end user on how the system works. Likewise, the system documentation can be used to orient new members of the information technology department or the design team in order to speed up the process of understanding the business systems that the business supports.

NOTE

Documentation should be an ongoing process; if not, it can become an overwhelming and never-ending endeavor. The documentation phase should be used to collect all previous documentation and produce a set of detailed documentation for the system users and for end users. Documentation should be written so that the end user can easily read and understand how things work. It might also be considered to create online help for the end user instead of providing a hard copy of the documentation.

Transition Phase

The transition phase is exactly what it sounds like. Transition includes the precaution taken after the design phase to provide a smooth transition for the physical database that has been implemented and tested into production. The basic processes that must take place during the transition phase include product testing, loading or converting data, and end-user training. The product must be tested before it is actually made available to the end user in production environment. The complete product consists of the complete back-end database and the database application interface.

During product testing, a user or group of users test the accuracy of the database application interface against the back-end database. The objective is to ensure that the application works properly according to the requirements and rules defined in the requirements document. The database itself should be tested for accuracy in regards to the way data is stored and accessed in the database. It is better to spend more time testing during transition, and possibly even direct effort back to the design of the database structure, than to give the end user a database or application that does not meet the requirements set forth during the strategy and analysis phases.

The user must be trained to properly use the system. Learning how to use the new system might put the end user under much stress, which makes the documentation phase of the design process even more important. If documentation has been written thoroughly, the work involved to train the end user will be minimized. End-user training is more directly associated with the application interface than with the back-end database. Although it might be important for the end user to understand how data has been grouped in the database, or which database is used to retrieve certain data, the focus is more on the application. The end user is concerned with how the application is used to access the data. What menu options are there? What buttons need to be pressed to perform certain operations? How does the application display the data? After user training, the end user should have a broad understanding of the database and an excellent understanding of using the application to access the database.

Figure 4.2 illustrates how data is used during the transition phase. Sample data might be used in order to test the database application against the back-end database. Sample data often includes a subset of production data. After product testing is complete, the real data must be loaded into a production environment that has been established. The live data might originate from one or more legacy systems. If the new system is the first automated system the company has used, data will have to be manually entered into the database using the application. The entry of data into the database by the end user is the first production task in many cases.

Production Implementation Phase

In the production implementation phase, both the database and the application that have been designed are ported to a production environment. The scope of work involved in converting a database and database application from the test environment to the production environment is typically a matter of copying the contents of the test environment into the production environment. When the production environment is established, the production data might need to be loaded in or converted from a legacy system before the end user can access the database.

Figure 4.2 illustrates how the end-user community uses a database application in order to access the production database. The database application that has been developed allows the end user to see the data in the database without having a knowledge of the actual structure of the database. A good database application should render the technical aspects of the database environment transparent to the end user.

Figure 4.2 also shows how changes might occur in a production database environment. For example, the end user might request a new feature to the database application, or might request new data to be stored in the database. At the time, a change request must first be approved by management. Part of the approval process should include management correspondence with the development team to ensure that the change request is feasible. After the change has been approved, it is first applied in the development environment. When changes have been completely added to the development environment, they are moved to the test environment where the application is tested thoroughly in conjunction with the modifications that have been made to the system. Finally, the changes that have been approved and tested successfully will be moved to the production environment, and are accessible to the end user.

Adapted Design Methods

All database design methodologies have the same goal in mind: to efficiently develop an accurate data model, and be capable of easily implementing the data model. Design methods can be adapted to meet the requirements of development software being used. A design methodology can also be tailored toward the experience and skills of the development team. An adapted design methodology adheres to the same principles of others, such as the traditional method, with customizations to design phases that can enhance overall productivity for a given situation. Although a design method can be selected and adapted to meet the needs of a particular situation, the overall goals and main deliverables should not be compromised. Remember that there is a grand difference between modifying the design process and compromising deliverables throughout the design process.

One adapted method is discussed in the Oracle Designer Handbook by Oracle Press. This method was selected because of Oracle Designer's popularity, although this method is not necessarily more appropriate than others. Keep in mind that design methods can vary depending on the automated design tools provided by different vendors. The Oracle Designer adapted design method is outlined in the following steps:

1. Strategy
2. Pre-analysis

3. Analysis

4. Pre-design

5. Design

6. Build

7. Test

8. Implementation

9. Maintenance

How has this design method been modified from the traditional and Barker methods? Again, the goals and basic deliverables of this modified development process are the same as most other methods. One of the main differences is that the analysis phase has been divided into pre-analysis and analysis, and design has been divided into pre-design and design. The pre-analysis phase is used to plan the actual analysis process to promote higher productivity during analysis. The same principle is applied to the design phase. Because the design of an information system is so costly, it is important to ensure that time and effort are not wasted. A distinct division might exist between the pre-analysis and analysis phases to guarantee that the development team is ready to proceed with analysis.

With this design method, an end-of-phase evaluation should occur to ensure that steps of the phase were followed, and that all deliverables were met. The end-of-phase evaluation is what determines whether the development team is ready to proceed to the next phase in the design process.

A completely separate test phase exists in this adapted design method because the testing of a product before it is released is so important. It is arguable that testing should be distinct from that of other phases. When product testing occurs, it is usually the assumption that the product has been completely developed, meaning that all business requirements have been gathered, a logical model has been established, and a physical model has been designed. Sometimes product testing is taken too lightly, therefore it is good to isolate testing from other phases.

Implementation of a database and application interface into a production environment occurs after the application has been thoroughly tested against the back-end database, and the development team and users are satisfied that all components of the application function as they should. Implementation usually involves porting the test database structure to a production environment, often using some form of export and import, or simply rerunning the DDL scripts used to create the database in the production environment. After the structure of the database has been created in the production environment, live data might need to be loaded into the database. As we mentioned earlier, it might be the end user's responsibility to load data into the database, perhaps by manually entering every record based on a set of documents. After the database itself has been prepared for use, the application might need to be loaded and configured for end-user access to the database.

4

THE DATABASE
DESIGN LIFE
CYCLE

Maintenance is a huge part of the life of most information systems. After a system has been designed, tested, and implemented, it must be maintained for the remainder of its life. Maintenance includes performance tuning and change management. Two levels of system maintenance that must occur are as follows:

1. Database maintenance—Involves the maintenance of the back-end database, related mainly to how data is stored in the database and how it grows after a given period of time. When new data is created in the database and old data is deleted, fragmentation occurs. One of the main tasks during database maintenance is to monitor the usage and growth of the database, and keep fragmentation to a minimum. Also, it is important to tune the database after it has been implemented to attempt to improve overall performance for the end user. Changes that might occur to a database throughout its life include the addition or deletion of database tables, columns, or indexes. It might be necessary to change any piece of the database structure as business and user needs change. Change requests are usually provided by the end user or the development team if an application change is also being made. Changes are implemented by the development team and the database administrator. Database maintenance is performed by the database administrator.

2. Application maintenance—Involves the ongoing maintenance of an application after it has initially been made available to the end user. Performance tuning an application might be related to the way the application accesses objects in the database. One of the most common performance problems associated with an application involves the underlying SQL and programming code. There are many ways to write code to perform the same task. For example, if a window in the application that reads the database retrieves data slowly on a consistent basis, the SQL query behind the window should be examined and tuned if necessary. Change requests are usually provided by the end user. Application maintenance is performed by application developers, although changes to the application might sometimes be recommended by the database administrator.

> **NOTE**
>
> Adapted design methods might be used based on the software development tools available, as well as the experience and skills of the development team.

Rapid system or software development might occur if a company is under a time crunch in order to produce a working information system. Rapid system development might require the steps that take place during the phases of the design methodology that you selected be condensed. The problem with rapid system development is that it is easy to skip important steps during the design process (or fail to spend ample time during a particular step), which might lead to an incomplete data model, and ultimately an application that does not meet users' needs. Rapid system development should be avoided if possible, but might be used for small systems that can easily be modified, or for temporary systems. For example, a temporary system might be developed quickly that automates the most critical user tasks while the *real* system is being developed. As with any design methodology that has been selected, it is important to spend adequate time planning for the project and gathering the necessary requirements for the system.

Overview of Design Processes

Regardless of the design methodology selected, the design process involves essentially the same process: creating a logical model and converting it into a working physical model. By now, you should have a good idea of the thought process that takes place by parties involved in system design.

The following subsections provide an overview of some of the steps taken during any design process that have not been addressed at this point. These steps are outlined as follows:

- Defining data
- Creating data structures
- Defining data relationships
- Determining views

Defining Data

Data consists of any information that a business is required to keep for any purpose. The object of any information system is to maintain information for an organization. A business might maintain internal or external information. For example, a company might keep track of health insurance claims submitted by many patients where care was administered by many providers and doctors, at multiple times, and at different locations. It is usually accurate to assume that—in most cases—no one person can accurately and completely define all data.

Questions such as the following must be directed to the right individuals and must be answered as completely as possible in order to define data structures:

- What type of data must be stored in the database?
- Is all data internal to this organization?
- What data is external to this organization?

4

- Who is the primary user of the data?
- Will there be different levels of users?
- How long must the data be kept?
- What methods will be used to retrieve and modify the data?
- What manual processes exist?
- What are the current responsibilities of the users?
- With whom do the users currently interact?
- What service or product is provided to the customer?

- How long will the data be stored before being archived or purged?
- What are the reasons for restricting certain users from modifying the data?
- Are data values character, numeric, or date and time?
- Must this information be unique? If so, why?
- Does this data depend on the existence of other data?
- Is this data referenced by other data?

Creating Data Structures

Defining the data and business rules is part of devising the logical model. Based on the data that has been defined, an entity relationship diagram might be produced to illustrate the groups of data that were defined. The purpose of the ERD is to show how data used by the organization has been categorized, and how data is related to other data.

The ERD is used to generate the physical model. The physical model consists primarily of tables—which are based on the entities (groups of data) defined during logical modeling—and should be shown in the ERD. After the tables have been defined, columns are defined, which more specifically identify rows of data, or records, that are stored in a particular table.

Some of the data rules that were defined are now used to finish defining the data structures. For example, if a certain value must be unique within the scope of a table, a primary key constraint or unique constraint might be placed on the column associated with the unique value. Before data structures have been completely defined, the development team will have considered the use or primary keys, foreign keys, unique constraints, check constraints, NULL values, and data types of all tables that have been defined.

Defining Data Relationships

Relationships are defined between groups of data during both the logical and physical modeling phases, although relationships are primarily established in the logical model. In fact, relationships between data should be established before entity attributes or table columns are defined. Typically, an entity is related to at least one other entity in a relational model.

When the logical model is transposed into the physical model, the relationships are inherited from the logical model. In fact, it is possible that no new relationships will be defined during the physical modeling of the database. In most cases, however, modifications will be made to some of the tables. For example, as tables are added or removed from the physical model, possibly because of normalization or denormalization, relationships between tables will need to be revised.

Table relationships are modeled in the logical model and implemented in the physical model using primary key and foreign key constraints. Each primary key value of a table must be unique. Foreign keys do not have to be unique, although a unique constraint might be placed on a foreign key column. The primary key represents the parent record, whereas the foreign key represents the child record of some primary key.

Four basic table relationships exist with the relational model. These relationships are

- One-to-one
- One-to-many
- Many-to-many
- Recursive

Briefly, a one-to-one relationship involves the existence of a maximum of one child record per parent record. With the one-to-many relationship, a parent record might have many child records. With the many-to-many relationship, a parent record might have many child records, as a child record might have many parent records. A recursive relationship represents a record that refers to another record in the same table.

Figure 4.3 illustrates three relationships. There is one address record per instructor. However, an instructor might have many skills. An instructor can teach many classes because a class can be taught by many different instructors; thus, there is a cross-reference table called INST_CRS_XREF. ERD details are discussed in detail in Chapter 9, "Entity Relationship Modeling."

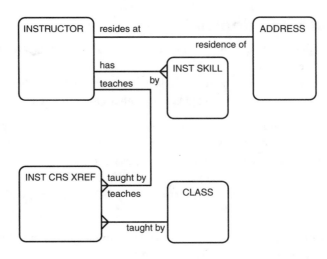

FIGURE 4.3
Illustration of common data relationships.

Determining Views

After the table structures have been completely defined in the physical model, views might be created based on database tables for a variety of reasons. Views are created based on the needs of the end user, which are determined during interviews and meetings with the intent of identifying how exactly the data will be retrieved. Views might be created from tables, or from other views. Some of the reasons views are created are

- To simplify the data the user sees
- For security purposes (to limit the data a user sees)
- To summarize data from multiple tables
- To improve query performance
- To provide the user with an alternative view of the data in the database

How do the users look at the data? Some users might need summarized information from several tables, whereas others require data from only certain columns in a single table.

Security features can be implemented using view definitions that limit users from seeing certain data. For example, a view might be created from a table with a limited number of columns. Instead of granting the user access to the base table, access is granted to the view.

There are some rules that go along with using views. Some of the most basic rules include the following:

- Avoid creating more than two or three levels of views (creating views of other views).

- Views should be schema-owned (part of the same schema in which the base tables reside).

- Document the use of views (without documentation, view management might be very difficult).

Figure 4.4 illustrates how a view can be created based on multiple tables. A view, though defined from many tables, acts as a single table itself. A view is defined with a SELECT statement, as shown in the figure. In this example, we have created a view called CLASS_VIEW which contains summarized class information from the six tables shown. In this example, the view is used to simplify and summarize data. Also, the query shown might be one that is frequently issued, so it is stored as a view definition in the database.

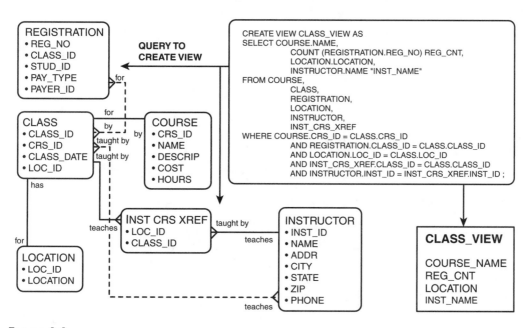

FIGURE 4.4

Defining a relational database view.

4

Redesign of an Existing Database

As businesses change, grow, downsize, and advance with technology, it frequently becomes necessary to analyze the effectiveness of the current database. As competitive as the market is for most businesses, it is critical to keep an edge over competition. One way to keep that edge is to stay current with technology and improve the efficiency of individuals within the organization by redesigning an existing information system that might have served its purpose years or even months ago, but could now stand some improvement.

Anytime a database is being redesigned, business process reengineering (BPR) may be involved. Figure 4.5 illustrates the concept of reworking existing processes and data definitions during BPR, defined in Chapter 1, "Understanding Database Fundamentals." The first part of the figure shows that business processes themselves might be added, removed, or changed in order to improve the way an organization conducts business. In Figure 4.5, the step 2 becomes step 2a and step 2b. Perhaps one of two actions is taken during step 2 based on certain criteria. For example, if a condition is TRUE, then step 2a is performed. Step 2b is performed if a given condition is FALSE. Sometimes, criteria for performing certain processes are not considered until after the database has been in production for some time and the users have had a chance to find deficiencies or inaccuracies. Additionally, data might need to be redefined. In Figure 4.5, the independent A table has been eliminated and combined with the data in the B table. The D table has been normalized into D1 and D2. Also, a new table called E has been created, which is related to table AB. Although this example is theoretical, the basic objectives of BPR should be clear.

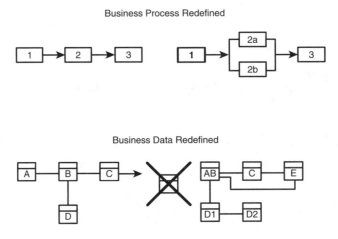

FIGURE 4.5

Business process re-engineering and database redesign.

Where does BPR begin? BPR begins with a system currently being used that might contain inadequacies. A BPR effort is usually triggered by one of the following:

- The end-user community complains that the system no longer meets their needs.
- The company has grown, which means more processes and data must be factored into the structure of the database and application interface.
- The company is looking to increase overall productivity.
- The database administrator has realized that database or application security does not exist.

- Nothing is wrong with the current system, but management wants to do things differently.

- The company is looking for ways to cut costs by automating processes.

- Management has budget dollars to spend.

Ironically, sometimes the last two triggering events go hand-in-hand. Regardless of the triggering event, more involvement is required of the end users, just as in the initial stages of any database design process.

The following information must be captured concerning the existing system before BPR begins:

- What are the current processes?

- How is the data currently stored?

- What inadequacies exist?

- What hardware and software are currently being used?

- Who are the users?

- How does the existing system perform?

The following information must be gathered to re-engineer the existing system:

- What is the remedy for existing inadequacies?

- What new processes exist?

- What are the proposed changes to the existing process?

- What changes will be required for the application to accommodate the new or changed processes?

- Is there new data involved?

- How will the new data be related to existing data?

- How will the new data be accessed?

- What changes will be required for the database structure to accommodate new data and relationships?

- Will existing hardware and software be adequate for the re-engineered system?

- Will there be any new users?

- Can changes be made to improve system performance?

The costs of re-engineering an existing system might be significantly less than the costs of developing a new system. Of course, the costs depend on the level of re-engineering. For example, if minor changes are to be made to the system, then it remains that most of the preliminary work has already been done in the initial design of the current system. However, if major changes are necessary, it might sometimes be easier to start with a clean slate because the numerous changes might be more difficult to manage, which could lead to the production of a piece of trash that serves the users' needs even less effectively than before. That is why BPR is a judgement call that should be made only after thorough discussion among management, the development team, and the end user.

Chapter 17, "Analyzing Legacy Databases for Redesign," takes a step-by-step approach toward the redesign and conversion of an existing legacy system into a new system using the relational model.

Overview of the Database Life Cycle

The database life cycle starts with a requirement to have information available for the operation of a business. At some point in the beginning, somebody decides that a new information system is needed. The company begins to plan for this proposed database, and resources are allocated for its development. This section describes the environments in which a database exists throughout its entire life.

There are several reasons that provoke the need for a database. Likewise, the need for a particular database implementation might perish for additional reasons. Some of these reasons are:

- The company changes the way it does business.
- New technology renders the existing database obsolete.
- An existing database needs to be re-engineered, but the costs would be far greater than designing a new database because of the volume of revisions involved.

The following subsections outline the considerations taken and questions that must be answered during the life cycle of any system. This section can be used as a reference to ensure that changes are properly applied and propagated to production throughout the life of a database. The following database environments are discussed:

- Development
- Test
- Production

Figure 4.6 illustrates the three minimal environments that should be used during the life of a database. The database is initially created in the development environment. The development environment should be used for nothing else; it is more of a staging area. After structures have been created or modified, the additions or changes are moved to the test environment, where any additions or modifications are tested for completeness and accuracy. After everyone is happy that any additions or changes are correct, any new modifications are applied to the production environment.

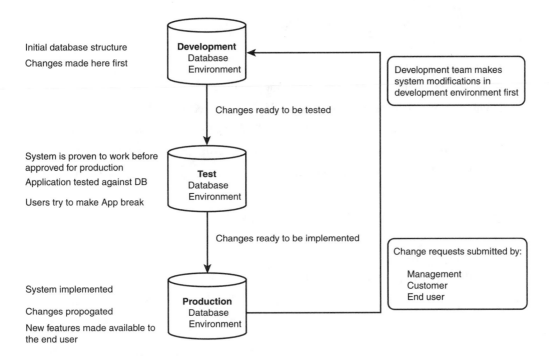

FIGURE 4.6

The database life cycle.

Figure 4.6 illustrates these three stages of a database's life. You can see that the natural flow of changes begins with development, moves to a test environment, and then is applied to the production environment. Each environment is discussed in greater detail in the following subsections.

Development Environment

The development environment represents the birth of an information system. In the development environment, all database objects are initially created, scripts might be developed, relationships are established, and the application is developed. No time limit on development exists other than the constraints dependent upon the milestones and deadlines that should be found in the design plan.

The development environment should be kept active throughout the production life of the database. Any new objects, changes to existing objects, or deletions should always begin in the development environment. It is important that all three database environments are kept in sync with one another in order to most easily manage system changes (new versions of the system) that occur, and this cannot happen if the development environment is not kept alive and used on a regular basis.

Following is a development evaluation checklist that might assist in determining if a database is ready to be tested:

- Are all processes reflected in the application?
- Are all business entities accounted for in the database?
- Do all data elements and processes defined allow new records to be entered?
- Do all data elements and processes defined allow existing records to be modified?
- Do all data elements and processes defined allow existing records to be deleted?
- Do all data elements and processes defined allow existing records to be queried?
- Are all table relationships accurate?
- Has referential integrity been applied?
- Have obvious indexes been created?
- Have views been created where needed?
- Does the database need to be normalized?
- Have all errors been accounted for and corrected during object creation?

Test Environment

After the database has been fully designed and created in the development environment, it is time to migrate all development structures into the test environment. During testing, the database and database application interface are tested for overall functionality and accuracy. The database should also be tested for performance, especially if it was a key concern to the customer when the system requirements were established.

When all database structures have been created in the test environment, test data must be loaded into the database to simulate the use of the database application in production. The data used during the test might be a percentage of the data that will actually be used in production, or might consist of a duplicate copy of production data. It is important to work with real data while testing to ensure that the database acts as expected, and that all modules of the end-user application function properly.

It is important to expose and correct system problems before the customer or end user has a chance to do so. If it is determined that corrections must be made, they are made in the development environment before being applied to the test environment. No changes are to be made directly to the test environment without first existing in the development environment. It is usually better to spend more time testing, making changes in development, and then testing again, than to give the end user a system that does not function as promised.

Who conducts testing? Typically, a team of end users might be designated to conduct the test because they are the individuals who understand the business and data the best (although, the development team should have a good understanding of the business and data by this point). During testing, scenarios are established and all aspects of the system are tested accordingly, to include usability, accuracy, and performance. If testing runs smoothly and the end users (testers) are satisfied that the test was successful; then full steam ahead to production.

The following test evaluation checklist might help determine if a database and application has been properly tested and if it is time to make the transition to production:

- How much time has been allocated to test the system?
- When is the system expected in production?
- Do any data relationships need to be modified?
- Are business rules being followed?
- How did the database application interface perform?
- Was the system tested with real data?
- Was the system tested with a realistic volume of data?
- Was data integrity compromised during testing?
- Were all changes tested thoroughly?
- Was the database queried after changes were made to data using the application interface (using a combination of the application and manual transactions and queries to ensure that the application is working properly)?
- Have all requirements for the system been double-checked for completeness?

Production Environment

Production is the point at which the database and application are made available to the end user. Real tasks are accomplished in the production environment that directly affect the way the business operates. Real users are working with real data, and interfacing with real customers. Now is not the time for the company to be embarrassed when it finds that the customer cannot be properly served. Now is the time to impress the customer with a system that works well and enhances the company's relationship with the customer by making life easier for all parties during real-world business transactions.

Although the production environment is considered to be the finished product, it is still subject to changes and improvements. Few systems, if any, are ever implemented into perfection in round one. Few systems ever actually see perfection. There is a difference between a perfect system and making the customer think you have a perfect system. It is a great practice to routinely search for ways to improve the new system because room for improvement inevitably exists.

The following production evaluation checklist might assist in the evaluation of a recent implementation, as well as the decision to make modifications in attempt to improve the system:

- Were there any errors during implementation?
- Does the end user have any complaints?
- How does the system seem to perform?
- Was all live data loaded or converted successfully?
- What is the average number of concurrent users?
- Are any areas for immediate improvement in database functionality or performance recognized?
- Are any areas for immediate improvement in application functionality or performance recognized?

Figure 4.7 depicts what might occur if changes are not tested, or not tested thoroughly. In this example, the base table CLASS is involved. Version 1 of the database involves the CLASS table, which apparently needs to be normalized. Version 2 has split the CLASS table into three different tables: CLASS, CLASS_TYPE, and CLASS_LEVEL. The purpose of this split is to eliminate the occurrence of the duplicate values for each level and type values. Suppose that this change was made directly to production without testing (which should not occur, but does occur more times than you might think). Notice that the view CLASS_VIEW is based on the CLASS table. In version 2, the CLASS_TYPE and CLASS_LEVEL do not exist in the CLASS table because normalization has occurred. The view should have been redefined to query all three tables, joining them together using the TYPE_ID and LEVEL_ID columns. Also, a user input form has been based on the CLASS table, which is now invalid as well. The table has been normalized, but the view is invalid, and the end user cannot use form. Now the view and form must be fixed, which might also affect other objects in the database, or forms in the application. The point is that all changes might not be so obvious; there might be ramifications to even the simplest change if not tested.

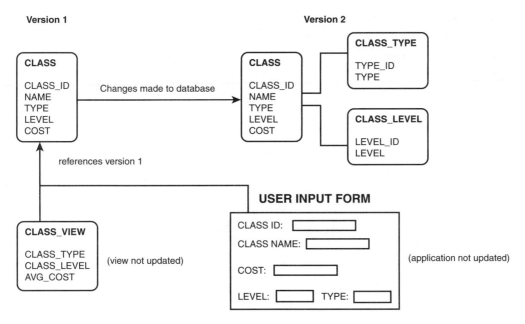

FIGURE 4.7

Production implementation with incomplete testing.

Summary

The system development process is used to design a database from a set of business rules, processes, and data that have been defined. A design methodology should be chosen to ensure that aspects of database design are considered, yielding a product of high quality. The traditional method has three simple phases: requirements analysis, logical modeling, and normalization. The Barker method, involving concepts and deliverables similar to those of the traditional method, has the following phases: strategy, analysis, design, build, documentation, transition, and production. An adapted design method is one that does not necessarily conform to the exact steps set forth by other selected methodologies. An adapted method might be used based on the exact requirements of the system, the development software being used, and the experience of the development team. Each method might have different phases (or different names for the phases), but all have the same goal.

Some of the most fundamental concepts of database design include the definition of data, rules, data structures, data relationships, and views. Business process re-engineering and database redesign might also be involved when designing a database. BPR involves the reworking of an existing system with the intent of improving existing processes and data storage methods.

After a database has been designed, it resides in one of three database environments: development, test, or production. Ideally, all three environments should exist for each database system. It is important to keep all three environments in sync with one another in order to properly manage system changes throughout a system's life. Changes should never be made directly to production. Once you have a good understanding of different methodologies, it will be easy to select one and adapt it to meet your needs if necessary. Then comes the interesting part—to begin modeling the system.

Analyzing and Modeling Business Requirements

IN THIS PART

Chapter 5, "Gathering Business and System Requirements," covers the process of gathering all the requirements necessary to design a database for an organization.

Chapter 6, "Establishing a Business Model," discusses the basic concept of interpreting the information gathered from interviews in order to begin to model the business.

Chapter 7, "Understanding Entities and Relationships," discusses data elements, or entities, and the different relationships that might exist between data in an organization.

Chapter 8, "Normalization: Eliminating Redundant Data," covers the concept of reducing or eliminating the amount of redundant data in the database. This chapter provides an overview of the normal forms, which measure the level of database normalization. This chapter also covers denormalization, which is the allowance of redundant data to improve performance.

Chapter 9, "Entity Relationship Modeling," explains how Entity Relationship Diagrams (ERDs) can be created to illustrate an organization's data. This chapter includes common conventions for diagramming entities and their relationships to one another.

Chapter 10, "Modeling Business Processes," explains how business processes can be modeled. This chapter also discusses how business processes can be used to validate completeness of entities that have been defined.

Gathering Business and System Requirements

IN THIS CHAPTER

Suppose that a couple is in the market for a new home and opts to build versus purchase an existing home. The couple has a vision of a dwelling that will meet certain standards to improve their quality of life. They perceive many features and conveniences that will improve the new home drastically as compared to their current dwelling. They know what they want; but of course, someone else will actually build the house. The couple also thinks they know what steps must be taken to build the house, how long it should take, and how much it will cost (or how much they are willing to spend).

A problem has arisen: a new house is needed that must meet certain requirements. Many questions related to the problem follow. Who will build the house? How will the house be built? When must the house be built? What is the budget for the house? How much is the bank willing to loan? Are all desired features of the house doable? Of those doable features, which are practical, and what can the couple actually afford? Is the desired timeframe reasonable? Will a crew be available to work on the house to produce a finished product in the desired timeframe? How long will the couple stay in the house? Do they plan to have kids? All these questions are merely preliminary issues that must be addressed before the house can be designed and built.

This scenario is comparable to that of designing a database. Before a database can be designed, all the requirements for the database must be gathered. A house can easily and quickly be built that does not satisfy the needs of the couple; in a similar manner, a database can be thrown together haphazardly that does not meet the customer's needs. Most of the questions raised in this scenario are common sense to most people, and can be paralleled to the preliminary questions involved to gather requirements in order to build a functional information system.

Because building a house is probably the greatest cost a couple might ever incur, in a similar manner, the cost involved in designing an information system is great. By following the guidelines as outlined in this chapter, the process of database design should be as cost-effective as possible for the firm spearheading the design effort, as well as for the customer.

Types of Requirements

As mentioned frequently throughout this book, the process of gathering requirements is imperative to the successful design of any database. Chapter 4, "The Database Design Life Cycle," discusses different design methodologies, each methodology relying heavily on the requirements gathering process. Chapter 4 explores the process of gathering requirements from a broad perspective according to each design methodology outlined. The focus here is to describe in great detail all considerations that comprise the requirements gathering process, regardless of the design methodology selected.

By now, you should understand that the basic requirements are the rules, processes, and data within an organization that are used to devise an information system. Two types of requirements are used to design an information system: business requirements and system requirements. Briefly, business requirements refer to those details that are related to how a business functions on a daily basis. System requirements are those details, many of which are associated with business requirements, that are used to actually design the system.

The process of gathering requirements is broken into the following three stages:

- Establishing business requirements
- Establishing system requirements
- Performing requirements analysis

Requirements analysis, which is thoroughly explained later in this chapter, is the process of reviewing the activities that took place and the data that was gathered during requirements gathering. Requirements analysis is a final evaluation that should take place before database design begins.

Business Requirements

As mentioned, business requirements relate directly to the tasks performed by individuals within an organization. Business requirements deal with how the business functions currently, as well as how the business plans to work or conduct business in a future. As technology and information needs are constantly advancing, it is very important to consider the future needs of the business, which turns out to be a common point of failure for many inexperienced firms attempting to design a database for the first time. All organizations deal with data, whether an existing information system is in place or not. It is the responsibility of the development team to find out what the data is and how the business uses the data.

Data and processes within an organization are always closely related. Processes can be used to determine data, as data can be used to determine processes. In fact, it is important to compare processes to data during modeling to ensure that all requirements have been completely gathered. This check-and-balance system will be discussed more thoroughly in the requirements analysis section of this chapter.

Processes are performed by individuals who belong to organizational units. An organizational unit is normally a department within an organization. For example, common organizational units that exist in many organizations include human resources, data entry, customer service, accounting, mail room, and management. During the business requirements gathering portion of the design process, the main goal is to break an organization into organizational units and associate data and processes with each organizational unit. Some processes that are performed can be specific to a particular organizational unit, or can be shared between organizational units. Likewise, data can also be shared, and usually is to some degree.

After the basic data and processes are determined, business rules must also be determined. Business rules are directly associated with data and processes that are used to manage the data.

Different forces are involved in the establishment of business rules. Primarily, business rules are molded around the data by the customer because the database belongs to the customer. Business rules established affect the way data can be accessed for operations such as queries, inserts, updates, and deletions. Business rules also help determine how data relates to other data, and will eventually be used to design entities and their relationships. Business rules are also the greatest factor in determining the use of referential integrity in a database.

Some of the following very basic questions can be used to begin the process of determining business requirements:

- Who will perform the tasks?
- How are tasks performed?
- What different organizational units will deal with business data?
- What processes are specific to certain organizational units?
- What data is associated with each individual process?
- How do the processes interact with one another?
- How do the organizational units interact with one another?
- What outside factors exist that affect business processes and data?

Later in this chapter, you learn how to communicate with various parties in order to properly gather the requirements for a business.

System Requirements

System requirements cannot be determined without the existence of business requirements because business requirements are used to establish the needs for an information system. If a new system is being designed, the requirements for the system are based solely on the business requirements that have been defined according to the needs of the end user. If a system is being modified or redesigned, the requirements for the system are based on business requirements, the requirements of the old system, the needs of the end user and business, and proposed remedies for deficiencies in the old system.

With the assumption that all business requirements have been completely gathered, the development team should feel confident about the conversion of business needs into system needs. The most difficult part of designing a system is outlining the requirements and devising a plan in which to design the system. The process of defining system requirements should, without question, simplify the process of physically designing the database. If business needs have been converted into system needs accurately, the physical design of the database should nearly take care of itself. There should be much tedious work involved in the physical design of a database, which is why most developers tend to use some form of automated design tool.

Some of the following very basic questions can be used to begin the process of determining system requirements based on the business requirements that have partly been defined.

- How do the defined business requirements relate to the needs that a user has for a system?
- How will business needs be converted into system needs?
- Which processes are the most critical?
- Are all defined business processes associated with the needs of the system?
- Will all organizational units share the same system?
- Will information be gathered from an existing system?
- From what types of systems will information be gathered and used to populate the new system?
- Can processes, outlined in business requirements gathering, be simplified through the use of the system?
- Who are the users of the new system?
- If the end user and the customer are different individuals, how will these individuals interact with one another?

Overview of Requirements Analysis

Supposing that all business and system requirements have been completely defined; it is time to start modeling the database. However, before modeling and design begin, requirements analysis must first occur. Requirements analysis is the process of analyzing the business and system requirements that have been established. Requirements analysis is a sort of evaluation of the work that took place during the analysis phase (information gathering). Different parties should be involved in the requirements analysis process. As stated before, the end user and customer (keep in mind that they are sometimes the same individual) should have continual input in the development process. Management and members of the development team also play a role during requirements analysis.

The customer and end user are offered the chance to provide input by interviews and end-user feedback sessions that are administered by members of the development team. The customer should verify that all needs of the business have been considered, as the end user should verify that the needs of the information system have been properly converted from the needs of the business.

Members of the development team have deliverables that must be turned in to their supervisor or the team leader. The team leader is responsible for insuring that all objectives have been met within the scope of the work has been assigned to the team. The team leader also has deliverables that are passed up to the project lead, who passes deliverables up to management. The project lead determines if the objectives have been met for the project from an overall perspective. Management ensures that the objectives of the project have been met as promised to the customer.

Determining Business Requirements

Now that the basic definition and concepts concerning gathering business requirements have been explained, we can explore the steps involved in actually gathering these requirements. It is important that the development team is educated before requirements gathering is attempted. Additionally, a plan should be devised to guide members of the development team through the initial information gathering phase. The preliminary steps—that should be taken before the command "ready, set, interview" is issued and the gun is fired—include the following:

1. Research of the business is conducted.
2. An interview plan is established.
3. A template is created with basic questions that trigger more specific questions.

Before attempting to interview anyone, a research study should be conducted of the business so that the interviewers understand what types of questions to ask the individuals being interviewed. Before performing any type of work for a client, preliminary research is important to show the client that you're concerned with the needs and goals of the business. Performing research ahead of time will allow the development team to be more organized when compiling interview questionnaires and will save more time during the actual interview process. This will make everyone happier because less time will be spent sitting in a meeting room behind closed doors.

As you have already learned, much planning goes into a database design effort. Planning for interviews is no different. Some sort of plan, however brief it might be, should be devised to organize the series of interviews that are to take place. The interview plan can include topics such as the individuals to be interviewed, the individuals conducting the interviews, cross interviews, and end-user feedback sessions throughout the design process.

After the interview plan has been devised and the interview teams have been formed, a template with basic questions can be developed for the system interviewers in the interview process. The template should have very basic questions that will be used to trigger more specific questions. Actually, it might be better to conduct a preliminary interview using the basic questions outlined in the interview template, and then the answers to the basic questions are used to derive more specific questions to be asked during a second interview. Breaking the initial interview process into preliminary and secondary interviews provides the interview team with more time between interviews to gather their thoughts and formulate a more complete list of questions to extract the required information from the interviewed parties.

The following subsections cover the various determinants for gathering business requirements, which include

- Evaluating the origination points of information
- Management's knowledge of the business goals
- Customer's knowledge of requirements, processes, and data
- End user's knowledge of processes and data
- Existing processes in place

Who Has "Say So?"

One question that must be answered before gathering business requirements is "Who has say so?" Who knows the business? Who knows the data best? Who has the authority to make decisions based on the goals and objectives of the business and the way the system is designed? Various individuals are allowed input into the requirements that are used to model the business and the system. The primary informational resources for requirements gathering include the following:

- The customer
- The end user
- Internal management
- External management

The different types of information that can be gathered from the users in the previous list are explained in detail in the following sections. In addition to compiling a business model based on the information gathered from these individuals, the derived information will also be used to begin creating documentation for the business—if it does not exist—and for the new system. Now is the time to begin the documentation process. Also, it is important to interview different types of parties individually. For example, management and end users should be interviewed individually because their goals and perceptions of the new system might differ dramatically. This does not mean that a kickoff meeting cannot be conducted for the project to include all parties involved. In fact, it might be best to involve all parties in an initial interview or group discussion, as well as having a sort of grand finale meeting at the end of the information gathering phase.

Keep in mind that the customer and end user might or might not be the same individual. The following subsections depict scenarios in which the customer and end user might be the same individual, or different individuals. Also notice in the following subsections that different types of management might be involved (internal and external).

Customer and End User Are the Same

In this scenario, imagine that an information system is being designed for the human resources department for a company. The customer is the individual for which the information system is designed. The end user is the individual who uses the information system to manage data.

In this case, the individuals in the human resources department comprise both the customer and the end user. The data is owned by the HR department, and will be managed by individuals in the HR department. For this type of system, it is important that HR works closely with the data. It would not make sense to hire an outside agency to manage the data.

Only local management is involved in this scenario. Management includes the hierarchical management structure within the organization, from the board of directors, down to departmental managers and supervisors. Management in the HR department should have the most input for the information system for obvious reasons. Upper management might help provide guidance to ensure that the new system is aligned with the overall goals of the business.

Customer and End User Are Different

Imagine the need for an information system that requires the involvement of an outside agency to manage the data. For example, picture a state's Medicaid insurance management program. Each state owns medical claims data, concerning individual patients who qualify for Medicaid, and the medical insurance claims made by patients. The state has its own employees who deal with the overall management of the program, specializing in the interaction with Medicaid candidates and overseeing Federal and State regulations.

For various reasons, the customer (state employee) might need assistance in managing the data. Some of these reasons might include lack of adequate staff, lack of experience using information systems, and lack of technological expertise. Although most anyone can quickly learn to use an information system that has been properly developed, time might be lacking to perform mundane tasks such as entering mass volumes of data. In a situation such as this, millions of claims might be made by patients each year. The assistance of an outside agency might be needed to manage the mass volumes of data generated. This way, the customer can focus on his primary responsibilities to ensure that the organization functions efficiently, while data entry clerks and medical claims specialists deal with mass data modifications triggered by medical claims, new patients, complaints, deaths, and so forth.

The state employee (customer) still needs access to the data, but mostly through the use of queries. Transactions and batch processing are conducted by the end user (provided by an outside agency), which can be supplied by the company designing the system, or can be outsourced from a temporary agency or another firm specializing in data management.

Two levels of management have a heavy impact on the design of the database. Management includes internal and external management. Internal management is the management of the firm responsible for managing the data. In this case, internal management is associated with the end user, who performs the transactional work and batch processing. External management is the management within the customer's organization. Although the end user directly deals with the data on a daily basis, keep in mind that the data is owned by the customer. The customer's management will have definite input on the requirements of the data and the uses of the proposed database. Both levels of management and users provide input for modifications that need to be made to the database in the near future. Both levels of management will also help determine if the objectives of the information system have been met according to the goals of the organization. It is important that both levels of management work together in order to meet the goals set forth for the database.

Interviewing Management

Because management makes most of the major decisions in an organization, it is important to get management's viewpoint of the goal of the proposed database. Management has the authority to approve and disapprove projects, and manage allocation of resources for projects. The success of any business is dependent on the quality of the management, which is why management is the first to be replaced when the goals set forth by the board of directors are not being met, or when a company's stock plummets. As previously mentioned, the end user and customer might belong to different organizations. In the case in which the end user and customer differs, management from both organizations must be interviewed. Customer management best understands the goals of the business, and end user management best understands the methods used to manage the data for the customer.

High-level business goals are determined by the board of directors, and are filtered down into appropriate sectors of management. Management sets departmental goals that support the main goals of the business. How does the goal of the proposed database compare to the goals of the business? Management can best answer this question because they have a better understanding of the "big picture" as compared to most database users. Although managers have areas of specialization, a good manager knows a little about everything and is able to fit all the pieces of the corporate puzzle together in order to optimize the activities that occur within his particular department.

Although managers are trying to do their job, they are under constant pressure from upper management. Upper management is under constant pressure to provide the best possible service or product to the customer. This rising pressure is usually triggered by changing goals, business needs, and opportunity for business growth. Customers' needs change and expectations escalate as technology advances, which rolls down through all levels of management. Because of the pressure placed on management, unnecessary pressure and unreasonable demands are often placed on employees. Unfortunately, the affected employees are usually members of the development team. Be aware that excessive pressure on the development team can cause the quality of the end product to decrease.

In addition to the stress management is under, management must also abide by budgetary constraints that are set forth by upper management. The budget is a major factor when designing a database. An inadequate budget will affect one or more of the following: the size of the development team, the allocation of funds for hardware and software used during design, the use of consultants to assist with design, and the amount of time allocated for the design project.

The two basic types of managers are as follows:

- Technical
- Non-technical

Technical management is management with technical experience related to required skills of employees in the department. For instance, say that John started out as a programmer, moved into a development position, was promoted to a team leader, and eventually became a manager. John has the same technical skills as his staff, and has a better understanding of the daily operations that take place within his department. Let's say that Mary was hired in as a manager from an outside agency. Although Mary is an excellent manager, she has never held a technical position. She has always been heavily involved in management.

Benefits and drawbacks to both types of management exist that might be relevant to a database design effort. John is technically minded, so he can more efficiently distribute the work and be more involved than Mary to get the design effort off to a good start and ensure that the process runs smoothly. However, because John is technical, his standards for the staff might be higher than Mary's standards, and John might tend to micromanage. Mary on the other hand, might be capable of providing superior managerial support to her employees without micromanaging, but might not know the first thing about database design, or even databases. A major advantage that technical management has over non-technical management is the ability to more effectively interact with parties concerning the needs of the database being designed.

Following are some of the issues with which management is most concerned in association with the need for a database:

- Fulfilling promises to the customer
- Providing better service to the customer
- Meeting contractual requirements
- Meeting business goals
- Making sure that the database adheres to company standards
- Making sure that costs aren't extended beyond budgetary constraints
- Making management's job easier
- Increasing overall productivity

- Optimizing payroll expenses
- Distributing the workload
- Training the development team
- Training the end users
- Transferring knowledge between teams, users, and the customer
- Making sure that documentation is accessible for training and transfer of knowledge

Following are some important questions that should be directed to management during the interviews:

- From your perspective, what are the goals of the business?
- From your perspective, what are the goals of the proposed database?
- Why is the database important from your standpoint?
- How will the database affect management?
- How will the database affect the customer?
- What is the expected life of the database?
- Have upgrades been forecasted for the near future?
- How do different departments interact?
- How is data transmitted between departments?
- What are the different user groups of the database?
- What is management's expectations of the system?
- What promises have been made to the customer?
- What are the plans for user training?
- Are sufficient resources available for the database?
- When is the drop-dead date for the database?

Following are common management pitfalls that adversely affect database design if not taken into consideration.

- Sometimes expect too much of development team, which can lead to unreasonable promises made to the customer.
- Might not fully understand the needs of the end user.
- Might not fully understand the needs of the customer.
- Pressure received from upper management.
- Non-technical management might not understand all the work that is involved in database design.

- Technical management might tend to micromanage the database design effort, hindering progress.
- If non-technical management tries to get too involved in the design, much time will be spent explaining and justifying, which slows work.

Interviewing the Customer

Two statements are sometimes used to describe a customer for any business: "the business exists because of the customer" and "the customer is always right." Both statements apply to customers needing databases, to a certain degree. The business of developing a database exists because of the customer, as the customer's business exists because of its customer. Saying that customers are always right is stretching it, but it is important to treat customers like they are always right. The customer is right until the integrity of the data is jeopardized—at which time you must be strong enough to be straightforward with the customer and offer suggestions in a tactful manner without character degradation. Customers are right in that they have a database need, they know the data, and they should get what they ask within the realm of a useful database, within reason. If a database has been produced with which the customer is not satisfied, logic says that the customer's needs were not properly gathered, which falls back into the responsibility of the development team.

Sometimes the customer asks for something, but wants something else—or so it seems according to the interpretations of the development team. How are the wants and needs retrieved from the customer? Customers know what they want, but how do they convey their needs to the development team? More appropriately, how does the development team extract the required information from the customer? First, the interviewers must learn to speak the customer's language. Sometimes the customer does not know what to ask for. It is important to communicate with the customer on his level. Take time to understand the customer's business and needs. Don't expect the customer to be technically minded enough to volunteer all the information needed to design a database.

Who is the customer? The customer might be a primary end user of the database or a secondary user of the database. If the customer is the primary user of the database, he is responsible for transactional processing, batch processing, queries, and backups. If the customer is a secondary user of the database, he might only need to query the database to make business decisions, while an organization manages the data (transactional activity, batch processing, database administration). More likely than not, the customer will require some level of access to the data in order for the business to operate.

The following relationships the customer has should be identified and expanded on as much as possible during the interview process:

- Who is the customer's customer?
- How does data relate to the customer's customer?
- What is the customer's relationship with the end user?

Be patient with the customer during interviews. Nobody understands the data, the flow of the data, and the importance of data like the customer. Afford the customer with the chance to speak and listen intently. Ask questions concerning the business and the customer's requirements based on the information the customer gives you. The basic information the customer volunteers should be used to generate important interview questions to gather detail.

Although, the customer should be allowed to speak, he should also listen to the interviewers. Even though it is important that the interviewers listen to the customer and be very attentive, they should be in full charge of the interview. The interviewers are the ones in control of the interview process, and should tactfully make this fact known to the customer. The customer might not know what information to volunteer in all cases. That is why the interviewer should take control and steer the interviews in the direction that will unveil responses to all issues that have surfaced, and those issues that will surely surface throughout the design process.

Interview various individuals within the customer community as much as possible. Different individuals might have different opinions and perspectives of the business, and might have different needs concerning the way the data is stored and accessed. The interview team should measure all responses to interview questions, and compare obvious differences between the same interview questions. If obvious differences in answers and opinions exist, it is important to determine why they exist. Consistent answers to interview questions will provide a clear understanding of the business requirements.

Different individuals from the development team should interview the customer. Using different interviewers helps provide different types of questions. Also, the degree of unbiased questions and opinions formulated by the design team will be reduced more than if only one person conducts the interviews. It is also imperative to win the customer's confidence. If you have won the customer's confidence, the customer will trust you to design a system, with little resistance along the way. Force yourself to get along with the customer, although sometimes it might seem impossible.

Following are some of the issues with which the customer is most concerned:

- Contractual requirements are met with their customer.
- Acceptable overall database performance is achieved.
- Acceptable database and application response time is achieved.
- The database actually meets all business needs.
- The database and application are user friendly.

- The data is easily accessed as necessary.
- The customer is able to serve its customer efficiently.
- The new database enhances the customer's business.
- Documentation is accessible for database and application architecture and basic usage.
- Quality—of the product or service provided to their customers—is improved.

The following questions should be directed to the customer in regards to the daily functions performed:

- What are the primary goals of your business?
- Who are your customers?
- What services or products do you provide?
- How do you interact with other individuals in the organization?
- From your perspective, what are the goals of the proposed database?
- What are the different activities that take place on a daily basis?
- Who performs these activities?
- How do these activities relate to the data?
- Are activities manual or automated processes?
- Can the processes be refined?
- What manual processes can be automated?
- What problems exist with current automated processes?
- What is the triggering event for each business process?
- What is the expected outcome of each business process?

The following questions should be directed to the customer with regard to the data:

- What is the data?
- How is the data used to support the business?
- Who uses the data?
- What business processes require what data?
- How long must the data be kept?
- When can data be purged or archived?
- How timely should archived data be accessible?
- How often will archived data be accessed?
- Is the data static, or will it change often?

- How will the data grow over a period of time?
- How do you expect data needs to change over a period of time?
- How much data do you have?
- Where does the data originate?
- Are there any existing data sources?
- Who should have access to the data?
- How is data currently protected?

NOTE

In large organizations and government agencies, politics is a huge driving force. Politics dictates the data that is stored, how long the data is stored, who is allowed access to the data, the existence of and relationship between business processes, and most definitely business rules.

Interviewing the End User

In review, the end user might be one with the customer, or might be a different individual altogether. If the end user is part of the customer community, the issues within this section will also apply to the interview of the customer. Even if the customer and end user are the same, it is still a good approach to distinguish between customer-based interview questions and user-based interview questions. Customer-based interview questions are associated with business requirements, where user-based interview questions should be directed toward the end user's needs and methods for accessing the database. It is important that the system meets the needs of both the customer and the end user.

NOTE

Even if the end user is a separate individual from the customer, the end user is still considered a customer of the technical development team.

End users come in all forms, shapes, and sizes, such as the following:

- Data entry clerks
- Customer service representatives
- Accountants

5

GATHERING BUSINESS AND SYSTEM REQUIREMENTS

- Lawyers
- Management
- Medical claims specialists
- Web users

All types of end users and prospective end users must be identified. If a database does not currently exist, there will only be prospective end users. If a legacy database exists, end users can be interviewed to provide feedback concerning the performance and usability of the existing database, as well as input on features they would like to see in the new database and application.

If there is an existing database, what tools are currently available to the end user? What deficiencies exist according to the end user? The end user is mostly concerned with the application, which is used to interact with the database. End user comments about the application help the development team make intelligent decisions that affect the design of the database. According to the end user, what are the possible improvements to the database and application as related to the way the data is stored and accessed, the way the data is related to other data, and the overall performance of the database?

The following questions should be directed to the end user with regard to the daily functions performed by the user:

- What is your primary job function?
- What else do you do?
- How do you do it?
- What tools are currently used to perform your job?
- Is a database currently used?
- What improvements could be made to the functions you perform?
- What improvements can be made to current tools or databases?
- How do you interact with other individuals in the organization?
- From your perspective, what are the goals of the business?
- From your perspective, what are the goals of the proposed database?

All end users need to access the data regardless of their individual needs or their job specifications. The specifics of the end users' responsibilities drive the needs for a database and the details of the application used to communicate with the database. The following questions should be directed to the end user with regard to the data:

- What is the data?
- Who uses the data?

- Why is the data accessed?
- How is the data used?
- How often is the data accessed?
- When does the data change?
- What is the approximate growth rate of the data?

Following are some of the issues with which the end user is most concerned:

- The database and application are user friendly.
- Manual tasks have been automated as much as possible.
- Acceptable response time is achieved.
- The database and application enhances the job at hand.
- The inner workings of the database and application are transparent.
- Minimal effort should be spent learning the new database and application.
- Documentation is accessible for training and reference.
- Technical support is available.

> **NOTE**
>
> During interviews, listen intently to the end user. Don't fall into the trap that many members of the development team encounter by letting egos interfere with the flow of the interviews. Remember that the end user has a vital function and responsibility to the company just as the individuals in the technical development team do.

Studying the Existing Processes in Place

An essential piece of requirements gathering is studying existing processes. Whether a database currently exists, business processes will exist that affect the design of the new database. Based on the need of a new database, processes can be added, eliminated, or refined. Processes must be defined by management, the customer, and the end user. The developer does not define process details, but rather captures all the steps involved in each process, called process steps. Interviews should reveal all processes and their relationships to one another. Interviews should also reveal the need for new or refined processes in conjunction with the goals of the proposed database.

Following are considerations for evaluating existing processes:

- Has a walk-through with the customer and end user been performed for each process?
- How are business transactions currently handled?

- What is the goal of each process?
- Are the goals currently being met?
- How will the goals change based on the need for a new database?
- What unnecessary process steps currently exist?
- Which process steps are mandatory for the framework of the new database?
- Do the processes defined imply the use of data that has not yet been defined?
- Can processes be streamlined so that users can make better use of their time?
- What processes can be automated that are not already?

Business requirements are those requirements that are related directly to business processes, business data, and business rules. Business requirements, once established, are used to define system requirements. System requirements are those requirements that related to the system, referring to the database and the application interface through which the user accesses the database. These requirements are discussed in detail in the following sections.

Analyzing Business Requirements

The initial interviews have been conducted. Now, what is done with all the information that has been obtained? Before the development team can begin modeling and designing a database, developers must have a solid understanding of the business data and how it is used. The process of deciphering the requirements that have been gathered is called requirements analysis. As with any portion of the database design process, it is important to first develop a plan. An analysis plan should be devised to guide the developers through requirements analysis.

The analysis should outline the following information.

- Interview details
- Personnel and time resources required
- Review of the legacy system
- Deliverables (diagrams)
- Tasks assigned and to whom
- Dates and deliverables for user feedback sessions

After all business requirements have been gathered, the information must be analyzed by the development team. Diagrams can be drawn to illustrate the data and processes within an organization. Following are some of the most common diagrams used to analyze business requirements:

- Entity relationship diagrams (ERDs)—Define the data and show relationships between data.

- Process Models—Show process steps involved in each process.
- Data flow diagrams—Show how data moves through an organization, from processes to data stores.
- Function hierarchy diagrams—Show how processes are related to one another.

All possible business rules should be shown in an ERD. Business rules determine the relationships between entities in the ERD. Rules that cannot be shown in the ERD are written in a text document and later used when designing the database and end-user application. ERDs are directly used to design the database, where the various process diagrams are mainly used to design the end-user application. The process diagrams are also used to ensure that all data is accessible, thus helping determine that the data has been completely defined.

NOTE

Chapter 9, "Entity Relationship Modeling," provides an understanding of entity relationship diagrams, and shows how to apply the concepts in this chapter to create ERDs. Chapter 10, "Modeling Business Processes," shows how to model business processes and functions.

Some of the questions that should be raised—when analyzing requirements to determine if all requirements have been gathered, and if those requirements make sense—include:

- Do the responses to all interview questions make sense?
- How will the interview responses be used to achieve a business model?
- What are the priorities for beginning to develop a business model?
- What processes trigger other processes?
- Does each process have an outcome or a consequence?
- Does it make sense how processes access data?
- Is all data that has been defined accessible?
- As an outsider looking in, does there appear to be any loopholes in the processes that might affect the design of the database?

User feedback sessions are a must, as well as a critical aspect of requirements analysis. Thinking that only one set of interviews are required before attempting to design a database will only set you up for failure. It is important to keep the appropriate parties involved after the initial interviews. Let the customer see your perception of the business. It is very likely that the end user, customer, and management will have more input throughout the analysis and design process. It is up to the interviewers to ask the right questions to extract as much information as possible from the individuals who know the most about the business. After the development team thinks the business is understood and diagrams have been drawn, it is important to get the interviewees involved again. During user feedback sessions, the user and customer are shown the work that has been achieved based on the requirements that have been gathered. The best way to ensure a successful design is to have the end users' and customer's stamp of approval on each deliverable of the design process that pertains to the completeness of the database. After a user feedback session, be prepared and willing to make adjustments to work that has been accomplished. Figure 5.1 illustrates interviews, business modeling, and obtaining feedback from the customer and end user.

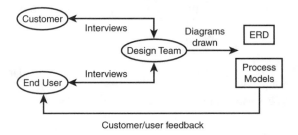

FIGURE 5.1

Getting feedback after interviews.

NOTE

Although the actual design has not actually begun at this point, all the work performed during analysis will be used to design the database. The developers should be meticulous, and pay close attention to detail. If every angle is not studied and the project prematurely proceeds to design, interviews and analysis will have to be conducted again, which equates to wasted time and effort and deadlines that will be unreachable.

Determining System Requirements

System requirements refer to the combination of the back-end database and the application interface to the database. The database is responsible for storing the data. The application is a mechanism through which the end user can interact with the database. A typical application is comprised of ad hoc queries, reports, and user input forms.

References to the user application will be made throughout this book because the database and application compliment one another, but keep in mind that the main focus is on the design of the database.

Although at this point in the design process, the focus is still on gathering the requirements for the business, the developers should look ahead and begin thinking about how these requirements will apply to the database. How will the business rules, processes, and data affect the forward motion of the design of the database? Although the processes of gathering requirements and beginning to define system requirements are distinct from one another, the transition between the two should be smooth. Once again, we point out the importance of completely gathering business requirements because a lack thereof will definitely create a bumpy road between gathering business requirements and determining requirements for the database.

System requirements are derived from the information gathered from the interviews. In other words, business requirements are converted into system requirements. The conversion of business requirements into system requirements involves the following steps, which are explained afterward:

- Identifying the data
- Grouping the data that has been defined
- Establishing a list of fields
- Establishing data relationships

Identifying the Data

A significant part of the interview process includes the identification of business data. Data will be found throughout the notes taken during the interviews. Required data to be stored or captured must be broken down into basic related groups. It is important to ensure that all data has been defined. How will you know that all data has been defined? You might not at first. Although this question must be raised, the answer cannot be determined until the business has been completely modeled, which will come later. The comparison of data and business processes helps determine the completeness of data. All data should be affected by at least one business process that has been defined. What is the use of data if it cannot be accessed? Additionally, most business processes imply the need for data. What data is required for each process? If a business process does not require data, the process will not be required to design the database.

Data can exist in a variety of forms. Data can currently exist in a legacy database or on paper in a file cabinet. You should understand how data is currently stored, and how it will be stored after the creation of the new database. Presumably, as much data as possible will be stored in the database. Although the total elimination of paperwork is unlikely, it is reasonable to assume that it's possible to greatly minimize the amount of paperwork needed. Some data can be stored in the database and on paper. For example, if a prospective employee submits a resumé to human resources, information about the prospective employee's skills are entered into the database, and the original resumé is stored in a file cabinet. By law, hard copies of other documents might be required.

Establishing Groups of Data

Defining the main groups of data is similar to composing a jot list because a jot list identifies all the main points associated with a topic. In this case, the jot list is the notes taken during interviews. Preliminary groups of data, referred to as entities, are established using the data collected from the interviews. Establishing entities involves breaking the data down into logical categories, which should be a no-brainer for the development team in the sense that this information should have already been defined by the interviewees. Some categories of data will be related to one another and others will not. Some of these categories of data might be directly related to business processes that are defined, whereas others might not. Entities that are defined during information gathering are later transformed into database tables during database design.

Examples of basic groups of data for our sample company, TrainTech, include

- Class information
- Student information
- Instructor information
- Class materials
- Class schedules
- Accounts receivable
- Accounts payable

Examples of basic groups of data for an online bookstore might include:

- Book information
- Author information
- Publisher information
- Distributor information
- Order information

- Product inventory
- Product returns
- Accounts receivable
- Accounts payable

Establishing a List of Fields

Now that the data has been categorized into different groups, some general and other very specific, it is time to break the data down into more detailed units of information. Based on the primary entities that have been defined, a list of fields must be defined for each entity. As noted earlier in this book, a field is called an attribute from a technical standpoint. A field is an individual unit of specific information that is associated with an occurrence of information in the entity. Likewise, an entity can be defined as a collection of fields that specifically define a logical grouping of data.

For example, the human resources department for a company must track employee data. Therefore, the basic type of information stored is employee information. Within the scope of employee information, many groups of data must be established. Some of these groups of data include basic personal information for employees, employee pay information, employee resumé, employee benefits, and employee tax information. For each group of data established, fields must also be established. As each entity within the organization is unique, so must be all fields within a given entity.

For example, fields within the pay category of data might include an identifier that refers to a specific employee, the employee's position within the company, the department in which the employee works, the pay information whether it's salary, hourly, bonus, or commission, the pay effective date, and so forth. The employee benefit entity might entail the following information: an identifier that refers to a specific employee, the type of health insurance elected, dental insurance elected, the deductible amount, the employer contribution toward benefits, the number of employee dependents, and so on.

> **NOTE**
>
> From the user perspective, the term field is correct. When discussing modeling, the term attribute is correct. In this section, we will use the term field because this part of the analysis process involves interaction with the customer and end user. An entity must have at least one field, but it is normally comprised of many fields.

Looking back to the entities established in the previous section, the following list of fields can be derived from the entity associated with class information:

- Class identifier
- Class name
- Cost of class
- Description of class
- Class prerequisites
- Class materials
- Class instructor

In association with instructor information, the following specific information might be required:

- Instructor identifier
- Instructor name
- Address
- Phone
- Skills
- Certifications
- Hire date
- Pay rate

In association with book information, an online book store might require the following information:

- Book ISBN
- Book title
- Description
- Category
- Publisher
- Author
- Publication date
- Cost
- Page count
- Related titles

After a list of fields has been established, all data within the organization should be accounted for, whether dealing with data associated with manual processes, or data currently used by a legacy system. The list of fields established for entities are used to generate detailed ERDs.

The detailed ERDs should completely illustrate all data needed to design a database for an organization.

Establishing Relationships

Before determining data relationships, it is important to identify all data first. Relationships allow one or more entities to be related. Without the ability to relate data among entities, all data and fields would be required to reside in a single entity, which means that the amount of redundant information stored will be maximized. Relationships determine how data from one entity can be associated with another entity. Relationships also determine how data from one entity can refer to (access) data in another entity. In order for relationships to exist between entities, entities must have fields that are common to one another.

Although many entities that have been identified will not have direct relationships to other entities, all entities should be related to at least one other entity, creating an indirect relationship between entities.

For example, consider the following entities and brief lists of fields:

- Class schedule (class, date, location, instructor)
- Registration (class, student)
- Instructors (instructor, address, pay rate)
- Students (student, address)

Instructors are associated with classes, classes are associated with registration, and students are associated with registration. Instructors and students are not associated with one another directly, but one can easily determine the students who are taught by a particular instructor by finding out what classes an instructor teaches, and then by finding out what students are registered for the classes taught by the instructor. Relationships such as these are typical in a relational database. This scenario represents two types of relationships found in a relational database: one-to-many and many-to-many relationships. A one-to-one relationship does not exist in this scenario.

The following one-to-many relationships exist:

- Class schedules are associated with many registrations.
- A student might have registered for many classes.

The following many-to-many relationships exist:

- Instructors can teach more than one class, and a class can be taught by more than one instructor.
- An instructor can teach many students, and a student can have many instructors.

5

Business rules affect the relationships that might exist between data. Consider the following business rules:

- A class might be scheduled many times throughout the year.
- A class must have a lead instructor.
- An instructor must teach at least one class.
- Many students can register for a class that has been scheduled.
- A class might have an assistant instructor, depending on the student enrollment.
- No more than 15 students can register for a given class.
- A class will be canceled if less than 5 students are enrolled for a given class.

The first five business rules determine data relationships. The fifth business rule also affects the logic in the user application. The last two business rules do not affect the design of the database or the data relationships, but affect the design of the user application that accesses the data. Take time to compare the business rules with the sample relationships discussed.

> **NOTE**
>
> Different types of relationships will be discussed in detail in Chapter 7, "Understanding Entities and Relationships." Understanding relationships is crucial when creating ERDs.

Determining the Direction of Database Design

At some point toward the end of information gathering and requirements analysis, the direction taken for the remainder of database design must be taken into consideration. Currently, all business requirements should be defined. In review, these business requirements include the data (entities and lists of fields), business rules, and business processes. Interviews have been conducted with the customer and end user, as well as management. Diagrams have been drawn to depict the business information gathered. These diagrams are used to enhance the development team's understanding of the business so that a database can be accurately designed. These diagrams are also used to conduct user feedback sessions, to obtain approval for the work accomplished from all appropriate parties. Back and forth, this process goes, until everyone is satisfied that all business requirements are completely gathered for the proposed database. After all information has been gathered, it is simply a process of putting the pieces together. Imagine putting a puzzle together, only to find out after hours of work that a piece has been missing all along.

Following are considerations in determining the direction of any database design effort after information has been gathered. These considerations can be taken before interviews are conducted; just be aware that database design cannot proceed until the following issues are resolved.

- Database model to be used
- Implementation to be used
- Establishment of naming conventions and standards
- Establishment of milestones and deliverables
- Assign roles to members of design team

These considerations are addressed in the following subsections.

Determining the Type of Database Model

Hopefully at this point, a database model has already been selected. In most cases in today's world, the choice will be the relational database model. The model that best suits the needs of the business must be selected. As previously mentioned, this book is based on the concepts of designing a database to fit the mold of the relational database.

It is very unlikely that the flat-file database, network model, or hierarchical model will be the best choice for an organization. As time passes, more companies will be paralleling their strategy for storing data with object-oriented (OO) and object-relational (OR) technologies. In our opinion, the transition most companies will take toward OO and OR databases will not happen for several years, during which time these new technologies will have applied standards, have been tested more thoroughly, and have had more successful real-world implementations.

Selecting an Implementation

It is easy to select a database model. After a database model has been selected, an implementation must be selected. If the relational database model is being used, a *relational database management system (RDBMS)* must be selected. If you are not familiar with any particular RDBMS, making a selection can be very difficult at first because so many relational database vendors exist.

Some common relational database management systems include

- Oracle—Commonly used by medium- to large-sized organizations (mainframe, client/server, Internet)
- Microsoft SQL Server—Commonly used by medium- to large-sized organizations (client/server)

5

- Microsoft Access—Commonly used by smaller organizations for personal applications (personal)
- DB2—Commonly used by small- to large-sized organizations (mainframe, client/server, Internet)
- Informix—Commonly used by small- to large-sized organizations (mainframe, client/server, internet)
- Sybase—Commonly used by small- to large-sized organizations (mainframe, client/server, internet)
- MySQL—Commonly used by personal applications

Setting Naming Conventions and Standards to Be Used

Naming conventions and development standards are not so important during information gathering, but must be established before beginning to model and design the database. Consider the following when establishing naming conventions and standards.

- How will entities be named?
- How will attributes be named?
- How will tables be named?
- How will columns be named?
- How will other database objects be named?
- What abbreviations will be used?

Common sense should prevail when naming any database related object. All names should be descriptive. At this point in the design process, avoid using abbreviations that might make a name obscure. If abbreviations are used, an approved abbreviation list should be created.

Entities and attributes should have long, descriptive names. Remember that the main focal point of information gathering and requirements analysis is understanding the business.

When business objects are converted into database objects, it may be more important to abbreviate names to simplify code and meet the storage requirements of the RDBMS. For example, some RDBMSs restrict the length of a database object name to thirty characters. Also, it is a common rule that database object names cannot contain any spaces, although an underscore can be used to achieve the same effect. An example is

EMPLOYEE PAY (entity name) becomes EMPLOYEE_PAY (table name).

Following are sample rules we like to use when naming database related objects:

- The name should be in singular form (CUSTOMER).
- The name should contain spaces if more than one word for entities, and should contain underscores in the place of spaces for tables.

- Names should be capitalized.
- Identifiers use the word ID.
- If abbreviations are used, be consistent.
- Don't prefix column names with the table name, or abbreviation for the table name (for the department name, use NAME, not DNAME).

It is important that naming conventions are established, followed, and enforced for consistency throughout the design and life of a database. Adherence to naming conventions promote ease in the development of the database, the application, and the management of an existing database. Defining and enforcing naming conventions is one of an organization's first steps towards a successful database implementation.

Setting Milestones and Deadlines

Now, milestones must be set for the tasks that will be performed following the initial gathering and analysis of information. Time frames must be set for every task that is required. What happens after information has been gathered? The business is modeled based on the provided information from management, the customer, and the end user. What then? With the assumption that all business perspectives have been considered, it is time to begin thinking about the system—more specifically, the database. How will the database be designed based on the information that has been gathered? The most powerful tool used to proceed with the design of the database is the ERD. From the basic ERD, detail can be added to fully identify all structural elements of the proposed database (tables, columns, primary keys, foreign keys, and relationships).

Sample major milestones for a database design effort:

1. Design team is formed.
2. Project kick-off meeting is conducted.
3. Strategy plan is devised.
4. Interview plan is devised.
5. Interviews are conducted.
6. Lists of fields established.
7. Initial ERD is built.
8. Process models, data flow models, and function hierarchy diagrams are drawn.
9. User feedback sessions are conducted.
10. Detailed ERD is built.
11. User feedback sessions are conducted.

12. Cross-check ERD with processes is created.

13. User feedback sessions are conducted.

14. Design of the physical model begins.

15. Further normalization of the physical model occurs.

16. Views are designed.

17. The database is generated.

18. The database is tested with the user application.

19. Production implementation occurs.

The time frame for the milestones should be aggressive, yet realistic. These are just common milestones to most database design projects. More milestones might be established between each step in this example. The project manager is ultimately responsible for ensuring that all milestones and corresponding deadline dates are set. The project manager is also responsible for distributing the workload among members of the design team, as discussed in the next section.

Assigning Roles to Members of Design Team

After all appropriate information has been gathered for the proposed database and the milestones have been set, work must be distributed to members of the design team. The project manager must be aware of how all tasks are developing at all times in order to effectively manage the workload. The project manager must also be aware of any problems that have surfaced which might affect deliverables and deadlines. Some problems might be serious and cause deadlines to be reset, or might require work to be redistributed to different members of the design team.

As discussed in Chapter 3, "Database Design Planning," a design team is established. The design team might be broken down into multiple teams, with team leaders. The project manager assigns roles to each team and distributes work to each team leader. The team leaders distribute work to members of the team. Deliverables are sent by the team members up through the chain of command. Before requirements analysis, tasks are assigned to the design team to accomplish interviews, draw diagrams to model the business, and conduct user feedback sessions. After requirements analysis is complete, tasks are assigned to begin modeling the database.

Preliminary Documentation

As important as documentation is, so many people fail to document their work. Lack of documentation causes duplicated effort and wastes valuable time. Documentation is an on-going process, which means that in order to be managed properly, it must be integrated from the beginning and constantly revised throughout the life of a database. Documentation should exist from initial planning and design to the discontinuance of the database.

During the life of any database, documentation proves invaluable to the following parties:

- Management
- Design team members
- New design team members
- Customer
- End user

Management should be provided documentation that outlines the work accomplished during a design effort. Through the use of the documentation, management should gain an understanding of the layout of the database and measure the worth of the database as it applies to the goals of the business. Documentation is provided to customer management and management above the design team. The customer documentation should pertain to the business and the application of the database to meet the goals of the business. Design team management should be provided documentation concerning the existing state of the database and all deliverables, so future design efforts of the current or new database can be more easily managed. Documentation is valuable to individual design team members because they must learn and maintain an understanding of the business during development. As new members are added to the design team, they need to be brought up to speed as quickly as possible, especially when dealing with high-priced consultants. The documentation compiled throughout the design effort will be used in the end to formulate end-user documentation that can be used during training and as a reference to the end user.

NOTE

Documentation is accumulated during the design phases and life of a database. Documentation should be modified as long as changes are being made to the database.

A lack of documentation is one of the major pitfalls of

- Database design
- Database implementation
- End-user training
- Transition during database changes
- Job turnover and training

5

GATHERING BUSINESS AND SYSTEM REQUIREMENTS

Documentation involved in the information gathering stage of database design includes

- A high-level work plan
- A strategy document
- A detailed requirements document

High-level Work Plan

A high-level work plan should be composed by the design team at the beginning of the database design effort. This work plan should be high-level, covering the major steps that will be taken to meet the goals of the database from a broad perspective. The high-level work plan is the "big picture," which must be viewed before interviewing, modeling, and designing can commence. This work plan will help determine how the organization will proceed with the project, and will also help determine the outline for additional documentation throughout design.

This plan should include

- The major steps projected to design the database
- The major tasks that will be involved during design
- Identification of major milestones
- Identification of major deliverables
- Outline of the resources required for the project
- Estimate of the personnel required for the project
- Estimate of the desired time frame to completion of the project

Strategy Document

A strategy document can be created, which outlines the system requirements from a high level. This document is similar to the high-level work plan in the sense that it is a big picture. The strategy document is a big picture of the business requirements that will be used to design the database. Only the most critical requirements should be included in the strategy document. The strategy document is important because it helps the customer and design team better understand the requirements for a database, while promoting confidence and allowing individuals to "buy in" to the project. Information gathered from initial interviews is used to create the strategy document. The strategy document should be used as a tool during an initial user feedback session.

Diagrams that should be included in the strategy document are

- High-level entity relationship diagrams (entities and relationships only)
- High-level business process models (main processes only)

Detailed Requirements Document

A detailed requirements document must be created before the design team becomes serious about proceeding with modeling and design of the project. The detailed requirements document is based on the strategy document, but must be more refined, depicting a detailed representation of all business requirements that will be used to design the database. As much detail as possible should be included in this document.

The detailed requirements document should include

- A detailed listing of database requirements that pertains to all appropriate organizational units within the organization
- All available legacy database documentation that pertains to the new database
- Business goals
- Outline of all design phases, milestones, and deliverables
- Objectives for each design phase
- The business rules as gathered from interviews (many business rules reflected in diagrams)
- Detailed diagrams as drawn during requirements analysis

Diagrams that should be included in the requirements document are

- Detailed entity relationship diagrams
- Detailed business process models
- Hierarchy of business processes
- Data flow diagrams

Diagrams can be used to cross-check the work accomplished during information gathering. For instance, it is common to cross-check business processes with data (entities) that have been defined. The existence of entities that are not associated with at least one process is normally an indication that all requirements have not been gathered.

Evaluating Analysis

When speaking of analysis, most people think of gathering information, or requirements, and analyzing those requirements in order to begin modeling a database. This chapter discusses the process of gathering requirements and beginning to analyze those requirements. In subsequent chapters, we will show how to actually convert the requirements into diagrams and eventually design the tables that comprise the database. Before getting too anxious and starting to model the database prematurely, the development team should take a step back, take a deep breath, and review the activities of analysis. The military calls this process an "after action review."

Database designers refer to this process as evaluation of analysis, which is a way of preparing for the next phases, database modeling and design, by reviewing the results of the analysis phase.

When evaluating analysis, or the work achieved so far, it is most important to check the requirements for completeness. Although completeness is checked many times up to this point, this is the last chance you will have to verify the completeness of the information gathered before modeling the database. Of course, requirements can always be established or redefined throughout database design, but not without taking a step back. It is best to follow all steps outlined in the design methodology used for any changes or additions to existing requirements to ensure that all deliverables and diagrams are consistent.

Involve the customer, end user, and management as much as possible during the evaluation of analysis. Begin by reviewing the interviews, the questions asked, and the responses obtained. Review the goals set forth for the database, and ensure that the interviews were conducted appropriately to gather the required information. Allow all parties to take part in the evaluation, reviewing all deliverables one last time as if issuing a stamp of approval.

Because a significant part of information gathering and requirements analysis involves drawing diagrams, the most important action taken during evaluation is to review all diagrams used as deliverables. The diagrams should be checked for consistency and accuracy according to the requirements that have been established. Are the diagrams accurate representations of the business, and the business's needs for a database? With regard to processes (functions), the evaluation of the analysis is complete when all the business requirements related to the database are mapped to a function, and each system requirement is associated with a function. With regard to data, all data and data-related business rules must be incorporated into the ERD.

NOTE

If inadequacies in requirements are found, they should be addressed as early as possible in the design process to minimize the overall effects on work and time involved to implement changes. For instance, more work will be required if the database has already been designed, and missing requirements are found that will alter the structure of the database. If a process or entity is added or changed, all appropriate diagrams should be modified to avoid confusion in the future.

ERDs should be checked to ensure that data has been completely defined. Process models are checked to ensure that all processes related to the database or application have been defined. Data flow diagrams are checked for accuracy for data access by processes. Function hierarchy diagrams are checked to ensure that all processes, or functions, are properly related to one another. If using an automated design tool, reports can be run to check the completeness of analysis. For example, some tools can generate matrix reports that illustrate entities that are affected by processes, and processes that affect entities. This type of report is an excellent tool to use to check for completeness concerning accessibility of data.

The following considerations should be taken to measure the completeness of information gathering and requirements analysis:

- Have all steps been followed so far?
- Is the direction of design still within the scope of the mission statement and objectives?
- Have all requirements been gathered in order to design a database?
- Is the Entity Relationship Diagram (ERD) correct?
- Is the function hierarchy correct?
- Are all database requirements on schedule for implementation?
- Do the requirements make sense to the development team?
- Were all deliverables acceptable to customer, end user, and management?
- Were all objectives of requirements analysis met?
- Are all appropriate parties comfortable with moving forward?

Summary

Taking time to gather the requirements that an organization has for a database is the most important part of design because a database cannot be created without these requirements. Without completely gathering requirements, a database can be created, but can lack a great deal of functionality to the end user, or can even be unusable. The different types of requirements discussed were business requirements and system requirements. Business requirements are those related to the functionality of the business. Business requirements are used to establish system requirements. System requirements are the requirements of the database and the end-user application based on the needs of the business. Requirements analysis is the process of analyzing the requirements that have been gathered, and converting the business requirements into system requirements.

Business requirements are obtained through interviews with management, the customer, and the end user. Interviews are conducted by various members of the design team. When conducting interviews, it is important that there is a variety of both interviewers and interviewees, in order to view the business from different perspectives, thus completely gathering all requirements. After all requirements are gathered, the design team draws various diagrams which depict the data and processes that belong to the business. The most typical diagrams, which are quite vague at this point, include entity relationship diagrams (illustrate the data), process model diagrams, function hierarchy diagrams, and data flow diagrams. Detail is added to diagrams when converting business requirements into system requirements. For example, after a list of fields is determined for a given entity, attributes are added to the entity on the ERD. System requirements are defined by identifying the data, breaking the data into logical groups, creating a list of fields for groups of data, and establishing data relationships.

Before information gathering and requirements analysis are complete, and the next major phase, modeling, is encountered, precautions must be taken to ensure that the project is moving on the right track. Before modeling begins, standards and naming conventions must be established so that all work is performed consistently. It is also important to begin documenting the activities conducted. The diagrams drawn comprise a significant part of documentation, which will be used by the design team, management, the customer, and the end user. Finally, all work performed is evaluated to ensure that the project is indeed moving in the right direction. The evaluation of analysis includes reviews of the interviews and all deliverables at this point. Because it is often easy to get off track, it is important to verify that the focus of the project is still based on the original goals set forth for the system. If for some reason the goals of the system have changed from the time of their definition to now, it will be necessary to restart the process of gathering requirements to guarantee completeness.

Establishing a Business Model

IN THIS CHAPTER

A model is an abstract representation of an object. It can be a powerful tool for predicting the response of an object to a stimulus. Except for the simplest examples, the response of actual objects might be surprising and counterintuitive. In many cases, such surprises can have disastrous effects. War gaming might offer the clearest example. Such trials allow battle field commanders to hone strategy and tactics without the need for expensive and deadly trial and error. Therefore, when predictability is important, a model can serve as a powerful planning tool. In addition, the model allows the user to engage in trial and error, or other explorations, without the time, expense, and (sometimes) danger of actual system use.

Such is the importance of establishing a business model for database design.

A business model is essentially an overall picture of an organization, including its data and the processes that are performed by individuals within the organization. A business model starts out simple, eventually branching out into specific detail that is used to transform business concepts into an information system (database and application interface). As you recall from Chapter 5, "Gathering Business and System Requirements," information is divulged from key players in an organization in order to design a database. This information that is gathered is first used to model the business so that it can be checked by the key players for completeness and accuracy before database design commences.

> **NOTE**
>
> This chapter contains references to *system* and *information system*, which vaguely refer to the combination of the back-end database (tables) and the front-end application (end-user interface to the database), respectively. At this point in design, it is still important to consider the system when considering modeling. During physical design (table definitions and application code), it is more realistic to focus on either database design or application design in a more exclusive manner.

Understanding Business Modeling Concepts

Precise definitions are essential to a discussion about modeling. The definitions serve as a touchstone in the application of modeling business concepts to complex objects. Business concepts are based on information extracted from interviews that are conducted during the information gathering phase of database design. The definitions of this topic are a distillation of explanations from the dictionary and technical standards. They are as follows:

A *process* is a sequence of related actions and responses with a well defined beginning and end.

To expand on the previous reference in the chapter introduction, a *system* is a self-contained object with well-defined boundaries (interfaces) and behaviors.

NOTE

These definitions are very practical because they offer testable criteria. If the starting point of a sequence of events is unclear, it cannot be a process. Similarly, if the interfaces of an object are indefinable, it will be impossible to treat the object as a system for the purposes of modeling.

Formal methods make an important distinction between behavioral and physical models. A behavioral model captures the response of a system to an input from the perspective of an outside observer. This model does not necessarily consider the internal structure of the system. Instead, the concern is simply to produce correct output and timing response. The physical model involves equations for the internal structure of the system. This approach might be necessary when high accuracy results, especially timing, are necessary. A hybrid approach is also possible in which the modeler decomposes the system into structural elements and constructs behavioral models for these subsystems.

As the definitions in the introduction of this topic suggest, the focus of modeling is careful definition of system interfaces and behaviors. This chapter describes some techniques for establishing model diagrams. This serves as a basis for an overview of business models and their constituents.

Using the Information Gathered

In the previous chapter, we discussed methods for extracting important modeling and design information from the customer, management, and the end user. Now, how is the information used? Obviously, the information is used to build the proposed database, but first it must be interpreted so that data elements and processes can be modeled.

This part of the design process is still considered analysis, which makes sense because the designer is trying to interpret the overwhelming amount of information received. Figure 6.1 illustrates the basic thought process implemented in the utilization of the information gathered in interviews, in accordance with business modeling.

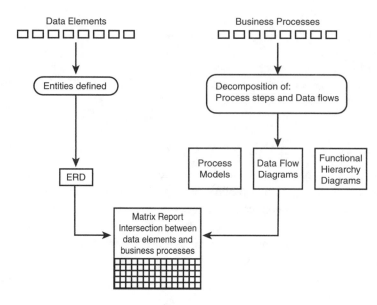

FIGURE 6.1

Transformation of information into the business model.

In Figure 6.1, defined data elements become entities, and processes as described by the users of the data must be decomposed into process steps and data flows. Entities are modeled using an Entity Relationship Diagram (ERD), which shows their relationships. Entities are decomposed and related appropriately to simplify the distribution and management of data. Processes and data flows are modeled by drawing process models, data flow diagrams, and functional hierarchy diagrams. These diagrams are used to show not only how processes are related to one another, but also how processes affect data elements. A matrix report can be generated to compare the ERD with the different process models to ensure that all possible interactions between data elements and process steps have been considered.

The following section discusses the act of modeling the business based on information gathered in the form of diagrams.

Business Model Diagrams

A diagramming method is a valuable modeling tool because it succinctly and precisely captures relationships among elements of a system. Verbal descriptions are often too ambiguous or wordy to be the basis of a design. People want to see pictures because pictures render easier visualization of the system and increase overall understanding. Diagrams play the greatest role in the designer's understanding of the business concepts that must be molded into a system.

Flow diagrams are a time tested, general mechanism for diagramming system behaviors. These consist of a sequence of interconnected blocks of various types, such as decision points (branches), inputs, outputs, and processing. Figure 6.2 shows a simple example for the calculation of a square root.

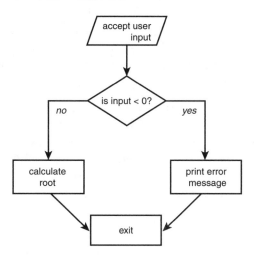

FIGURE 6.2

Simplistic process flow diagram.

Flow charts can work well with simple systems, but they present an important drawback in more complicated cases. The flow chart combines the depiction of data flow and control mechanisms, potentially rendering such diagrams hopelessly intractable. Instead, a diagrammatic method should produce simple, understandable representations. The traditional method of reducing complexity is "divide and conquer." In this case, the flow chart must separate into many types.

For this reason, data flow diagrams have become an important aspect of modern design methods. Although the formalities can be arcane, the essential features involve

1. Describing the structure and content of the data
2. Identifying how the data enters and leaves the system
3. Isolating those sub-elements of the system that use or modify the data

The data description is specific to a system design, but it could involve many factors. The goal is to look for patterns in the data and match them to the system structures for the most efficient processing. In addition, the data elements should be simple enough to be easily manageable. It is common to diagram data elements, or entities, using an entity relationship diagram. The fundamental purpose of the entity relationship diagram is the illustration of an organization's data elements and their relationships to one another.

The data flow design should also consider interfaces. Certain data elements must use particular interfaces for greatest efficiency. One approach is to break inputs into blocks targeted to elements that use or modify the information.

The system design should be as simple as possible so that it is understandable. Einstein, when once asked about mathematical modeling, replied that the model "should be as simple as possible, but no simpler." This response is more than simply humorous. It can be just as dangerous to model too little of the system behavior as too much. The balance point in data modeling is achieved when users are convinced that the model captures system behavior accurately. Obviously, simplicity is a tremendous aid in logic debugging.

After the designer weighs such decisions, it should become apparent that certain blocks of information travel through the system through the same paths. In addition, the blocks might even have the same structure even though actual entries differ. In such cases, it is possible to formally define a data structure, which is a powerful method of defining an interface. Data structures enable code reuse, simplify debugging, and lower maintenance costs. They also form the basis of the formal definition of the system interface. The jargon of formal modeling identifies such constructs as data objects.

NOTE

Data structures form the basis of the system interface, or the boundaries which are used to define the system. Data structures relate directly to an organization's data. Data objects are data modeling constructs that represent data structures.

The system model must also decompose the processing of data into manageable parts. Once again, data flow, complexity, performance, and timing are key considerations in such decisions. System elements are referred to as *entities*.

Consider a very simple example. Based on command inputs, a small electric motor within the toy locomotive moves the train on the track. In addition, a position sensor electrically locates the train. Finally, a remote monitor makes it possible to announce the train position.

The system model might consist of two elements—the control and monitor portions. These interact internally in ways that are not necessary for a top-level model to know. Interfaces must be present for the commanded position (input), actual position (input), and a motor control signal (output). The monitor portion might digitally broadcast the two inputs.

Although the structure of the data objects is simple, this example illustrates the mapping of objects to interfaces. The system produces two types of output data, control and monitor. For the sake of reduced complexity of implementation, separating these into distinct interfaces offers advantages.

Formal methods focus on two aspects of the system model. These are the data flow (in terms of structures) and the system elements (entities). The interaction among the system elements and data structures leads to another diagramming technique known as Entity Relationship Diagrams.

> **NOTE**
>
> This chapter discusses only the basic concepts of modeling business objects. Chapter 7, "Understanding Entities and Relationships," explains data elements, or entities in more detail, leading to Chapter 9, "Entity Relationship Modeling." Chapter 10, "Modeling Business Processes," discusses process modeling in more detail, showing process models, data flow diagrams, and functional hierarchy diagrams; all of which might be used to ensure the completeness of a database design effort.

Common Business Models

A universal model for all business processes is much too ambitious. Instead, it is common to break business applications into sub-domains. Some of these apply to all businesses, whereas others do not. These include

- Financial
- Inventory
- Project management
- Marketing
- Security

For the sake of efficiency, many businesses now rely on electronic processing of financial information. This might include payroll, tax reports, income and expense reports for stockholders, and many others. Once again, it might be most efficient to separate these for the sake of reducing complexity. However, it is usually necessary to link them because they are related. For example, payroll processing generates results needed for tax reports.

For some businesses, inventory control is the most important aspect to sales. A grocery store manager, for example, wants fresh food to sell, so it is important to know how long ago the current products arrived. It is equally important to track sales so that the store does not deplete its inventory. In addition, it is important to account for the supply chain because orders might take longer at certain times of the year. All these considerations are important elements of a behavioral model.

Other types of businesses have no need of an inventory model. A service provider, such as a consulting group, has no inventory to sell. For such companies, project management tools might be more significant. These allow senior managers to check on contracts placed, completion estimates, and marketing projections.

Marketing activities might be the subject of another modeling effort. One important area is *contact management*. This includes identifying and qualifying sources of new business and follow-ups with previous customers. The new sources may be sales contacts developed by the marketing group. On the other hand, the contacts might be a response to advertisements. It is important to track such responses in order to fine-tune the advertising efforts. Modeling of the marketing group, therefore, might have interfaces to advertisers, current customers, and new leads. The primary output, the basis of a *metric*, is contracts placed that are measured in terms of dollar value and length of performance.

Security might be another application. One example of this is logging building access electronically. This offers a backup record for access to equipment, documents, and computer systems. Some companies also couple building access logs to time-keeping systems. The goal of such information exchange is usually not checking employee tardiness, but rather to ensure the accuracy of payroll and other related systems.

The concept of metrics is an important consideration when building a model. Metrics are just measures of performance. However, capturing the metrics is often an important consideration in defining model interfaces. The metrics are crucial to improving performance of a group, so company wide distribution and usage of a particular model is critical. As mentioned previously, the metric for the marketing group is usually in terms of contracts placed. Similarly, the metrics for project management are usually dollars spent versus available and schedule completed versus tasks scheduled. The metrics for the financial system are timeliness and accuracy. The earlier discussions also suggest metrics for inventory and security systems.

Models of business processes are an important tool for corporate planning. They serve as the basis for computer-based implementations that offer more efficient data management. The result is better responsiveness and avoidance of information overload. In the highly competitive business world, this approach can be the difference between success and failure.

Sample Elements in a Business Model

Earlier discussions provide the steps involved in building a model—defining the system boundaries and then breaking it up into tractable components. Data flow among components and the system is an important characteristic. After a process model is refined, it represents a powerful tool for studying how the company conducts business. Until business practices are clearly defined and understood, an information system cannot be designed.

Consider an example from the financial management area. For simplicity, the example involves a checking account, savings account, and credit card. This might be an adequate model for a cash-based, service business. As discussed earlier, though, product sales demand consideration of interfaces to the inventory system. The data flow analysis involves building all the possible tracks by which money can flow among these. The goal is to offer an instantaneous, accurate account balance as well as long-term trends checking. Long-term trends might be related to statistical or historical data.

Each sub-element has inputs and outputs. In the case of the savings and checking accounts, the inputs are income, interest, and fund transfers between the two. The credit card inputs are payments and interest. Outputs for the savings account are cash withdrawals, service fees, and fund transfers. The checking account outputs are checks written, automatic withdrawals, cash transfers, and service fees. Finally, it is useful to consider credit card purchases as an output.

The three accounts interact by money transfers. For example, the owner might make payments on the credit card balance using checks. The funds for the checks might stem from a transfer of money from the savings account. Of course, the savings account contains these funds as a consequence of income. Figure 6.3 offers a diagram of this interaction.

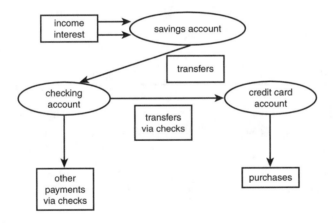

FIGURE 6.3

Cash flow model.

Money also flows to other accounts such as the payroll system. For the sake of reducing complexity, many companies rely on separate systems for payroll and accounts. In fact, some companies contract out to a payroll service. This has the effect of reducing payroll to simply another expense category.

For each account, the balance is simply computed as

```
balance = (start balance) + (all inputs) - (all outputs)
```

However, finer resolution is usually desirable. For example, it is useful for purposes of tax accounting to break the outputs into expense categories such as those of Table 6.1. Similarly, it is important to classify the inputs, being careful to separate interest from ordinary income.

TABLE 6.1   Expense Categories

Category	Explanation
Computers and software	Office equipment
Consultants	Non-payroll reimbursements for contract services
Electronic mail	Connection service fee
Insurance	Business liability, other
Mail	Stamps, other postage
Meals, entertainment	Marketing
Mileage	Repayment for use of personal vehicle for business
Office supplies	Expendables such as paper
Payroll	Payments to employees, benefits, taxes
Professional	Accountant, lawyer
Telephone	Office telephone
Travel, non-meals	Transportation, hotel

In terms of formal modeling, the entity is a "financial account" of which this model has three instances. These, of course, are savings, checking, and credit. A financial account has one input port and one output. Its behavior is to produce the balance described previously.

The relationship among sub-elements is somewhat arbitrary, but when established, should be enforced. The model of Figure 6.3 captures the policy decisions (business rules associated with account management) that

- Ordinary income is always a deposit to savings, never checking or credit.
- Cash withdrawals are always taken from savings.
- Funds transfers from savings provide the money for checking.
- Credit card payments are always by check.

Figure 6.3 describes three data elements, or entities: savings account, checking account, and credit card account. Processes determine how these data elements are accessed, and how data flows; hence, a data flow diagram.

The benefits for enforcing such processes come monthly and at tax reporting time. With such procedures in place, it is simple to reconcile bank and credit card statements. At tax time, expense reports, interest income, and other relevant material is easily obtainable. Such a system is essential to achieve accuracy and responsiveness.

The abstract model of a financial account is a tool that forces managers to reason precisely about company policy involving these accounts. It might be advantageous to allow cash withdrawals from checking, for example. However, the linkage among the models illustrates that fewer data paths result in analysis that is easier to understand.

Summary

Business modeling is the transition point between gathering information from interviews and actually designing a database. Business modeling uses gathered information in order to model the business from a logical standpoint. In order to model a business, various diagrams are drawn that represent key components which belong to an organization in relation to the organization's need to store information. These key elements include mainly data elements and processes.

A data element represents an organization's data, and is modeled by breaking data elements into what are called entities. Entities are those objects graphically shown in an entity relationship diagram. Processes are decomposed into process steps and data flows. Processes define how individuals within an organization operate in order to accomplish their daily tasks. Processes are represented in diagrams such as process models, data flow diagrams, and functional hierarchy diagrams. The implication of the need for a database implies that a significant amount of these tasks affect data. Therefore, both data (entities) and processes must be modeled, and relationships must be defined between them. The next several chapters discuss entities, processes, and logical modeling in more detail.

Understanding Entities and Relationships

IN THIS CHAPTER

Initially, identification of entities should be a freewheeling process. There are no stupid questions or dumb ideas as we attempt to identify and capture the potential entities for our system. In a new system, look for the nouns in the descriptions of the new and of the old system, old system reports, and user interviews as a source of potential entities. Entities are defined throughout the information gathering phase of design, originating from user interviews and legacy documentation if available.

At this point, you should have a basic understanding of entities. This chapter intends to complete the understanding of entities through a study of entity relationships. This chapter also includes information on the use of entities after logical modeling, and the use of data with regard to entity relationships. After you have a solid understanding of entities and their relationships to one another, you can begin modeling the logical database based on information gathered from interviews and requirements analysis.

Overview of Entities and Entity Relationships

As you should already understand by now, entities represent an organization's data. When designing a database, you might be surprised at how much data actually exists. As you will deduct after interviews, many entities will need to be defined to track all data that has been defined. An entity should be created for each category of data defined.

NOTE

The intent of this chapter is to enhance your understanding of entities and their relationships to one another. Defining entities, defining entity relationships, and relationship modeling are not covered here, but in Chapter 9, "Entity Relationship Modeling." However, it is important to understand the concepts covered in this chapter first.

Of all entities defined by the design team, many of the entities will be related to one another. In fact, it is a rarity that an entity is not related to at least one other entity. An entity can be related either to only one other entity, or to many entities. One entity can be defined to which all other entities are related, allowing an indirect relationship to exist between all entities. The main question this chapter would like to address is, "how are the entities related?"

Because an entity represents data, we are talking about data related to other data. An occurrence of data in an entity can be related to a record in a file cabinet. Suppose that one file cabinet stores resumes, each folder in the cabinet containing a resume for an individual. Suppose that another file cabinet maintains files containing employee information. We know that all resumes kept by a company don't correlate to the hiring of an employee. Yet, we don't want to store an employee's resume in the employee file if we already have a resume file. That would be twice as much paperwork to store resumes for employees. Instead, the files in both cabinets are stored alphabetically. If you wanted to pull an employee file along with the employee's resume, you would refer to both file cabinets using the employee's name. Thus, the information (resume data and employee data) stored in both cabinets is related by the employee's name.

Let's talk more about the relationships that might exist between the files in both cabinets. A resume is first submitted by a candidate for employment. If the candidate is hired, an employee file is opened, so a file exists in both the resume and employee cabinets. However, only one file should be in each cabinet for a particular individual. We can deduce that a file must first be in the resume cabinet before a file is created in the employee cabinet. In other words, a file in the employee cabinet should not exist if no file exists in the resume cabinet for that person. If so, procedures were apparently not followed. If the candidate is not hired, a file should not be created in the employee cabinet. If an employee is fired or quits, the file can be pulled from the employee cabinet, but the resume will remain in the resume cabinet. The employee file can now be transferred to a third cabinet that tracks former employees. Now we have three cabinets that are related to one another. The resume cabinet is related to the employee cabinet and the former employee cabinet. The employee and former employee cabinets are not related to one another. Now, think of each cabinet as an entity.

We have defined the following three cabinets:

Cabinet #1	Resumes
Cabinet #2	Employees
Cabinet #3	Former employees

Based on our discussion in the previous paragraph, the following relationships exist between the cabinets:

A resume *may* correspond with only one employee file.

A resume *may* correspond with only one former employee file.

Employees *must* have only one resume.

Former employees *must* have only one resume.

Notice that words of optionality are italicized in the previous list. *May* implies that a relationship may not exist for a given occurrence of data, and *must* implies that a relationship must exist. For example, a resume may not correspond to a file in the employee cabinet. All these relationships are discussed in detail in this chapter.

Cardinality is the term used to describe the number of occurrences of data that might exist which are associated with occurrences of data from another entity. *Optionality* is the term used to describe whether a relationship is optional, or must exist.

> **NOTE**
>
> Complete relationships are bidirectional, meaning that a relationship is attached to each entity. Cardinality and optionality might differ between related entities.

The following subsections discuss these entity relationships (the first five relationships deal with cardinality):

- One-to-one
- One-to-many
- Many-to-many
- Recursive
- Mandatory
- Optional

One-to-One Relationship

A one-to-one relationship represents a relation between entities in which one occurrence of data in one entity might have one occurrence of data in the related entity. Entity A might have only one occurrence of related data in entity B, and entity B might have only one occurrence of related data in entity A.

Figure 7.1 illustrates a one-to-one relationship, which shows sample data. Notice that all employees listed under Employee Data have a corresponding occurrence of data (record) under Employee Pay Data. It makes sense to track an employee's name, address, and other personal information only one time. It also makes sense that every employee should have a pay record, but only one pay record.

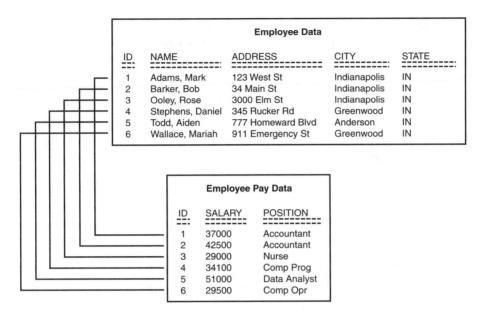

FIGURE 7.1

Sample one-to-one relationship.

> **NOTE**
>
> A relationship represents rules concerning data that belongs to an organization. Relationships represent the nature of related data, and are enforced by placing constraints on columns after entities have been mapped to tables, as explained in Chapter 12, "Integrating Business Rules and Data Integrity."

Other examples of one-to-one relationships include the following:

Entity A	Entity B
Product information	Inventory information
Customer information	Customer profile
Book information	Detailed book description
Author information	Author biography

One-to-Many Relationship

In most relational databases that we have seen, the one-to-many relationship seems to be the most common relationship that exists. A one-to-many relationship represents a relation between entities in which one occurrence of data in one entity might have one or more occurrences of data in the related entity. For example, entity A might have several occurrences of related data in entity B.

Figure 7.2 illustrates a one-to-many relationship, which shows sample data. Here, we have employee data and employee bonus data. Based on an employee's performance, a bonus might be rewarded from time to time. Some employees might have never been issued a bonus, some employees might have been issued a bonus on one occurrence, and some employees might have received multiple bonus checks.

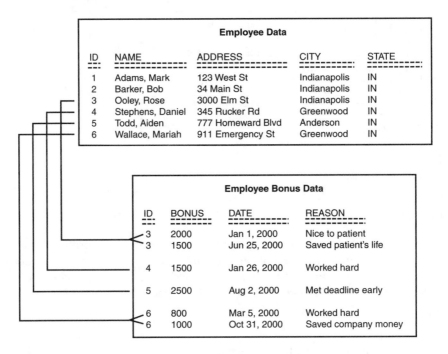

FIGURE 7.2
Sample one-to-many relationship.

Bonus information, although related to an employee's pay, still warrants a separate entity from the employee pay entity. Why? Both the bonus and employee pay entities are related to the employee entity. An employee can only have one pay record, which is associated with the employee's salary. An employee might have many bonuses over a period of time. You can see that there are two relationships involved here:

- One-to-one between employee and pay data
- One-to-many between employee and bonus data

Based on these two relationships, we have opted to reserve an entity for only bonus information. Based on the fact that two relationships exist between the data, we can say that two different groups of data, or entities exist (referring to pay and bonus).

Other examples of one-to-many relationships include the following, where Entity A contains one record and Entity B contains many records per occurrence in Entity A.

Entity A	Entity B
Customer information	Order information
Product information	Order information
Student information	Class registration
Instructor information	Class information
Author information	Book information
Publisher information	Author information
Publisher information	Book information

Many-to-Many Relationship

A many-to-many relationship exists if multiple occurrences of related data are allowed to exist between two entities, in either direction. For instance, entity A might have many occurrences of related data in entity B, and entity B might have many occurrences of related data in entity A.

Figure 7.3 illustrates a many-to-many relationship, showing sample data in which two basic entities exist for instructor and class data. An instructor might teach many classes, and a class can be taught by many instructors. A class can be taught during the day or in the evening. Multiple instructors exist as backups to one another, and for scheduling purposes. By studying the relationship between the two entities and sample data in the figure, you can see that Ryan Stephens teaches the Intro to SQL and Intro to DBA classes. If you are looking for the classes a particular instructor teaches, you would look under Instructor Data. If you are looking for instructors who teach a particular class, you would look under Class Data. By looking for Intro to SQL under Class Data, you can see that Chuck Mesecher, Ron Plew, and Ryan Stephens all teach that class. Although this is a simple figure, you can probably see how confusing a many-to-many relationship might be to maintain. In fact, the design shown here is far from optimal. But at this point, it is adequate to illustrate how many-to-many data relationships exist.

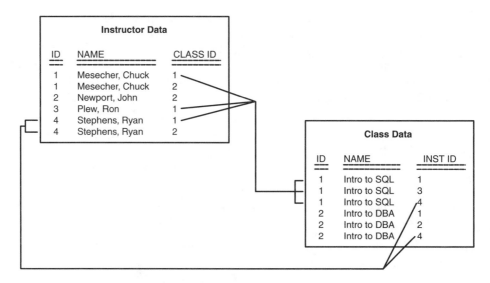

FIGURE 7.3

Sample many-to-many relationship.

NOTE

As a general rule, direct many-to-many relationships should be avoided. This many-to-many relationship is a poor design, mainly because of redundant data. Later in this chapter, we will show how to solve the problem of maintaining the same information while avoiding a direct many-to-many relationship.

Other examples of many-to-many relationships include the following:

Entity A	Entity B
Instructors teach many classes	Classes taught by many instructors
Instructors teach many Students	Students taught by many instructors
Doctors treat many patients	Patients treated by many doctors

Recursive Relationships

Sometimes it makes sense to relate data to other data in a single entity. A recursive relationship is a circular relationship that exists between two attributes in the same entity. Recursive relationships are rare, but useful. The most common example used to illustrate a recursive relationship is employee and manager names. Every employee has a manager, who is also an employee.

Figure 7.4 illustrates a recursive relationship to derive a manager's name from employee data. In this example, we have added an attribute called MGR ID to Employee Data. Notice that every employee has a value associated with MGR ID except for Mark Adams, who happens to be the big cheese. The value associated with MGR ID happens to be a value associated with an occurrence of ID. It is not necessary to store a manager's name separate from employees because a manager must also be an employee. In the figure, we are seeking the Daniel Stephens' manager. First, Daniel Stephens' record must be found. Once found, the value associated with MGR ID is found. The value of MGR ID is used to reference ID. After the matching ID is found, the manager's name is apparent.

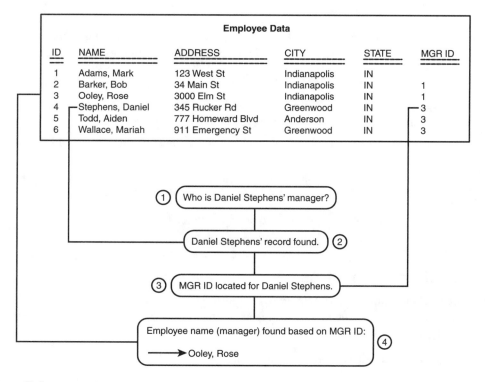

FIGURE 7.4
Sample Recursive Relationship.

> **NOTE**
>
> A recursive relationship is one in which an entity is related to itself, allowing for data to be stored and extracted in a hierarchical format. One attribute simply references another attribute in the same entity. In order for a value to be valid for MGR ID, a corresponding value must be found under ID. In other words, a value cannot exist under MGR ID if it does not exist under ID first.

Other examples of recursive relationships include the following:

- Chain of command in the armed forces
- Team leaders within an organization
- Products that might be sold separately or as accessories to other products

Mandatory Relationships

A mandatory relationship represents data that is required to have associated data, or you could say that a relationship must exist. A mandatory relationship typically uses the word *must*.

Following are examples of one-sided mandatory relationships:

- An employee pay record must match an employee personnel record. (An employee pay record cannot exist without a corresponding employee personnel record.)
- An order must be placed by a customer. (Every order must be associated with one customer.)
- An order must correspond to an available product. (Every order must be associated with one product.)
- An author must be associated with one or more publishers.
- A book must be associated with one or more authors and one or more publishers.

Optional Relationships

An optional relationship does not require a relationship to exist, which means that data might exist that isn't directly associated with data from another entity. An optional relationship typically uses the word *may*.

Following are examples of one-sided optional relationships:

- A customer may place one or more orders. (A customer may not be required to place an order, but may cease to be considered a customer after a certain period of time with no account activity.)

- A product may be ordered by a customer. (Products may exist that have never been ordered.)

- An insured individual may place a claim. (An individual may have health insurance and never have a medical claim.)

- An employee may be awarded a bonus. (Some employees may be awarded bonuses, whereas others are not.)

Now that we have discussed relationships of both optionality, here are some examples of complete relationships:

- Each employee pay record must match an employee personnel record, and each employee personnel record must have a corresponding pay record. Furthermore, it can be said that each employee must have both a personnel and pay record.

- Each student must be registered for one or more classes, and each class may have one or more registered students.

Transformation of the Entity in Design

What becomes of entities? After the logical model is complete, entities are transformed into database tables. The relationships defined for entities are carried over into the physical model (tables). Attributes become table columns. In the physical model, relationships are defined and enforced by placing constraints on columns, consisting mainly of primary key and foreign key constraints.

The transformation of entities into tables occurs one of two ways: manually or through the use of an automated design (AD) tool. The manual conversion of entities to tables involves the developer typing the CREATE TABLE statements (standard command used to create relational database tables) based on *Entity Relationship Diagrams (ERDs)* that are drawn, either manually or using and AD tool. AD tools can be used to automate the conversion of entities into table structures. AD tools will generate the physical model based on the logical model. In the physical model, the developer can easily make adjustments to table structures, add columns, and create indexes and views. With the click of a button, an AD tool will generate the DDL (data definition language), or CREATE commands to build the tables, indexes, views, and any other object defined.

Figure 7.5 illustrates the conversion of entities into tables. We are using two of the entities previously defined in this chapter. Entities do not actually contain data, they represent data. We have shown sample data just to help you visualize the entities. The figure shows how data types are applied to columns in a table, which represent the type of data that can be inserted into a column.

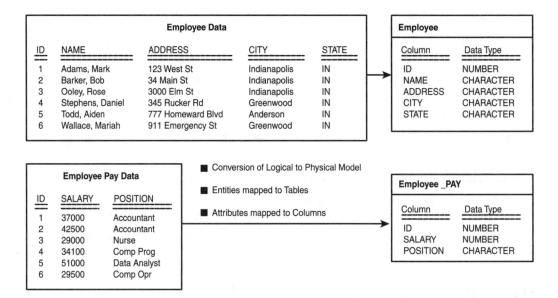

FIGURE 7.5

The entity to table conversion process.

In the physical model, table structures can be refined in the following ways:

- Tables can be added and removed.
- Columns can be added and removed.
- Further normalization or denormalization can occur.
- Data types, domains, and constraints are added to columns before final code generation.
- Views can be added.

How Will the User Access the Data?

A resultset is the data retrieved from a database query, or a subset of data from the base table(s). If data is accessed together, entities (become tables) will have to be joined together (data merged) to get the complete resultset. A resultset might consist of one row of data, or millions of rows, such as with a large query.

When designing a database, it is important to understand how the data will be accessed and used by the end user. Figure 7.6 shows how two groups of data can be merged in order to return a requested resultset. The requested resultset in this case is the name of the nurse, assuming that there is only one nurse in this simplistic example. First, the position called "Nurse" must be found under Employee Pay Data. After "Nurse" is found, the value associated with ID is found, which references the ID under Employee Data, and directs us to the name we were searching for: Rose Ooley.

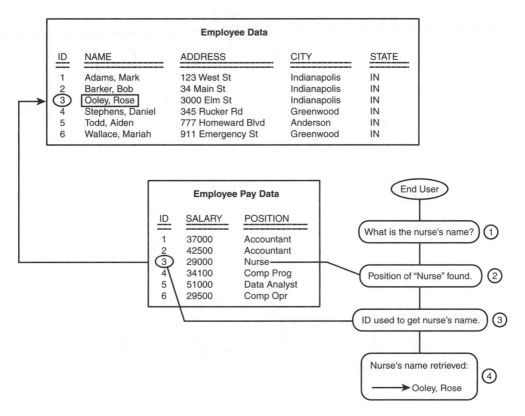

FIGURE 7.6

Merging data to resolve a query.

Having a knowledge of how data will be accessed and used will help the development team properly design the database by logically grouping related data and establishing relationships between entities.

Suppose that Employee Data becomes a table called EMPLOYEE and Employee Pay Data becomes a table called EMPLOYEE_PAY. The SQL query used to derive the answer to the question in Figure 7.6 would appear as follows:

```
SELECT NAME
FROM EMPLOYEE,
     EMPLOYEE_PAY
WHERE EMPLOYEE.ID = EMPLOYEE_PAY.ID
  AND EMPLOYEE_PAY.POSITION = 'Nurse';
```

Note

This SQL statement is used to query the database for an employee's name based on the criteria that the individual's position is "Nurse." SELECT tells what columns to return, FROM tells the database in which tables to look for the data, and WHERE is used to place conditions on the data returned, including the join condition between the two tables.

A join operation is used in this SQL statement to merge the data between two tables. Probably the most common method for joining tables is the use of a condition in the WHERE clause. If a join operation is not included in the query, all rows of data in the first table will be merged with all rows of data in the second table. The actual join operation is

```
WHERE EMPLOYEE.ID = EMPLOYEE_PAY.ID
```

Note

Although this is not a SQL book, it is hard to fathom successfully designing a relational database without a good knowledge of SQL in addition to a clear understanding of an organization's business rules, processes, and data. A knowledge of SQL should definitely be a prerequisite to actually designing a relational database. Attempting to design a relational database without an understanding of SQL is comparable to a doctor attempting a surgery without an understanding of human anatomy.

The following subsections cover the following topics, which must be discussed and understood before continuing with our discussion of design:

- Avoiding poor relationship constructs
- Understanding relationships and table joins

Avoiding Poor Relationship Constructs

As we have preached throughout the book, the key to successfully designing a database is to know the data and how it is used by an organization. Divide the data logically into entities, and then establish relationships between entities that have related data.

TIP

Following are some additional tips for avoiding poor relationship constructs:

- Avoid direct many-to-many relationships.
- Create a join entities when necessary to simplify the process of merging related data.
- Avoid the storage of redundant data.

Figure 7.7 shows the solution to the problem that surfaced with the many-to-many relationship between Instructor Data and Class Data previously in this chapter. With the join entity that is introduced in the figure, the user can more easily navigate between the two main entities to find the desired information. To find the classes that Ryan Stephens teaches, the ID under Instructor Data is matched with INST ID under Classes that Instructors Teach, and then the CLASS ID under Classes that Instructors Teach is matched with ID under Class Data. If searching for instructors who teach a particular class, just go the opposite direction, beginning with Class Data, transitioning through Classes that Instructors Teach, to Instructor Data.

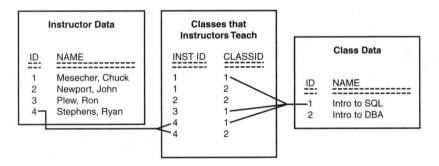

FIGURE 7.7

Resolving the many-to-many relationship.

The main benefit of including a join entity is the reduction of redundant data, which you should know by now is one of the foremost goals of designing a database. With the join entity, instructors are stored once, as are classes, even though an instructor can teach many classes and a class can be taught by many instructors. The product of this join entity is two one-to-many relationships.

The primary relationships in Figure 7.7 are as follows:

- An instructor can have many entries under Classes that Instructors Teach.
- A class can have many entries under Classes that Instructors Teach.

Instructor Data and Class Data are no longer directly related to one another. They are indirectly related, only through Classes that Instructors Teach.

> **NOTE**
>
> A join entity created to eliminate a many-to-many relationship between two entities yields two one-to-many relationships, leaving the original two entities unrelated to one another in a direct manner.

Understanding Relationships and Table Joins

When data is merged without a join operation, all rows of data from the first table are merged with all rows of data from the second table. This is called a Cartesian Product, and should be avoided 99% of the time, or thereabouts. However, there are uses for the Cartesian Product when desiring to show all possible combinations between multiple table data. For example, suppose one table contains possible first names and another table contains possible middle names. A Cartesian Product between these two tables would show every possible combination of the two names for a full name, minus the surname. This example is shown later in this chapter.

The most common types of join operations include the following, and are briefly discussed in the next subsections:

- Equi join (test for equality)
- Non-equi join (test for non-equality)
- Outer join (inclusion of missing values)
- Self join (recursive relationships)

Table 7.1 lists the most common join operations based on relationships defined for entities.

TABLE 7.1   Relationships and Typical Join Operations

RELATIONSHIP	*TYPICAL JOIN OPERATION*
one-to-one	equi join
one-to-many	equi join
	outer join
many-to-many	equi join
	non-equi join
recursive	self join

It was previously stated that this is not a SQL book, but it is also true that SQL is the standard language used to access data in a relational database. An understanding of the access methods of data plays an important role in the design of the database, although it is arguable whether to include SQL code showing examples of joins in this chapter. We feel that the SQL code is a bonus to the readers to increase their understanding of relational databases, and to show how entity relationships and SQL access methods to data affect one another. It is difficult to understand entity relationships without examples of real data.

> **NOTE**
>
> The following subsections show examples of join operations to assist in your understanding of data relationships in a database. The intent here is not to teach SQL, but to use some simple SQL queries to help you to visualize how relationships affect access to data. We would never recommend anyone attempting to design a relational database without a clear understanding of these relationships.

Applying the Concept of an Equi Join

An equi join is used to compare for equality when merging data from multiple tables. This type of join is by far the most common. The following PLAYER table lists players of sports, and the SPORT table lists sports that are played.

Consider the following query. We are selecting all columns from the PLAYER table. Note that the asterisk represents all columns in SQL. All rows are selected from the table because a WHERE clause is not supplied.

```
SELECT * FROM PLAYER;
```

The output of the query is as follows. Note that there are five unique names, each with their own ID.

```
        ID NAME
---------- ----------
         1 JOHN
         2 DANIEL
         3 TINA
         4 LINDA
         5 ANDY
```

The following query selects all columns and all rows from the SPORT table.

```
SELECT * FROM SPORT;
```

The output of the query is as follows.

```
       ID NAME
---------- ---------------
        1 BASKETBALL
        2 BASEBALL
        3 VOLLEYBALL
        4 TENNIS
```

As you can see, it is possible for a many-to-many relationship to exist between PLAYER and SPORT because a player can play many sports, and a sport can be played by many players.

To avoid a many-to-many relationship, we have created a join table called PLAYER_SPORT, which is related through a one-to-many relationship to each one of the original tables. Following is a query from PLAYER_SPORT.

```
SELECT * FROM PLAYER_SPORT;
```

The output of this query is as follows.

```
      P_ID       S_ID
---------- ----------
         1          1
         2          1
         3          3
         5          2
```

By looking at the sample data, you will see that some players listed do not play any sports, and that some sports listed are not played by anyone. The following SQL query can be used to derive a list of the sports played by each player. An equi join is used to merge data between the three tables. Notice that the original tables are both joined to PLAYER_SPORT.

The following query makes use of the join table, which will be used to link PLAYER and SPORT to show all players of each sport.

```
SELECT PLAYER.NAME, SPORT.NAME
FROM PLAYER,
     SPORT,
     PLAYER_SPORT
WHERE PLAYER.ID = PLAYER_SPORT.P_ID
  AND SPORT.ID = PLAYER_SPORT.S_ID;
```

The output of the equi join query is as follows.

```
NAME       NAME
---------- ---------------
JOHN       BASKETBALL
DANIEL     BASKETBALL
TINA       VOLLEYBALL
ANDY       BASEBALL
```

Understanding Entities and Relationships

CHAPTER 7

179

7

UNDERSTANDING
ENTITIES AND
RELATIONSHIPS

Applying the Concept of a Non-equi Join

A non-equi join is a test for non-equality, which is essentially a Cartesian Product, minus the rows that are actually common between the tables. In the following example, we have two tables: FNAME and MNAME. These tables contain possible names that can be used as a first or middle name for a baby girl.

The following SQL statement queries the FNAME table.

```
SELECT * FROM FNAME;
```

The output of this statement is as follows.

```
NAME
----------
MARIAH
DAWN
TINA
LINDA
```

The following statement queries the MNAME table, which happens to have the same data as the FNAME table.

```
SELECT * FROM MNAME;
```

The output of this query is as follows.

```
NAME
----------
MARIAH
DAWN
TINA
LINDA
```

Suppose that we want to generate a list of all possible combinations of these names in order to name a baby. First, we use a non-equi join.

```
SELECT FNAME.NAME "First",
       MNAME.NAME "Middle"
FROM FNAME,
     MNAME
ORDER BY FNAME.NAME;
```

The output of this query is as follows.

```
First       Middle
----------  ----------
DAWN        MARIAH
DAWN        DAWN
DAWN        LINDA
```

```
DAWN       TINA
LINDA      MARIAH
LINDA      DAWN
LINDA      LINDA
LINDA      TINA
MARIAH     MARIAH
MARIAH     LINDA
MARIAH     TINA
MARIAH     DAWN
TINA       MARIAH
TINA       LINDA
TINA       TINA
TINA       DAWN
```

After reviewing the data, you probably noticed names such as "DAWN DAWN" and "TINA TINA." You probably would not want to give a duplicate name such as these. A non-equi join, shown in the next example, can be used to show all possible combinations of the first and middle name, where the first and middle names are not the same. The following example uses the exclamation mark to negate the join condition in the WHERE clause.

```
SELECT FNAME.NAME "First",
       MNAME.NAME "Middle"
FROM FNAME,
     MNAME
WHERE FNAME.NAME != MNAME.NAME
ORDER BY FNAME.NAME;
```

The output of this revised query is as follows.

```
First      Middle
---------- ----------
DAWN       MARIAH
DAWN       TINA
DAWN       LINDA
LINDA      MARIAH
LINDA      TINA
LINDA      DAWN
MARIAH     DAWN
MARIAH     TINA
MARIAH     LINDA
TINA       MARIAH
TINA       DAWN
TINA       LINDA
```

Applying the Concept of an Outer Join

An outer join is a type of equi join that is used to show all data from one table, even if corresponding data is not found in a second table. Outer joins are most commonly used with tables having one-to-many relationships. In the following example, we have employee information and bonus information. As mentioned earlier, some employees might be awarded a bonus, whereas others are not. Additionally, some employees might be awarded multiple bonuses over a period of time. Thus, you can conclude that we have a one-to-many relationship between EMPLOYEE and BONUS.

The following simple query selects all columns and all rows from the EMPLOYEE table.

```
SELECT * FROM EMPLOYEE;
```

The output of this query is as follows.

```
    ID NAME          MGR_ID
---------- ---------- ----------
     1 ROSE
     2 CHRISTY            1
     3 RON                1
     4 ANDY               3
     5 RYAN               3
```

Now, we query the BONUS table in the same manner.

```
SELECT * FROM BONUS;
```

The data in the BONUS table appears as follows. You can associate a bonus amount with an employee using the ID column.

```
    ID        AMT
---------- ----------
     1       1000
     2        500
     4       1500
     2        700
```

If we wanted a list of all employees and the bonuses they have been paid, we can use the following SQL query with an equi join.

```
SELECT EMPLOYEE.NAME, BONUS.AMT
FROM EMPLOYEE,
     BONUS
WHERE EMPLOYEE.ID = BONUS.ID;
```

The output of this query follows.

```
NAME          AMT
---------- ----------
ROSE          1000
CHRISTY        500
CHRISTY        700
ANDY          1500
```

Notice in the resultset, however, that the employees Ron and Ryan are not listed because they have not been issued bonuses. What if we wanted to show all employees, whether a bonus has been awarded? The following example makes use of the Oracle (+) operator in order to denote that an outer join operation should take place. (Note that some implementations might have different operators for outer join operations.)

```
SELECT EMPLOYEE.NAME, BONUS.AMT
FROM EMPLOYEE,
     BONUS
WHERE EMPLOYEE.ID = BONUS.ID(+);
```

The output of this outer join query is as follows. Notice that all employees are shown, whether a bonus has been awarded.

```
NAME               AMT
---------- ----------
ROSE              1000
CHRISTY            500
CHRISTY            700
RON
ANDY              1500
RYAN
```

Applying the Concept of a Self Join

A self join is the only way to compare data to other data in a table. Self joins are used exclusively for tables that have a recursive relationship to themselves, meaning that a column in a table is related to another column in the same table. The following EMPLOYEE table has an ID column and a MGR_ID column. The MGR_ID column references the ID column because a manager must also be an employee.

Again, we have the same simple query that selects all columns and rows from the EMPLOYEE table.

```
SELECT * FROM EMPLOYEE;
```

The output of this query is as follows.

```
        ID NAME             MGR_ID
---------- ---------- ----------
         1 ROSE
         2 CHRISTY             1
         3 RON                 1
         4 ANDY                3
         5 RYAN                3
```

By reviewing the data, you can easily determine, for example, the manager of Andy, by finding Andy's record, locating the value associated with MGR_ID for Andy, and then matching that value with the corresponding valued under ID to find the manager's name. In SQL, you select the table twice, assign the table a different alias for each time selected, and then join the appropriate columns. Essentially, a self join is the same as an equi join of two different tables.

The query resembles the following:

```
SELECT E1.NAME "Employee", E2.NAME "Manager"
FROM EMPLOYEE E1,
     EMPLOYEE E2
WHERE E1.MGR_ID = E2.ID;
```

The output of this self join query shows a nice list of all employees who have managers, and their managers' names.

```
Employee    Manager
----------  ----------
CHRISTY     ROSE
RON         ROSE
ANDY        RON
RYAN        RON
```

Summary

Entities are those objects we define that represent organizational data. After entities are defined, they are drawn out in an Entity Relationship Diagram (ERD), or used to logically model the business requirements. Before drawing an ERD, it is imperative to understand the relationships that might exist between entities. Cardinality refers to the number of occurrences of data that can be associated with a given occurrence of data. For example, data in one entity can have several occurrences of related data in another entity. Optionality refers to mandatory and optional relationships. If a relationship is mandatory, corresponding data must exist in the related entity. If a relationship is optional, corresponding data is not required in the related entity. The types of relationships that exist in a relational database include one-to-one, one-to-many, many-to-many, and recursive.

After entities are defined and all parties involved in the design effort are satisfied with the logical model, a transformation occurs. Although a detailed discussion of the transformation of entities into tables is well ahead of the game at this point, it is important for you to understand how an entity will be used after logical modeling because the relationships defined for entities carry over as entities become tables. When tables are created and populated with data, users must access the data. It is important to understand how the data will be used when designing the database, and optimizing entity relationships. In order to understand entity relationships, it is helpful to visualize the data that these entities represent.

The subsequent chapters in this section of the book focus on the act of performing logical modeling. ERDs and process models will be generated to represent the data that was defined during interviews. The entities and relationships discussed in this chapter will be used to understand an ERD, and eventually, table design.

Normalization: Eliminating Redundant Data

IN THIS CHAPTER

In review, normalization is the process of reducing the redundancy of data in a relational database. Redundant data refers to the data that is stored in more than one location in the database. Data should not be redundant, which means that the duplication of data should be kept to a minimum for several reasons. For example, it is unnecessary to store an employee's home address in more than one table. With duplicate data, unnecessary space is used. Confusion is always a threat when, for instance, an address for an employee in one table does not match the address of the same employee in another table. Which table is correct? Do you have documentation to verify the employee's current address? As if data management is not difficult enough, redundancy of data could prove to be a disaster. On the other hand, there are also benefits to databases that have not been normalized, mainly related to increased database performance.

This chapter focuses on the process that a developer might take to normalize a database during design. Many issues must be confronted during database design that might have an impact on normalization. In this chapter, the following topics are discussed in detail:

- Overview of normalization, including the advantages and disadvantages of normalization
- Discussion of the NORMAL FORMS, or levels of normalization
- Definition and discussion of denormalization, and the associated benefits

Overview of Normalization

Normalization is the application of a set of simple rules called FIRST, SECOND, and THIRD NORMAL FORM to assign attributes to entities in the ERD. Although there are additional levels of normalization beyond THIRD NORMAL FORM such as Boyce-Codd, FOURTH, and FIFTH levels of NORMAL FORM (which we will discuss), normalization of a production relational database generally stops at the THIRD NORMAL FORM.

> **NOTE**
>
> Naming conventions are one of the foremost considerations when you are designing a database. The use of naming conventions eases the task of normalization greatly. You want to give your tables names that describe the type of information they contain. A company-wide naming convention should be set, providing guidance in the naming of not only tables within the database, but also users, filenames, and other related objects. Designing and enforcing naming conventions is one of a company's first steps toward a successful database implementation.

The normalization process is fundamental to the modeling and design of a relational database. Its purpose is to eliminate data redundancy, avoid data update anomalies that can occur in unnormalized databases (databases that have not been normalized), and to simplify enforcement of integrity constraints. Later, the advantages and disadvantages of normalization of a database will be discussed. We will also compare data integrity versus performance issues that pertain to normalization.

A database that is not normalized can include data that is contained in one or more different tables for no apparent reason. This is not optimal design with regard to security reasons, disk space usage, query retrieval speed, efficiency of database updates, and most importantly, data integrity. A database before normalization is one that has not been broken down logically into smaller, more manageable tables.

For example, study the data in Tables 8.1 and 8.2.

TABLE 8.1   PEOPLE

NAME	ADDRESS	CITY	STATE	ZIP
STEVE SMITH	123 BROADWAY	INDIANAPOLIS	IN	46227
MARK JONES	456 MAIN ST	INDIANAPOLIS	IN	46238

TABLE 8.2   OCCUPATIONS

NAME	OCCUPATION
STEVE SMITH	COMPUTER PROGRAMMER
MARK JONES	DATABASE ADMINISTRATOR

In Tables 8.1 and 8.2, the full name of an individual is stored in more than one table. The primary concept behind a relational database is the ease of maintaining relationships. The full name only needs to be stored in one location. In this case, the full name is redundant in the second table, which means that if STEVE SMITH has a name change, his name must be changed in both tables, or the data will be inconsistent.

Also, study the data in Table 8.3.

TABLE 8.3   EMPLOYEES

NAME	DEPARTMENT
STEVE SMITH	MARKETING
MARK JONES	MARKETING
BILL WILLIAMS	DATA ENTRY
JENNY KRAFT	CUSTOMER SERVICE
AIDEN TODD	ACCOUNTING

In this example, the redundant data happens to be stored in the same table. Each employee is assigned a department. There are a limited number of departments, much less than the total number of employees. Why should the department be spelled out for each employee? Every time a new employee is entered into the database, the department is also entered. What happens if the department is not always spelled the same, abbreviated, or misspelled?

Suppose that two records were entered into the database as follows:

NAME	DEPARTMENT
MARIAH WALLACE	CUSTOMER SERVICE
DANIEL STEPHENS	CUST SVC

When required data to be entered is left up to the end user, there is a substantial possibility of inconsistency. The customer service department was spelled out for the first record, but abbreviated for another record. What if the end user wants to list all employees who work in customer service? If searching for customer service, does the end user specify CUSTOMER SERVICE, CUST SVC, CUSTOMER SVC, or CUST SERVICE (we think you get the point)? If a table is designed similar to this one and the end user does not correctly supply all valid department names as search criteria, the data returned will be incomplete. One solution is to code edits in the user application; but if data changes, the application needs to be re-coded. The only true solution is to normalize the database.

Consider the following similar example. In one table in an unnormalized database, an individual's name could read STEVE SMITH, whereas the name of the same individual reads STEPHEN R. SMITH in another table. If you search for data by last name, all the SMITHs will be returned, but the two entries might appear to belong to two different individuals. Even though it might be clear that both entries belong to the same individual (perhaps through an identifier such as PERSON_ID), it is still unclear as to which name is spelled correctly.

When considering normalization, some user-related design considerations include

- What data should be stored in the database?
- How will the user access the database?
- What privileges does the user require?
- How should the data be grouped in the database?
- What data is the most commonly accessed?
- How is all data related in the database?
- What measures should be taken to ensure accurate data?

Advantages of Normalization

Normalization provides numerous benefits to the design of a database, the design of an application, and the implementation of the production database. Some of the major benefits include

- Greater overall database organization will be gained.
- The amount of unnecessary redundant data is reduced.
- Data integrity is easily maintained within the database.
- The database and application design processes are much more flexible.
- Security is easier to manage.

Organization is brought about by the normalization process, making everyone's job easier—from the end user who accesses tables to the database administrator (DBA) who is responsible for the overall management of every object in the database. Data redundancy is reduced, which simplifies data structures and conserves disk space. Because duplicate data is minimized or completely eliminated, the possibility of inconsistent data is greatly reduced.

If a database has been normalized and broken into smaller tables, you are provided with more flexibility as far as modifying existing structures. It is much easier to modify a small table with a small amount of data than to modify one large table that holds all the data. With smaller tables, it is much easier to logically separate and find columns, especially when coding the end user application, or querying the database. Additionally, security is also improved in the sense that the DBA can grant access to limited tables to certain users. Security is easier to control when normalization has been accomplished.

8

NORMALIZATION:
ELIMINATING
REDUNDANT DATA

> **NOTE**
>
> The advantage of normalization will be a cleanly designed relational database model with all the entities identified, as well as flexibility and easy change both for the database itself and for applications that run against it. The primary product of each level of normalization is the creation of entities that meet certain criteria on how data is to be stored. A database that has not been normalized tends to experience problems because of data redundancy or incorrect dependencies between data through parent and child relationships.

The process of converting one entity into multiple entities in order to normalize the original is called decomposition. An unnormalized single entity will be decomposed into two or more normalized entities via the application of normalization rules. For example, a model in THIRD NORMAL FORM (the third level of normalization) will have no repeating or redundant data attributes and will have entities with attributes fully dependent on that entity's entire primary key and not on each other. More examples of each level of normalization are discussed later in this chapter.

Disadvantages of Normalization

The disadvantage of normalization is that it produces a lot of tables with a relatively small number of columns. These columns then have to be joined using their primary/foreign key relationships in order to put the information (we've so carefully normalized) back together so we can use it. For example, a query might require retrieval of data from multiple normalized tables. This can result in complicated table joins. The required tables for the query were probably one before decomposition (normalization).

> **NOTE**
>
> Although most successful databases are normalized to some degree, there is one substantial drawback of a normalized database: reduced database performance. The acceptance of reduced performance requires the knowledge that when a query or transaction request is sent to the database, there are factors involved such as CPU usage, memory usage, and input/output (I/O). A normalized database requires more CPU, memory, and I/O to process transactions and database queries than unnormalized and denormalized databases require. A normalized database must locate the requested tables and then join the data from the tables to either get the requested information or to process the desired data.
>
> At the fine tuning level, a DBA will often look at a particularly taxing query and try to find ways to reduce the number of I/Os. In a flat file call, the required information is usually one I/O. In a fully normalized database, multiple I/Os can occur. Some users tend to think of today's powerful processing and storage systems in terms of bandwidth. In databases, I/Os per second is also a very huge performance consideration.

Decomposition of tables has two primary impacts. The first is performance. All the joins required to merge data slow processing down and place additional stress on your hardware. The second impact challenges developers to code queries, that return desired information, without experiencing the impact of the relational database's insistence on returning a row for every possible combination of matching values if the tables are not properly joined by the developer. Additional rows that are returned because of tables that are not properly joined (using their key values) are extraneous nonsense. This collection of extraneous data is called a Cartesian Product. In the middle of a processing day, a poorly written ad hoc query can bring even the mightiest system to its knees. The cost of extra code to join tables, however, is a small price to pay to maintain the integrity of the data.

Overview of the NORMAL FORMS

NORMAL FORM is a way of measuring the levels, or depth, to which a database has been normalized. A database's level of normalization is determined by the NORMAL FORM. The NORMAL FORMS discussed in this chapter are as follows:

- The FIRST NORMAL FORM
- The SECOND NORMAL FORM
- The THIRD NORMAL FORM
- The Boyce-Codd NORMAL FORM
- The FOURTH NORMAL FORM
- The FIFTH NORMAL FORM

The three most common NORMAL FORMs implemented in production databases are the FIRST, SECOND, and THIRD NORMAL FORMS. Of normal forms, each subsequent normal form depends on normalization steps taken in the previous normal form. For instance, in order to normalize a database using the SECOND NORMAL FORM, the database must initially be in the FIRST NORMAL FORM.

The process of normalization has an initial requirement that each instance in an entity has an attribute or combination of attributes that uniquely identifies it from any and all other instances of that entity. In short, every instance in the entity must have a unique identifier (UID) or primary key before you implement FIRST NORMAL FORM. Each NORMAL FORM builds on the previous. FIRST NORMAL FORM must be complete before you can begin SECOND NORMAL FORM, and second must be complete before you can begin third. Boyce-Codd builds on THIRD NORMAL FORM. FOURTH NORMAL FORM builds on Boyce-Codd. FIFTH NORMAL FORM builds on FOURTH NORMAL FORM and so on.

As mentioned previously, we generally stop at THIRD NORMAL FORM for production systems. Forms above THIRD NORMAL FORM, as you'll see in our discussion in the next subsection, tend to be conceptually difficult and applicable to only a limited number of situations. The return on applying them generally doesn't justify the cost or the effort involved in their application. THIRD NORMAL FORM is the standard. The concepts of forms above THIRD NORMAL FORM might be applied in specific instances, however, to overcome specific problems.

As mentioned, prior to application of FIRST NORMAL FORM, there must be an attribute or combination of attributes that is a unique identifier (UID), or primary key that uniquely identifies each instance of the entity. No two instances of an entity can have the same UID. All attributes within an entity must depend on the UID. This is a prerequisite to starting the normalization process.

NOTE

The phrase "the key, the whole key, and nothing but the key" is an adaptation stolen from our court system. But it is a good reminder of what is involved in FIRST, SECOND, and THIRD NORMAL FORM.

FIRST NORMAL FORM: The Key

The objective of the FIRST NORMAL FORM is to divide the base data into logical units called entities, or tables. When each entity has been designed, a primary key is assigned to it.

The entity has a UID (key) and all attributes must be single valued. A repeating or multivalued attribute is an attribute or group of attributes that will have multiple values for one occurrence of the UID. You would have to repeat the attribute(s) multiple times in the entity structure in order to capture all the possible occurrences of the event being modeled. The solution is to move repeating attribute(s) to their own entity and create a relationship between the two decomposed entities. Working with tables in design, you'd move the repeating columns to their own table along with a copy of the original entity's UID as a foreign key. As you look at an entity, ensure that each entity attribute is single-valued with no repeated attributes allowed. Note the following example:

The entity INSTRUCTOR_SCHEDULE is meant to track instructors and the courses they teach by semester. The instructor_id is the UID for this entity. Note that the pound sign is typically used to identify the primary key for an entity.

INSTRUCTOR_SCHEDULE

#instructor_id

fname

mi

lname

year

semester

department1

course1

section_id1

department2

course2

section_id2

INSTRUCTOR_SCHEDULE

department3

course3

section_id3

Because the instructor teaches multiple classes each semester, the class attribute and its attendant department and section attributes would need to have more than one value (be multivalued) in the entity structure. Another way of saying this is that the class attribute would repeat as Class1, Class2, Class3, and so on. The issue is the requirement for multivalued attributes—not whether you've taken the extra step of creating them. In either case, the repeating attributes need to be moved to their own entity.

In the previous example, department(1-3), course(1-3) and section_id(1-3) are multivalued attributes or repeating columns. This is a violation of the FIRST NORMAL FORM normalization rule. The solution is to place department, course, and section in their own entity, COURSES_TAUGHT, with a relation to the decomposed INSTRUCTOR entity.

INSTRUCTOR	*COURSES_TAUGHT*
#instructor_id	#course
fname	#department
mi	#section
lname	#semester
	#year
	instructor_id

SECOND NORMAL FORM: The Whole Key

The objective of the SECOND NORMAL FORM is to take data that is only partly dependent on the primary key and enter it into another table.

The entity is in FIRST NORMAL FORM and if an entity has a composite UID (that is, it takes more than one attribute to make an instance of the entity unique), all the non-UID attributes must be dependent on all the UID attributes—not just one or some of them.

Let's look at our prior example. The COURSES_TAUGHT entity has a composite UID consisting of course, department, section, semester, and year required to uniquely identify an instance.

INSTRUCTOR	*COURSES_TAUGHT*
instructor_id	#course
fname	#department

INSTRUCTOR	COURSES_TAUGHT
mi	#section
lname	#semester
	#year
	instructor_id

Say that someone wants to add an attribute called department_address to the COURSES_TAUGHT entity. Because such an attribute would be dependent only on the attribute department and not the whole composite UID, it would be a violation of SECOND NORMAL FORM and that attribute would not be allowed for this entity. As in FIRST NORMAL FORM, the solution for violation of SECOND NORMAL FORM (attributes in an entity that are not dependent on an entire composite UID) is to move the offending attribute(s) to another entity and establish a relationship between the two entities.

INSTRUCTOR	COURSES_TAUGHT	DEPARTMENT
#instructor_id	#course	#department _id
fname	#department_id	department_name
mi	#section	department_address
lname	#semester	
	#year	
	instructor_id	

THIRD NORMAL FORM: And Nothing but the Key

The THIRD NORMAL FORM's objective is to remove data in a table that is not dependent on the primary key. The entity is in SECOND NORMAL FORM and a non-UID attribute can't depend on another non-UID attribute. All non-UID attributes should depend directly on the whole UID and not on each other. Put another way, attributes don't have attributes of their own. If attributes do have attributes, they're really entities.

For example, the EMPLOYEE entity has an attribute called category. Category initially has potential values of technical, management, administrative, or professional.

EMPLOYEE
#employee_id
last_name
first_name
mi
ssn
category

Later, however, we decide to add an attribute called category_level, which further qualifies category into a more detailed subgroup based on expertise level with potential values of 1 for a beginner, 2 for a middle level, and 3 for an expert.

EMPLOYEE
#employee_id
last_name
first_name
mi
ssn
category
category_level

Category_level is dependent first on category. Category_level is only dependent on the employee_id entity UID through category. An attribute dependency on the UID—which is not direct but only passes through another attribute that is dependent on the UID—is called a transitive dependency. Transitive dependencies are unacceptable in THIRD NORMAL FORM. Category and category_level need to be moved from the EMPLOYEE entity to their own EMPLOYEE_CATEGORY entity as a violator of THIRD NORMAL FORM.

EMPLOYEE	*EMPLOYEE_CATEGORY*
# employee_id	# category
last_name	# category_level
first_name	# employee_id
mi	
ssn	

> **NOTE**
>
> As previously mentioned, Boyce-Codd, FOURTH NORMAL FORM, FIFTH NORMAL FORM, and higher levels of normalization are usually not applied to production relational databases. We will briefly describe them here, for information purposes.

Boyce-Codd NORMAL FORM

Boyce-Codd NORMAL FORM is in effect when an entity is in THIRD NORMAL FORM, and every attribute or combination of attributes (a determinant) upon which any attribute is functionally dependent is a candidate key (that is, unique). An attribute or combination of attributes upon which any attribute is functionally dependent is also called a determinant.

Functional dependency can be described as follows. If column2 is functionally dependent on column1, it means that each value in column1 is associated with one and only one value in column2 at a particular point in time. A particular value for column1 will always have the same value in column2. The reverse is not true, however. A particular value for column2 can have multiple corresponding values in column1.

If there is only one determinant upon which other attributes depend and it is a candidate key (such as the primary key), THIRD NORMAL FORM and Boyce-Codd NORMAL FORM are identical. The difference between THIRD NORMAL FORM and Boyce-Codd NORMAL FORM is that Boyce-Codd requires all attributes that have other attributes with functional dependencies on them (are determinants) to be candidate keys and THIRD NORMAL FORM does not. Boyce-Codd, with this subtle difference, is in effect a stronger version of THIRD NORMAL FORM.

FOURTH NORMAL FORM

FOURTH NORMAL FORM is in effect when an entity is in Boyce-Codd NORMAL FORM, it has no multivalued dependencies, and neither of the following conditions exist:

1. The dependent attribute(s) is not a subset of the attribute(s) upon which it depends (the determinant).

2. The determinant in union (combination) with the dependent attribute(s) includes the entire entity.

A multivalued dependency is a situation in which two or more attributes are dependent on a determinant and each dependent attribute has a specific set of values. The values in these dependent attributes are independent of each other.

In Table 8.4, we create a SALES_REGION entity that includes attributes for sales persons and customers. This is an example of a multivalued dependency.

TABLE 8.4   SALES_REGION

SALES_REGION_ID	SALES_PERSON	CUSTOMER
1	Mary	Joe
1	Mary	Julie
1	Tom	Joe
1	Tom	Julie

CUSTOMER is functionally dependent on SALES_REGION_ID, and SALES_PERSON is dependent on SALES_REGION_ID. Neither SALES_PERSON in union with SALES_REGION_ID nor CUSTOMER in union with SALES_REGION_ID are the whole entity and neither CUSTOMER nor SALES_PERSON are subsets of SALES_REGION_ID. This entity is violating FOURTH NORMAL FORM. The problem is we would have to create a row for every possible combination of sales person and customer to ensure consistency for the resulting table. Although this might be what the developer intended, it would produce redundancy with other table's data and could be accomplished as well with relations.

FIFTH NORMAL FORM

FIFTH NORMAL FORM (also called project-join normal form) is in effect when FOURTH NORMAL FORM is in effect and the entity has no join dependencies that are not related to that entity's candidate keys.

When we decompose (break up) entities as we apply normalization rules, we should be able to reconstruct the original entity by doing joins between the two resulting entities without losing any data and without generating extra and generally incorrect rows. This is called a lossless-join.

An entity is in FIFTH NORMAL FORM when it cannot be decomposed into several smaller entities, which have different keys from the original without data losses. If data was lost after decomposition, a lossless-join would not be possible. If all the decomposed entities use one of the original entity's candidate keys as keys, joins of those entities would result in a lossless-join. With respect to the original entity, it would still be considered to be in FIFTH NORMAL FORM without decomposition.

8

NORMALIZATION:
ELIMINATING
REDUNDANT DATA

> **NOTE**
>
> Again, NORMAL FORMs above THIRD are largely in the realm of the theoretician. As a practical matter, THIRD NORMAL FORM is the limit for normalization of production databases.

Denormalization

Denormalization is the process of taking a normalized database and modifying table structures to allow controlled redundancy for increased database performance. There are costs to denormalization, however. Data redundancy is increased in a denormalized database, which might improve performance but requires more extraneous efforts in order to keep track of related data. When denormalization is employed, it's usually a derivative of normalized data, so that even if an atomic unit of data exists in several places, it is derived form one source. When a database has been denormalized, you must consider how the redundant data will be managed.

Application coding renders more complications because the data has been spread across various tables and might be more difficult to locate. In addition, referential integrity is more of a chore; related data has been divided among a number of tables. A happy medium exists in both normalization and denormalization, but both require a thorough knowledge of the actual data and the specific business requirements of the pertinent company.

Denormalizing a database: Why would you ever want to do that? Attempting to improve performance is the only reason to ever denormalize a database. A denormalized database is not the same as a database that has not been normalized. Denormalizing a database is the process of taking the level of normalization within the database down a notch or two. Remember, normalization might actually slow performance with its frequently occurring table join operations. Denormalization might involve recombining separate tables, or creating duplicate data within tables. This will reduce the number of tables that need to be joined in order to retrieve the requested data, which results in less I/O and CPU time.

> **NOTE**
>
> After initial database design has occurred, some reversal of normalization (denormalization) might take place in the data model in order to improve performance of the physical system as it supports running applications. Generally, denormalization is undertaken because of performance problems relating to insufficient processing speed or power for high volume or high complexity application functions. It's necessary to get an application to meet functional speed requirements or to cut the load on a laboring CPU. Also, OLAP systems such as data warehouses will often find their base data in one or more production OLTP systems, then create new tables for the warehouse from aggregations of the base tables as well as denormalization of base table structures.

Acceptable database performance is at the mercy of the end user's perception. Perception quickly becomes the end-user's reality. The database must perform well enough to effectively enhance the end-user's job and allow the end user to be as productive as possible. Performance is normally measured according to the database activity that is occurring, such as

- Large queries
- Batch transactions
- Small transactions
- Small queries

> **NOTE**
>
> Management of expectations (of the users, the developers, database administration, and management) is one of the greatest challenges of any design/implementation strategy. Expectations might be based on perception of database, software, and development team capabilities, which might be inaccurate. It may be necessary to help all parties maintain a realistic focus for the design project.

The end user normally deals with small transactions and small queries. For example, when a customer calls to a bank, the end user (bank teller or loan officer) might query the database to retrieve the customer's information. The end user might first verify the customer's account balance. This is an example of a small query because only one record is being retrieved in comparison to possible millions. A small transaction might consist of a change to the customer's information, such as the home address, or a transfer from a line of credit. In this case, the end user expects response time to be timely, usually within a couple of seconds. Response time is how long it takes for information to be returned from a query, or verification that a transaction has taken place successfully. Large queries and batch transactions deal with throughput, the speed at which mass volumes of data can be accessed. Keep in mind that some databases (transactional) rely on acceptable response time, whereas other databases (such as data warehouses) rely on acceptable throughput.

Denormalization has a price and should be undertaken only to the degree required to obtain necessary performance. Denormalization generally involves one of these three tasks:

- Replicating some data columns to several tables in order to have them more easily accessible without multi-table joins. This can include data columns themselves or foreign key columns. With replication of data columns, the data is often available to the application without joins. Additional foreign key columns can potentially allow direct connections between tables rather than multiple joins including tables that are only providing a connection, but carry a large time cost in the join.

- Pre-calculation and storage of derived data such as summary calculations or concatenations can speed processing. Create special purpose tables that contain precalculated information required by a commonly run report or create tables that contain data often needed for queries.

- Undoing some decomposition of entities to avoid the price of multiple joins. This would primarily be undertaken for tables that have one-to-one relationships.

Although denormalization will often provide necessary performance help, it comes with a price. The data model becomes much less flexible and more complex. Maintenance becomes more difficult. Changes to the database and its applications are more difficult when the complexity arising from data replication must be considered. Although database reads (selects) might be considerably faster after denormalization, there is often a negative performance impact on writes (inserts and updates) arising from the need to update replicated data in several places. Combining tables puts back the data redundancy and may create problems they were normalized to overcome. With all this negativity in mind, understand that denormalization is often necessary as a last measure to improve database performance. If denormalization is implemented carefully and tested thoroughly, most negative impacts can be minimized.

Nonetheless, in the final analysis, a database design and applications that depend on it must perform fast enough to meet user requirements. If the application is not running fast enough, tuning the database and application hasn't helped and increasing hardware resources or network bandwidth hasn't helped or isn't an option, denormalization might be a necessary tool. It is not, however, the first place to look for a solution to performance problems.

Sample Normalization Exercise #1

This section illustrates a normalization exercise. We have begun with a portion of a raw database, and have achieved the THIRD NORMAL FORM. This section steps through the most common NORMAL FORMS (1-3) according to the given scenario, and shows how redundant data can be reduced or completely eliminated in some cases.

Suppose that a database is being designed for an online bookstore called BOOK-ZOO.COM. BOOK-ZOO.COM must track information about books, authors, customers, and orders. Following is a subset of required information (not yet normalized) that must be modeled into a database:

> AUTHOR
> NAME
> PUBLISHER
> BOOK1
> EDITION1
> DESCRIPTION1
> COST1
> BOOK2
> EDITION2
> COST2
> DESCRIPTION2

In order to achieve the FIRST NORMAL FORM, data has to be broken into logical units, each having a primary key, and ensuring that there are no repeated groups in any of the tables.

Instead of one large entity that might have repeating attributes for multiple books the author has written, we now have two concise tables, as follows:

AUTHOR	BOOK
#AUTH_ID	#ISBN
NAME	#EDITION
PUBLISHER	NAME
ADDRESS	COST
	DESCRIPTION

Before the AUTHOR entity was normalized, an attribute existed for every possibility of a new book. If normalization did not occur, attributes might have to be added to the entity if the author writes a new book. Without normalization, the structure of the entity depends on the data that will be contained. Just remember that attributes represent specific categories of data, not data itself. After the original AUTHOR entity is normalized, a record is simply added to the BOOK entity if an author writes a new book. The database is now in the FIRST NORMAL FORM.

Now, take a look at BOOK:

BOOK
#ISBN
#EDITION
NAME
COST
DESCRIPTION

The primary key is comprised of the combination between ISBN and EDITION. The ISBN identifies each book and the EDITION identifies the edition of the book. For example, many books have second and third editions. The name of the book remains constant regardless of the edition, but the cost and description might change with each subsequent edition. Therefore, we have attributes that are dependent on only part of a multivalue primary key. The SECOND NORMAL FORM is achieved by separating attributes that are only dependent on part of a primary key, as follows:

BOOK	EDITION
#ISBN	#EDITION
NAME	COST
	DESCRIPTION

Now, we find that a problem still exists with redundant data. Many authors might have the same publisher, therefore, the PUBLISHER might appear many times in the AUTHOR entity.

Why not create a separate entity called PUBLISHER, and create a relation between AUTHOR and PUBLISHER based on the UID of PUBLISHER, PUB_ID? By doing this, we have normalized the database to the THIRD NORMAL FORM.

AUTHOR	PUBLISHER
#AUTH_ID	#PUB_ID
NAME	NAME
PUB_ID	ADDRESS

Personal author information depends on the primary key, or AUTH_ID, so that information remains in the AUTHOR entity. On the other hand, the information that is only partly dependent on the AUTH_ID (each individual author) is used to populate PUBLISHER. Notice that both entities contain the column PUB_ID. This is the primary key in PUBLISHER and should be a foreign key in AUTHOR that references the PUB_ID in PUBLISHER. PUB_ID is used to match corresponding data between the two entities.

This was merely a simple example to increase your understanding of normalization. Normalization is difficult for most people to understand, but it is a critical part of database design. It is most important to understand the first three NORMAL FORMs.

Sample Normalization Exercise #2

This section illustrates a normalization exercise. We have begun with a portion of a raw database, and have achieved the THIRD NORMAL FORM. This section steps through the most common NORMAL FORMS (1-3) according to the given scenario, and shows how redundant data can be reduced or completely eliminated in some cases.

Suppose that a database is being designed to manage projects staffed by a consulting company. The consulting company works on many projects. A project is associated with a client's need. For example, a client might require a Java developer to design a Web page. Another client might need three SQL programmers. Yet another client might need system administration support, database administration support, and several programmers. Therefore, we can assume that a project may consist of one or more positions.

Without normalization, the raw data appears as follows:

PROJECT
#PROJ_ID
NAME
DESCRIP
STATUS
POS_ID1

PROJECT

POS_DESCRIP1

POS_RATE1

POS_START_DT1

POS_END_DT1

POS_STATUS

POS_ID2

POS_DESCRIP2

POS_RATE2

POS_START_DT2

POS_END_DT2

POS_STATUS2

Recalling that the FIRST NORMAL FORM should eliminate multi-valued attributes, we can separate position information associated with each project based on the knowledge that each project could consist of many positions.

The FIRST NORMAL FORM appears as follows:

PROJECT	*PROJECT_POSITION*
#PROJ_ID	#PROJ_POS_ID
NAME	PROJ_ID
DESCRIP	DESCRIP
STATUS	RATE
	START_DT
	END_DT
	STATUS

Projects and positions are only related through PROJ_ID.

Notice that each project and project position have a status. Let's say that the value of status will be OPEN if a project or position is available but not filled, CLOSED if a project or position is no longer available, or FILLED if a project or position is available but has been filled by a consultant. There is no need to store the full name of the status for every occurrence of a project or position.

Recalling that the objective of the SECOND NORMAL FORM is to take data that is only partly dependent on the primary key and enter it into another entity, consider the following breakdown of our two entities.

PROJECT	PROJECT_POSITION
#PROJ_ID	#PROJ_POS_ID
NAME	PROJ_ID
DESCRIP	DESCRIP
STATUS_ID	RATE
	START_DT
	END_DT
	STATUS_ID

STATUS_CODE
#STATUS_ID
STATUS

The status is only partly dependent on a project or a position. Although the status name is not stored with each project or position, it can easily be derived by comparing the STATUS_ID between PROJECT and STATUS_CODE, for instance.

Recall the objective of the THIRD NORMAL FORM: to remove data in a table that is not dependent on the primary key. All non-UID attributes should depend directly on the whole UID and not on each other. For example, the STATUS_ID attribute does not depend wholly on the UID for either of the other two entities. The STATUS_ID attribute can actually be removed from both PROJECT and PROJECT_POSITION, and moved to its own entity.

To achieve the THIRD NORMAL FORM, our entities are decomposed as follows:

PROJECT	PROJECT_POSITION
#PROJ_ID	#PROJ_POS_ID
NAME	PROJ_ID
DESCRIP	DESCRIP
	RATE
	START_DT
	END_DT

STATUS_CODE	PROJ_POS_STATUS
#STATUS_ID	#PROJ_ID
STATUS	#PROJ_POS_ID
	STATUS_ID

The value of the fourth entity, PROJ_POS_STATUS, is this: STATUS_ID need only be stored per position, which is associated with a project. If the status of a position is OPEN, then the status of the project as a whole is OPEN. The primary key for PROJ_POS_STATUS is the combination of PROJ_ID and PROJ_POS_ID, ensuring that only one status is recorded for each individual position.

The data found in tables with this THIRD NORMAL FORM design might look similar to Tables 8.5 through 8.8.

TABLE 8.5   PROJECT

PROJ_ID	NAME	DESCRIP
1	Aiden, Inc.	DBA support
2	Tom's Tools	Web development
3	Aiden, Inc.	Database design

TABLE 8.6   PROJECT_POSITION

PROJ_POS_ID	PROJ_ID	DESCRIP	RATE	START_DT	END_DT
1	1	DBA	65.00	06/25/00	01/18/01
2	2	Java Prog	55.00	03/31/00	07/12/00
3	3	Project Mgr	70.00	09/26/00	01/26/01
4	3	Developer	50.00	09/26/00	01/26/01

TABLE 8.7   STATUS_CODE

STATUS_ID	STATUS
1	OPEN
2	CLOSED
3	FILLED

TABLE 8.8   PROJ_POS_STATUS

PROJ_ID	PROJ_POS_ID	STATUS_ID
1	1	1
2	2	2
3	3	3
3	4	3

Redundant data has been eliminated from this design, as it is easier to see with data. The following status can be concluded by studying the sample data for these normalized tables. All the following information is obtained by using PROJ_POS_STATUS.

The DBA position for Aiden, Inc. is open.

The Java Programmer position for the Tom's Tools Web development project is closed. Maybe the contract was not renewed after the end date, or maybe the consulting company was not able to fill the position.

Both the project manager and developer positions for Aiden, Inc. for the database design project have been filled.

Normalization Self-test

Carefully study the following table structures, then determine the NORMAL FORM, if any, applied to the tables. In the following table structures, the possibilities are unnormalized, FIRST NORMAL FORM, SECOND NORMAL FORM, and THIRD NORMAL FORM.

Scenario #1

PRODUCT	ORDER
#PROD_ID	#ORD_NO
PRODUCT	#PROD_ID
DESCRIP	ORD_DT
COST	QTY
	AMOUNT

Scenario #2

CLASS_PREREQUISITE	INSTRUCTOR_SKILL
#CLASS_ID	#INST_ID
NAME	NAME
DESCRIP	SKILL1
PREREQ1	SKILL2
PREREQ2	SKILL3
PREREQ3	

Scenario #3

ORDER	ITEM
#ORD_NO	#ITEM_NO
ORD_DT	ORD_NO

ORDER	ITEM
AMOUNT	PROD_ID
PAY_TYPE	QTY

Scenario #4

PERSON	ADDRESS	STATE
#PERS_ID	#ADDR_ID	#ST_CD
NAME	ST_ADDR	STATE
SEX	CITY	
DOB	ST_CD	
ADDR_ID	ZIP	
	PHONE	

Scenario #5

ORDER	PAYMENT_TYPE
#ORD_NO	#PAY_TYPE_ID
ORD_DT	PAY_TYPE
AMOUNT	
PAY_TYPE_ID	

Scenario #1 Explanation:

The PRODUCT and ORDER tables are in the FIRST NORMAL FORM in this example. No repeating groups are found. However, ORDER has a composite key of ORD_NO and PROD_ID, because each order can have multiple products. The ORD_DT column is dependent on ORD_NO, and the QTY column is dependent on PROD_ID.

Scenario #2 Explanation:

These tables are unnormalized because repeating groups are found in each table. To achieve the FIRST NORMAL FORM, prerequisites should be separated from individual class information, and instructor skills should be separated from instructor names.

Scenario #3 Explanation:

The ORD and ITEM tables in this example are in SECOND NORMAL FORM. This is a decomposition of Scenario #1. Because an order might consist of multiple products, the individual product information can be separated from the main order information into its own ITEM table. There are no repeating groups and there are no multiple key dependencies.

Scenario #4 Explanation:

The PERSON and ADDRESS tables are in THIRD NORMAL FORM, because no repeating groups of data are found, no multiple key dependencies are found, and redundant data has been minimized by storing the STATE_DESCRIP in its own table. The redundancy of CITY can be debated even though it has fewer unique values than STATE_DESCRIP.

Scenario #5 Explanation:

This scenario is a further decomposition of the SECOND NORMAL FORM in Scenario #3. The ORDER and PAYMENT_TYPE tables are in THIRD NORMAL FORM. The valid number of unique pay types is limited, so the repeating data can be minimized in the ORDER table by storing only an identifier for the payment type and storing the PAY_TYPE itself in its own table.

Summary

Normalization is the process of reducing or completely eliminating the occurrence of redundant data in the database. Although in most cases redundant data is not completely eliminated, the greater the reduction of redundancies, the easier data integrity is to maintain. Normalization improves on the structure of a database, but unfortunately, has consequences. The drawback of normalizing a database is the inevitable degradation of database performance. When data is normalized, multiple entities are created that are related through unique identifiers (UIDs). In order to retrieve desired data, entities must be merged. The merging of entities (tables) to access data is called a join operation. Join operations require significant overhead, mainly related to how data is read from its physical location on disk and married with other related data from another physical location. A tradeoff must take place between the performance of the database and the manageability of the database.

NORMAL FORMs represent the level to which a database has been normalized. The NORMAL FORMs discussed in this chapter include the FIRST NORMAL FORM, SECOND NORMAL FORM, THIRD NORMAL FORM, Boyce-Codd NORMAL FORM, FOURTH NORMAL FORM, and FIFTH NORMAL FORM. The first three NORMAL FORMs are the most common, and are standard for production database implementations. The other NORMAL FORMs are mainly theoretical, and are sparsely used in production databases. In order to apply a NORMAL FORM, the database must currently exist in the state of the previous NORMAL FORM.

Denormalization is the process of recombining attributes in a database that has been normalized. Basically, redundant data is allowed in the database for the purpose of improving performance. A denormalized database differs from a database that has not been normalized. Denormalization has drawbacks as well, such as increased redundancy, increased storage requirements, and increased difficulty in the management of data integrity. Unfortunately, there are only guidelines for normalizing a database. All databases differ; therefore, the developer must take time to learn the data, relationships, and data usages in order to effectively normalize a database for a combination of optimal performance and manageability.

Entity Relationship Modeling

IN THIS CHAPTER

Entity relationship modeling is the process of visually representing entities and attributes that are defined as a result of interviews, one of the initial steps during the business-analysis process. The entity relationship diagram (ERD) is an iterative tool and process that models logical data structures during the analysis phase of system development. ERD components are data entities, the attributes of those entities, and the relationships among the entities. The complete ERD is used later in database design to physically design database tables.

The creation of an ERD first involves the identification and definition of entities. As you should recall, entities are classes of things of importance about which data must be stored or manipulated in the course of business processes. Entities are the nouns of your information system. EMPLOYEE, CUSTOMER, PRODUCT, and INVOICE would all be probable examples of entities. Not all nouns are of significance to a business, and case-by-case decisions must be made as to what entities need to be in your logical model. An entity is not a single individual or example but instead a class or category of things. A single, specific occurrence of an entity is an *instance*. Other terms for an instance are *record* and *tuple*. In physical design, a logical instance will become a physical row. For example, John Smith, the employee, is an instance of the entity EMPLOYEE. He is not an entity himself. Any entity for which there is just one instance is not an entity.

The ERD's great advantage is that it is simple enough that both technical and nontechnical people can quickly learn to use it to communicate productively about data requirements. Yet, it is enormously powerful in its capability to capture and communicate data about data (metadata) on an evolving information system's data requirements. It is also flexible enough to easily support the rapid, iterative change that comes as development teams hone in on their ultimate logical model. The ERD's relative simplicity, power, and flexibility makes it an excellent tool for communicating complex data-definition issues among the technical developer and functional user teams that develop most new systems.

NOTE

ERDs contain metadata, or data about other data. For example, ERD data include boxes, names, and lines. The data that a line represents is the relationship between two entities in the ERD. An entity name represents a table that will be created later, which will also contain data of its own.

NOTE

There are many different ERD formats and syntaxes developed by different vendors and academicians. These ERD formats are conceptually and procedurally nearly identical but use different symbols, syntaxes, and formats to represent conceptually identical logical objects. For the sake of simplicity and consistency (and because it's the one we know best and the one used by Oracle corporation), we use the symbol set and method from Richard Barker's *CASE*METHOD Entity Relationship Modeling* (Addison-Wesley, 1989) in our discussion of ERDs.

This chapter focuses on the explanation of modeling entities in a diagram (ERD), the steps involved in ERD modeling, and how an ERD is used during database design. First, it is important to understand how an ERD applies to logical database design.

Logically Modeling Business Entities

Data modeling is an iterative process through which you define in detail a logical representation or model of the data requirements for a new or upgraded information system. You try to capture the data requirements for real-world processes in your data model. The tool or process most commonly used in initial data modeling of the logical data structures required for relational database systems is the *entity relationship diagram* (ERD). The ERD process models logical data structures during the analysis phase of system development. ERD components are data entities, the attributes of those entities, and the relationships among the entities.

NOTE

ERDs are platform independent and can also be used with network or hierarchical databases. ERDs can also be used to help model business concepts outside of the scope of relational databases, such as with XML (Extensible Markup Language) and other Web-based languages. This chapter, however, will discuss ERDs in the context of a relational database.

Physical structures such as tables, columns, and foreign keys are defined later in the design phase of the development process, based on the logical objects that are the product of the ERD. Logical entities from the analysis phase will become the basis for physical tables in the design phase. Logical attributes will become physical columns, and logical relationships may become physical foreign keys.

The logical-to-physical transition is not a one-to-one correspondence, however. Some logical entities may not make it to the physical design at all. Multiple logical entities may be combined into single, physical tables for reasons of performance or convenience.

The ERD is a tool used in the analysis phase of development to model in an unconstrained logical environment the initial design of your data structures. During the design phase, the physical reality of storage and performance requirements may well require modifications to the logical design. Still, most of what is done in the logical model will carry over into the physical. That's why it's important to do a good job with the ERD.

> **NOTE**
>
> In the case of a really bad design, you might reach a point in which no amount of hardware or tuning will save you, and the model must be redesigned from the beginning. The ERD is essential in both design and redesign.

Constructing Entities in the ERD

Initially, identification of entities should be a freewheeling process. There are no stupid questions or dumb ideas as you attempt to identify and capture the potential entities for your system. In a new system, look for the nouns in the descriptions of the new and the old systems, old system reports, and user interviews as sources of potential entities. The idea is to capture as many potential entities as possible and let the ERD process weed out entities so that the first-cut ERD can evolve into a complete product. You should be patient with entities that initially appear as if they won't make the cut. They may prove to be useful later as the model evolves.

As you develop applications within large enterprise systems (where your application will coexist with other applications in a common database environment), early in your project you will need to come up with naming conventions for your entities and indeed all your objects to avoid confusion and make your system consistent and therefore easier to manage, maintain, and use. Different developers will go entirely different and inconsistent directions in naming items if you don't set standards, and problems will result.

The first step in creating an ERD, then, is to capture an unconstrained group of entities that represent all the business objects in your data model and either draw them into your ERD or input them into the ERD using an automated design (AD) tool. Over time, as you work on your data model, that group of entities will evolve toward completion. As the process continues, you might find yourself creating, deleting, and modifying entities in the ERD to fit the business requirements.

In the CASE*METHOD methodology, entities are represented in ERDs by "soft" (rounded-corner) boxes. These boxes can be of various sizes, depending on how much of what's inside them you want to display. Inside an ERD entity box is placed a singular, unique entity name in uppercase. Figure 9.1 shows an entity called INSTRUCTOR. This entity represents information about instructors, such as name, contact information, skill set, and so forth. Attributes are determined later in the modeling process, only after all entities and their relationships have been defined.

INSTRUCTOR

FIGURE 9.1

A CASE*METHOD representation of an entity.

Entity attribute names are included inside the entity box. This is discussed later in the chapter after relationships are covered. In your first effort at an ERD (the strategy ERD in Oracle's methodology), attributes are largely optional. Initially you're trying to capture the entities and the relationships between them.

Figure 9.2 illustrates the difference between what are called *supertype* and *subtype* entities. In this illustration, EMPLOYEE is the supertype entity—the main category of information. The subtype entities of EMPLOYEE include SALARIED_EMPLOYEE, HOURLY_EMPLOYEE, and OTHER_EMPLOYEE, because there are different types of employees.

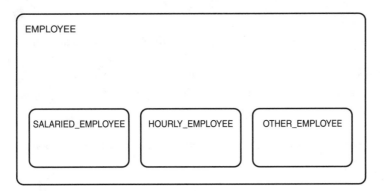

FIGURE 9.2

A CASE*METHOD representation of a supertype entity.

9

NOTE

A supertype entity has some attributes that are at the supertype level. Subtypes share the supertype attributes and may have attributes of their own. Subtypes can be further subdivided into subtypes of their own, but it is not advisable to nest subtypes deeper than three levels. Include the subtype OTHER if you're not sure that all the possible supertype instances are covered in one of its defined subtypes.

An entity may be a supertype entity, which means that it is an entity with mutually exclusive subtypes.

Defining Entity Relationships

Once you have identified a list of potential entities and placed them into an ERD, the next step is to identify the relationships between the entities. Relationships are the verbs of your system. Again, as you'll recall from Chapter 7, "Understanding Entities and Relationships," a relationship is a bidirectional connection between two entities or between an entity and itself. Relationships are represented by lines between entities in an ERD. Chapter 7 discussed the concept of entity relationships. This chapter shows how to establish and model these relationships in an ERD.

> **NOTE**
>
> A relation between entities includes a verb name for each entity's participation in the relationship, an optionality shown by whether or not the portion of the connecting line nearest the entity is broken, and a cardinality or degree shown by either a single line (one and only one) or a three-line "crow's foot" (one or more) at the connection points of the line to the entities.

Figure 9.3 shows two entities: INSTRUCTOR and DEPARTMENT. This is a many-to-one relationship (same as one-to-many relationship) because an instructor may be employed by only one department, but a department might be comprised of many instructors. Notice that there's a solid line between the two entities, designating a mandatory relationship. The relationship is mandatory in the sense that an instructor must be employed by a department, and a department must have at least one instructor. The crow's foot is adjacent to the INSTRUCTOR entity, meaning that many occurrences of an instructor may be associated with one occurrence of a particular department.

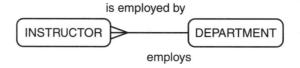

FIGURE 9.3
An example of entities with a relationship.

The relationship example from the INSTRUCTOR side in Figure 9.3 would be read as follows:

> An instructor is employed by one and only one department.

The relationship example from the DEPARTMENT side in Figure 9.3 would be read as follows:

> A department employs one or more instructors.

According to the CASE*METHOD, the steps in creating entity relationships are as follows:

1. Check to see if a relationship exists.
2. If a relationship exists, identify a verb for each direction of the relationship.
3. Identify an optionality for each direction of the relationship.
4. Identify a degree for each direction of the relationship.
5. Validate the relationship by reading it.

These steps are covered in the following subsections, with examples included.

Check to See if a Relationship Exists

Does a relationship exist? A common tool used to help define entity relationships is a simple, hand-drawn table. Take the entities and list them across the top and down the left side of a piece of paper. At each intersection point of the matrix you've created, you can evaluate each pair of entities to see whether there is a relationship. Note those that do. In some cases, an entity will have a relationship with itself. This is called a *recursive relationship*. In the following table, you can see how easy it is to determine relationships in this manner. For example, each instructor is related to a department and students. None of the entities in this table are related to themselves. Wherever a relationship is discovered (noted by "yes" at an intersection point in the table), a relationship will need to be defined, based on cardinality and optionality, and then modeled.

	instructor	*department*	*student*
instructor	none	yes	yes
department	yes	none	yes
student	yes	yes	none

Identify the Verbs for the Relationship

If there is a relationship, identify a lowercase verb name for each direction of the relationship. Active verbs for at least one direction are best. Verbs such as *has*, *is associated with*, or *is related to* should be avoided due to their lack of clarity. The following table illustrates how relationships and their verbs can be determined using a simple matrix.

	instructor	*department*	*student*
instructor	none	is employed by	teaches
department	employs	none	is major of
student	is taught by	majors in	none

Identify the Optionality

Identify an optionality for each direction of the relationship. The optionality of a relationship is either *must be* or *may be*. Mandatory (must be) relationships are represented by solid lines. Optional (may be) relationships are represented by broken lines. The part of a relationship line between entities that's closest to an entity reflects the optionality for that entity's portion of the relationship.

Modeling Mandatory Relationships

A mandatory relationship is one that must exist between two entities. Figure 9.4 illustrates a relationship between INSTRUCTOR and STUDENT. This relationship is a mandatory relationship between both entities. Note that both sides of the relationship line are solid.

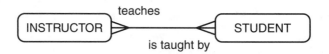

FIGURE 9.4

An example of entities with a mandatory relationship.

This example would be read as follows:

> Each instructor must teach one or more students, and each student is taught by one or more instructors.

The assumption here is that an instructor must instruct and a student must be instructed. That's why the mandatory relationship exists.

Modeling Optional Relationships

An optional relationship is one that might or might not exist between two entities. For example, an instance in one entity might or might not have a corresponding instance in another related entity. Figure 9.5 shows an optional relationship between DEPARTMENT and STUDENT. Note that both sides of the relationship line are broken.

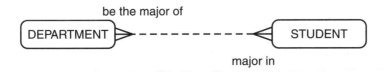

FIGURE 9.5
An example of entities with an optional relationship.

This example would be read as follows:

> Each department may be the major of one or more students, and each student may major in one or more departments.

A department could exist without students who major in it, and some students may not yet have declared a major. Therefore, the optional relationship exists in both directions.

Modeling Mandatory and Optional Relationships Together

Both a mandatory and optional relationship can exist between two entities. Figure 9.6 shows related entities with different optionalities. This relationship is mandatory from the perspective of the instructor but optional from the perspective of instructor skill. Note that the side of the relationship line nearest the instructor is not broken, indicating a mandatory relationship. Also, the side nearest the instructor skill entity is broken, indicating an optional relationship.

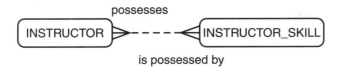

FIGURE 9.6
An example of entities with an optional relationship on one side and a mandatory relationship on the other. This example would be read as follows:

Each instructor must possess one or more instructor skills, and each instructor skill may be possessed by one or more instructors.

The rationale is that each instructor must have at least one skill, but a particular required skill may be held by no instructor if it's new or the prior expert quit or retired.

> **NOTE**
>
> Remember that the part of the line closest to the entity is the part that applies to its optionality.

Identify a Degree

Identify a degree (also called *cardinality*) for each direction of the relationship. Degrees of a relationship are either *one and only one* or *one or more*. Degrees of 0 (no required relationship) are handled by "may" optionality, which means that associated data is not required in the second entity.

A "one and only one" degree is represented by a single line coming from the entity box on the side of the relation opposite the entity that's the starting point for reading the relationship. "One or more" is represented by a crow's foot (see the previous three-clawed examples) coming from the entity box on the side of the relation opposite the entity that's the starting point for reading the relationship.

You should choose a standard as to the direction in which the crow's feet point in the layout of your ERD. Generally, the convention is "crows fly east or south." This means that you should place your entities on your ERD so that the claws of the crow's feet point up or to the left. Following this standard will put the busier, high-volume entities in the upper left and the low-volume entities in the lower right of the ERD. This also puts the children in foreign key parent/child relationships in the upper left and the parents in the lower right. In both cases, the convention eases the reading of the ERD, thus improving communication. "Crows fly west or north" is used in other ERD methods and works about as well, but in reverse. The key is consistency, using one way or the other.

Three types of potential degree/cardinality two-way relationships exist:

- Many-to-one (M:1) relationships
- Many-to-many (M:M) relationships
- One-to-one (1:1) relationships

Many-to-one (M:1) relationships are common in logical models, but mandatory M:1 relationships in both directions are fairly rare. When you reach the physical design stage, the "M" (crow's foot) side of the relationship will become a foreign key relationship for that entity, with the entity on the "1" side. The "1" is on the parent side, and the "M" (crow's foot) is on the child side.

Degree of One and Only One

A degree of one and only one means that multiple instances in an entity cannot be related to an instance in the original entity. In Figure 9.7, the relationship has an optionality of *mandatory* and a degree of *one and only one* from the perspective of the product, and it has an optionality of *optional* and a degree of *one or more* from the perspective of the vendor. Note that the indicator of the degree is on the opposite side of the relationship line from the entity that's the starting point of the relationship.

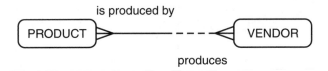

FIGURE 9.7
An example of entities with an M:1 relationship.

This relationship would be read as follows:

> Each product must be produced by one and only one vendor, and each vendor may produce one or more products.

Degree of Many

A degree of many occurs when an instance in one entity can have multiple related instances in another entity. Many-to-many (M:M) relationships are very common and are usually optional in both directions but may be mandatory in one direction. M:M relationships are invalid in the model and need to be resolved to two M:1 relationships. If necessary, this may mean creating a new entity with an M:1 relationship with each of the entities to resolve the M:M relationship. Recall the M:M relationship created in Chapter 7 that was resolved by creating a new entity common to both entities involved in the M:M relationship. This new entity is called an *intersection entity*. Usually, M:M relationships mean you don't know enough about the entities and relationships involved at this point and need to discover the entities you've missed. They're okay initially, but they have to be resolved as you work on your data model. The initial three examples provided are all M:M relationships. In the following paragraphs, you'll see an example of resolving one of these M:M relationships into two M:1 relationships using an intersection entity.

The original example of many instructors teaching many students may seem correct at first glance, but it is not very useful in a data model other than as a starting point. In Figure 9.8, an entity called COURSE is used as an intersection entity to resolve the M:M relationship to two M:1 relationships.

9

ENTITY
RELATIONSHIP
MODELING

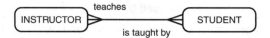

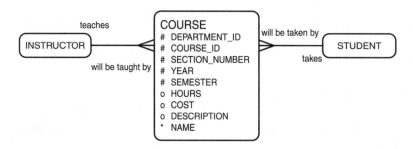

FIGURE 9.8

Resolving an M:M relationship.

By making a composite unique identifier for the course intersection entity that uniquely identifies a particular presentation of a course (department, course, year, semester, and section), you can connect both a particular instructor and a particular student to that particular unique course presentation and establish 1:M relationships for each of the former participants in the M:M relationship. Intersection entities will often add a time element in order to establish precision and uniqueness for a relation.

One-to-one (1:1) relationships are rare. Entities that seem to have 1:1 relationships might be the same entity or one is a component of the other.

Figure 9.9 depicts an example of a 1:1 relationship, if it's assumed that the car can't have two engines and that it must have one engine to be considered a car.

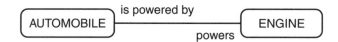

FIGURE 9.9

A 1:1 relationship.

A better example of a 1:1 relationship might be current husband to current wife (in most places).

Validate the Relationship

Validate the relationship by reading it aloud to ensure that it makes sense. If a relationship does not make sense to an end user or management, it should be reworded.

Relationships are read in the following format:

	OPTIONALITY		*CARDINALITY*	
Each	must		one or more	
EntityA	may	"Rname"	one and only one	EntityB

For example, each customer *may* order *one or more* products. In this example, "Rname" represents the relationship name.

Relationships are read in both directions, as shown in the following table:

	OPTIONALITY		*CARDINALITY*	
Each	must		one or more	
EntityB	may	"Rname"	one and only one	EntityA

For example, each product *may* be ordered by *one or more* customers.

Relationships have an additional feature called *transferability*. If EntityA and EntityB have a transferable relationship, one instance in EntityA can be transferred from one instance of EntityB to another. A "provides service" relationship between a CUSTOMER entity and a SALES_PERSON entity is probably transferable. A "belongs to" relationship between entity EMPLOYEE and entity SALARY_AND_BENEFITS is probably not transferable.

An entity may have a relationship with itself. As you'll recall from Chapter 7, this is referred to as a *recursive relationship*. A line is still drawn with optionality and cardinality expressed as in other relationships, but in this case the line is drawn from one side of the entity to another side of the same entity. This produces a relationship line that curves back onto the same entity. Such a line is referred to as a *pig's ear*.

Figure 9.10 shows an example of a recursive relationship. It's read as follows:

> Each employee may manage one or more employees, and each employee is managed by one and only one employee.

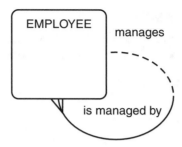

FIGURE 9.10

A recursive relationship.

> **NOTE**
>
> Common recursive entity relationship uses are to show hierarchies, lists of products on orders, and parts that are subcomponents of other parts.

An *arc* is two or more mutually exclusive relationships between an entity and two or more other entities. Of those relationships that are part of the arc, only one may exist for a particular instance of the original entity. All relationship optionalities for the end of the relationships that the arc spans must be the same—all optional or all mandatory. In physical design, a foreign key is established within the original table for each of the remote tables related to via the arced relationships.

Figure 9.11 illustrates an arc—a representation of a recursive relationship. The course entity would be related to three different program entities: undergraduate, graduate, and adult education. Only one of these three program areas would be a primary proponent of or sponsor for a particular course. The relationships shown on the arc are mutually exclusive.

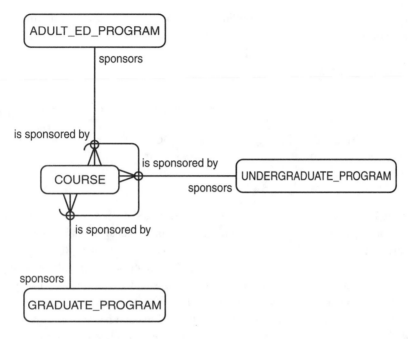

FIGURE 9.11
An arc distinguishing multiple relationships to COURSE.

Defining the Attributes for an Entity

Once you have your entities and their relationships captured in your ERD, the next step is to identify and capture the attributes of your entities. Your first task will be to identify a unique identifier attribute or combination of attributes for each entity. Every entity must start with a unique primary key.

Up to this point, the level of detail has been somewhat limited. Adding attributes will add significant detail to the model. Entity attributes are details about or descriptions of an entity that need to be recorded for use in processing. The entity EMPLOYEE for example, might have attributes such as first_name, last_name, middle_initial, ssn, and date_of_birth. Attributes describe, quantify, or qualify an entity by listing its features of interest or answering questions about an entity instance, such as who, what, when, where, and how many.

Adding attributes will also be the impetus that causes your entities to evolve as you apply guidelines and normalization rules pertaining to assigning attributes to entities. A list of attribute guidelines follows. As you identify and assign attributes to your entities, consider and apply these guidelines.

9

**ENTITY
RELATIONSHIP
MODELING**

As a development team or even as an individual developer, come up with and enforce attribute-naming conventions for your system. Words fully spelled out with some standard, clear, and mutually agreed upon abbreviations, with an underline separating the words, is a common convention. Whatever works for you is fine.

> **NOTE**
>
> One of the keys to database design is consistency. Consistent attribute names make it easier for your users and developers to use the system.

Create the attribute names in plain English so that the users and other developers can understand them. Be clear and specific with attribute names. For instance, create Annual_Performance_Bonus, not just Bonus. This is especially true of date attributes. Use Date_Invoice_Received, not just Date_Received. Avoid cryptic abbreviations, technical jargon, or other generally meaningless attribute names that may be fine for you but will just irritate and inconvenience other people trying to work with the system. These entities will become tables, and the attributes will become columns that are used by many people. Poorly named attributes will make it harder for users already overworked to do their jobs. Coincidentally, these users will like you and your system less in direct proportion to just how bad those attribute names are.

> **NOTE**
>
> Be clear and specific when naming attributes. Remember that your work in the ERD will carry over into table design. Avoid cryptic abbreviations, technical jargon, and other generally meaningless wording. Poorly named attributes make life more difficult for everyone in the long run.

You might think that column names aren't important to anyone other than you as the developer. The users just see a screen format with labels the system provides them, and other developers ought to be clever enough to interpret your abbreviations. However, some sophisticated users will likely use tools such as COGNOS or Oracle's Discoverer to generate ad hoc but nonetheless high-priority reports. What's more, a year later you, yourself, probably won't be clever enough to interpret your abbreviations, let alone some poor developer trying to maintain your system.

We once saw a table used as an interim storage location for data going through a complex transformation process, from one column format to another column format, with meaningless column names—something like A, B, C, D, and so on. The developer probably figured that nobody would see the table but him, so why worry about designing it properly? We discovered the table because the process in which access to the table was an interim step wasn't working, and we'd been tasked with trying to help fix it. Meaningless column names and poor documentation made helping with the maintenance of that process nearly impossible. Another lesson to learn from this is that no entity, even one only used as workspace behind the scenes by your application, is unimportant.

NOTE

Having advocated long and descriptive attribute names, try not to make them any longer than you have to in order to clearly communicate what the attributes represent.

In general, you should break attributes up into their smallest logical pieces. For example, use first_name, last_name, and middle_initial rather than just name. This will help later in the physical database when you want to do searches or sorts on last names and they aren't buried somewhere in a single-name column. The same is generally true for attributes such as address. Attributes such as social security numbers, phone numbers, and ID numbers for parts, invoices, or people are generally not broken up, even though their subcomponents may have meaning on their own. You might leave names and addresses as single attributes in the logical model and break them up on the physical side, or you might break them up right off.

Attribute and column names should not include space for hyphens, commas, or other formatting punctuation. Such items are not stored in the database and are not allowable characters for most relational database management systems (RDBMSs). Sometimes, entity and attribute names include spaces. When you're converting entities to tables and physically designing those tables, spaces that are found in entity and attribute names are replaced with underscores. An underscore is typically an acceptable character to be stored in a database, and it achieves the same visual effect as a space for readability.

9

ENTITY
RELATIONSHIP
MODELING

NOTE

When naming entities and attributes, choose a naming standard that specifies the maximum length of a name to be a few characters less than the maximum size technically possible for your database system. Doing this will give you a little room for future emergency changes.

An entity must have attributes; otherwise, it's not an entity. The exception to this involves certain intersection entities used to resolve M:M relationships. However, as you go through the process of assigning attributes and normalizing the logical model, entities that lack attributes initially may pick some up. Early on, don't drop entities just because they don't have attributes yet.

Also, don't include the entity name in its attribute names. Doing so is redundant. A probable exception to this is the primary key UID attribute(s), which may be sent to other entities/tables as a foreign key during physical design.

NOTE

Developers should agree to enforce naming conventions, comments, and documented alterations for the sanity of those who come later as well as the current staff. That way, if a developer knows all tables are created in a very specific way consistently, he will likely know the name of a table without looking it up—or he'll know what the table does through the description.

Study the following basic table structures:

PRODUCT	ORDER
ID	ID
NAME	PROD_ID
DESCRIP	DATE_ORD
COST	QUANTITY

In this example, both primary keys are named *ID* and may be distinguished as PRODUCT.ID and ORDER.ID. PROD_ID must also be stored in ORDER so that a product may be associated with an order.

Consider the following relationship:

ORDER.PROD_ID references PRODUCT.ID.

What you have here is a one-to-many relationship. Each product has only one entry in PRODUCT but may be many entries in ORDER, because a product can be ordered multiple times. To avoid confusion, primary and foreign keys should be named consistently throughout the database. A better naming scheme for these columns (which start as entity and attribute names) follows:

PRODUCT	ORDER
PROD_ID	ORD_ID
NAME	PROD_ID
DESCRIP	DATE_ORD
COST	QUANTITY

What you don't want to see is something like this:

PRODUCT	ORDER
PROD_ID	ORD_ID
PROD_NAME	ORD_PROD_ID
PROD_DESCRIP	ORD_DATE_ORD
PROD_COST	ORD_QUANTITY

In a standard relational database, there should be no attributes that are the results of calculations based on or concatenations of other attributes. These derived attributes are redundant with the columns they are derived from. This requires unnecessary storage and leads to possible data inconsistencies when the original attributes get updated but the derived attributes do not. Warehouse applications, however, will often have entities with attributes that are the result of presummarization as a precursor to a physical design that includes presummarization as a means to speed performance. Precalculation of derived attributes is also a common denormalization step if performance becomes an issue.

An attribute should be in only one entity to avoid data redundancy. The issue here is not the attribute name but rather the actual data element that the name represents. Don't store the same data item in two entities, whatever you name it. Your application would have to maintain this item twice, and there is always the possibility that one or the other will get out of sync. Replication of data attributes is also a common denormalization step if performance becomes an issue, but this should be viewed as a necessary evil of physical design and not included in a logical model.

You will need to identify the data types and sizes of your attributes. A *data type* is the kind of data represented by an attribute. Character, number, and date are all examples of data types. A common mistake for beginners is to place noncalculating numbers, such as phone numbers and SSNs, into numeric columns or dates into character columns. Noncalculating numbers should be characters, and dates should be dates. SQL syntax and system processing of the data will be different based on the data types, and it is important to assign them correctly. Size is also important. Ensure that number attributes have sufficient size overall and a sufficient number of decimal places to the right of the decimal point to meet requirements.

> **NOTE**
>
> When you're assigning data types to attributes or columns, the only attributes that should be assigned a numeric data type are those that contain values that are treated as numbers, such as those values used in calculations. All other attributes should be assigned a character or date data type, as appropriate.

Most (some ERD methods say *all*) of your attributes should be defined by a domain on these points. Prior to creating attributes, identify and define a complete list of domains that will be applied to your attributes.

A *domain* is a set of business data validation rules, data range limits, and data type and data format standards that will be applied to attributes of common types. It may also include a list of acceptable values. For example, you might define the domain "money" with a number data type, a range from 0 to 1000000000.00, and a format that includes two decimal places. You would then use this domain for all your money-related attributes in all your entities. Another example might be the domain "state," which includes a list of all the states as acceptable values with a character data type and a size of 2. Domains are very helpful in creating consistency at the attribute level within your model. Make and use as many domains as possible.

> **NOTE**
>
> Domains are useful for maintaining consistency and speeding up database design. Consistency is maintained because similar attributes can inherit the traits of a domain and then be fine-tuned. The use of domains speeds up design because less work is involved in defining individual attributes once domains have been established.

Given all these considerations, it is time to begin identifying attributes and assigning them to entities. The first step is to ensure that each entity has a unique identifier (UID), which is unique for every instance in the entity. The UID may consist of one or more attributes and cannot be duplicated within an instance of an entity once applied to an entity. The UID may represent actual data as long as it is unique. Attributes such as ssn and part_number can be UIDs. In this case, you're using what is termed an *intelligent key*. Intelligent keys are used occasionally. However, keep in mind that a person's SSN is private data and that part numbers can change if you change your inventory system. Short, system-generated numeric keys (dumb keys) are more often utilized for the UID. The UID for an entity is tagged with a pound sign (#) in the entity box on an ERD.

Assign additional attributes to the entities based on the information you want to capture on that entity. You will need to assign each attribute a domain or a specific data type, size, and other characteristics of its own. As you work, you will identify new potential domains. Create and use them.

You will need to decide whether each attribute is optional or mandatory. A *mandatory attribute* means that the column cannot be null (empty or unknown). It is a required column. Mandatory attributes are tagged with an asterisk (*) in an ERD. Optional attributes can be null and are tagged with the letter *o* in an ERD.

> **NOTE**
>
> It is important to determine whether an attribute is optional or mandatory. If you incorrectly choose mandatory, your users will be unable to add a row without putting some kind of data—generally some nonsense—into it. If you incorrectly choose optional, your users will be able to add a row without putting some required information into it.

Once you have assigned attributes to the entities in your ERD, apply the first, second, and third normal form normalization rules (described in the Chapter 8, "Normalization: Eliminating Redundant Data") to each of the entities in your model. This normalization and resulting decomposition of your entities is a complex process and will produce major iterative changes in the entities and their attributes.

Figure 9.12 illustrates an ERD containing examples of entities with attributes and indicators of UIDs (#), required columns (*), and optional columns (o).

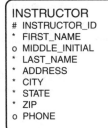

F!GURE 9.12
Entities with attributes.

How an ERD Is Used

A complete enterprise system ERD provides a picture of the logical side of your database. Such an ERD is a good planning and integration tool for defining on an enterprise level the overall and potentially shared data requirements for multiple, separate but coexisting information systems within the enterprise. An ERD is also good for showing the scope of data requirements for an individual information system project within the enterprise. Complete system ERDs can be invaluable to the sophisticated user trying to create ad hoc reports or spot potential new or optimal uses for the data this system will capture.

ERD uses can range from simple back-of-the-envelope ERDs used as the basis for communication between developers and between developers and functional users, to ERDs produced by fully integrated GUI components of sophisticated automated design (AD) products such as Oracle's Designer. The ERD tool included in Designer is used for detailed definition of logical business entities, entity attributes, and relationships between entities. The Designer ERD tool lets the developer draw ERDs ranging from the simple to the highly complex in level of detail in an easy-to-use point-and-click environment. Designer captures the metadata (data about data) represented by the detailed data structures that the developer defines in the ERD within a central repository (one that's shared by all developers). That metadata later will be transformed within Designer into a physical database design model, and from that physical design model the tool will generate the SQL Database Definition Language (DDL) that, when run, will create, object by object, a complete Oracle relational database. All this originates from an ERD.

Typical ERD Symbols

The most common symbols used to create an ERD are shown in this section. These symbols have been discussed throughout this chapter in examples that use them. Figure 9.13 shows the symbols most typically used during entity relationship modeling.

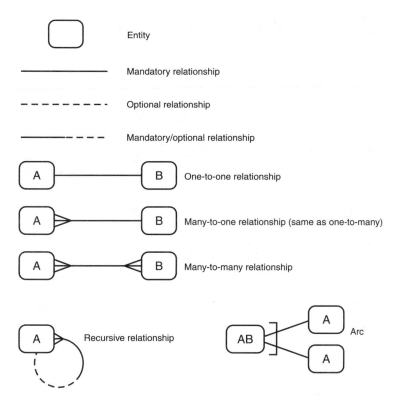

FIGURE 9.13

Common ERD symbols.

Figure 9.14 shows an enlarged entity from an ERD. Attributes have been defined for this entity. Note the use of the #, *, and o characters to define attributes. When an ERD is complete, all entities should look similar to this one.

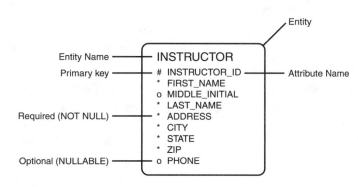

FIGURE 9.14

Detail of an entity's components.

An ERD for the Sample Company TrainTech

Remember TrainTech? Figure 9.15 is an ERD that covers the requirements for this training company. Looking at the figure, you can see that the information is based on courses that are offered, taught by instructors, and taken by students.

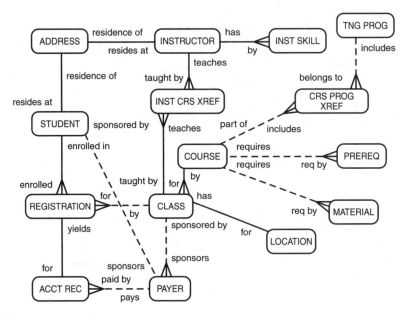

FIGURE 9.15

ERD for our sample company.

In Figure 9.15, COURSE is used to track individual courses that are offered. CLASS represents an occurrence in which a particular class is taught. CLASS has several branches: LOCATION, PAYER, and REGISTRATION. Each class is taught at one location. Each class also has one or more registrations, which are associated with individual students. Finally, somebody has to pay for the class. The payer might be an individual student or a company sponsoring a student, which is why PAYER and STUDENT are related.

On the flip side of CLASS are the instructors. There is a many-to-many relationship between INSTRUCTOR and CLASS, because a class may have more than one instructor, and an instructor may teach one or more classes. INST CRS XREF is an intersection entity used to decompose the many-to-many relationship into two one-to-many relationships. An instructor has one home address but may have many skills that determine the classes he or she is qualified to teach.

Courses that are taught also have required information in addition to classes that are scheduled. Courses have prerequisites, which in some cases refer to other courses that are offered. Courses also have corresponding material, such as textbooks and lab workbooks. Courses may also be part of a program, such as a database-management program or a software-development program.

Although the example in this section does not show the attributes for each entity, you should have a good idea of the attributes that apply to each. In order to further your understanding of this example, it would be beneficial for you to define the attributes for the entities shown in Figure 9.15.

Summary

Entity relationship modeling is the process of visually representing entities that are derived from user interviews. Entities represent organizational data and are later used to physically design database tables. An entity relationship diagram (ERD) is a diagram of an organization's entities, entity attributes, and entity relationships. An ERD is used to organize a database-design effort to ensure that the complete data is modeled so that the finished product, the database, is as accurate and complete as possible.

Defining entities and their relationships is a process that can be summarized by the five simple rules outlined in the CASE*Method methodology, by Richard Barker of Oracle Corporation. The five basic rules for defining entity relationships follow:

1. Determine whether a relationship exists.
2. Designate a verb name for the relationship.
3. Identify the optionality for the relationship.
4. Identify the cardinality for the relationship.
5. Validate the relationship by reading it out loud.

Using a standard set of symbols, an ERD can be created with ease, assuming that interviews have been thoroughly conducted and the design team was able to make sense of the gathered information. It is easiest to use an automated design (AD) tool to design a database. It is fairly simple to draw an ERD with an AD tool, store models, recall and make changes to these models, and convert the logical design (ERD) into the physical design (table structures). Once an ERD has been created, the organization's data and the relationships that exist should be fully understood by the development team, management, and functional users alike.

9

ENTITY
RELATIONSHIP
MODELING

Modeling Business Processes

IN THIS CHAPTER

A *business process* is a function or related block of work that a business needs to accomplish in the course of meeting its business goals. The definition of business processes begins at a very general level, with a few root processes. Most business organizations, for instance, have some level of accounting, finance, human resources, research and development, operations, and marketing processes.

These general processes are then further decomposed into lower-level processes. Accounting, for instance, can be decomposed into accounts payable, accounts receivable, payroll, and so on. Processes on this level are then further decomposed. Accounts payable, for instance, can be further decomposed into processes such as receive invoice, verify receipt of product with operations, and send payment. Then, these processes can yet again be decomposed. Send payment can be broken down into receive disbursal approval, print check, prepare envelope, place check in envelope, and mail envelope.

Processes, then, are tasks a business must do in the course of doing business. Processes can be and are as general as "accounting." However, the complexity represented by so general a process is beyond easy comprehension. The processes are therefore decomposed, level by level, eventually down to the level of specificity of "mail envelope." Everyone can understand that. Each level of specificity has its use, depending on the perspective and requirements at the time. The intent of this chapter is to show how processes can be modeled to increase overall understanding of the proposed database. A database cannot be properly designed without clear comprehension of both the data and the processes, or *tasks*, performed to access the data.

> **NOTE**
>
> There are several references to Oracle's automated design tool, Designer, in this chapter. We are not advocating the use of Designer to design a relational database; it just happens to be the AD tool with which we are most familiar. Numerous AD tools are available, many of which have features that are similar to those shown in the examples in this chapter.

How Do Business Processes Affect Database Design?

Business processes are the real reason databases exist. Whether you start with defining optimal data structures and develop processes that meet business requirements that use those data structures or define the processes first and then develop data structures to support those processes is still open for debate. Historically, the latter has been done. Today, however, the trend is toward the former, but there are still open discussions either way.

Whichever side you choose—data or process—the two must work so closely together that it will often be difficult to tell which came first anyway. Once defined, entities and processes must be compared; this is done by assigning data usages. A *data usage* is a means through which a process accesses an entity. Usages can be defined at both the entity and attribute levels. For example, a process may be associated with an entity, or more specifically, only certain attributes within a particular entity.

> **NOTE**
>
> Automated design tools allow you to assign entity usages to processes. For example, Oracle's Designer lets you assign entity usages through the use of either the Data flow Diagrammer or the Function Hierarchy Diagrammer.

As you identify data entities in your ERD and processes in your process model, a tool called a CRUD (Create, Retrieve, Update, Delete) matrix will be used to cross check your entities and your processes. You put your processes across the top and your entities down the left side of a piece of paper (or an automated design tool does it for you). Then you note whether an entity's instances are created, retrieved, updated, or deleted by the processes in the intersection points between each process and entity in the matrix.

Table 10.1 shows an example of a CRUD matrix.

TABLE 10.1   Sample Matrix to Cross Check Processes and Entities

Entities	Hire	Fire	Update Info
EMPLOYEE	CR--	-R-D	-RU-
EMP_PAY	CR--	-R-D	-RU-
BONUS	----	----	CRUD
INSURANCE	CR--	-R-D	-RU-
RET_401K	CR--	-R-D	-RU-

Each entity must have processes that create, retrieve, update, and delete its instances. Each of these functionalities must occur. If not, you're either missing a process or you don't need the entity. On the other hand, processes that don't touch an entity also need justification of their existence.

The bottom line is that processes and data entities feed on each other, and it's nearly a chicken-and-egg question as to which comes first. Both will evolve and impact each other. Consider the impact on a process that the many decompositions of entities resulting from normalization will have. Every new entity will have new processes or modified old ones that allow creation, retrieval, updates, and deletions of its instances.

Defining Business Processes

A first cut at defining business processes is pretty simple. You define the high-level functions and either draw a picture of them or input them into an automated design (AD) tool such as Designer. As you decompose the processes, which you must do in order to accomplish anything useful, you'll find that the complexity grows almost exponentially with each level of decomposition. You probably got this idea from the previous, relatively simple decomposition examples. This complexity is why using some AD tool becomes a near necessity with even medium-sized projects. It is perhaps possible to crosswalk 100 entities and 600 processes via a CRUD matrix without the use of an AD tool, but it is certainly a daunting prospect—and that's a medium-to-small project.

When you're modeling business processes, all the following must be defined in order for the model to be complete:

- Organizational units
- Processes
- Process flows

Given that you start with the process model format (which focuses on processes, not data flow), your initial effort in developing a process model is to define organizational units (OUs). You need to first capture the formal organizational chart into organizational units within your model. You then need to add in any informal or undefined organizational units that reflect reality if not found in the organizational chart.

Once you have organizational units in place, you can start defining processes and assigning them to the OU that does them. Start at the highest level. A process is a verb phrase. A process does something. Once you establish processes, you then define process flows. Process flows are nouns. They represent a flow of data that is the output of one process to another process for which it is input. Data flows are how processes interact with one another. When you complete a higher level, you decompose each individual higher-level process one at a time in order to complete the next level below it in the decomposition. In Designer, this is called *opening the process down*. Returning to the higher level is called *opening up*.

The execution of a process is initially kicked off by something from outside the process. It might be receipt of an invoice, a phone order, or a customer appearing in person. Whatever that external event is, it is called a *triggering event* or *trigger*. Once the triggering event occurs to initiate the first process, data will flow between the processes on that level until each process is complete. If the process produces a particular product that is needed by another process, the results of the process may go into a construct called an *output*. The results of a process may also include an update of another process model construct called a *data store*.

> **Note**
>
> Organizational units represent departments in a company that perform certain tasks. These tasks are referred to as *processes* or *functions*. Most processes performed will eventually become part of the process-flow diagram.

Overview of Process Modeling

A *process model* is an effort to capture real-world processes, ranging from the overwhelmingly general to the painfully specific, into a logical representation that can then be studied and manipulated to support different and better ways to accomplish these tasks. Not all processes have or need information system support. Automated or not, they should be included in the model.

Business processes are modeled for the following reasons:

- Understanding business processes
- Reengineering/improving business processes
- Graphically representing interaction between organizations within the company
- Illustrating the duration of a process cycle
- Developing a business process flowchart
- Crosschecking with entities to ensure completion

Most business processes these days, however, are automated. Applying information system support to business processes in new ways has been the source of many of the productivity gains that have led to the ongoing success story for American business. Applying massive and immediate business process changes using information systems is the basis for business process re-engineering (BPR).

There are three commonly used methods for presentation of business models. All three represent the same processes. Largely, they are different ways of looking at the same thing, with some additions in capability and syntax for each. These three models are discussed in the following subsections:

- The process model
- The function hierarchy
- The dataflow diagram

10

The Process Model

The first method for modeling business processes is the process model. The process model allows you to assign processes to particular business units (*organizational units*) and show flows of data between those processes and therefore within and between the organizational units. In Oracle's Designer product, the process modeler also allows you to allot resources to a process.

> **NOTE**
>
> The process model allows you to assign processes to organizational units within your enterprise.

Figure 10.1 shows a simple process model that includes processes performed by two different organizational units: ACCOUNTING and OPERATIONS. When a vendor sends an invoice, this process is triggered. First, an invoice is received along with the product. The product and quantity on the invoice is checked against the actual products received. Upon verification, payment is sent to the vendor for the product, while OPERATIONS updates the inventory of the product in the database. The large arrow pointing to the Receive Invoice process represents a triggering event. A box is used to designate each process, whereas the arrow lines represent flows between processes. Notice that a rounded box encloses INVENTORY. A rounded box designates a data store or an entity.

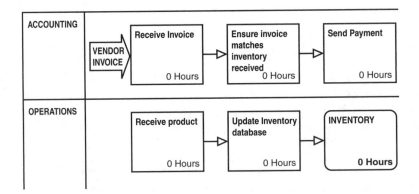

FIGURE 10.1

Process model depicting organizational units and processes.

Figure 10.2 shows a breakdown of the Send Payment process step from the previous figure. Send Payment has substeps and has been decomposed as shown in the figure. The processes shown here are child processes of the root process Send Payment.

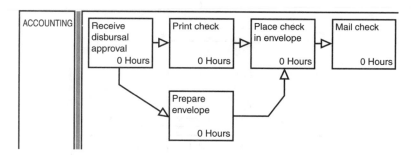

FIGURE 10.2

Process decomposition of Send Payment.

The Function Hierarchy

The second method for presenting process models is the function hierarchy diagram (FHD). The FHD is best for displaying the process hierarchy. An FHD can show processes in various levels of decomposition, depending on the point of interest at the time.

> **NOTE**
>
> The functional hierarchy diagram allows you to look at your process model as a hierarchy of tasks.

A functional hierarchy diagram is shown in Figure 10.3. The root process, or function, is Accounting. Accounting has one child function, which in turn has three child functions of its own. Notice the plus (+) and minus (-) signs next to some of the functions. The plus sign allows a function to be expanded (show child functions), and the minus allows a function to be collapsed (hide child functions). Figure 10.4 shows how the Manage Accounts Payable function has been expanded. Figure 10.5 shows how the Send Payment function has been expanded.

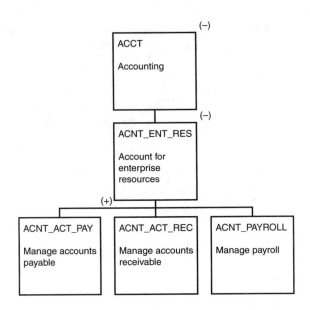

FIGURE 10.3

Function hierarchy diagram.

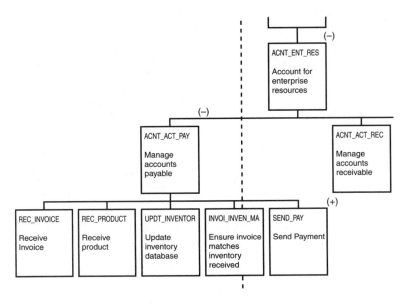

FIGURE 10.4

Expansion of a child function.

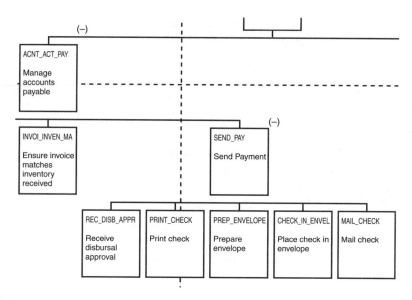

FIGURE 10.5
Expansion to the lowest level.

NOTE

In the function hierarchy diagram, notice that process flows are not shown. The concern in the FHD is on function relationships, not necessarily the flow. An FHD is an excellent tool to use to show how functions (processes) are related to one another.

The Data Flow Diagram

The third method for presenting process models is the traditional data flow diagram (DFD). The DFD shows processes and data flows like the process modeler, but it also assigns a numeric ID number to each process. Using the generic process model example discussed earlier, the high-level processes would be DFD level 0, each with its own unique identifying number to the left of the decimal place with a zero to the right.

Process	Level
Accounting	1.0
Finance	2.0
Human resources	3.0
Research and development	4.0

To further decompose accounting, you would use the accounting processes "1" on the left and a unique number as the first digit on the right. This would be a level-1 DFD.

Process	Level
Accounts payable	1.1
Accounts receivable	1.2
Payroll	1.3

These processes can then be further decomposed. To further decompose accounts payable, you would use the accounting process's "1" to the left of the decimal place and the accounts payable process's "1" as the first digit on the right. You would then add another decimal point and a unique number for each process beneath accounts payable as the second digit on the right of the decimal place. This would be a level-2 DFD with two numerals to the right of the first decimal place.

Process	Level
Receive invoice	1.1.1
Verify receipt of product	1.1.2
Send payment	1.1.3

These processes can yet again be decomposed. You could decompose send payment 1.1.3 by adding a decimal place and unique number for each process beneath send payment. This would be a level-3 DFD, and its decomposition is shown in the following example.

Process	Level
Receive disbursal approval	1.1.3.1
Print check	1.1.3.2
Prepare envelope	1.1.3.3

DFD is the oldest method for processing modeling. Extensive rules are defined for the creation of DFDs that are derived from years of experience using them. The logical organization brought with the numbering system also can be valuable.

The DFD is the traditional method for process modeling, and it assigns a numeric ID to each process based on its parent process and its sequence as related to other processes on the same level.

Figure 10.6 illustrates a data flow diagram based on the process that has been discussed so far this chapter. The main process shown in this DFD is "manage accounts payable" (1.1.1). Notice that the step number is annotated in the upper-left corner of each function. Functions are represented by rounded boxes. Data stores (entities) are represented by open-ended rounded boxes. Process and data flows are represented by arrows. This diagram contains much of the same information found in the process model. The focus here is to define data access (data usage) by associating functions and entities.

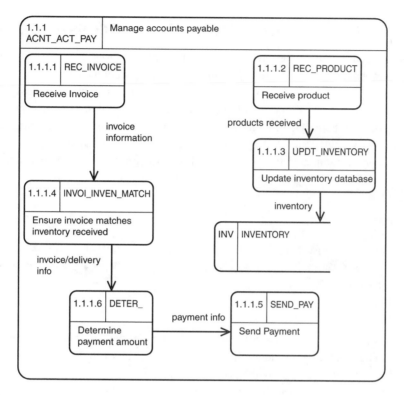

FIGURE 10.6

Data flow diagram.

A data flow diagram can be created to illustrate the functions, flows of data, and data stores associated with a database system being designed. A data flow diagram is used to show how information moves through an organization.

> **NOTE**
>
> Earlier in this chapter, the use of a CRUD matrix to associate processes and entities was mentioned. The CRUD can be drawn by hand or generated by an automated design (AD) tool. In order to generate a CRUD with an AD tool, information must be entered into the tool, normally using the DFD. Although all AD tools will vary, consider this example: When using Oracle's Designer, a developer can double-click a process in the DFD and select the accessible entities from a drop-down list that appears. Processes can be associated with whole entities or, more specifically, individual attributes within an entity.

What Does One Gain from the Process Model?

The business process model is an invaluable tool in communicating process requirements between developers and users and in capturing them once communicated. Users, the people who truly understand the current processes, can look at the description of processes from the model to see if you, as a developer, really have captured the processes the new system needs to accomplish. As with the ERD, a picture is worth a thousand words. User feedback sessions utilizing the process model as the starting point for discussions are invaluable as you develop the model. Once you've completed the model, it will hold the process requirements agreed to by developers and users as analysis turns to design and then to implementation.

> **NOTE**
>
> A good developer/consultant will get to know the nature of the business and really understand the business itself before beginning to use the process model or asking questions of the user.

The process of creating the model will help the design team develop a better understanding of the business. The great depth of detail that must be captured as you decompose each process will show the designer exactly how the processes are working and, on occasion, how they're not. It will also often show opportunities for getting rid of duplicated efforts and gaining economies of scale by combining duplicate processes on an enterprise level or establishing new processes that combine several of the old processes more efficiently and effectively. The process model graphically illustrates the flow of data within the system. Often, this will be helpful in identifying ways to make those flows more effective. Unused weekly reports may disappear. Entire applications may be found that are making no real contributions.

As mentioned earlier, the process model can illustrate entity usage via a CRUD matrix. This is a great help in designing the data model.

Finally, if you have been able to use a CASE tool, it will document in detail the process model you have created and the users have agreed to. CASE has its proponents (it supports iterative work well, captures enormous amounts of detail, generates code, generates documentation, assists in developing standard analysis and design processes, and so on) and detractors (it's expensive, it has a huge learning curve for developers, and its repository is sufficiently demanding that it nearly demands its own UNIX box for a host and a dedicated repository staff of two or three for a large project). Both groups are right. Still, if you're working with a medium-to-large project and want to be competitive, you need to use CASE. It's benefits more than outweigh its admittedly steep price.

Typical Process Modeling Symbols

Some common symbols used to create process models to capture an organization's needs are shown in this section. These symbols have been discussed throughout this chapter, as examples have been shown using these symbols. Figure 10.7 shows these symbols. The symbols include those used for modeling processes and data flows.

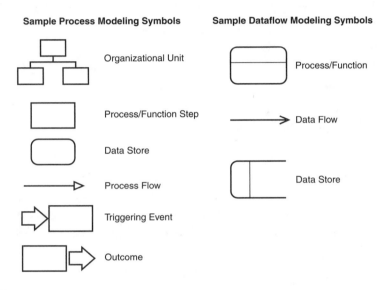

FIGURE 10.7

Common process-modeling symbols.

Using Process Models in Database Design

Process modeling is used in a direct manner to build an application interface that the end user utilizes to access a database. As you can see, entity relationship modeling and process modeling go hand in hand to assist the development team during the design of a database. Process modeling is important for database design in that you can use process models to check the completeness and accuracy of entities that have been defined.

A matrix diagram or report (check the availability of this report with the automated design tool your using) can be used to crosscheck data usages and relationships between elements in the repository for your application. Data usage tells you how certain data is accessed and utilized by an application. Some processes may utilize a lot of data, whereas others do not access data at all. All processes should be modeled, but only those process that have a need to access data will be used to design the application. All processes help determine the completeness of the ERD. The completeness of the ERD must be carefully checked before the design effort progresses to the physical design of the database.

Some recommended reports that may be generated after business processes and entities have been modeled include those listing the following items:

- Entities and their attributes
- Entity definitions
- Attribute definitions
- Domain definitions
- Attributes in domains
- Function (process) to entity matrix (intersection)
- Function (process) to attribute matrix (intersection)
- Function hierarchies
- Data flows without attributes or entities

Figure 10.8 illustrates a sample matrix diagram from Oracle's Designer, depicting business functions on the side axis and entities on the top axis. After glancing at this diagram for a second, you should have gathered that the definitions of these processes and entities are incomplete.

Business Functions	ORDERS	RETURNS	VENDORS	INVENTORY
PROCESS	CR			RU
ORDER RECEIVED				
ORDERS				
ORD FORM FILLED				
ORDER FORMS				
ORDER FORMS				
DATA ENTRY	CR			RU
ORDER				
VENDOR				
DE NOTIFIES MR				
PROCESS				
RET PROD REC				
VEND NOT IF				
VEND REPLACES				

FIGURE 10.8

Matrix diagram of processes and entities.

> **NOTE**
>
> Remember about this about CRUD:
>
> - C stands for Create
> - R stands for Retrieve
> - U stands for Update
> - D stands for Delete

You can use this diagram in two ways, both of which complement one another:

- Read processes first
- Read entities first

You can begin with a process and read across through all entity intersections with that process. For example, the PROCESS (process order) function currently accesses the ORDERS and INVENTORY entities. When an order is processed, orders may be retrieved and new orders may be created. Also, the inventory of a product ordered may be retrieved and updated, reflecting a deduction in the quantity ordered. The PROCESS function does not utilize the RETURNS and VENDORS entities.

You can also start with an entity and read down through all process intersections with the entity. For example, INVENTORY is accessed by the PROCESS function (data can be retrieved and updated). INVENTORY is not accessed by ORDER RECEIVED (although after all definitions are complete, ORDER RECEIVED may access this or another entity). The main point is to ensure that each entity is utilized by at least one process and that each process utilizes at least one entity. The lack of at least one intersection between entities and processes is a good indication that all entity and attribute definitions are not complete.

Process Models for the Sample Company TrainTech

As you recall, TrainTech is a growing computer training company. TrainTech has a need to track classes that are scheduled and taught, instructors that teach, students that register for classes, and, of course, accounting. Table 10.2 is a decomposition of the processes performed by employees of TrainTech.

TABLE 10.2 Sample Decomposition of TrainTech Processes

1.	Class registration	1.0
	Telephone registration	1.1
	Receive call	1.1.1
	Verify space availability	1.1.2
	Obtain personal info	1.1.3
	Obtain payment info	1.1.4
	Reserve class seat	1.1.5
	Issue confirmation	1.1.6
	Internet registration	1.2
	Receive email form	1.2.1
	Verify space availability	1.2.2
	Verify personal info	1.3.3
	Verify payment info	1.3.4
	Reserve class seat	1.3.5
	Issue confirmation	1.3.6
	Class cancellation	1.3
	Phone notification	1.3.1
	Verify phone number	1.3.1.1
	Call student	1.3.1.2
	Email notification	1.3.2
	Verify email	1.3.2.1
	Notify student	1.3.2.2
2.	Accounting	2.0
	Accounts payable	2.1
	Receive invoice	2.1.1
	Verify receipt of product	2.1.2
	Send payment	2.1.3
	Print check	2.1.3.1
	Prepare envelope	2.1.3.2
	Mail envelope	2.1.3.3
	Accounts receivable	2.2
	Invoice customer	2.2.1
	Print invoice	2.2.1.1

	Prepare envelope	2.2.1.2
	Mail invoice	2.2.1.3
	Process payment	2.2.2
	Receive payment	2.2.2.1
	Deposit payment	2.2.2.2
	Payroll	2.3
	Figure payroll	2.3.1
	Distribute payroll	2.3.2
	Print check	2.3.2.1
	Prepare envelope	2.3.2.2
	Mail envelope	2.3.2.3
3.	Class management	3.0
	Instructor management	3.1
	Hire instructor	3.1.1
	Fire instructor	3.1.2
	Update instructor info	3.1.3
	Course management	3.2
	Add class	3.2.1
	Requisition	3.2.1.1
	Approval	3.2.1.2
	Develop class	3.2.1.3
	Remove a class	3.2.2
	Requisition	3.2.2.1
	Approval	3.2.2.2
	Update class info	3.2.3
	Update materials	3.2.4
	Update prerequisites	3.2.5
	Class scheduling	3.3
	Check lab availability	3.3.1
	Verify instructor	3.3.2
	Verify location	3.3.3
	Schedule class	3.3.4
	Order materials	3.3.5

10

MODELING
BUSINESS
PROCESSES

Figure 10.9 illustrates the organizational units and the main processes involved, as show in the previous table. One process is handled by CUST SVC, and the other two processes are handled by OPERATIONS. Figure 10.10 shows a breakdown of the class registration process.

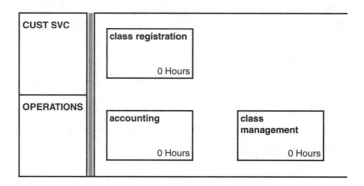

FIGURE 10.9

TrainTech's basic process model.

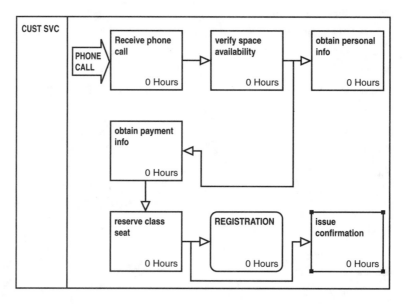

FIGURE 10.10

Decomposition of the class-registration process.

Figure 10.11 illustrates TrainTech's processes (functions) in a hierarchical format. Although not all processes have been modeled at this point, you can see how the hierarchy is beginning to form based on the original process model. The process model was used as a basic starting point.

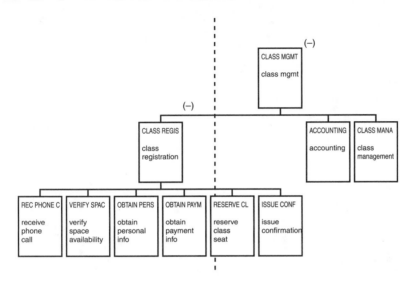

FIGURE 10.11

TrainTech's function hierarchy diagram.

Finally, the data flow diagram in Figure 10.12 is derived, once again, from the basic process model. Again, the class-registration process was selected. Notice the process steps that have been annotated in the rounded boxes. They should match the process steps that were defined in the previous table.

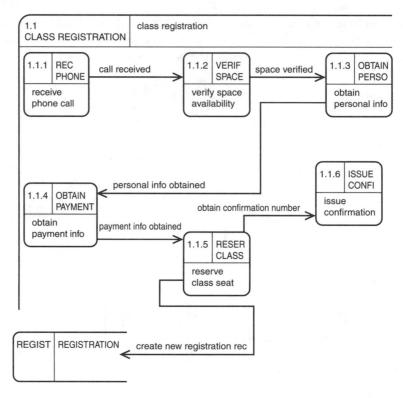

FIGURE 10.12

TrainTech's data flow diagram.

Summary

You might be able to design a database without producing process models, but you can't design a database without considering the business processes that take place. A database exists for the end user. The end user has a job to perform that, with or without the use of an automated database system, always requires at least one process. The database must be designed to fit the mold of the requirements implied by these processes. Therefore, business processes drive the need for a database.

Whether using an AD tool or not, the development team should create process models to ease its efforts in understanding how the data fits together with the processes. The three basic models used to visually represent business processes are the process model, the function hierarchy diagram, and the data flow diagram. The process model shows processes (starting with a root process), organizational units that perform processes, flows between processes, and data stores.

Data stores refer to entities that have been defined. The functional hierarchy diagram shows all processes, also called *functions*, that have been defined in a hierarchical format so that it is easy to determine the relationship between processes. The data flow diagram also shows processes, their flows, and their associated data stores. The DFD is used primarily to show how data flows within an organization. Data usages can be defined that determine how processes may access entities and attributes (data).

With a clear understanding of the processes that comprise an organization, the development team will feel comfortable that the end product (the database) is as complete and accurate as possible.

Designing the Database

PART

III

IN THIS PART

Chapter 11, "Designing Tables," begins discussing the physical design of a relational database. In this chapter, entities are converted into tables. Attributes are converted into columns, and they are assigned data types and primary key constraints.

Chapter 12, "Integrating Business Rules and Data Integrity," takes physical table design to another step. Now, constraints are applied to table columns to enforce business rules that were defined when gathering the business requirements. Some of the constraints discussed in this chapter include primary key, foreign key, unique, and check constraints.

Chapter 13, "Designing Views," discusses the definition of views, which provide users with perspectives of the data different from what is shown in the tables that have been defined. Views have many uses, and should be considered during design, although they can be created throughout the life of a database to satisfy the enduser's needs.

Chapter 14, "Applying Database Design Concepts," provides a case study of a company needing a database. The owner of a grocery store supplies information that will be used to design a database to automate the management of the growing data. This case study covers the database design process up to this point in the book.

Designing Tables

IN THIS CHAPTER

Tables are the fundamental logical building blocks of relational databases. A table is a grouping of columns of data that pertains to a single particular class of people, things, events, or ideas in an enterprise about which information needs to be stored or calculations made. As an example, the phone book is a table containing data about phone numbers and about people or businesses who have phones. The phone book table's columns would represent peoples' and business' names, addresses, and phone numbers. The phone number and other columns of information pertaining to a specific phone is a row in the table. There are other terms that are used to describe columns, rows, and tables, depending on which relational database system (RDBMS) you're using. Columns can also be referred to as *fields* or *attributes*, and rows can be called *records* or *tuples*. A table itself can also be called a *relation*.

In database design, tables are derived from entities that were defined during logical modeling. Likewise, columns are derived from these entities' attributes. So, you can see the importance of the care taken during information gathering and logical design. This chapter begins by discussing the different types of tables found in a relational database and then progresses through the considerations made when designing tables. Table design is the first part of physical design, and it's one huge step taken toward the finished product. When physical design begins, it is assumed that the business has been successfully modeled and is ready to be converted into a database.

Types of Tables

As stated, the table is the primary unit of storage in any relational database. Although a relational database might be comprised of various other objects, design always begins with the table and branches out from there. Entities become tables and are often referred to tables, even during logical design, because you cannot hide the fact that an entity really is a table, but in a physical form. Whereas entities represent data, tables actually store data. An end user will never access an entity for data but instead will access a table. Entities are related to one another, but tables are joined together so that related data can be merged. Table joins are made possible through the relationships defined during entity relationship modeling.

There are different types of tables in a relational database, each of which has its own part in the representation of an organization's data. The different types of tables are based on the defined entities and the kinds of relationships that exist among them.

Here are the four types of tables discussed in the following subsections:

- Data tables
- Join tables
- Subset tables
- Validation tables

Data Tables

A *data table* contains rows of information about a person, place, event, or thing of importance to an enterprise. This is by far the most common type of table. The other classes of tables described later are data tables as well. The following table types are placed into additional classes due to some database function they meet in addition to holding data.

A data table represents a single class of things of significance in the database. A data table has a primary key column or combination of columns (a composite key) that uniquely identifies each instance of the class. All other table columns are dependent on that primary key and only on that primary key.

A data table should have no columns that consist of data derived from calculations or concatenations on other data columns.

Good candidates for data tables include the following:

- INSTRUCTORS
- CUSTOMERS
- STUDENTS
- COURSES
- MATERIALS
- EMPLOYEES
- PRODUCTS

A data table has no repeating columns. An example of a repeating column in the following table would be if an instructor is an independent contractor who works for several companies, and the table contains a column for each company for which the instructor works:

INSTRUCTORS
INSTRUCTOR_ID
INSTRUCTOR_LNAME
INSTRUCTOR_FNAME
INSTRUCTOR_SSN
INSTRUCTOR_CATEGORY
EMPLOYER1
POSITION1
EMPLOYER2
POSITION2
EMPLOYER3

INSTRUCTORS

POSITION3
EMPLOYER4
POSITION4

This could be corrected by establishing a new table where there is no repeating column but instead a new row for every position. This concept was covered during the discussion of normalization in Chapter 8, "Normalization: Eliminating Redundant Data." The following tables illustrate how the previous table can be normalized to eliminate repeating columns.

INSTRUCTORS	*INSTRUCTOR_POSITIONS*
INSTRUCTOR_ID	INSTRUCTOR_ID
INSTRUCTOR_LNAME	EMPLOYER
INSTRUCTOR_FNAME	POSITION
INSTRUCTOR_SSN	
INSTRUCTOR_CATEGORY	

Join Tables

A *join table*, also known as an *intersection table* or *linking table*, is used to resolve a relationship between two other tables that would otherwise have a single many-to-many relationship into two one-to-many relationships. Because many-to-many relationships are initially pretty common in the logical design and must be resolved prior to creating tables, most databases will have some join tables.

For example, an instructor will teach many courses during his or her career, and a course will be taught by potentially many instructors. A direct link between an INSTRUCTORS table and a COURSES table will be a many-to-many relationship, and there will be no easy way to directly identify every time an instructor has taught a class. Here's an example:

INSTRUCTORS	*COURSES*
INSTRUCTOR_ID	COURSE_ID
INSTRUCTOR_LNAME	COURSE_NAME
INSTRUCTOR_FNAME	DPT_ID
INSTRUCTOR_SSN	

The following statements are true about these tables:

- Instructors will teach one or more courses.
- Courses will be taught by one or more instructors.

A COURSE_SCHEDULE intersection (join table) can be placed between COURSES and INSTRUCTORS, with the primary keys from the COURSES and INSTRUCTORS tables in it as foreign keys. You can then add columns to the intersection table so that each row in the join table will support a unique connection between the two tables with the many-to-many relationship. In the following example, you need COURSE_ID, SECTION, SEMESTER, and ACADEMIC YEAR columns to uniquely identify a particular presentation of a course. These columns comprise a composite primary key for COURSE_SCHEDULE.

INSTRUCTORS	*COURSE_SCHEDULE*	*COURSES*
INSTRUCTOR_ID	COURSE_ID	COURSE_ID
INSTRUCTOR_LNAME	INSTRUCTOR_ID	COURSE_NAME
INSTRUCTOR_FNAME	SEMESTER	DPT_ID
INSTRUCTOR_SSN	SECTION	
	ACADEMIC_YEAR	

You now can make two one-to-many relationships based on the COURSE_SCHEDULE join table—one from INSTRUCTORS to COURSE_SCHEDULE, and one from COURSES to COURSE_SCHEDULE.

The following statements are now true about the previous tables:

- A course section during a particular semester and academic year will be taught by one and only one instructor.

- A course section during a particular semester and academic year will be a presentation of one and only one course (a course may be taught during many semesters).

Take a look at the next example. Here are two tables, CARS and PARTS, that would otherwise generate a many-to-many relationship if it were not for the intersection table CAR_PARTS. Each car consists of many parts, but like parts may be used for many different models.

CARS	*CAR_PARTS*	*PARTS*
MODEL_NO	MODEL_NO	PART_NO
BRAND	PART_NO	NAME
MAKE	QTY_REQ	DESCRIPTION
STYLE		
YEAR		
DESCRIPTION		

Subset Tables

In some cases, a general-purpose table will have columns that do not apply to some sub-classes or subsets of all the instances of the table. In the following example, instructors in INSTRUCTOR_CATEGORY classified as "adjunct" or "associate" would be primarily employed elsewhere than the college. This information would need to be captured for them, but the columns involved would be null for all the full-time instructors.

INSTRUCTORS
INSTRUCTOR_ID
INSTRUCTOR_LNAME
INSTRUCTOR_FNAME
INSTRUCTOR_SSN
INSTRUCTOR_CATEGORY
PRIMARY_EMPLOYER
PRIMARY_POSITION

By creating a new subset table called ADJUNCT_EMPLOYMENT, which can be joined to INSTRUCTORS by INSTRUCTOR_ID, you can avoid all those null columns. The common columns for all instructors, whether a university employee or adjunct instructor, remain in INSTRUCTORS. Only those unique to the subset and the linking primary/foreign key relationship column used with the join are moved to the subset column, as shown here:

INSTRUCTORS	*ADJUNCT_EMPLOYMENT*
INSTRUCTOR_ID	INSTRUCTOR_ID
INSTRUCTOR_LNAME	PRIMARY_EMPLOYER
INSTRUCTOR_FNAME	PRIMARY_POSITION
INSTRUCTOR_SSN	
INSTRUCTOR_CATEGORY	

Validation Tables

A *validation table* or *lookup table* contains a list of acceptable values for the columns of some other table or tables. It is used to support data integrity or business rules by providing a list of acceptable values to the user or to check input against the validation table to ensure the input is in the range of acceptable values. Validation tables are often called *code tables* as well.

Good candidates for validation tables include the following:

- DEPARTMENTS
- POSITIONS

- STATE_CODES
- MARITAL_STATUS

For example, data in the STATE_CODES table might appear as follows:

STATE_CODES

STATE	STATE_DESCRIPTION
AL	ALABAMA
AS	ALASKA
AZ	ARIZONA
AR	ARKANSAS
CA	CALIFORNIA
CO	COLORADO

The application may query the STATE_CODES table in order to validate a state that is input by the user. Additionally, the STATE_CODES table may be joined to the EMPLOYEES table, for example, by the STATE column. Note the structure of the following table:

EMPLOYEES

EMP_ID
LNAME
FNAME
MNAME
ADDRESS
CITY
STATE
ZIP

The full state name need not be spelled out for each employee in the EMPLOYEES table. Only the two-character code for the state should stored with employee records, which may be used to reference the full state name in the STATE_CODES table. For instance, it may be desirable to print the full state name on a report, but it is needless to redundantly store the full state name in the database. Again, recall the discussion of normalization in Chapter 8.

Basic Table Structure

The basic structure of a table is quite simple. A table consists of columns and rows, as defined early in this book. A table column is derived from the entity attributes defined during the logical design of the entity that was the table's precursor. Each table column is a description, qualification, or quantification of some feature of an instance of the entity the table represents. The column is the smallest division of meaningful data in the database.

Ideally the following statements would describe columns, although there may be some changes that arise due to denormalization (denormalization will be discussed a bit later):

- Columns contain a single data value.
- Columns have the same data type and maximum size for each row in the table.
- Columns are already broken down into their smallest logical components (for example, first_name, last_name, middle_name).
- Columns are not duplicated in more than one table. There is no redundant data other than foreign key columns.
- Columns do not contain data that is the result of calculations or concatenations from other data columns.

A row is a primary key value and columnar data associated with a particular instance of a table. Rows are created for each instance of the class represented by the table. In other words, when an employee is hired into a company, a row of data (record) is created for the new employee in the EMPLOYEES table. Figure 11.1 illustrates the basic structure of a table in a relational database. This is how an end user visualizes a table.

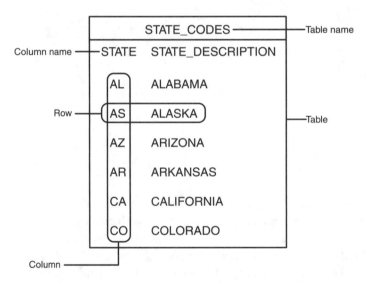

FIGURE 11.1
Basic relational table structure.

The STATE_CODES table shown in Figure 11.1 is both a data table and a validation table. It is a data table in the sense that it stores information for all states. It is a validation table because it is used to validate values entered into other tables. The validation occurs through a foreign key constraint that is set up in another table that references the STATE_CODES table. Foreign keys are discussed in more detail in the following chapter.

Defining Your Tables

Figure 11.2 illustrates a simple ERD with five related entities. These entities will become different types of tables, two of which (EMPLOYEE and STATE_CODE) were discussed previously in this chapter. The main table in this figure will be EMPLOYEE.

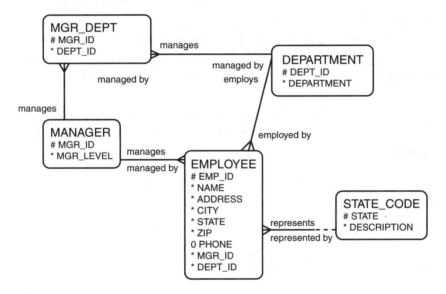

FIGURE 11.2

A simple ERD depicting various entity types.

The following statements are true about the entities shown in Figure 11.2:

- Each employee must have a manager.
- Each manager must manage one or more employees.
- Each employee state code must represent a state.
- Each state description may be represented by one or more employee state code.
- Each employee is employed by a department.
- Each department employs one or more employees.
- Each manager must manage one or more departments.
- Each department must be managed by one or more managers.

The following table lists the entities, the prospective tables, and the table types:

ENTITY	TABLE	TABLE TYPE(S)
EMPLOYEE	EMPLOYEES	Data
MANAGER	MANAGERS	Data, subset
STATE_CODE	STATE_CODES	Data, validation
MGR_DEPT	MGR_DEPT	Data, join
DEPARTMENT	DEPARTMENTS	Data, validation

These tables are about employees. An employee may also be a manager. Managers may manage at different levels, such as the department level, multidepartment level, and organizational level. Therefore, a manager may be in charge of multiple departments (a department may have multiple tiers of management), thus justifying the need for the join table between MANAGERS and DEPARTMENTS.

The following CREATE TABLE statements can be used to define the tables in the selected relational database management system (RDBMS). Compare the following CREATE TABLE statements to Figure 11.2.

```
CREATE TABLE MANAGERS
(MGR_ID          VARCHAR(9)    NOT NULL,
MGR_LEVEL        VARCHAR(1)    NOT NULL);

CREATE TABLE MGR_DEPTS
(MGR_ID          VARCHAR(9)    NOT NULL,
DEPT_ID          VARCHAR(2)    NOT NULL,
MGR_MGR_ID       VARCHAR(9)    NOT NULL,
DEPT_DEPT_ID     VARCHAR(2)    NOT NULL);

CREATE TABLE DEPARTMENTS
(DEPT_ID         VARCHAR(2)    NOT NULL,
DEPARTMENT       VARCHAR(30)   NOT NULL);

CREATE TABLE EMPLOYEES
(EMP_ID          VARCHAR(9)    NOT NULL,
LNAME            VARCHAR(30)   NOT NULL,
FNAME            VARCHAR(30)   NOT NULL,
MNAME            VARCHAR(30)   NOT NULL,
ADDRESS          VARCHAR(30)   NOT NULL,
CITY             VARCHAR(30)   NOT NULL,
STATE            VARCHAR(2)    NOT NULL,
ZIP              VARCHAR(5)    NOT NULL,
PHONE            VARCHAR(10),
MGR_ID           VARCHAR(9)    NOT NULL,
DEPT_ID          VARCHAR(2)    NOT NULL,
MGR_MGR_ID       VARCHAR(9)    NOT NULL,
ST_CODE_STATE    VARCHAR(2)    NOT NULL);
```

> **NOTE**
>
> Notice in the CREATE TABLE statement for EMPLOYEES that NAME was broken up into three separate columns: LNAME, FNAME, and MNAME. This is a good example of how tables are refined during physical design.

```
CREATE TABLE STATE_CODES
(STATE VARCHAR(2)     NOT NULL,
DESCRIPTION     VARCHAR(30)     NOT NULL);
```

These CREATE TABLE statements could have been typed manually based on information in the ERD, or they could have been generated automatically by using an automated design (AD) tool. In Oracle's Designer, a Server Model Diagram can be generated that looks very similar to the ERD. The Server Model Diagram shows tables, columns, and relationships. From the Server Model Diagram, columns can be added and removed, constraints can be added and removed, data types can be defined, and so forth. Each AD tool will be different but should include features to automate the conversion of entities into tables as well as ease the overall tasks of physical design.

The following subsections discuss considerations for designing tables, whether you're performing the physical design manually or with an AD tool. Later, this chapter discusses attribute-to-column transformation and considerations for specifying a field list for a table.

Reviewing Naming Conventions

The precursors for table-naming conventions should already have been established in entity-naming conventions. These naming conventions should be adhered to and carried out throughout the database-design process. Naming conventions help promote consistency for table and column names, thus decreasing the chance of confusion among developers. With consistency comes an increased chance for greater accuracy and overall understanding of the tables defined.

If you are a medium-to-large enterprise, establishing a two-or-three-character initial identifier for the objects created by each of the various development teams may prove useful. This identifier may be used to represent the various enterprise departments involved and will keep the departments from stepping on each other's toes with their table names, thus simplifying central DBA management by letting the overall system DBA know who to call when there's a problem with a particular table. This identifier also eliminates the possibility of conflicting (nonunique) table names if multiple departments or applications share the same database environment.

For example, a Human Resources application may have table names with the following prefixes:

> HR_EMPLOYEES
>
> HR_EMP_PAY
>
> HR_BENEFITS
>
> HR_401K

A product-order application may be associated with tables with names as follows:

> ORD_EMPLOYEES
>
> ORD_CUSTOMERS
>
> ORD_PRODUCTS

Notice that it is now clear to which application each of these tables belongs. Also notice that the two EMPLOYEES tables have unique names because prefixes are used to distinguish them (HR and ORD).

NOTE

Table names should be in clear language with no acronyms and minimal abbreviations included. Underscores are often useful for separating words in the name, such as with INVOICE_RECEIVING_REPORTS.

Common naming conventions for tables include the following:

- Table names should be unique within your enterprise.
- Table names should be as descriptive, yet as concise, as possible.
- Leave the word *table* or *file* or any other generic term stating that this is a table out of the name.
- Establish a standard maximum table name length a few characters less than the technical name length imposed by the RDBMS. This will provide some flexibility in table naming as the system evolves.
- Don't create tables with limiting names—for example, CENTRAL_REGION_INVOICES. An INVOICES table with a REGION column will let you put all invoices in a single table.
- Table names should be plural.

Establishing a Table List

Common sense tells us that a table list originates from the logical model, or *ERD*. This ERD, as you recall, originates from information gathered during interviews about the data associated with an organization. Remember that entities are logical, whereas tables are physical or physically contain data. An automated design (AD) tool may be used to generate this table list. This generation is called a *conversion*, or *transformation*, from the logical model to the physical model. When you're using an AD tool to establish a table list, the attributes are also converted into columns (list of fields).

Once a table list has been established, it may be necessary to add or remove tables to complete the database definition for the organization. Tables may be added and removed due to new-found needs or tables that are not really needed. Tables may be added and removed due to further normalization or denormalization of the existing database structure. Normalization occurs during logical modeling, but remember that structures can always be refined at this point. Denormalization normally occurs during physical modeling, or sometimes after the database has been implemented. Denormalization also commonly occurs when extracting and recombining data from tables to be used for reporting in a decision support database.

Determining Column Specifications

During the process of creating entities, you assigned attributes to the entities. Attributes are characteristics of an entity that quantify, describe, or qualify the entity. Entity attributes become table columns, more commonly referred to as *fields* by end users and application developers. Referential integrity is used to enforce data integrity on tables. With columns or fields, data integrity can be enforced by the use of field-specification constraints.

Most specifications of columns occur during logical modeling in the ERD, as attributes are defined for entities. In the ERD, primary keys are identified as well as required and optional attributes. A required attribute represents a column that must have an associated data value for every occurrence of data (row) in the table.

Relationships are also modeled in the ERD, which are converted in foreign keys during table design. If great care has been taken during the creation of the ERD, most of the work required to convert entities to tables will have been accomplished. However, it is still necessary to review the logical model during physical design and go through the motions for defining tables and columns to ensure greatest accuracy for the finished product.

> **NOTE**
>
> Naming conventions are established early in the game and must be followed through-out database design. It is sometimes too easy as you near the end to become relaxed and compromise standards that were set early in order to complete the job on time.

Here are the levels of column specifications discussed in the following subsections:

- General level
- Physical level
- Logical level

General Level

The general level of column specification represents the need for a column name in association with the table to which it belongs. The name of the column should be unique within the database, unless the column has been propagated to other tables as a foreign key. Some columns, such as LNAME and FNAME, may be found in multiple tables but are qualified by the table to which they belong. It is most important—and required by the RDBMS—that a column name be unique within the scope of the table. If all column names are unique to their tables, all columns are unique in the database. This is true because all table names must be unique in the database, and a table is used to qualify a column. In other words, you must go through the table to get to a column in the table.

Columns are reference via SQL as follows:

```
TABLE_NAME.COLUMN_NAME
```

or

```
EMPLOYEES.LNAME
```

All the following column names are technically unique:

```
EMPLOYEES.LNAME
```

```
EMPLOYEES.FNAME
```

```
CUSTOMERS.LNAME
```

```
CUSTOMERS.FNAME
```

Physical Level

The physical level of column specification refers to the data type of the column. The data type represents the acceptable character set and size for values associated with the column.

Here are the most basic standard data types for relational databases:

- Character values
- Numeric values
- Date and time values

Data types are specific to RDBMS software, but generally include most of the following:

- Fixed-length and variable-length character data
- Integer and floating-point numbers
- Date/time
- Long character data
- Long binary data, which stores documents, pictures, and sound
- Boolean (true or false)

Character sets indicate whether the column will support only English ASCII characters or provides support for multibyte characters, such as those in the Japanese alphabet. Size is how large the column can be. The definition of the size controls the precision (number of digits) and scale (digits to the right of the decimal point) of numbers. It controls the length of fixed-length character columns and the maximum length of variable-length character columns.

Table 11.1 shows sample columns, data types, precision and scale values, and sample data.

TABLE 11.1 Sample Columns and Data Types

Column	Data Type	Data (Example of Max Value)
LNAME	VARCHAR2(10)	RICHARDSON
ORD_DT	DATE	01-JAN-2000
SALARY	NUMBER(6)	999999
HOUR_RATE	NUMBER(4,2)	99.99

In this table, the precision (or the allowed size of a column) is specified in parentheses after the data type name. The last example in the table includes two numeric values in parentheses, separated by commas. These values represent the precision and scale.

Logical Level

Logical specification indicates whether the field has a role as a primary or foreign key. It states whether values in the field must be unique and whether the field can be null. Logical specification also establishes any default values and any range of acceptable values or a domain for the field.

Care should be taken here. A value of NULL in a column indicates that the column is unknown or empty. A column with a NOT NULL constraint is a required column. If a value is required here for processing, the column must be NOT NULL. Primary key columns, for instance, are NOT NULL by default. On the other hand, if a column is not required and you define it as NOT NULL, your users will have to put a value into that column in order to add a row, whether or not they have a valid value for the column. If they don't have a value, they'll make one up, thus wasting their time putting inputting fake data as well as the DBA's time in trying to correct the resulting junk data.

> **NOTE**
>
> Only define a column as being NOT NULL if it is absolutely required; although you will find that most columns will probably be defined as NOT NULL in a normalized database. Unnecessarily defining columns as NOT NULL will result in junk data, wasted space, and confusion.

If you provide a list of accepted values, either as a check on or aid to data entry, be sure you have all the potential values on the list. Again, users being users, if they can't pick the right value, they'll pick the closest one they can and move on. A list of acceptable values is either controlled using a check constraint or by referencing a validation table using a foreign key constraint. Also, a default value can be used. A default value is automatically input into a column if no value is specified. For example, in a multinational company that does the vast majority of its business in the United States, a default value of United States might be appropriate.

> **NOTE**
>
> The integration of constraints during table design is discussed in detail in the following chapter.

Establishing a Column List

As the table list is derived from the entity list, the field list for each table is derived from the attributes listed for the associated entity. Again, most of this work should be done during logical modeling, but it should be refined and finalized during physical design.

As discussed, when listing and defining columns, you must establish the following information:

- Name of the column
- Data type
- Nullability
- Key values
- Applicable constraints
- Allowed data values
- Allowed duplicate values

The following subsections define column specifications for the EMPLOYEES table (refer to the EMPLOYEE entity in Figure 11.2). The EMPLOYEE entity in the figure lists the following attributes:

```
EMP_ID
NAME
ADDRESS
CITY
STATE
ZIP
PHONE
MGR_ID
DEPT_ID
```

Column Names

As explained, column names should be descriptive, concise, and represent the lowest level of data associated with an instance in the entity or table.

The column names are based on the attribute names but are refined as necessary during table design. For example, study the following refined column list:

```
EMP_ID
L_NAME
F_NAME
M_INIT
```

ST_NUM

STREET

APT

PO_BOX

CITY

ST

ZIP

AREA_CD

PHONE

MGR_ID

DEPT_ID

The name has been broken out into its smallest components (last, first, and middle), the address has been broken down (street number, street, apartment, and P.O. box), and the area code has been separated from the phone number. Notice that all columns are no longer than they really need to be, yet it is still easy to figure out how columns are associated with the data.

Data Types

Given the previous column list, data types should be established, as follows:

Column Name	Data Type
EMP_ID	NUMBER(5)
L_NAME	VARCHAR2(20)
F_NAME	VARCHAR2(20)
M_INIT	VARCHAR2(1)
ST_NUM	VARCHAR2(10)
STREET	VARCHAR2(20)
APT	VARCHAR2(5)
PO_BOX	VARCHAR2(10)
CITY	VARCHAR2(30)
ST	VARCHAR2(2)
ZIP	VARCHAR2(5)
AREA_CD	VARCHAR2(3)
PHONE	VARCHAR2(7)
MGR_ID	NUMBER(5)
DEPT_ID	NUMBER(2)

A few things might surprise you about the data types selected for the columns in this list. For instance, why are columns such as AREA_CD, PHONE, and ZIP not assigned numeric data types? Although these columns will always contain numeric values, they are never treated as numbers, which means they are not used in calculations or summaries. The EMP_ID column is defined as numeric because a value will be generated by the database for the column for each row of data.

NULL Values

Now, it's time to determine where NULL values are allowed. The keyword NULL indicates that a column is optional or may contain NULL values. The NOT NULL keyword indicates that data is required for the column for all rows of data, meaning that NULL values are not allowed.

Column Name	Data Type	Nullability
EMP_ID	NUMBER(5)	NOT NULL
L_NAME	VARCHAR2(20)	NOT NULL
F_NAME	VARCHAR2(20)	NOT NULL
M_INIT	VARCHAR2(1)	NULL
ST_NUM	VARCHAR2(10)	NULL
STREET	VARCHAR2(20)	NULL
APT	VARCHAR2(5)	NULL
PO_BOX	VARCHAR2(10)	NULL
CITY	VARCHAR2(30)	NOT NULL
ST	VARCHAR2(2)	NOT NULL
ZIP	VARCHAR2(5)	NOT NULL
AREA_CD	VARCHAR2(3)	NOT NULL
PHONE	VARCHAR2(7)	NOT NULL
MGR_ID	NUMBER(5)	NULL
DEPT_ID	NUMBER(2)	NOT NULL

The way this table is designed so far, address-related columns must be defined as NULL (optional) because an employee may use a P.O. box instead of a home address. It is possible that any or all address-related columns will be used for a particular individual. MGR_ID is defined as NULL because all employees will not have a manager (that is, if the highest-level manager is considered).

Key Values

Key values must now be determined or verified if already determined by the ERD. Key values are related to primary keys, foreign keys, and unique keys. In the following example, notice that an SSN column has been added. Because all social security numbers must be unique, a unique key for the SSN column has been designated to eliminate the chance for duplicate values.

Column Name	Data Type	Nullability	Keys
EMP_ID	NUMBER(5)	NOT NULL	PRIMARY
SSN	VARCHAR2(9)	NOT NULL	UNIQUE
L_NAME	VARCHAR2(20)	NOT NULL	
F_NAME	VARCHAR2(20)	NOT NULL	
M_INIT	VARCHAR2(1)	NULL	
ST_NUM	VARCHAR2(10)	NULL	
STREET	VARCHAR2(20)	NULL	
APT	VARCHAR2(5)	NULL	
PO_BOX	VARCHAR2(10)	NULL	
CITY	VARCHAR2(30)	NOT NULL	
ST	VARCHAR2(2)	NOT NULL	
ZIP	VARCHAR2(5)	NOT NULL	
AREA_CD	VARCHAR2(3)	NOT NULL	
PHONE	VARCHAR2(7)	NOT NULL	
MGR_ID	NUMBER(5)	NULL	FOREIGN
DEPT_ID	NUMBER(2)	NOT NULL	FOREIGN

Key values can be either natural or artificial when referring to primary keys. A *natural value* refers to a value that is actually part of the organization's data set. For instance, if you were to use SSN as the primary key for this table, you would have a natural key because each SSN is actually data. However, in this case an artificial key called EMP_ID is used. EMP_ID does not represent any important data; it is only a numeric value that is generated by the system to uniquely identify every row of data in the table.

NOTE

The allowance of duplicate values is handled primarily by primary key constraints and unique constraints.

Column Constraints

In addition to primary key, foreign key, and unique constraints, other constraints may be created in order to control the integrity of the data stored in the tables. Check constraints can be placed on columns to identify a static list of valid values for column data. Constraints can also be placed at the application level as a checks-and-balances system for enforcing data integrity at the database level.

Table Design Considerations

The vast majority of the work in identifying and defining database tables is done during logical modeling and design of the entities from which physical table structures are derived. During logical design, you identify and capture in a logical model the entities (things of significance) in the real-world system you need to model through your database and the applications that utilize it. Examples of entities would be students, customers, employees, products, and orders. Much of logical database design revolves around identifying the entities in the system and then identifying the descriptive facts about these entities that will be included as attributes. Attributes of a student entity might be last name, first name, middle initial, address, date of birth, social security number, and so on. During logical design of relational databases, many of the initial entities identified in the data model will be further broken up into two or more additional entities, each with fewer attributes, by iteratively applying a set of logical rules to the entities in a process called *normalization*.

Logical entities from the logical design phase are transformed into tables. The biggest difference between entities and tables is that entities are logical structures only. They represent a class of items the database must logically model but do not contain any specific examples or instances of that class. Entities have no data rows. Tables are still logical structures, but they contain many rows of data and are tied closely to the physical files utilized by the RDBMS to actually store the data on the database's host computer. Data for a particular table will be stored in a particular physical data file or combination of physical data files that the table is associated with in a manner dependent on the particular RDBMS being used.

NOTE

The biggest difference between entities and tables is that entities are logical structures only, representing data. Tables contain data, although they are still technically logical structures because they are used to organize and represent the physical placement of data on a disk drive.

Some entities will come through the transformation design process to tables relatively unchanged. In such cases, the structure of the table and its columns will look almost exactly like the logical entity and its attributes from which the table is derived. The notable addition to even those tables that are relatively unchanged will likely be the inclusion of foreign key columns in the table needed as part of the underpinnings for referential integrity constraints within the database.

The following subsections discuss these table design considerations:

- Referential integrity
- The importance of the logical model in table design
- Denormalization during design

Referential Integrity in Table Design

Referential integrity is the glue that binds the tables of a database together. One of the columns of a table or a combination of table columns in a row will make up a unique identifier or primary key for each and every row in the table. In addition, the primary key column (or columns) or other non-key columns from the parent table (the "one" side in a one-to-many relationship or one of the "one" sides in the occasional one-to-one relationship) is propagated to the structure of the child table as a foreign key column, and joins between the two tables are generally done based on equality of the parent and child key relationship columns. In addition to the foreign key relationship being the basis for joins, prior to adding a row to the child table, the RDBMS will check the parent table column that the foreign key column of the child table refers to in order to ensure that the parent table column has a row that includes the specific foreign key column value in the row you're trying to add in the new child table row. If the parent table doesn't have that exact value in the column that the child foreign key refers to, the proposed new row in the child table will be rejected.

An example of declarative referential integrity would be a products table with a primary key of product_id and an orders table where column product_id is a foreign key referring to the products table's product_id column. When you try to add a row to orders (the child in this relationship), the RDBMS will check to ensure that the product ID you are adding to the new orders row already exists in a row in the parent table's product_id column and rejects the new orders row if it doesn't. The effect of this foreign key relationship is that an order can't be placed for a product_id that doesn't exist in the products table.

In this example, RDBMS referential integrity constraints are used to enforce business rules. Such referential integrity constraints are proliferated throughout well-designed databases. Whether you're accessing the database using Access, a C program, or an application, referential integrity will, once created, always be there. Data-quality integrity constraints built into applications can be overcome by simply accessing the database other than through the application. Referential integrity constraints are a key part of data table design.

Importance of the Logical Model in Table Design

A table's logical structure (column names, column data types, and column sizes) is derived from the logical entity structures defined during logical database design as you build an entity relationship diagram (ERD). Logical design produces an unconstrained logical data model of an enterprise's data requirements. Table structures are those unconstrained entity structures transformed with the consideration of the physical database design, such as with the association between data storage and application performance. The ERD entities are transformed into the logical structure for the tables of a relational database. Entity attributes will become table columns. Entity unique identifiers will become table primary keys. Entity domains will become table data constraints. Entity relationships will become table primary and foreign key referential integrity constraints.

Logical database entity design is not constrained by concerns for physical performance. Its purpose is to correctly model the data structure requirements for the business processes the database must support and to do away with data redundancy and other data structure errors. Normalization does away with redundant data columns. A particular data column is stored in a single table to simplify updates and prevent errors when one table gets updated and the other doesn't. Derived data columns that are the result of calculations on other columns or concatenations of other columns are also not allowed in a normalized structure. The normalization process produces many tables with relatively few columns.

Tables are logical objects whose design takes into consideration the logical data model and the capabilities and limitations of the physical host machine. They are the embodiment of the logical entities created during logical design. Due to the close connection to the physical side of the database and the resulting performance concerns, tables in a mature database design will not be a direct translation of the logical entities defined during logical design. Tables must also be configured so that data and referential integrity are maintained and so that applications running against them perform fast enough to satisfy the users. The ties to the physical side of the database will cause many modifications to the logical structure of entities during the transformation to tables in order to gain acceptable or optimal performance for the applications that run against the database.

Denormalization During Physical Design

When performance is taken into consideration in table design, a process called *denormalization* may be applied. In denormalization during table design, you give up some of the advantages of third normal form in order to get better physical performance. The normalization of entities in the logical model to best design and capture a relational database's data requirements will be undone to the degree necessary to get adequate performance from the table structures. This process of undoing some entity normalization during table design is called *denormalization* and involves putting some entity structures that were taken apart by normalization back together again in tables, thus allowing some redundant data columns among tables and perhaps allowing some presummarized columns or data columns derived from existing data columns.

The rationale for denormalization is that there's a performance cost to joining two or more tables based on the equality of primary key or other parent and foreign key columns so you can put columns from each of these tables on a screen or report at the same time. It takes time to do the join. If that join time is too long for the users, the table structures can be changed to provide the data required without using the join. This could be accomplished by adding redundant columns in one of the tables with the required data or recombining tables that were broken up by normalization so that data is now in the same table and doesn't require a join. The cost of such denormalization is managing and ensuring the update and consistency of the redundant or derived data.

> **NOTE**
>
> Before you denormalize a database, check to ensure that the performance you perceive can be gained can't be obtained by some other method, such as indexing the tables, using views, or optimizing the use of hardware devices.

The following are questions that can be raised during physical design to help determine the necessity of denormalization:

- Did you design the database badly? Is the join you need between two tables going through four intermediate tables to get the connection? Perhaps an additional foreign key to create a direct connection between the two tables will solve the problem.

- Are the host hardware and OS set up optimally? (See the discussion of OS block size, later in this chapter.) Could you add RAM or processors to the host? Allocating RAM for database use is the single most common solution to any performance problem. Databases love RAM.

- Can you add more or faster processors to the host? Parallel processing with multiple host processors can greatly speed performance, as well.

- Is your database operating on a host that is already overworked by other applications? Could the database be moved elsewhere, where there is less contention for computer resources, such as CPU and RAM? If possible, it is best to place large databases on dedicated host machines.

- Is the RDBMS set up optimally? Is there additional host RAM that could be allocated to the database? Is the RDBMS block size large enough?

- Can the application be tuned? Are there indexes on the columns being used for the joins or searches? Is the RDBMS using them? Indexes greatly speed up join performance, especially if the query can be satisfied within the index itself without even going to the table.

- Is the network saturated or are there just too many router hops between the user and the host? You should either improve the network, move the database to a host nearer the user, or rewrite the application to a thinner client with more processing occurring on the server. Additionally, the application can be written such that the recordset is called from the database before the application screen is painted. This way, after the screen is painted, the data is there and ready for use (the perceived wait is less to the end user).

Denormalizing table structure changes with the costs inherent to them are made to get better performance by avoiding the time cost involved in joining the separate tables or performing calculations at application runtime. You denormalize only to the degree necessary to get required performance and only if there's no other solution to the performance problem. There are good reasons why third normal form is the normalization standard for production, relational, online-transactional-processing databases. It avoids inconsistent and redundant data. It avoids columns that are mostly nulls. Undoing some of the normalization process needs to be done only sparingly and on a case-by-case basis, driven by the need to meet performance requirements. If the need to stray from THIRD NORMAL FORM keeps surfacing within the needs of an organization, a separate decision support system (DSS) might be required. The DSS system should be nothing more than the aggregations, roll-ups, and denormalized tables required for a specific department in order to twist the data in different ways for analysis.

> **NOTE**
>
> The key point in table design is to stick as much as possible to the entity structures that come from the logical database design model while making table structure modifications necessary to take advantage of the capabilities of the physical host system or RDBMS or to avoid system or RDBMS weaknesses.

Storage Considerations

Part of table design is considering storage for tables. Storage primarily refers to the specific data that will be stored in a table. That's the first step. Once a table has been converted from an entity and then refined during table design, other storage considerations should be taken, such as the size of the data and the estimated growth of the data over certain periods of time.

Before the database is ever created, the block size must be determined. This does not affect the design process but should be in the back of the DBA's head. The block size, although it does not affect database design, will definitely affect the performance of the finished product. Operating systems and the RDBMS will have a block size. A *block* is the size in bytes of a single physical read or write operation. The block size is a key performance issue. A larger block size, at least to a point, is generally better than a smaller block size, because it is then implied that more data can be read and written at once. The block size for the host operating system is part of the initial set of an operating system disk. The RDBMS block size is part of the initial RDBMS install. Default block sizes tend to be relatively small, so research the block size for your host and RDBMS before you install your database software and create the database. Changing the block size usually requires reinstallation or re-creation of the database.

The following topics are discussed in more detail in the following subsections:

- Estimated growth and sizing of data
- Actual growth of data and continual monitoring
- The use of views versus replication
- How levels of RAID affect storage

Table Growth and Sizing

Because both the database and operating system read and write in blocks, a certain number of blocks (space) are allocated when a table is created. As mentioned, there is always a default block size, which is relatively small. When a table is created, it takes an initial extent, which consists of one or more database blocks. The initial extent is the initial space allocated for a table for physical disk pages, or operating system blocks. As a table grows (more rows are inserted into the table), more extents are taken (more physical disk space allocated), which causes the data to be physically spread across the disk drive. Data growth leads to fragmentation if it's not taken into consideration. This goes back to understanding the data that will be kept in each table. The sizing of all tables will be different based on the columns that are found in the tables and the average length of a row of data in the tables.

If a new database is being designed, it may be difficult to estimate the size of the data because it is unknown. If a legacy database is being redesigned, then data already exists. Therefore, the current size of data is known, making it much easier to estimate the growth of data based on past statistics. If the size of data is known, it is typically a good practice to size a table so that all data will fit into a single extent, thus eliminating fragmentation.

> **NOTE**
>
> Table sizing is a common shortcoming of most developers with which we have worked. The DBA usually inherits this responsibility. The key to table sizing is knowing the data. Unfortunately, there are a lot of unknown factors when designing a database, especially if there's no legacy data to use as a guide.

Actual Growth and Monitoring

The estimated size of data and its growth usually turns out to be quite different than actual size and growth for new systems. We have witnessed two extremes regularly when involved in the design and creation of a database. Either way too much space is allocated or not nearly enough space is allocated. Both cause problems but can usually be rectified without affecting the availability of the database or the integrity of the data.

Sometimes, developers tend to request much more space than is needed in attempt to "reserve" the space for their projects. For example, suppose 1GB of space was reserved for a database, but well after implementation, only one-tenth of that space was utilized. Unless sudden growth is expected in the near future, the amount of space originally requested may not be justified. On the other hand, developers and DBAs sometimes tend to ignore the importance of table sizing, which leads to small default sizes, a great deal of fragmentation, misuse of space, and poor database performance. It's a shame for a database that's well thought out and designed to be neglected in the area of sizing, which will offset the performance measures gained through a good design.

After the database has been built and made available in production, the usage and size of data should be monitored by the DBA and application administrator. The DBA is usually responsible for all databases, which house tables for all applications associated with an organization. An application administrator may be assigned to manage each application as far as data usage, data loads, application functionality, change requests, and even user management.

NOTE

Most DBAs find their time limited to monitor and performance tune the database in addition to their other responsibilities associated with managing an organization's data. Try to get the low hanging fruit first in a production environment, and then work on more difficult tuning issues as time permits. Even a small change can yield significant benefits. Also keep in mind that even if the database has been well planned and designed, the end environment for the database might differ from that which was originally planned. This shouldn't happen, but an organization's needs seem to change, even during the design process.

A common question dealing with the growth of data over time is this: How long should data be kept? It is sometimes unnecessary to keep gobs of data online that will probably never be used. Take historic data from three years back, for example. Data such as this may be accessed, say, once every few months to pull data for reports. To save online storage and improve overall database performance, historic data can be archived to tape or some alternative hardware device, and it can eventually be purged from the database. The question of "how long" can only be answered by the individuals who best understand the use of the data (usually the end users).

Views Versus Replication

Tables contain physical data and therefore require storage space in the database. Other objects, such as indexes and snapshots, also require storage. These objects are created to improve database performance. Indexes are created to speed up data lookup, and snapshots are created to replicate data. A *snapshot* is what it sounds like—a snapshot of how the data looks in one or more tables for a given point in time. Data is sometimes replicated to speed up a massive amount of queries against data.

Views can also be created to replicate data. Views can definitely improve the performance of the database, although sometimes not as well as snapshots. Views actually refer to one or more base tables, so the data associated with a view is also tied to one or more tables and therefore not separate. Data that is stored in snapshots is retrieved from one or more tables but is stored separate from tables, which may provide better performance benefits. One of the advantages that views have over snapshots is the fact that no additional storage is required for views.

Also, as stated earlier, a data table should have no columns that consist of data derived from calculations on or concatenations of other data columns. This is where views come into play. A view (virtual table) can be created that has virtual columns appearing to be summaries or calculations of other columns. Views have many more benefits. Defining views is a significant part of database design. Views are discussed in depth in the following chapter.

RAID

Most medium-to-large databases will use RAID (Redundant Arrays of Inexpensive Disks) for disk storage. RAID 0 is a file system with a single set of disks with the data striped across them. Striping can speed up disk I/O by allowing multiple disks and disk controllers to share the read/write work. RAID 0 has the potential I/O advantages of striping, good performance, and speed of access but no data redundancy. If a disk goes bad, there is no way to restore the data from the disk, and there will be data loss and downtime with any disk failure while a new disk is installed and the database is restored from tape.

RAID levels 1 to 5 provide data redundancy in case of disk failure. Data redundancy will keep the database from failing even if a disk fails by running off the good copy on a mirrored disk set or allowing rapid re-creation of files based on parity information calculated and stored during database writes. Redundancy is provided by having the data written to multiple disks, either by mirroring drives (RAID level 1) or by having a drive or drives with striping of data across several physical drives. Parity information is stored which allows rapid re-creation of files in the event of disk failure, by taking information from the surviving disks and the parity information to re-create the lost or damaged files.

In RAID 1, full data redundancy is provided by mirroring all disks. This method is expensive, requiring twice as much disk space as there is data. No striping or parity information is involved in RAID 1. In the striping RAID levels (2 to 5), a parity check is maintained so that stripes can be recalculated and reproduced based on information stored on good disks if a disk fails. In RAID 2, 3, 4, and 5, data redundancy is provided through parity checks that are calculated for various levels of data. The parity checks can be used to re-create the data in question without mirroring, so this method requires less disk space than RAID level 1. However, the need to calculate the parity checks will generally make writes slower. In RAID 3, parity bytes are stored on one physical disk with bit-level parity. In RAID 4, parity bytes are stored on one physical disk but with block-level parity. In RAID 5, redundancy is provided by parity checks as in RAID 3 and 4, but parity information is stored along with the data and is hence striped across several physical disks.

There are benefits and disadvantages to using RAID. In general, RAID level 1 or 0+1 is most useful for systems where complete redundancy of data and prevention of any downtime is a must and cost of disk space is not an issue. For large systems or systems where cost is an issue, the mirrored RAID 1 and 0+1 levels may not be feasible due to their high requirements for physical disks. Mirroring will, however, keep the system up, and writes under RAID 1 are no faster and no slower than those to normal, non-RAID disks. RAID 0+1 has the performance advantages of striping without the write issues arising from RAID-related parity-check calculations.

For the levels of RAID 2 to 5, which require calculation of a parity check, writes will tend to be slower and reads will be faster than under "normal" file systems. Writes will be slower the more frequently parity information is calculated and the more complex the parity information is. Depending on the ratio of reads to writes in your system, I/O speed may have a net increase or a net decrease. RAID can improve performance by distributing I/O, however, because the RAID controller spreads data over several physical drives; therefore, no single drive is overburdened.

RAID 1 or 0+1 should be used for high-priority systems or for some commonly written-to system-related data files, such as those for temporary spaces or redo logs. RAID 0+1 provides the RAID 0 advantages of striping but then provides data redundancy by mirroring the striped drives. It is, in a sense, the best of both worlds. RAID 5 should not be used for write-intensive files, because the continuous calculation of parity information can make writing data to disk slower and produce inadequate performance. It can, however, be used easily for systems that are read intensive but written to fairly rarely. Databases can be set up with appropriate mixes of RAID, depending on the function of the particular data files. RAID 0+1 (striping of mirrored drives) is generally a good solution for high-priority, write-intensive files, and RAID 5 is good for read-intensive files. A mix will allow you some redundancy while avoiding some cost.

> **NOTE**
>
> Hardware RAID performs much better than software RAID. If you plan some form of system redundancy, off-site storage controllers are a must. Metadata/RAID characteristics must be kept with the storage. Based on user needs and business requirements, higher levels of availability might dictate exactly what storage implementation is needed.

> **NOTE**
>
> Some storage concerns tend to be RDBMS specific. If your RDBMS allows you to set aside data space for future additions of data to current NULL or VARCHAR columns, as Oracle does using its percent free parameter, you should include consideration of that parameter in your table design. This will help keep data for a particular row contiguous on the disk.

Ownership of Tables

Placing all the tables for a particular application under a single owner is the standard method for table ownership. Although many developers may be involved in the design of a database, when the database is actually built, tables are created by one database user. In review, the owner of tables in a database is called the *schema owner*. The *schema* is the collection of tables and other objects that are associated with an application. These objects must be owned by only one user in order to promote effective database management. Having one owner simplifies management of rights (privileges) on the tables for the database users and management of tables by the DBAs. Placing application tables under different schema owners complicates the system and should be done only in rare cases where some operational concern justifies the effort and increased overhead in management.

A different schema owner should exist for separate applications or database design projects. Association of data to a schema owner is the easiest way to separate databases that are not related to one another. That is not to say, however, that an object (such as a table join) in one schema cannot somehow be associated with an object in another schema. By separating database tables through the use of schemas, management is made easier. Also, users' jobs that require access to more than one schema or application are made easier.

The schema owner (also called DBO, or database owner, in Sybase and MS SQL Server) is responsible for managing security within the scope of the schema. The schema owner must grant object-level privileges to users to allow access to data and revoke privileges to remove access. A system manager/administrator account exists in all RDBMS implementations, which has full database access, with the exception of managing schema security in some cases. The implementation of database security is discussed in detail in Chapter 15, "Implementing Database Security."

Table Design for the Sample Company TrainTech

Figure 11.3 is an ERD for the sample company TrainTech. Everything in the ERD is based around courses that are scheduled and taught. A class represents an occurrence of a particular course or when a course is taught. A course may be taught several times per year, by many different instructors, and in many different locations.

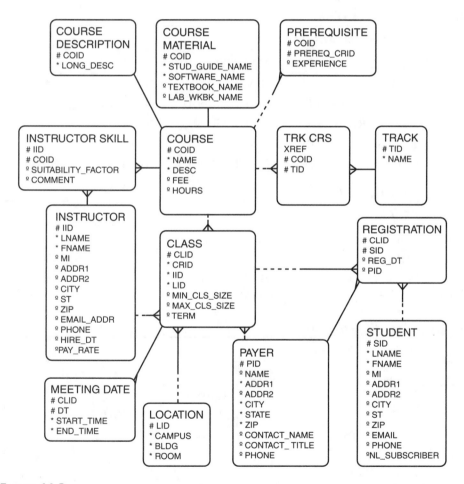

FIGURE 11.3

Detailed ERD for TrainTech.

The following is a listing of tables that were designed based on the information in the ERD. This is a mandatory step that must take place before the logical model can be converted and eventually implemented. The information that follows can simply be plugged into CREATE TABLE statements in order to actually build the tables that comprise the database.

ENTITY:	***COURSE DESCRIPTION***			
TABLE:	*COURSE_DESCRIPTIONS*			
	COLUMN	*DATA TYPE*	*NULLABILITY*	*PK*
	COID	NUMBER(5)	NOT NULL	#
	LONG_DESC	VARCHAR(50)	NOT NULL	

ENTITY:	***COURSE MATERIAL***			
TABLE:	*COURSE_MATERIALS*			
	COLUMN	*DATA TYPE*	*NULLABILITY*	*PK*
	COID	NUMBER(5)	NOT NULL	#
	STUD_GUIDE_NM	VARCHAR(50)	NOT NULL	
	SOFTWARE_NAME	VARCHAR(50)	NULL	
	TEXTBOOK_NAME	VARCHAR(50)	NULL	
	LAB_WRKBK_NAME	VARCHAR(50)	NULL	

ENTITY:	***PREREQUISITE***			
TABLE:	*PREREQUISITES*			
	COLUMN	*DATA TYPE*	*NULLABILITY*	*PK*
	COID	NUMBER(5)	NOT NULL	#
	PREREQ_COID	NUMBER(5)	NULL	#
	EXPERIENCE	VARCHAR(100)	NULL	

ENTITY:	***INSTRUCTOR SKILL***			
TABLE:	*INSTRUCTOR_SKILLS*			
	COLUMN	*DATA TYPE*	*NULLABILITY*	*PK*
	IID	NUMBER(5)	NOT NULL	#
	COID	NUMBER(5)	NOT NULL	#
	COMMENTS	VARCHAR(100)	NULL	

ENTITY:	**COURSE**			
TABLE:	COURSES			
	COLUMN	DATA TYPE	NULLABILITY	PK
	COID	NUMBER(5)	NOT NULL	#
	NAME	VARCHAR(50)	NOT NULL	
	DESCRIP	VARCHAR(200)	NOT NULL	
	FEE	NUMBER(8,2)	NOT NULL	
	HOURS	NUMBER(2)	NOT NULL	

ENTITY:	**TRK CRS XREF**			
TABLE:	TRK_CRS_XREF			
	COLUMN	DATA TYPE	NULLABILITY	PK
	COID	NUMBER(5)	NOT NULL	#
	TID	NUMBER(5)	NOT NULL	#

ENTITY:	**TRACK**			
TABLE:	TRACKS			
	COLUMN	DATA TYPE	NULLABILITY	PK
	TID	NUMBER(5)	NOT NULL	#
	NAME	VARCHAR(50)	NOT NULL	
	DESCRIP	VARCHAR(200)	NOT NULL	

ENTITY:	**INSTRUCTOR**			
TABLE:	INSTRUCTORS			
	COLUMN	DATA TYPE	NULLABILITY	PK
	IID	NUMBER(5)	NOT NULL	#
	LNAME	VARCHAR(20)	NOT NULL	
	FNAME	VARCHAR(20)	NOT NULL	
	MI	VARCHAR(1)	NULL	
	ADDR	VARCHAR(30)	NOT NULL	
	CITY	VARCHAR(30)	NOT NULL	
	ST	VARCHAR(2)	NOT NULL	
	ZIP	VARCHAR(5)	NOT NULL	
	EMAIL	VARCHAR(40)	NULL	

ENTITY: **INSTRUCTOR** *Continued*

TABLE:	*INSTRUCTORS*			
	COLUMN	*DATA TYPE*	*NULLABILITY*	*PK*
	PHONE	VARCHAR(10)	NULL	
	HIRE_DT	DATE	NOT NULL	
	PAY_RATE	NUMBER(8,2)	NOT NULL	

ENTITY: **CLASS**

TABLE:	*CLASSES*			
	COLUMN	*DATA TYPE*	*NULLABILITY*	*PK*
	CLID	NUMBER(5)	NOT NULL	#
	COID	NUMBER(5)	NOT NULL	
	IID	NUMBER(5)	NOT NULL	
	LID	NUMBER(5)	NOT NULL	
	MIN_CLS_SIZE	NUMBER(2)	NOT NULL	
	MAX_CLS_SIZE	NUMBER(2)	NOT NULL	
	TERM	NUMBER(2)	NOT NULL	

ENTITY: **REGISTRATION**

TABLE:	*REGISTRATIONS*			
	COLUMN	*DATA TYPE*	*NULLABILITY*	*PK*
	CLID	NUMBER(5)	NOT NULL	#
	SID	NUMBER(5)	NOT NULL	#
	REG_DT	DATE	NOT NULL	
	PID	NUMBER(5)	NULL	

ENTITY: **MEETING_DATE**

TABLE:	*MEETING_DATES*			
	COLUMN	*DATA TYPE*	*NULLABILITY*	*PK*
	CLID	NUMBER(5)	NOT NULL	#
	MEET_DT	DATE	NOT NULL	#
	START_TIME	VARCHAR(10)	NOT NULL	
	END_TIME	VARCHAR(10)	NOT NULL	

ENTITY:	**LOCATION**			
TABLE:	LOCATIONS			
	COLUMN	DATA TYPE	NULLABILITY	PK
	LID	NUMBER(5)	NOT NULL	#
	CAMPUS	VARCHAR(30)	NOT NULL	
	BLDG	VARCHAR(30)	NOT NULL	
	ROOM	VARCHAR2(30)	NOT NULL	

ENTITY:	**PAYER**			
TABLE:	PAYERS			
	COLUMN	DATA TYPE	NULLABILITY	PK
	PID	NUMBER(5)	NOT NULL	#
	NAME	VARCHAR(30)	NOT NULL	
	ADDR	VARCHAR(30)	NOT NULL	
	CITY	VARCHAR(30)	NOT NULL	
	ST	VARCHAR(2)	NOT NULL	
	ZIP	VARCHAR(5)	NOT NULL	
	CONTACT_NAME	VARCHAR(30)	NOT NULL	
	CONTACT_TITLE	VARCHAR(30)	NULL	
	PHONE	VARCHAR(30)	NOT NULL	

ENTITY:	**STUDENT**			
TABLE:	STUDENTS			
	COLUMN	DATA TYPE	NULLABILITY	PK
	SID	NUMBER(5)	NOT NULL	#
	LNAME	VARCHAR(20)	NOT NULL	
	FNAME	VARCHAR(20)	NOT NULL	
	MI	VARCHAR(1)	NULL	
	ADDR	VARCHAR(30)	NOT NULL	
	CITY	VARCHAR(30)	NOT NULL	
	ST	VARCHAR(2)	NOT NULL	
	ZIP	VARCHAR(5)	NOT NULL	
	EMAIL	VARCHAR(40)	NULL	
	PHONE	VARCHAR(10)	NULL	
	NEWS_LETTER	VARCHAR(1)	NULL	

Again, keep in mind that the exact syntax for every RDBMS might differ, as well as the available data types to define columns. The VARCHAR data type is referenced in ANSI documentation, but its name might vary per implementation. It is most important that you understand the steps to derive the information shown in this example. Substituting values into command syntax is the easy part.

Summary

Logical modeling is the most important part of database design in regard to completely capturing the data-storage needs of an organization. At some point, the logical model must be completed and attention directed to the aspects of physical design. Physical design is where the development team gets serious about converting the information gathered and modeled for an organization into an actual database, and the first step is to begin designing tables. As you know by now, entities represent data. Entities are converted into tables. All along, you know that entities will become tables and that attributes will become columns, just as you know a caterpillar will evolve into a butterfly.

Four basic types of tables may be found in a relational database. The first is the data table. All tables are actually data tables because they contain information pertinent to an organization. The second type is the join table. The join table is used to resolve a many-to-many relationship between two tables. A join table will produce two one-to-many relationships, thus reducing the amount of redundant data that would normally be required with a many-to-many relationship. The third type is a subset table, which contains information that pertains to only a subset of rows found in the parent table. Finally, validation tables are used to store long descriptions of names and for validation of data when entering new data into a column.

Whether you're using an automated design tool or relying on manual processes to design a database, table design is based directly on the work performed during logical design. In fact, most work should have been achieved during logical design. More upfront thought takes places in the logical stage, whereas more tedious work is involved in physical design to achieve the final product. The physical design of tables consists of converting table structures from entities and reviewing table structures, such as the need for additional tables and columns or the lack of need for certain tables and columns. This leads to further normalization or a process called *denormalization*. Denormalization is the process of undoing normalization, or recombining data in one or more tables, solely for the purpose of boosting overall database performance. Denormalization should only be considered if all other means of improving performance have been exhausted.

During physical design, table structures should be studied and refined as much as necessary until the development team is comfortable with the database that is about to be produced. Integrating the use of constraints to manage data integrity is also an important part of database design. Views are also defined during physical design for a variety of purposes. The further design of tables using constraints and views is discussed in the following two chapters.

CHAPTER 12

Integrating Business Rules and Data Integrity

During database design, each phase and each step of each phase should blend into the subsequent phases and steps as smoothly as possible. During physical design, which begins with table design, you take another look at the logical ERD because it should currently represent the data needs for the organization. You'll begin to extract the information you placed into the ERD so that it can be used to define the tables, which are defined as the fundamental storage facilities for any relational database. Once you have initially designed the tables, you should see that many of the constraints necessary have already been defined. However, it's time to take a closer look at these constraints in preparation to refine them and add as many features as necessary in order to protect the organization's data.

As you should recall from previous chapters, *business rules* are those rules that determine how an organization operates and utilizes its data. Business rules affect how data flows through an organization, how it's propagated to database tables, and how it may be accessed and manipulated. *Data integrity*, in review, is the process of ensuring that data is protected and stays intact through defined relationships, promoting data consistency and overall accuracy of data throughout the database.

The following sections of this chapter discuss how business rules affect the physical database. You'll learn how information is extracted from the logical model to derive the physical model, progressing from basic table design to the definition of constraints and other mechanisms that provide the capability to manage the integration of business rules and data integrity.

How Do Business Rules Affect the Database?

Business rules start out as simple business processes that evolve over time through the implementation of an organization's policies and operational procedures. With an organization's decision to design a database with which to automate tasks and maintain data, interviews are eventually administered by elected individuals of the development team who attempt to extract as much information from the data users as possible. A great deal of this information includes business rules, in addition to business processes and data.

Without the existence of business rules, there would be a total lack of control. Processes would exist with no direction for the management of data. Without rules, users would be walking around aimlessly like zombies, working with data that would eventually lose all meaning, after progressively deteriorating into complete junk with no apparent use to the organization. Business rules are the glue that holds an organization's data together. This is why it is so important to ensure that business rules are carried over into table design from the logical model. When this far in the design game, it is no time to compromise the database objectives as set forth in the beginning.

During database design, business rules are primarily integrated through the use of database constraints. Technically speaking, database constraints consist of the following:

- Primary keys
- Foreign keys
- Unique constraints
- Check constraints
- Data types
- Data precision and scale
- NULL/NOT NULL

Most of these constraints were discussed in a fair amount of detail in the previous chapter. In review, a *primary key* is a value that's used to uniquely identify every row of data in a table. Primary keys are implemented at the table level. A primary key constraint is created to enforce the concept of row-level uniqueness based on a column value. A *foreign key* is a child value that references a parent value in another table. A foreign key constraint ensures that a foreign key references a primary key. Primary and foreign keys are the basis for referential integrity, and their use in collaboration with one another is discussed in more detail in this chapter.

> **NOTE**
>
> *Referential integrity* is the concept of managing parent and child records in the database to ensure data consistency. Primary and foreign keys are the basis for the implementation of referential integrity.

Only one primary key may exist per table, although a primary key might consist of a combination of two or more columns. A unique constraint can be specified for a non-primary key column to ensure that all values in the column are unique. For instance, if the social security number for employees is stored, a unique constraint would be appropriate on the SSN column. A telephone company might apply a unique constraint to the PHONE_NUMBER column because all customers must have unique telephone numbers.

A check constraint may be defined for a column to ensure that the value inserted into the column for a row of data matches one of the specified values, as listed in the check constraint. For example, a check constraint may be added to the GENDER column of the EMPLOYEES table to ensure that a value of either MALE or FEMALE is entered into the column. Whereas check constraints may be used to validate values based on a static list, a validation table may be used to validate values based on those that reside in the table.

Table 12.1 shows the purpose of the different types of database constraints.

TABLE 12.1 Constraints and Their Uses

Constraint Type	Uses
Primary key	Column uniqueness
	Row uniqueness
	Row identifier
	Designates parent record
Foreign key	Designates child record
	Used for validation purposes
Unique	Column uniqueness
Check constraints	Validation of data input
	Static list of valid values
NOT NULL	Disallows the input of NULL values

The constraints mentioned in this section can be specified using an automated design (AD) tool or manually. If specified manually, SQL code is typed to define the constraints in addition to the SQL that will be used to create the table structures themselves. If an AD tool is used, the SQL will be generated automatically based on the options specified during physical design. Regardless of the means used to generate the Data Definition Language (or *DDL*, a sublanguage in SQL used to define database structures), the SQL code will have to be executed to build the database. The following subsections show examples of the SQL code used to define database constraints.

Application of a Primary Key Constraint in SQL

The following EMPLOYEES table has an obvious single-column primary key candidate of EMP_ID. Every employee should have his or her own identification, whether system generated or based on social security number. If an identifier such as EMP_ID did not exist in the initial table design for some reason, an ID should be added to identify employee rows in the table.

EMPLOYEES
EMP_ID
LNAME
FNAME
MNAME
ADDRESS

CITY

STATE

ZIP

PHONE

The SQL to define this primary key is as follows:

```
ALTER TABLE EMPLOYEES
ADD CONSTRAINT EMPLOYEES_PK
PRIMARY KEY(EMP_ID);
```

For the following three tables, primary key selection may not seem so straightforward to an individual not familiar with relational databases:

INSTRUCTORS	INST_SKILL_XREF	SKILLS
INSTRUCTOR_ID	INSTRUCTOR_ID	SKILL_ID
LNAME	SKILL_ID	SKILL
FNAME		DESCRIP
MNAME		
ADDRESS		
CITY		
STATE		
ZIP		
PHONE		

In the INSTRUCTORS table, the obvious primary key column is INSTRUCTOR_ID. In the SKILLS table, SKILL_ID is obviously the primary key. Considering only the INSTRUCTORS and SKILLS tables, you would have a many-to-many relationship, because an instructor can have many skills, and a skill can be associated with many instructors. In this example, a join (or *intersection table*) called INST_SKILL_XREF has been included. This join table contains only the columns necessary to form a relationship between INSTRUCTORS and SKILLS, only now you have two one-to-many relationships, because INSTRUCTORS and SKILLS are not directly related to one another. They are related only through INST_SKILL_XREF. The definition of a primary key is one or more columns that make a row of data in a table unique. The combination of INSTRUCTOR_ID and SKILL_ID in the join table make every row of data unique because it is unnecessary for an instructor to be associated with the same skill more than once. Therefore, the primary key in this case consists of two columns.

The SQL to define the primary key for the join table is as follows:

```
ALTER TABLE EMPLOYEES
ADD CONSTRAINT INST_SKILL_XREF_PK
PRIMARY KEY(INSTRUCTOR_ID, SKILL_ID);
```

> **NOTE**
>
> Multiple-column primary (composite primary keys) are common in join tables.

Application of a Foreign Key Constraint in SQL

The following two common tables illustrate a basic parent/child relationship. The parent table is EMPLOYEES, which contains the base personal data for each employee. The child table is EMPLOYEE_PAY, containing company-related pay information for each employee. All employees must have a row of data in both tables, thus creating a one-to-one mandatory-to-mandatory relationship. Either table could have technically been the parent table, but EMPLOYEES is chosen because the employees' names are stored there. The EMP_ID column is the primary key in both tables; neither table should have more than one row of data per employee. Because the EMPLOYEE_PAY table is treated as the child table, the EMP_ID column in EMPLOYEE_PAY is designated as a foreign key, which references EMP_ID in EMPLOYEES. What that means is this: A row must be inserted into EMPLOYEES for an employee before a row can be inserted into EMPLOYEE_PAY, and a row for an employee in EMPLOYEES cannot be removed without the corresponding row in EMPLOYEE_PAY being removed first.

EMPLOYEES	*EMPLOYEE_PAY*
EMP_ID	EMP_ID
LNAME	HR_RATE
FNAME	SALARY
MNAME	HIRE_DATE
ADDRESS	DEPENDENTS
CITY	WITHHOLDING
STATE	
ZIP	
PHONE	

The SQL to define the foreign key for the EMPLOYEE_PAY table is as follows:

```
ALTER TABLE EMPLOYEE_PAY
ADD CONSTRAINT EMPLOYEE_PAY_EMP_ID_FK
FOREIGN KEY (EMP_ID) REFERENCES EMPLOYEES (EMP_ID);
```

The join operation between these two tables in a SQL query is as follows:

```
EMPLOYEES.EMP_ID = EMPLOYEE_PAY.EMP_ID
```

A similar scenario involves the following two tables: PRODUCTS and ORDERS. A one-to-many relationship is involved between these two tables because a product may have only one entry in PRODUCTS but may have many entries in ORDERS. In other words, a product may be ordered by customers many times (the more the better for sales). The primary key in PRODUCTS is PROD_ID, and in ORDERS it's ORD_NO. The PROD_ID column in ORDERS is a foreign key that references PROD_ID in PRODUCTS. Products that do not exist cannot be ordered. Business rule or common sense?

PRODUCTS	*ORDERS*
PROD_ID	ORD_NO
PRODUCT	PROD_ID
DESCRIP	ORD_DT
COST	QUANTITY

The join operation between these two tables in a SQL query is as follows:

```
PRODUCTS.PROD_ID = ORDERS.PROD_ID
```

Application of a Unique Constraint in SQL

In the following example, notice that an SSN column has been added to the EMPLOYEES table. SSN is an excellent candidate for a unique constraint because all social security numbers are unique. Depending on circumstance, PHONE could also be unique. However, using PHONE in this case might not be a great idea because a requiring a unique PHONE NUMBER would disallow residents of the same address from being co-employees. If you were keeping track of customers for a telephone company, phone number would be a better candidate for a unique constraint because only one individual's name is associated with the phone bill.

EMPLOYEES
EMP_ID
LNAME
FNAME
MNAME

EMPLOYEES   *Continued*

SSN

ADDRESS

CITY

STATE

ZIP

PHONE

Another good example of a unique constraint (in addition to the primary key in the table) is the serial number for a product, as shown in the following table:

PRODUCTS

PROD_ID

PRODUCT

SERIAL_NUM

DESCRIP

COST

The SQL to define the unique constraint for the PRODUCTS table is as follows:

```
ALTER TABLE PRODUCTS
ADD CONSTRAINT PRODUCTS_SER_NUM_UNIQ
UNIQUE (SERIAL_NUM);
```

Application of a Check Constraint in SQL

In the following example, a GENDER column has been added to the EMPLOYEES table. The gender of an employee should either be MALE or FEMALE. You could define a check constraint for GENDER as well as STATE.

EMPLOYEES

EMP_ID

LNAME

FNAME

MNAME

SSN

GENDER

ADDRESS

CITY

STATE

ZIP

PHONE

Here are two possible constraint definitions for the EMPLOYEES table:

```
ALTER TABLE EMPLOYEES ADD CONSTRAINT CHK_EMPLOYEES_STATE
CHECK (STATE = 'IN');

ALTER TABLE EMPLOYEES ADD CONSTRAINT CHK_EMPLOYEES_GENDER
CHECK (GENDER IN ('MALE','FEMALE'));
```

Extracting Business Rules from the Logical Model

They say a picture is worth a thousand words, which is probably why it's recommended that you visually represent an organization's needs before attempting to design a database for the organization. So far, this chapter has discussed the application of constraints to manage business rules through data integrity concepts. Now, it's important to decipher the business rules in the diagrams created during logical model in order to extract all business rules. Not only will all business rules be extracted, but others will surely be defined. As new rules are defined, it's important that you update the logical models so that they're in sync with the work that's being performed during the physical design phase.

In the ERD, business rules are interpreted from relationship lines that are drawn. The different relationships (one-to-one, one-to-many, and many-to-many) determine the uniqueness of data as well as child record references to parent records. For instance, a one-to-one relationship represents uniqueness in both tables, whereas a one-to-many relationship represents uniqueness in the first table only. This uniqueness represents either a primary key constraint or a unique constraint. The child record always represents a foreign key constraint. Required and optional attributes are defined that determine the nullability of columns associated with a table.

In the ERD, relationships are shown between different entities, or *data*. In the process model, relationships are shown between processes and data. The process model helps determine the proper order of updates that occur to data. The process model is used in two basic ways: to crosscheck the completeness of the data model and to generate the front-end user application through which the end user will access the database. The process model deals with relationship-specific business rules, table-level rules, and column-level rules. The process model first relates processes to data and then can be used to show not only what data a process accesses but how the data is accessed. For instance, Process A might access all columns in Entity A but only one column in Entity B. Process B might access all columns in both entities. Of the columns that are accessed by the processes, the types of access that could occur include creation of new data (C), which refers to the insertion of data, not the creation of database objects, retrieval of data (R), update of data (U), and deletion of data (D). This is all determined by the process model and used to complete the design of the database and begin the design of the front-end application.

> **NOTE**
>
> Some developers fail to realize the importance of the process model when designing a database. The data and process models must work in conjunction with one another in order to ensure a complete transition of an organization's needs into a fully functional database system.

The Nature of the Data

There is no way to properly design a database without a thorough knowledge of the nature of the data. The nature of the data deals with the type of data, the appearance of data, and how the data is used by the end user. Unfortunately, the true nature of the data may be unknown before actual implementation. That's why so many changes are made to a database (and application) after implementation. Changes should always be expected, and thus part of the plan to design and implement the database (and design, test, and implement, and so on).

The nature of data falls into four fundamental categories, most of which have already been discussed. The following topics are discussed in the next few subsections, which cover the nature of data and its importance in database design:

- Data type of data
- Uniqueness of data
- Case of data
- References to data

Again, most of this information about the nature of data should be defined in the ERD, but it should be further defined during initial table design and refined throughout the rest of the physical design process.

Data Type of Data

One of the first steps when defining attributes of entities, and columns of tables, is to assign an applicable data type to the column based on the specific data that will be stored. The data type automatically constrains the data that may be entered into a column. A precision, or *size*, may also be assigned to columns (*must* be assigned in most cases). Some implementations have default precisions for data types if not specified. A scale may also be associated with a column in collaboration with the precision. Once the data type, precision, and scale are set for a column, the end user is very limited as to what can be entered. If a value of the wrong data type is entered, the RDBMS should return a message to the user while rejecting the data.

Uniqueness of Data

Normalization is the process of reducing or eliminating redundant data stored in the database. Normalization forces the use of primary key and foreign key constraints to enforce referential integrity. If these constraints are not created, referential integrity will not be enforced, and redundant data may be allowed into tables that are supposed to be normalized. Primary keys enforce the entrance of only unique values into a column, as do unique constraints.

> **NOTE**
>
> Foreign key constraints are not used to control uniqueness but rather to reference unique data or primary keys. Parent records should be unique, whereas child records may be many.

Case of Data

Everything discussed in this book points to the idea of protecting an organization's data by promoting consistency and accuracy throughout the database. Once aspect of data's nature that must be considered is the case of the data. Should data be stored in upper, lower, or mixed case? In the real world, we have seen all three in different systems, and even combined aimlessly into the same system. Consistent storage and entering methods lead to consistent data. The use of uppercase seems to be the most common approach by organization concerned about consistent data, although if everything is stored in uppercase, the readability of everyday mixed case is defeated. Mixed-case storage is also common because it depicts more realistic data that everyone uses on a daily basis. Lowercase storage is rare, but it achieves the same level of consistency as all uppercase storage.

Table 12.2 illustrates the importance of case—RDBMSs tend to be case-sensitive with the data they store.

TABLE 12.2   Constraints and Their Uses

Value 1	Statement	Value 2
SMITH	Is not equal to	smith
SMITH	Is not equal to	Smith
SMITH	Is equal to	SMITH
SMITH	Is equal to	UPPER(SMITH)

Case is most important when using SQL to make comparisons between criteria and table data in order to process or retrieve specific data for a report. If data is not properly compared, then all data might not be considered for a transaction or query. In the table, you can see how the difference in the case of data is treated. Luckily, SQL provides an UPPER function that can be used to convert data for comparison purposes. Case of data can also be controlled by specifying an available character set when installing your database software and creating the database.

To join columns that may be inconsistent (even though the use of an index to search for the data may be suppressed), you could use the following logic:

```
WHERE UPPER(EMPLOYEES.NAME) = UPPER(CUSTOMERS.NAME)
```

If you do not know the case of data, or if it is inconsistent, you could use the following logic in a transaction or query:

```
WHERE UPPER(CITY) = 'INDIANAPOLIS'
```

So how does all this affect database design? Before design is complete, the case of the data must be factored in so that database-level constraints (such as check constraints), triggers, and any mechanisms at the application level can be coded properly to most effectively manage the data. Standards should be established on how data will be used, and this information should be conveyed to the end user via training and documentation.

NOTE

Inconsistency of data must be avoided. The case of data is elementary, but it has a tremendous impact on the management of a relational database. If the case of the data is not considered, SQL statements that make data comparisons for data retrieval or updates may retrieve an incomplete data set. The case of the data can be controlled through the use of check constraints, database triggers (discussed later in this chapter), application code, application edits, and user training.

NOTE

Unicode is an encoding system that provides a unique numbers for every character, regardless of the platform, database software, or language. With Internet and business-to-business development increasing, companies are beginning to express more of a need to represent characters in a standard format, more efficiently enabling the transmission of data. Also, XML is becoming a large part of Internet development and very often requires moving data between heterogeneous systems such as Oracle and SQL Server, whether from business to business, or within an organization.

References to Data

Finally, the nature of data is seen through its relationships with other data, as defined initially in the ERD. This is called *referential integrity*. Previously in this chapter, you learned about the designation of primary key and foreign key constraints, which serve the purpose of managing parent and child relationships.

In review, parent and child relationships occur with the following entity (table) relationships:

- One-to-one relationships
- One-to-many relationship

Remember that many-to-many relationships should be converted to two one-to-many relationships, which represent parent/child relationships, using a join table.

Maintaining Historic Data

The topic of historic data always raises an age-old question: How long should data be kept? People often have the tendencies to be pack rats, refusing to let go of their precious data. But really, how long is the data needed? By keeping unnecessary amounts of data (say, 10 years worth, totaling a few billion records or several hundred gigabytes of storage), two things will happen (not necessarily in the following order):

- You will run out of free disk space for new data.
- Overall database performance will suffer drastically.

This is why it is important to consider data archival, or even data purging, to free up resources used by old data and make room for the new. The process of archiving and purging can even be automated, although it should be closely monitored.

The following are some questions that should be answered to help you determine the need to archive and purge data:

- How long should data be kept online?
- What data is important to keep?
- What is used to determine whether the organization's data is historic?
- How long should data be archived?
- Where should data be archived?
- When should data be purged (no archive or after archive)?
- How timely must data be retrieved from archives if needed?
- How often is data expected to be retrieved from archives?

Table 12.2 depicts a sample plan for archiving and purging data for an online bookstore's ordering system.

TABLE 12.2   Plan for Data Archival and Purging

DATA	STORAGE PLAN
Current year	Online
2 to 3 years old	Archive to alternate server or tape; readily available
4 to 7 years old	Archive to tape and store
7+ years old	Purge

NOTE

You may also consider partitioning online tables by date in order to narrow down data searches to smaller subsets of data, thus improving performance. Views can also be used to create logical partitions of data. Views are discussed in the following chapter.

Enforcing Business Rules

Once business rules are modeled, they are designed (or you might say, *built into the physical table structures*). Business rules are primarily comprised of database constraints at the physical level. It is easy to enforce business rules if they're properly defined, because the RDBMS will do all the real work for you. The RDBMS will make sure users follow the rules established by constraints when new data is entered or existing data is updated or deleted. There's some work that should be performed in order to ensure that business rules and the organization's policies are followed and that changes can be implemented when necessary in order to improve the integrity and overall use of the data for the end user.

At the database level, business rules are enforced using the following items:

- Database constraints
- Audit scripts to monitor data
- Database triggers

> **NOTE**
>
> Quality assurance (QA) reports can be generated from the database to monitor the use of data to help determine if policies are being followed and proper care is taken with the data. QA reports are an essential supplement to the database and application features that provide data integrity.

At the application level, business rules are enforced using these items:

- Application constraints and edits
- Application triggers
- User training to provide an understanding of business policies

It is important that the features of the selected RDBMS are used to their full extent to protect data and that the application is coded so that its data integrity complements that of the database. With a combination of both database and application constraint integration, data integrity will be optimized.

> **NOTE**
>
> Once business rules have been defined and designed into the database, they are for the most part enforced automatically by the RDBMS.

It cannot be stressed enough the importance of maintaining referential integrity in the database, without relying on features coded into the application. Poorly coded applications can wreak havoc when the business rules that manipulate data are not in the engine itself. The enforcement of business rules cannot be guaranteed by the RDBMS if they themselves are not actually stored in the database. The following subsections discuss the enforcement of business rules at the database level in more detail in relation to the use of triggers and validation tables.

Using Triggers to Enforce Business Rules

A *trigger* is an object of stored programming code in the database that's executed (fired) automatically by the RDBMS based on a given event that occurs. Events refer to data-manipulation commands, such as INSERT, UPDATE, and DELETE. Triggers have several uses, one of which is to manage referential integrity (parent and child relationships between data). For example, suppose an end user attempts to remove an employee pay record. A trigger may exist that looks for a deletion of an employee pay record and, upon such event, fires and first removes the parent record containing the employee's personal data. Suppose that a new employee is added to the database. A trigger may exist that, upon entry of a new employee, fires and creates a default pay record for the new employee.

> **NOTE**
>
> The use of triggers to manage data is supported by the latest American National Standards Institute (ANSI) SQL standard. However, there are many different implementations of SQL, all of which have varying syntax. Vendors provide extensions to standard SQL so that program code can be stored in the database. For example, Oracle's extension to SQL is called *PL/SQL*. Microsoft's SQL Server extension is known as *Transact-SQL*. See your RDBMS documentation for CREATE TRIGGER syntax.

Triggers are also used for updates to historic-type tables for quality assurance (QA) purposes and for the validation of data. Suppose a transactional history table has been designed that stores information about the transaction being performed (INSERT, UPDATE, or DELETE), the user performing the transaction, the old data, and the new data. A trigger can be created that will fire every time a transaction is performed, inserting the appropriate information into the transactional history table, but only after the transaction is final (meaning a COMMIT has been performed). A query can then be written to produce a QA report from the transactional history table and given to a QA specialist, who is in charge of browsing over the transactions that occurred, looking for obvious mistakes during data entry and possibly comparing new data with source documents. QA queries may also be run periodically to spot-check all data to reduce the amount of junk in the database.

Using Validation Tables to Enforce Business Rules

Validation tables are used mainly for two purposes (both of which work hand in hand with one another):

- To ensure data consistency through validation
- As a code table to reduce data redundancy

Validation tables can be referenced as follows:

- Using a foreign key constraint
- Using a trigger or stored procedure
- Embedded in application code

The following is incorrect syntax for referring to a validation table:

```
CHECK (STATE IN (SELECT STATE FROM STATE_CODES))
```

This example will not work. Check constraints are used to validate against a static list of values. Validation tables contain data the may change at any given point in time. Validation tables allow for dynamic validation of values. Dynamic validation can be accomplished at the application level once validation tables are in place. For instance, Oracle Form Builder (development software used to create end-user input forms) allows a query to be used to define a list of valid values for a field on the form.

The following simple example makes use of two validation tables, called STATE_CODES and DEPARTMENTS, through the use of foreign key constraints that are defined in the EMPLOYEES table:

```
CREATE TABLE EMPLOYEES
(EMP_ID     NUMBER(5)      NOT NULL,
 L_NAME     VARCHAR(20)    NOT NULL,
 F_NAME     VARCHAR(20)    NOT NULL,
 ADDRESS    VARCHAR(30)    NOT NULL,
 CITY       VARCHAR(30)    NOT NULL,
 STATE      VARCHAR(2)     NOT NULL,
 ZIP        VARCHAR(5)     NOT NULL,
 DEPT_ID    NUMBER(5)      NOT NULL);

CREATE TABLE STATE_CODES
(STATE      VARCHAR(2)     NOT NULL,
 STATE_NM   VARCHAR(30)    NOT NULL);

CREATE TABLE DEPARTMENTS
(DEPT_ID    NUMBER(5)      NOT NULL,
 DEPT_NM    VARCHAR(30)    NOT NULL);

ALTER TABLE EMPLOYEES ADD CONSTRAINT EMPLOYEES_STATE_FK
FOREIGN KEY (STATE) REFERENCES STATE_CODES (STATE);

ALTER TABLE EMPLOYEES ADD CONSTRAINT EMPLOYEES_DEPT_ID_FK
FOREIGN KEY (DEPT_ID) REFERENCES DEPARTMENTS (DEPT_ID);
```

Using this logic, a user must enter valid values for STATE and DEPT_ID when creating a new employee record. An error will be returned upon insertion if at least one of the values entered for the two columns does not match a primary key value in the parent validation tables.

Integrating Business Rules at the N-Tier Level

The client/server environment traditionally involves a two-tier architecture, including the client as one tier and the host server as the other. Typically, the database resides on the host server, and the application resides on the client. To ensure optimal security and management of business rules, as much integration of security and business rules must be implemented at the database level. In some cases, business rules are also integrated at the client level in the end-user application. The rules stored in the application should be used only to enhance those stored on the database. Over-reliance on application features unnecessarily duplicates standard features of the RDBMS while failing to prove as effective in many cases.

N-tier database environments provide more layers in which to distribute database and application components. The "n" in n-tier refers to multiple tiers, implying three or more. In an n-tier environment, the client still makes requests from a host server, which usually houses the database with the desired information. One or more middle-tier components can be used to bridge the communication between the client and the server, particularly in the Internet environment.

The integration of business processes and rules is a growing trend in the e-commerce world. By distributing database and application components among several different tiers, performance might be significantly increased because resource loads are spread across multiple systems, where each component performs a specified task on its associated system.

In an n-tier environment, the middle tier acts as the link between the client and the database on the host server. The client is equipped with an application interface, or a standard Web browser in the Internet computing environment. The majority of the application logic (representation of business processes and rules) resides at the middle tier level, and submits requests to the target database on the host server. As in the traditional client/server environment, business rules and data integrity are integrated within the relational database.

Consider an example involving a Web application. The client (end-user PC) is equipped with a standard Web browser, such as Internet Explorer or Netscape. An application server serves as the middle tier component, linking the client to the database on a host server. The application server (middle tier) handles connectivity between the client and the server, using application forms coded using Java. The forms on the application server represent business process that access data, and include business rules to control data integrity. When the end user navigates to a URL on the Internet using the Web browser, the application server sends code (HTML, XML) back to the user's PC in order to display the form. The end user enters data appropriately on the form and submits a query, for example. The application server acts as the agent in submission of the query. The database on the host server satisfies the query request, and the final data results are returned to the end user on the form in the Web browser.

There is no replacement for storing business rules in the database in the form of constraints, triggers, and stored procedures. However, business rules can be stored at various levels in the n-tier environment in order to distribute the overall load on resources for a database application and ultimately improve performance for the end user.

Constraint Generation Using an AD Tool

Figure 12.1 shows the simple ERD from the previous chapter. By studying this ERD, you should be able to determine most of the constraints applicable at this point.

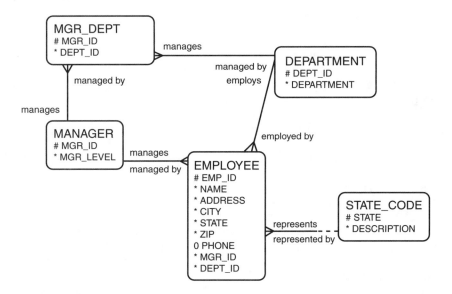

FIGURE 12.1
Simple ERD depicting various entity types.

The following is a listing of SQL code produced using the automated design tool Oracle Designer. This code, when executed, will create the constraints based on the information defined in the automated design tool. This code assumes that the tables have already been created. Adding constraints to tables changes table definitions; therefore, the ALTER TABLE command is used.

```
ALTER TABLE MANAGERS
 ADD CONSTRAINT MGR_PK PRIMARY KEY
  (MGR_ID);

ALTER TABLE MGR_DEPT
 ADD CONSTRAINT MGR_DEPT_PK PRIMARY KEY
  (MGR_ID);
```

```
ALTER TABLE DEPARTMENTS
 ADD CONSTRAINT DEPT_PK PRIMARY KEY
  (DEPT_ID);

ALTER TABLE EMPLOYEES
 ADD CONSTRAINT EMP_PK PRIMARY KEY
  (EMP_ID);

ALTER TABLE STATE_CODES
 ADD CONSTRAINT ST_CODE_PK PRIMARY KEY
  (STATE);

ALTER TABLE MGR_DEPT ADD CONSTRAINT
 MGR_DEPT_MGR_FK FOREIGN KEY
  (MGR_MGR_ID) REFERENCES MANAGERS
  (MGR_ID) ADD CONSTRAINT
 MGR_DEPT_DEPT_FK FOREIGN KEY
  (DEPT_DEPT_ID) REFERENCES DEPARTMENTS
  (DEPT_ID);

ALTER TABLE DEPARTMENTS ADD CONSTRAINT
 DEPT_EMP_FK FOREIGN KEY
  (EMP_EMP_ID) REFERENCES EMPLOYEES
  (EMP_ID);

ALTER TABLE EMPLOYEES ADD CONSTRAINT
 EMP_MGR_FK FOREIGN KEY
  (MGR_MGR_ID) REFERENCES MANAGERS
  (MGR_ID) ADD CONSTRAINT
 EMP_ST_CODE_FK FOREIGN KEY
  (ST_CODE_STATE) REFERENCES STATE_CODES
  (STATE);
```

Notice in this code that primary key and foreign key constraints are generated by the AD tool. The naming conventions this particular AD tool uses for constraints are NAME_PK for primary keys and NAME_FK for foreign keys. Even with the use of an AD tool, unique constraints, check constraints, and validation tables have to be specified manually, in addition to any relationships defined in the ERD.

Constraint Integration for the Sample Company TrainTech

Once again, it's time to come back to the sample company TrainTech. In the previous chapter, you studied the ERD with the intent of converting entities into tables (as shown in Figure 11.3).

Now, you'll take a look at the ERD in Figure 11.3 with the intent to extract the business rules modeled by entity relationships. What you see here are numerous potential primary and foreign key constraints. Using common sense, you can also determine where unique constraints, check constraints, and validation tables might be beneficial.

Using the ERD, you will define the following constraints in respective order:

- Primary keys
- Foreign keys
- Unique constraint candidates
- Check constraint candidates
- Validation table candidates

The following is a table list of the constraints that have been defined based on the ERD and the initial table designs created in the last chapter. It's recommended that you study each constraint and compare it to the ERD and the table definitions at the end of the previous chapter for increased understanding. Under each constraint type is a list of applicable tables in the left column. The applicable columns are listed in the right column.

TABLE 12.3   Sample Primary Key Candidates

Table Name	Primary Key Column(s)
COURSE_DESCRIPTIONS	COID
COURSE_MATERIALS	COID
PREREQUISITES	COID and PREREQ_COID
INSTRUCTOR_SKILLS	IID and COID
COURSES	COID
TRK_CRS_XREF	COID and TID
TRACKS	TID
INSTRUCTORS	IID
CLASSES	CLID
REGISTRATIONS:	CLID and SID
MEETING_DATES	CLID and MEET_DT
LOCATIONS	LID
PAYERS	PID
STUDENTS	SID

Table 12.4   Sample Foreign Key Candidates

Table Name	Foreign Key Column(s)
COURSE_DESCRIPTIONS	COID references COURSES.COID.
COURSE_MATERIALS	COID references COURSES.COID.
PREREQUISITES	COID references COURSES.COID.
PREREQUISITES	PREREQ_COID references COURSES.COID.
INSTRUCTOR_SKILLS	IID references INSTRUCTOR.IID.
INSTRUCTOR_SKILLS	COID references COURSES.COID.
TRK_CRS_XREF	COID references COURSES.COID.
TRK_CRS_XREF	TID references TRACKS.TID.
CLASSES	COID references COURSES.COID.
CLASSES	IID references INSTRUCTORS.IID.
CLASSES	LID references LOCATIONS.LID.
REGISTRATIONS	CLID references CLASSES.CLID.
REGISTRATIONS	SID references STUDENTS.SID.
REGISTRATIONS	PID references PAYERS.PID.
MEETING_DATES	CLID references CLASSES.CLID.

Table 12.5   Sample Unique Constraint Candidates

Table Name	Unique Constraint Column(s)
COURSE_MATERIALS	Change TEXTBOOK_NAME to ISBN.
	Define unique constraint for ISBN.
	Create TEXTBOOKS table:
	TEXTBOOKS
	ISBN
	TEXTBOOK_NAME
INSTRUCTORS	Add SSN column for pay purposes.
	Define unique constraint for SSN.
INSTRUCTORS	Define unique constraint for EMAIL.
STUDENTS	Define unique constraint for EMAIL.

TABLE 12.6 Sample Check Constraint Candidates

Table Name	Check Constraint Column(s)
PREREQUISITES	CHECK (EXPERIENCE BETWEEN 1 AND 100)
COURSES	CHECK (FEE BETWEEN 1 AND 2000)
COURSES	CHECK (HOURS BETWEEN 1 AND 40)
INSTRUCTORS	CHECK (ST = 'IN')
INSTRUCTORS	CHECK (PAY_RATE BETWEEN 20 AND 100)
CLASSES	CHECK (MIN_CLS_SIZE BETWEEN 1 AND 25)
CLASSES	CHECK (MAX_CLS_SIZE BETWEEN 1 AND 25)
CLASSES	CHECK (TERM IN (1,2,3,4,5))
REGISTRATIONS	CHECK (REG_DT BETWEEN '01-JAN-2000' AND '31-DEC-2010')
MEETING_DATES	CHECK (MEET_DT BETWEEN '01-JAN-2000' AND '31-DEC-2010')
PAYERS	CHECK (STATE IN (SELECT STATE FROM STATE_CODES))
STUDENTS	CHECK (STATE IN (SELECT STATE FROM STATE_CODES))
STUDENTS	CHECK (NEWSLETTER IN ('Y',NULL))

Validation Table Candidates

- Create a table to store state codes and state names.
- Create a table to store approved text books.
- Create a table to store approved software.
- Create a table to store approved student guides and lab workbooks.
- Create a table to store additional instructor skills that may not be associated with current classes.
- Create a table to store valid course fees.
- Create a table to store valid start and end times for classes.
- Create a table to store a complete list of campuses.
- Create a table to store a valid list of ZIP codes (acquire data from some third-party organization).

Summary

The first part of physical design involves the conversion of entities into tables and attributes into columns. Upon conversion, constraints will also be converted (if you're using an automated design tool) based on relationships that were defined in the ERD. The second part of physical design involves a review of the initial tables and refinement of those table structures to involve the remainder of the business rules that have not yet been integrated. Various mechanisms can be used to integrate business rules into database design at both the database level and application level. Although this is a database design book, it is important to understand some of the thought process that takes place when designing a front-end application, at least to the extent of the basic business processes and data usages. It is narrow minded to think only of the back-end database during database design because it is important to understand how the end user will use the data in order to derive an optimal design.

Business rules are implemented using mainly the following database constraints:

- Primary keys
- Foreign keys
- Unique columns
- Check constraints
- NOT NULL constraints
- Data type precision and scale

Referential integrity is managed through the use of foreign key constraints that reference primary keys in parent tables. If a relational database does not have a large number of foreign key constraints, then something is dreadfully wrong. Either relationships were not properly defined, the database has not been normalized, or the physical design of the tables is not complete.

The nature of data (the way data looks and acts) is also a factor. The nature of data, as defined in this chapter, is determined by the data type, the uniqueness of the data (primary keys and unique constraints), the case of data (upper, lower, mixed), and references to other data (foreign key constraints). In addition to these constraints, business rules can also be managed by utilizing triggers and validation tables. A *trigger* is a stored unit of programming code that fires when a given transaction occurs in the database. Triggers can be used to automate the process of maintaining referential integrity or for validation. Validation tables are also often called *code tables*. Validation tables reduce the amount of redundant data stored in the database and allow data entered into a column to be verified using a foreign key constraint before the transaction is finalized.

With this knowledge of physical design through the definition of tables, columns, and constraints, one of the next logical steps is the creation of views. The following chapter discusses view design and the many purposes for using views to represent data in your tables.

Designing Views

IN THIS CHAPTER

A *view* is a virtual table, which means that a view looks and acts like a table. A view is virtual in the sense that it has no physical limitations like a table—data is stored in tables and only used by the views to provide the user with an alternative representation of the data. To users, a view seems to be a database table with rows and columns that they can select from and can execute Database Manipulation Language (DML) commands (such as INSERT, UPDATE, DELETE) according to the privileges they have been granted on the view. A view, however, has no data of its own. It is instead the result of an SQL SELECT statement (also known as an *SQL query*).

There are many potential benefits to using views, many of which most people are unaware. The creation of views is a critical point in the physical design of the database, but more than likely, view definition and refinement will continue well after the database has been implemented and users find new ways to use data that meet the organization's needs.

After providing an overview of view usage, this chapter discusses view uses as related to database design as well as view usage during and after database implementation. View relationships are then discussed. Finally, there's a discussion of the maintenance of views and the avoidance of poor view design.

Overview of Views

As mentioned, a view is defined by a database query. The query SQL is stored in the database as a database object so that exactly the same SQL can be referred to by users and user applications as required by calling that view name. The users select data from a view exactly the same as they would a table. The result of the view query is presented to the users as if it were table data. When a user or the user's application executes a query or DML against a view, the RDBMS SQL engine substitutes the SQL used to define the view into the user's SQL command and then pulls the data from the underlying tables, which are the true source of the view's data.

A view selects desired columns or generates derived columns from a table, a view, or some combination of joined tables and/or views. A view also returns only specific rows from source tables and views selected based on the select criteria established by logical conditions and table joins contained in the stored view SQL statement. A view is merely a window to its base tables, from which the view receives its column structure and the data rows that fill the column structure.

Figure 13.1 illustrates the creation process and basic use of a view that has been defined. The top half of the figure shows a view creation based on selected data in a source table. The lower half of the figure shows how an end user accesses a view through a query. The user queries the view. The SQL query behind the view is executed and pulls data from the base table. Then it returns the data to the user. To the user, querying a view is no different than querying a table.

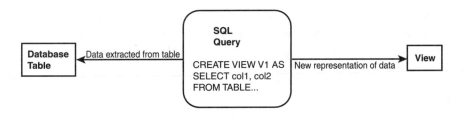

FIGURE 13.1

The view-creation process.

Views are memory objects only. They take up only the amount of disk space necessary to store the SQL upon which the view is based. Views are refreshed by the SQL engine every time they are accessed by a query, pulling the data from the underlying tables whenever users access them.

> **NOTE**
>
> The main difference between a table and a view is that a table contains actual data and consumes physical storage, whereas a view contains no data and requires no storage other than what's needed to store the query providing the view definition.

The following is an example of the SQL used to create a simple view. It's called a *view definition*. Note that the view definition consists mainly of a SELECT statement. The keywords CREATE VIEW "VIEW_NAME" AS are simply inserted before the SQL query.

```
CREATE VIEW JOB_VIEW AS
SELECT E.NAME, P.PAY_RATE, J.JOB_LOCATION, J.DATE
FROM EMPLOYEES E,
     EMPLOYEE_BENEFITS P,
     CONSTRUCTION_JOBS J
WHERE E.SSN = P.SSN
  AND E.SSN = J.SSN;
```

13

DESIGNING VIEWS

Once the view is in place, end users may access it, assuming that the appropriate object privileges have been granted to the end users. Object privileges may be assigned to and removed from users just as they are for tables. An end user might select data from the previous view as shown in the following query:

```
SELECT * from job_view;
```

The user front-end application may also access the view as it does tables. If so, the fact that a view is being accessed instead of a table is transparent to the user. The user does not care whether he is accessing a table or view as long as the desired data is returned from the database.

Why Use Views?

Views play a major role in the design and function of a relational database and in the applications that run against it. A normalized relational database will consist of many tables, each pertaining to a particular person, place, thing, or event of importance in the business system the database represents. Often these normalized tables have to be rejoined to create meaningful information for a particular situation. Views allow the SQL necessary to create the joins, select the required table columns, and establish criteria the rows must meet to be formally stored in the database for future use for a particular situation. Views can customize a single set of tables to meet many highly specific requirements from a wide variety of user groups. Because a particular view is stored in the database, it is standardized and therefore consistent for all users who access it. Using a view is also much simpler and convenient for users and applications than performing complicated queries themselves.

Views provide data independence for users and applications. The virtual tables a view creates can have columns with any name desired drawn from any combination of tables that can be joined. Different divisions within an enterprise may have different names for the same data. The view's ability to name columns as desired allows you to present the same tables to each of several different user groups with the column names the users are familiar with. The view columns can also be virtual columns derived from a concatenation of or calculations on existing table columns.

In summary, some of the major advantages of using views include the following:

- Views do not require physical storage.
- Views are stored in memory when accessed, providing increased performance over tables in some cases.

- Views can provide a different perspective of table data to satisfy reporting needs.
- Views can provide data independence for users and applications.
- Views simplify data usage.

In the event that table structures within the database change, views can present the data in the same format with the same column names that users are used to seeing, regardless of the table changes.

As related to database design, the subsections that follow describe the following view concepts:

- Data summarization
- Filtering data
- Database security
- Data conversion
- Data partitioning

NOTE

The definition of many views will take place after the first pass of design and implementation. The possible use of views will be discovered as users learn more about the data and how it is used to perform on the job.

Data Summarization

Views can also be used to show the results of complicated calculations or summary data. By using a view definition, data can be extracted from numerous database tables in just about any format imaginable. Figure 13.2 illustrates the use of views for the summarization of data. In this figure, a view is created to summarize product data found in four different tables. Instead of seeing individual rows of data every time a product has been ordered, for example, the user sees summarized information for each product based on inventory, orders, and returns.

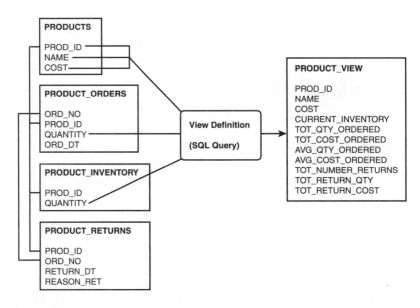

FIGURE 13.2

Using views for data summarization.

Summary views can be used as building blocks or necessary interim steps in even more complicated queries. For example, the following view, EMPLOYEES_BY_REGION, returns a single row per region ID, with the employee count for the region:

```
CREATE OR REPLACE
VIEW EMPLOYEES_BY_REGION AS
SELECT REGION_ID, COUNT(REGION_ID) EMPLOYEE_COUNT
FROM EMPLOYEES
GROUP BY REGION_ID;
```

The SALARY_BY_REGION view returns a single row per region ID, with the salary sum for the region:

```
CREATE OR REPLACE
VIEW SALARY_BY_REGION AS
SELECT REGION_ID, SUM(SALARY) SUM_SALARY
FROM BENEFITS
GROUP BY REGION_ID;
```

The AVERAGE_SALARY_BY_REGION view returns a single row per region ID, with the sum of the salaries by region obtained from the view SUM_SALARY divided by employee count for the region obtained from the view EMPLOYEE_COUNT. The view that returns that calculation, AVERAGE_SALARY_BY_REGION, is created by the following SQL:

```
CREATE OR REPLACE VIEW
AVERAGE_SALARY_BY_REGION AS
SELECT A.REGION_ID,
B.SUM_SALARY/A.EMPLOYEE_COUNT AVERAGE_SALARY
FROM EMPLOYEES_BY_REGION A,
SALARY_BY_REGION B
WHERE A.REGION_ID=B.REGION_ID;
```

Filtering Data

View SELECT statements include WHERE clauses, which allow you to create filter conditions. This enables users to quickly access a specific subset or class of instances of a particular business entity. Figure 13.3 illustrates the use of a view to filter data the user sees. Suppose certain users have no need to see sensitive data, such as SSN and salary. A view can be created to filter out those columns, presenting the user with only the required data.

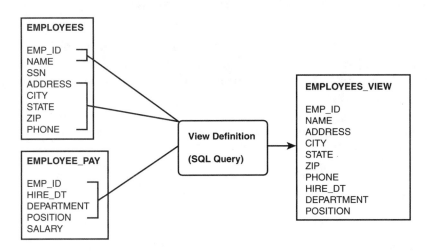

FIGURE 13.3
Using views to filter data.

In the following examples, a nontechnical accounting manager could hone in on various groups of accountants. The database has a single EMPLOYEES table, but the manager is generally interested only in accountants. A view called ACCOUNTANTS would show him just the accountants. The SQL code to define this view follows:

```
CREATE OR REPLACE VIEW ACCOUNTANTS AS
SELECT EMP_ID EMPLOYEE_ID, LNAME LAST_NAME,
FNAME FIRST_NAME
FROM EMPLOYEES
WHERE JOB_CATEGORY='ACCOUNTANT';
```

13

DESIGNING VIEWS

The simple SQL command SELECT * FROM ACCOUNTANTS; would provide the accounting manager with a list of all accountants.

Let's say that the database also has a performance-rating table with ratings of 1, 2, and 3 for good, average, and poor. A view showing accountants with a rating of 1 would show only the accountants that have a good current rating. Notice that the view SQL syntax also handles setting up the joins and the logical criteria rows must meet:

```
CREATE OR REPLACE VIEW GOOD_ACCOUNTANTS AS
SELECT A.EMP_ID EMPLOYEE_ID, A.LNAME  LAST_NAME, A.FNAME
       FIRST_NAME, B.RATING
FROM EMPLOYEES A, PERFORMANCE B
WHERE A.JOB_CATEGORY='ACCOUNTANT'
  AND (B.RATING=1 AND B.RATING_PERIOD='CURRENT')
  AND A.EMP_ID=B.EMP_ID;
```

A simple SELECT * FROM GOOD_ACCOUNTANTS; would provide the manager with a list of all accountants that have a 1 or good current rating.

Let's suppose the manager wants to know which accountants are high-salaried but marginal performers. A view that pulls data from the employee, performance, and benefits table with criteria of salary being over $50,000 and a current rating of poor would provide that information:

```
CREATE OR REPLACE VIEW OVERPAID_ACCOUNTANTS AS
SELECT A.EMP_ID EMPLOYEE_ID, A.LNAME LAST_NAME, A.FNAME
       FIRST_NAME, B. RATING, C.SALARY
FROM EMPLOYEES A, PERFORMANCE B, BENEFITS C
WHERE A.JOB_CAT='ACCOUNTANT'
  AND (B. LAST_RATING=3 AND B.RATING_PERIOD='CURRENT')
  AND C.SALARY>=50000
  AND A.EMP_ID=B.EMP_ID
  AND A.EMP_ID=C.EMP_ID;
```

Get the idea? If the manager typed SELECT * FROM OVERPAID_ACCOUNTANTS;, it would be a quick, easy way to figure out who to downsize.

Database Security

Views can be used to select columns from a table or a combination of joined tables that a particular user group needs to see, while leaving out of the view all the columns they don't need to see. Privileges granted for SELECT access and DML work the same for views as they do for tables. By creating a user view that has only the columns that a group needs to see and then granting SELECT and DML privileges as appropriate to the view and no SELECT or DML privileges to the underlying table or tables, you can keep a user group completely out of certain table columns. There may be columns that have private or sensitive data in them. By creating a view on a table while excluding sensitive columns from the view, users see only what they need.

NOTE

One of the main advantages of using views is for the enhancement of database security. Because views define a subset of data from one or more base tables, columns can be included or restricted from views. Without the use of views, end users are granted access on database tables. When views are used, end users can be granted access to only the views, and be restricted access to the underlying tables themselves.

Figure 13.4 illustrates the benefits gained by using views to control database security. In this figure, there are two different groups of users, each with a different level of data access. The first group must be able to perform transactional activity, whereas the second group needs only to query the database. The users who need full access are granted access to the database tables by the schema owner. The users needing only query access are granted access to the view, which may have filtered columns, as discussed in the previous section.

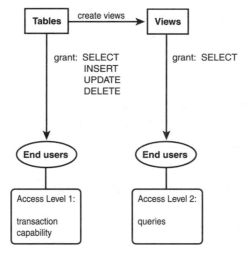

FIGURE 13.4
Using views to enhance security.

NOTE

Privileges are granted to and revoked from users for views just as they are with database tables. Remember that once a view is created, it is in essence, a table.

Rows of data can also be excluded from user views based on logical conditions in the view WHERE clause. In the previous example pertaining to accountants, users with access only to the ACCOUNTANTS view and not to the underlying tables would have access only to the specific accountant-related information provided by the view.

Data Conversion

Data conversion is related to filtering data because it represents the source data in a format that is more presentable to the end users for a given purpose. For example, suppose you have the following CUSTOMERS table:

CUSTOMERS
CUST_ID
L_NAME
F_NAME
M_NAME
ADDRESS
CITY
STATE
ZIP
PHONE

Suppose the mail room needs to print mailing labels to mail all customers the latest product catalog. A view may be created as follows:

```
CREATE VIEW MAIL_LABELS AS
SELECT L_NAME || ', ' || F_NAME || ' ' || M_NAME "LINE1",
       ADDRESS "LINE2",
       CITY || ', ' || STATE || ' ' || ZIP "LINE3"
FROM CUSTOMERS;
```

Customer data as represented in the MAIL_LABELS view would appear as follows:

MAIL_LABELS:

LINE1	LINE2	LINE3
Kruger, Freddy L	601 Elm St.	Indianapolis, IN 46211

When a query is executed against the MAIL_LABELS view, the output, used to print the mailing labels, would appear as follows if each column in the output was forced to print on a separate line:

Kruger, Freddy L
601 Elm St.
Indianapolis, IN 46211

Data Partitioning

Data can be partitioned, which means that subsets of data from a table can be stored separate from one another, with the intent of improving performance. Suppose you have an encyclopedia set. The set is organized in many volumes. For instance, all subjects beginning with the letter A would be stored in the first volume, the B's would be stored in the second volume, and so on. This type of organization makes information in the encyclopedia easier to find and speeds up the process as well. Imagine an encyclopedia that consists of only one massive volume and how much longer it would take you to find *caterpillar*. With a one-volume set, individuals would have to wait to use the encyclopedia, whereas with it split into multiple volumes, there is a decreased chance of waiting. Data partitioning adheres to the same principles.

Data can be partitioned in many ways, depending on the RDBMS selected, the operating system platform, and hardware. The previous chapter discussed Redundant Array of Inexpensive Disks (RAID) and how it may be used to partition data across hardware devices. There are other ways of partitioning data that are independent of the RDBMS, OS, or hardware. As long as a relational database is being designed, data partitioning can be accomplished using simple tables and views.

Figure 13.5 shows how data in a large table might be partitioned in order to improve database performance. The large table is split into three separate tables. All three tables will have the same structure (columns, data types, constraints), but certain criteria will be placed on data in the original table to populate each one of the partitioned tables. Once all three partitioned tables have been created, a view is created based on all three subsets of data from the original table. What does this gain? To the users, one object (the view) has all the data they need. The database will perform better because the data is physically separated, particularly if multiple users are accessing the data or small amounts of data (perhaps from just one partition) are selected on a regular basis.

13

DESIGNING VIEWS

> **NOTE**
>
> A strong fundamental knowledge of good design and partitioning concepts are absolutely key when building databases that will scale very high or span across multiple hosts. RDBMS partitioning features, when used for a well-modeled and properly partitioned workload, are extremely beneficial in performance tuning and guaranteeing high availability. If the implemented model does not take into account the working realities (capabilities) of the host operating system as it relates to properly partitioned tables, much of the efforts and cost of design will be in vain.

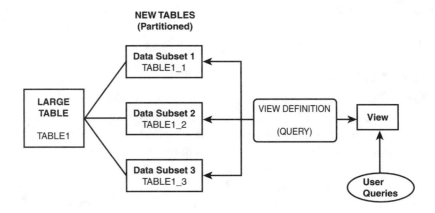

**NEW TABLES
(Partitioned)**

FIGURE 13.5

A view's role in data partitioning.

The previous chapter discussed data archival and purging for an online bookstore. Data archival and purging serves two purposes: to more adequately manage space consumption, and to improve performance of data retrievals. Given the same scenario, study Table 13.1 to see the storage plan for data in the organization. An online bookstore such as Amazon.com generates a tremendous amount of data based on orders that occur. Archival and purging of data should be a major consideration for any organization dealing with large amounts of data. It can either be handled now, in design, or later when problems occur. Why not be proactive?

TABLE 13.1 Plan for Data Archival and Purging

Data	Storage Plan
Current year	Online
2 to 3 years old	Archive to alternate server or tape; readily available
4 to 7 years old	Archive to tape and store
7+ years old	Purge

Table 13.2 proposes a plan to partition data for the online bookstore. Archiving and purging occurs for the purpose of space management. Partitioning is performed to improve performance. Notice that the organization of data in Table 13.2 corresponds with the way data is stored in Table 13.1. The rightmost column of Table 13.2 identifies the partition number of the data, which is just some arbitrary number assigned to different subsets of data based on the time period. The oldest year's data starts with partition number 1. The partition number is incremented up to the most current data, which has no partition number.

Table 13.2 Plan for Data Partitioning

Data	Storage Plan	Partition Number
Current year 2000	Online	N/A
Year 1999	Online	7
Year 1998	Online	6
Year 1997	Tape	5
Year 1996	Tape	4
Year 1995	Tape	3
Year 1994	Tape	2
Year 1993	Purged	1

Here is the plan. The oldest partition (lowest partition number) will be purged each year, making room for new data for the current year. For instance, in the year 2001, partition number 2 will be purged and partition number 8 assigned to year 2000 data. In 2002, partition number 3 will be purged and partition number 9 assigned to year 2001 data, and so forth. The idea is to maintain data only for the last seven years.

Year 2000 Partition Steps

The following is an example of the steps that might take place in order to create partitions for data if the current year is 2000. The following tables are created based on the original ORDERS table:

```
CREATE TABLE ORDERS_7 AS
SELECT * FROM ORDERS
WHERE ORD_DT BETWEEN '01-JAN-1999' AND '31-DEC-1999';

CREATE TABLE ORDERS_6 AS
SELECT * FROM ORDERS
WHERE ORD_DT BETWEEN '01-JAN-1998' AND '31-DEC-1998';

CREATE TABLE ORDERS_5 AS
SELECT * FROM ORDERS
WHERE ORD_DT BETWEEN '01-JAN-1997' AND '31-DEC-1997';

CREATE TABLE ORDERS_4 AS
SELECT * FROM ORDERS
WHERE ORD_DT BETWEEN '01-JAN-1996' AND '31-DEC-1996';

CREATE TABLE ORDERS_3 AS
SELECT * FROM ORDERS
WHERE ORD_DT BETWEEN '01-JAN-1995' AND '31-DEC-1995';
```

13

Designing Views

```
CREATE TABLE ORDERS_2 AS
SELECT * FROM ORDERS
WHERE ORD_DT BETWEEN '01-JAN-1994' AND '31-DEC-1994';
```

Export ORDERS_2, ORDERS_3, ORDERS_4, and ORDERS_5 to tape. Remember that because these partitions contain data two to three years old, they will be stored on tape. Once these partitions have been successfully archived to tape, they need not be stored online. The partition tables that have been archived to tape may now be dropped from the online database using the following commands:

```
DROP TABLE ORDERS_2;
DROP TABLE ORDERS_3;
DROP TABLE ORDERS_4;
DROP TABLE ORDERS_5;
```

Check constraints should be added to the online partitions to ensure that only the desired dates are stored in each partition table. Now that the partition tables have been created, data not belonging to the current year can be deleted from the original ORDERS table, as in the following SQL statement:

```
DELETE FROM ORDERS WHERE ORD_DT < '01-JAN-2000';
```

When new order information is entered into the database, the data is also entered into the original ORDERS table. By keeping the current year's information in the original ORDERS table, the application code will not have to be changed to point to the partitions for transactional activity. End users may need to query data not found in the original ORDERS table (the current year's data). A view can be created that combines the data from all table partitions. The application is coded to query the view instead of the ORDERS table or one of its partitions. The following CREATE VIEW statements exemplify how data can be logically grouped into a view. The application is kept simple by having one source that users access, while performance is improved because the data is physically separated, or *partitioned*, according to date.

```
CREATE OR REPLACE VIEW ORDERS_VIEW AS
SELECT * FROM ORDERS
UNION ALL
SELECT * FROM ORDERS_6
UNION ALL
SELECT * FROM ORDERS_7;
```

Year 2001 Partition Steps

This is simply an example of managing the partitions each subsequent year, with the oldest partition number being purged each year. The tape containing the ORDERS_2 table can be recycled. If the whole tape is not dedicated to ORDERS_2, the tape should not be recycled. Instead, only the information associated with ORDERS_2 should be removed from the tape.

Referring back to Table 13.2, partition number 6 is the oldest online data, which is now eligible for archival. Therefore, the ORDERS_6 table is exported and stored on tape. Now, the ORDERS_6 table should be dropped because it has been archived. This is done in the following code:

```
DROP TABLE ORDERS_6;
```

Now, another partition table, ORDERS_8, is created to store the most recent year's data. Remember to add a check constraint to the new online partition table (ORDERS_8) to ensure that only desired dates are stored in the table (in case somebody or some process tries to directly update the table). Here's how:

```
CREATE TABLE ORDERS_8 AS
SELECT * FROM ORDERS
WHERE ORD_DT BETWEEN '01-JAN-2000' AND '31-DEC-2000';
```

Because the data for the previous year's data has been partitioned (copied into a secondary table), the data can be removed from the original ORDERS table, as shown by the following code (as a reminder, only the current year's data is stored in the original ORDERS table):

```
DELETE FROM ORDERS WHERE ORD_DT < '01-JAN-2001';
```

Finally, the ORDERS_VIEW view is rebuilt to reflect the current table partitions:

```
CREATE OR REPLACE VIEW ORDERS_VIEW AS
SELECT * FROM ORDERS
UNION ALL
SELECT * FROM ORDERS_7
UNION ALL
SELECT * FROM ORDERS_8;
```

In summary, ORDERS_6 was archived and a partition called ORDERS_8 was added, which must be reflected in the view definition. The current year's definition in the view (ORDERS) will always stay the same.

View Performance and Other Considerations

Views, as defined, are stored queries. The same tuning considerations that enhance query performance will also increase a view's performance. However, tuning is RDBMS version specific. Placing indexes on appropriate join columns in the WHERE clause of a query will generally enhance performance in any Relational Database Management System.

View performance depends on the organization of the view definition itself and on the hardware, the RDBMS, and the database design. If the tables involved are large, several joins between tables are required, or the database host computer is already challenged in terms of CPU or memory utilization, view performance can quickly become an issue. A view is a constantly updated query, and it can be resource intensive depending on the nature of that query.

13

DESIGNING VIEWS

> **NOTE**
>
> We have found that the use of views at the application level (definition of views to resolve complicated and long-running queries) significantly improves performance. The combination of views defined during the design process and application views defined for the purpose of speeding SQL queries should be taken advantage of. In most systems we have seen, this is not the case.

In addition to view performance, there are two other basic considerations to keep in mind when designing views as part of your database. The following list outlines the considerations discussed in this section:

- Join operations in view definitions
- View limitations

Join Operations in View Definitions

Another relational database characteristic to remember as you design views is the use of joins when merging data from multiple tables. First, when multiple tables are joined, one row of output for every possible combination of rows from each table will result, based on the criteria provided in the WHERE clause. To demonstrate, the EMPLOYEES, BENEFITS, and DEPENDENTS tables will be used.

The three tables could be joined based on the equality of the EMP_ID column. There are two one-to-many relationships here. Each employee may have one or more benefits and may have one or more dependents.

EMPLOYEES *EMP_ID*	*BENEFITS* *EMP_ID*	*TYPE*	*DEPENDENTS* *EMP_ID*	*FNAME*
1	1	SALARY	1	MARY
2	1	BONUS	1	BILL
3	2	SALARY	2	TOM
	3	SALARY	3	CINDY
	3	BONUS	3	MICHAEL
	3	STOCK	3	BERNARD

Here's the SQL to create the view:

```
CREATE OR REPLACE EMPLOYEE_VIEW AS
SELECT A.EMP_ID, B.TYPE, C.FNAME
FROM EMPLOYEES A, BENEFITS B, DEPENDENTS C
WHERE A.EMP_ID=B.EMP_ID
  AND A.EMP_ID=C.EMP_ID;
```

The thing to remember is that there is only a single row for each employee ID in the EMPLOYEES table. By the time the joins have finished creating output rows for every possible EMP_ID match combination, employee 1 will have two benefits and two dependents. Employee 1 will end up having four output rows in the view. Employee 3, with three benefits and three dependents, will have a total of nine output rows in the view, which is misleading. Summary data based on joins of multiple tables with more than one one-to-many relationship has a very good chance of being inflated due to this repetition of rows. The output of a query against this view would appear as follows:

EMP_ID	TYPE	FNAME
1	SALARY	MARY
1	SALARY	BILL
1	BONUS	MARY
1	BONUS	BILL
2	SALARY	TOM
3	SALARY	CINDY
3	SALARY	MICHAEL
3	SALARY	BERNARD
3	BONUS	CINDY
3	BONUS	MICHAEL
3	BONUS	BERNARD
3	STOCK	CINDY
3	STOCK	MICHAEL
3	STOCK	BERNARD

Another concern related to view joins based on multiple tables is the problem with equi-joins, where if a particular row value does not find a match in any one of the tables being joined, the row does not appear in the output at all. Suppose employee 2 gets a divorce and no longer has any dependents. Study the following modified data:

| EMPLOYEES | BENEFITS | | DEPENDENTS | |
EMP_ID	EMP_ID	TYPE	EMP_ID	FNAME
1	1	SALARY	1	MARY
2	1	BONUS	1	BILL
3	2	SALARY		
	3	SALARY	3	CINDY
	3	BONUS	3	MICHAEL
	3	STOCK	3	BERNARD

The SQL used before would produce no rows of output for employee 2 because there is no match for employee 2 in the dependents table. To overcome this problem, you would need to create a view using an outer join, with the benefit of the outer join going to the EMPLOYEES table. Here's the code to create the view with an outer join in ORACLE SQL:

NOTE

An outer join allows you to see all data from one table, even if there are no corresponding rows of data in the second table. With an outer join, the test is for equality. As in the example, it may be necessary to generate a complete list of employees, whether or not an employee has any dependents. If a simple equi-join is used, no matches for an employee with no dependents will be found in the DEPENDENTS table. So only the employees with dependents will be shown in the query output. With an outer join, all employees, regardless of number of dependents, will be reported. Dependent information will also be shown with an outer join.

```
CREATE OR REPLACE VIEW EMPLOYEE_VIEW AS
SELECT A.EMP_ID, B.TYPE, C.FNAME
FROM EMPLOYEES A, BENEFITS B, DEPENDENTS C
WHERE A.EMP_ID=B.EMP_ID(+)
  AND A.EMP_ID=C.EMP_ID(+);
```

The character in ORACLE SQL used to represent an outer join operation is the plus sign. The plus sign is placed to the right of the column in the table that might not have matching rows to the base table. In this case, the base table is EMPLOYEES, because all employees must have a record here.

A similar outer join operation in SQL Server would appear as follows:

```
CREATE VIEW EMPLOYEE_VIEW AS
SELECT A.EMP_ID, B.TYPE
FROM EMPLOYEES A LEFT OUTER JOIN BENEFITS B
WHERE A.EMP_ID=B.EMP_ID(+)
```

The effect of the outer join would be that all rows from EMPLOYEES will be in the output, even if there is no match for an employee's ID in the other two tables. Only one table in the view can get the benefit of an outer join at a time. In this example, it is the EMPLOYEES table.

> **NOTE**
>
> Keeping in mind that ANSI SQL is merely a standard (guidelines), and not a language itself, remember that different vendors provide varying implementations of standard SQL features, such as outer joins.

View Limitations

If the intent is to use a view to support DML, limitations on DML updates to the tables behind views must be considered. These limitations are to a high degree RDBMS specific, but the following are examples of update limitations that might exist on the tables behind views:

- You cannot delete data using a view with a sub-SELECT in its WHERE clause.
- You can insert into or update only one table in a view at a time. There is only one updatable table in a view.
- Using DISTINCT in the VIEW SELECT query precludes UPDATE or DELETE DML on the underlying table.
- All NOT NULL columns in the underlying table must have a value in the INSERT row from the view if the INSERT is to work.
- There can be no updates on a virtual (a calculated or concatenated) view column.
- The tables behind summary views that include a GROUP BY clause cannot be updated.

View Relationships

There are just a few ways in which views may be related to one another or other objects in the database. Views may be related to either other views or tables in the database. There is no formal relationship between views as there are with tables. A view is ultimately based on one or more tables. The only formal relationships are those that exist between the tables (one-to-one,

13

one-to-many, and many-to-many), which are resolved when the query behind the view is executed. Because a view is a virtual table, virtual relationships may exist between views and tables.

Within a view definition, the following relationships may exist:

- Table-to-table
- Table-to-view
- View-to-view

Figure 13.6 illustrates the basis for view creation and the relationships that exist between views and tables. In the figure, Table 1 contains the source data used to define View 1. View 3 is also based on a table. View 2 gets its source data from Table 3 and View 1 (which gets its data from Table 1). View 4 gets its data from View 2 (which gets data from Table 3 and View 1) and View 3 (which gets its data from Table 2). You can see how relationships can become complicated if you are not careful.

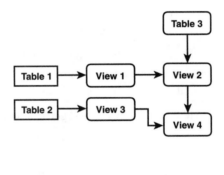

Figure 13.6

View creation and relationship scenarios.

A view that includes columns from multiple tables will require a join clause just as any query pulling data from multiple tables will. For example, study the following `CREATE VIEW` statement:

```
CREATE VIEW JOB_VIEW AS
SELECT E.NAME, P.PAY_RATE, J.JOB_LOCATION, J.DATE
FROM EMPLOYEES E, BENEFITS P, JOBS J
WHERE E.SSN = P.SSN;
```

Table-to-table joins generally will be equi-joins or outer joins, based on primary and foreign key relationships. These joins are unique at least on one side of the relationship. Joins between tables on non-key columns are also acceptable, but care should be taken to ensure that the results are meaningful in such a potential many-to-many relationship.

Joins between tables and views can be and often are made. The view is treated just like a table in the view-creation SQL. Grouped views (views including a GROUP BY clause) cannot be joined to a table in some RDBMSs. For example, study the following CREATE VIEW statement:

```
CREATE VIEW CITY_PAY AS
SELECT CITY, AVG(SALARY) "AVG_SAL"
FROM EMPLOYEE_PAY
GROUP BY CITY;
```

Joins between two views can also be made. Both views are treated like tables in the view-creation SQL. As with table-to-view relationships, a grouped view (a view including a GROUP BY clause) cannot be joined to another view in some RDBMSs.

Managing Views

Once views are created, they must be managed just like any other database object. Although database management is beyond the scope of this book, view management must be understood so that views may be defined properly during design.

Figure 13.7 illustrates the different levels of views that could exist in a database. The first level contains views whose definitions are based on only database tables. The second level has views dependent on other views, as does the third level. The reason that views should only be created two or three levels deep is simple. If, for example, Table 2 gets dropped, the following views are now invalid: View 2, View 3, View 5, and View 7. If View 1 is dropped, then Views 4, 5, 6, and 7 are made invalid. If a column definition is changed in Table 1, many views may be affected by the change.

The point being that if there are too many view levels, they become difficult to manage. If view definitions become invalid, queries and application programs may no longer work; or worse, the customer may think that data is missing. Luckily, you know that views do not actually contain any data, but their lack of validity may halt a production system if not properly managed. If a change is made to a base table or view, it is important to evaluate the effect on all database objects (tables and views) as well as any queries or application programs. This is all part of the change-management process, which is discussed in Chapter 16, "Change Control."

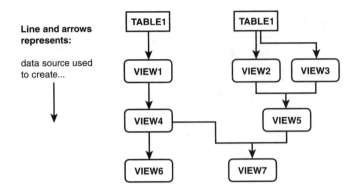

FIGURE 13.7

View management problems.

Views two levels deep (views whose source is another view) are usually okay as long as your machine has adequate resources and there are not too many joins of large tables involved. To avoid performance issues and to simplify view management, you probably should not go more than three view levels deep (a view selecting from a view that selects from a view).

Another concern for managing views deals with ownership. Suppose the owner (schema owner) of the base tables for a database application is called SCHEMA1. SCHEMA1 is responsible for managing grants and revokes of object privileges to and from tables in the schema to end users. Now, suppose that USER1 creates view on one of SCHEMA1's tables. In order for other users to see the data in USER1's view, USER1 must grant privileges on the view to the appropriate users. As you can imagine, control may be quickly lost as numerous users begin creating views, and then sharing those views with other users. In turn, users may begin to code queries or application components that reference views. Similar to the aforementioned problem of too many view levels, too many view owners likewise become a problem. As with any objects in a schema, it is the best practice for all views to be owned by a single user, preferably the original schema owner.

Avoiding Poor View Design

As with any other part of the database that is being designed, it is important to watch out for common failure points that organizations tend to have with views. In order to get good view performance, there are several things to avoid when you're designing views:

- Avoid trying to update tables through complex views. Updates through views are subject to complex rules, some of which have been mentioned already. Update rules vary considerably from RDBMS to RDBMS. Identifying the view-update rules for your RDBMS and applying them on a case-by-case basis to update requirements should be part of your design. The general guideline is that simple views are usually updatable and complex ones aren't. Complex views should be reserved for query-only operations.

- Views nested more than three views deep will probably have performance problems and will be very difficult to manage.

- Views with multiple joins to large tables will often be slow. Such views that do not have or do not utilize indexes on the join columns will be extremely slow.

- Views that include complex calculations will often be slow. Ensure that calculations are not executed on a larger set of rows in the view than is really necessary and that calculations are not more complex than necessary.

- Views should take advantage of the same RDBMS-specific tuning principles that are applied to any database query. Executing the query yourself, analyzing the results, and applying SQL tuning to the SQL in the view-creation script will usually provide a good view performance return for the tuning time invested. Views, by their nature, are often placed at key points in applications to perform calculations or present data in a particular format. Tuning views is often a cheap place to find improved application performance and is a good place to start looking if your application needs a performance boost.

View Definitions for the Sample Company TrainTech

There are a few potential view candidates for the sample company TrainTech. Again, refer to TrainTech's ERD, as shown in Figure 11.3 in Chapter 11, "Designing Tables," assuming that the finished table design and ERD match.

Some of the view candidates for our sample company TrainTech follow:

COURSE_VIEW
COID
NAME
FEE
TOT_TIMES_TAUGHT
AVG_CLASS_SIZE
TOT_STUDENTS_TAUGHT
TOT_REVENUE
AVG_REVENUE_PER_CLASS
NUMBER_OF_DAYS_SCHEDULED

13

DESIGNING VIEWS

STUDENT_VIEW
SID
LNAME
FNAME
MNAME
ADDRESS
CITY
ST
ZIP
PNONE
NUM_CLASSES_TAKEN
TOT_DOLLARS_SPENT

INSTRUCTOR_VIEW
IID
LNAME
FNAME
MI
HIRE_DT
YRS_EMPLOYED
PAY_RATE
TOT_CRS_CAPABLE_TO_TEACH
TOT_CLASSES_TAUGHT

All these views have some form of summarization and filtering. It is assumed that security is not so much an issue in this scenario. However, if the person in charge of scheduling classes should not see certain data (the instructor's pay rate, for example), then such columns should be filtered out using a view. For an organization such as this, partitioning is not necessarily a factor. This is a small training company. For a national or international training company, partitioning may be much more of an issue.

Summary

Tables are the primary storage mechanisms for any relational database, and views are virtual tables that allow users to see data given from different perspectives. Views do not contain any data. The only space required to store a view in the database is that required to store the SQL query that defines the view. When a view is queried, the view definition, a query itself, is executed by the RDBMS against the base tables that comprise the view.

Views have many uses in a relational database, all revolving around one basic concept: to present the data to the users in an alternative format with no impact on the physical structure or physical data. Some of the common purposes for creating views include data summarization, filtering data, database security, improving database and application performance, and data partitioning.

A view can be created from a table, from another view, or from any combination of related tables and views. When creating views, pay close attention to their relationships to one another and to the view levels. A view level of two or three should not be exceeded. If too many levels of views are created, it is difficult to determine the impact of a simple structure change to a table or view on which other views depend. If a view becomes invalid, the production database may not function as expected. Also, there may appear to be a problem with the data itself to the end users, who will demand an explanation.

Views are very significant components to the relational database, and they should be used, although their capabilities sometimes tend to be ignored. The design of views should at least be considered as part of the physical design of the database, particularly after all table definitions are complete.

13

DESIGNING VIEWS

Applying Database Design Concepts

IN THIS CHAPTER

So far, you have read about the process of designing a database to fit a relational model. As covered earlier in Chapter 3, "Database Design Planning," the basic phases of database design, as discussed in this book, include the following:

- Gathering requirements
- Building data models
- Designing the database

Chapter 4, "The Database Design Life Cycle," presented the Barker method, which included the following database design phases:

- Strategy
- Analysis
- Design
- Build
- Documentation
- Transition
- Production

The first four phases of the Barker method are covered extensively in this book, and the last three are referenced and discussed briefly, where applicable. Regardless of the methodology used to design a database, common sense dictates that information must be learned about the organization and captured through whatever means necessary, and the information must be transformed into a database. So far, a systematic approach to design has been taken to simplify the process. Much time was spent on information gathering and logical modeling, which help provide a clear understanding of an organization's needs. This is imperative to a successful design.

During the discussion of logical modeling, the main focal points included

- Gathering requirements via interviews
- Understanding entities, processes, and entity relationships
- Creating ERDs to visually represent an organization's data
- Creating process models to depict the processes performed by an organization and using the processes to determine how data is accessed

In terms of physical design, the main focal points included

- The design of tables
- The design of constraints to enforce business rules, as defined in ERDs and process models
- The design of views to provide alternate representations of an organization's data to the end user

The motivation for this chapter is to provide you with a case study, showing a quick design of a relational database from ground zero, and at the same time providing you with an increased understanding of the knowledge you've gained so far in this book.

Database Design Case Study

The following case study involves the need that a growing grocery store, Ronaldo Foods, has for a database in order to manage various information. The owner of the grocery store has decided to invest money into an information system. The following text in this section is a monologue spoken by the business owner, describing the business to a consulting firm as a preliminary step to designing the database. The following monologue takes place during the initial interview. During the monologue, the firm has listened intently and taken notes by hand, in addition to the approved use of a tape recorder.

PRACTICAL EXAMPLES

The monologue begins now.

When I first started the store, there was me, my wife, and a couple of teens working. We had the grocery department and the produce and deli departments. We had 150 to 200 customers, no advertising, nothing really special. The building had plenty of room to grow. We allocated space as the business grew. I kept the books, did the payroll, ordered the merchandise—did just about everything. Now, we just added a second store and have 125 employees—up from 55. We added a meat department, a flower department, a video section, and a summer garden section. I cannot keep the records and books for all this by hand anymore. I need to get with the times and enter the computer age. I need to replace my paper database with a computer database.

I need to keep track of the business. I need to keep information on my employees, the departments, sales, inventory, taxes, payroll, vendors, customers, advertising, accounts payable, and accounts receivable.

The goal of my business is to make money. I plan to do this by supplying a quality product at a reasonable price and giving good service. The database should keep all information about my employees, including name, home address, phone, emergency contact information, social security number, birthday, and employment data such as date started, pay rate, work department, previous departments worked, and anniversary date of hire.

I need information about each department, such as sales, inventory, who works in each department, supplies, and where to get them and how to get them, inventory as far as where to buy, from whom, actual counts of items, and inventory loss.

I need feedback information on our advertising, such as coupon counts, customer counts, advertised item counts, pricing, cost of advertising, who I advertise with, and contacts.

Other very important information that needs to be kept involves holidays and information such as sales, ads, help scheduling, and customer counts.

I run the business. I have department heads for each department. They order the merchandise and manage the employees who work for them. I have a store manager for each store who the department heads answer to. I set the ads up two months in advance with the store manager's input, who gets his input from the department heads. I also have a head cashier for each store who is responsible for keeping track of the sales, cash, bank deposits, cashiers, and sack boys.

We open at 7:00 a.m. and close at 11:00 p.m., Sunday through Saturday. The employees are scheduled on a weekly basis and come in various days and times. We have both full-time and part-time employees. I am the only "outside" employee who works both stores and performs duties for both stores. In my absence, one of the store managers will act for me.

The head cashier supervises the front-end help, which includes the cashiers and sack boys. She helps with the scheduling, keeps the customer lines going, keeps track of the receipts for the day's business, prepares the bank deposits, orders the change, and prepares weekly sales reports as well as monthly sales reports.

The produce manager schedules his help, orders the produce merchandise, sets the displays, meets with the store manager for advertising ideas, and supervises his help. During the summer months, the produce manager will also manage the garden shop.

The meat manager schedules his help, orders the meat product, orders supplies, sets the displays, meets with the store manager for advertising ideas, and supervises his help.

The deli and video managers perform the same type of duties.

The two stores' information will be kept separate, but together. Inventories should be able to be checked to help each other with overages and/or lack of inventory of sales items. There may be both permanent help or temporary transfers of help between the different stores.

The cashiers have a responsibility of checking out the customers. They ring up purchases and take cash, checks, or charge cards for the customers. Their cash drawers are to be to the penny. The cashiers are not to have more than $400 at any one time in their cash drawers. If a cashier has over $400, then she does a pickup. She counts out approximately $300 and calls the office cashier. The office cashier comes out to the register and picks up the cash and takes it to the office. The cashier will also assist the sack boys with bagging the groceries. The cashier will call for help when lines of customers build up or when customers require help with their groceries.

The sack boys are responsible for bagging the customers' groceries, carrying out the groceries for the customers, putting back items customers have changed their minds on, retrieving items that customers could not find or have forgotten, gathering carts from the parking lot, keeping bags available, keeping the front end clean, and checking prices for unmarked items or items for which the customer disagrees on the price.

The produce clerks work for the produce manager. They unload delivery trucks, prepare the product for sale, prepare the signs, and set up the racks with product for sale. During summer time, they assist with the garden shop, keeping their area clean and free of debris. The garden shop carries flowers, vegetables, and various supplies. Clerks water the plants, set up displays, and set up advertising and pricing signs. When product does not look so good, they mark it down for quick sale.

The deli clerks work for the deli manager. They unload delivery trucks, wait on customers, set up display areas with product, set up pricing signs, set up advertising signs, assist meat counter personnel with customers, and prepare special orders (meat trays, birthday cakes, and so on).

The meat department has two subdepartments: the sales people at the counter and the meat cutters. The counter people stock the meat case with product, set up advertising signs and pricing signs, constantly rotate product, wait on customers, assist deli clerks with customers, may assist with unloading product, and keep supplies filled. The meat cutters cut the meat for sale as well as weigh, price, and package the meat for sale. They unload deliveries and assist the counter people with customers. They also help load bulk sales for customers.

The video clerks work for the video manager. They wait on customers, restock returned movies, check for late returns, send out notices for late returns, stock new movies, and stock their grocery rack with candies and popcorn.

The office cashiers work for the head cashier. They make bank deposits, count the cashiers' cash drawers after their shifts, and wait on customers by writing money orders, cashing checks, selling stamps, issuing new check-cashing cards, and running the quick check. They also take change to the cashiers, count the pickups of cash from the cashiers, control the front end, call for help when needed, and count and deposit the candy and pop machine money. They also stock the cigarette rack and the health and beauty aids aisle.

Each store has one manager and two assistants who are in charge of the grocery department as well as assist in managing the store. The store manager is responsible for the smooth operation of the store, taking care of the customers, scheduling employees, counseling employees, interviewing prospective new hires, ordering products, overseeing the stocking of product, checking in deliveries, dealing with vendors, planning and setting up displays, implementing price changes, and helping with other departments when necessary.

We also have what we call the backdoor man. He is responsible for checking in all deliveries. He keeps the backroom clean and free of debris, and he keeps the area around the dumpster clean and free of debris. He also fills the candy and pop machines with product and takes the money to the office cashiers.

My wife and I keep the books and report everything to the accountant and the payroll service. We have plans to hire a payroll clerk after we open our next store. I meet with the department heads and management to set up the advertising and make holiday plans. I try to see as many customers as possible. I am making plans now to open three more stores within the next two years. Employee growth should double. Sales are expected to triple.

The monologue is complete.

Making Sense of the Regurgitated Information

If you know what information to look for, you can derive a great deal of information from the interview with the store owner. The information divulged by the store owner includes the following:

- Grocery store goal (mission statement)
- Departments (organizational units)
- Business data
- Business processes
- Business rules

If you were not able to identify most of the information in this list, you should reread the previous section before proceeding further. Look for key words that imply application to the topics in this list.

Isolating Individuals Associated with the Grocery Store

From the interview, you can conclude that the following types of individuals are associated with this particular grocery store, assuming that the information provided was complete:

- Business owner
- Wife (owner assistant or partner)
- Customers
- Store managers
- Store assistant managers
- Department managers

- Head cashiers
- Cashiers
- Office cashiers
- Sack boys
- Grocery department workers
- Produce department workers
- Deli department workers
- Meat department workers
- Flower department workers
- Video department workers
- Summer garden department workers
- Stock boys
- An accountant
- A payroll service
- A payroll clerk (near future)

The prospective users of the new database include the following people:

- Management
- Department management
- Cashiers
- Select department workers
- Payroll clerk

Finally, here are the types of employees:

- Full-time employees
- Part-time employees
- Temporary employees (transferred from another store)

The Interviewee's Interpretation of the Data Required

According to the store owner's monologue, he thinks that the following information needs to be stored in an automated database system. Only time will tell whether this list is complete:

- Employees
- Department sales
- Inventory

- Taxes
- Payroll
- Vendors
- Customers
- Advertising
- Accounts payable
- Accounts receivable

Formulating a Mission Statement and Design Objectives

The mission statement can be extracted directly from the owner's monologue. As you should recall, a mission statement refers to the goal of the proposed database. The design objectives, related to the mission statement, are detailed objectives of the proposed database, in relation to present-day and future needs.

The mission statement for Ronaldo Foods follows:

> An automated database system is needed to manage grocery store data, enabling the management of growing data and providing better service to the customer, thus increasing profits.

The design objectives for Ronaldo Foods follow:

- The manual processes involved in grocery management should be automated.
- Only internal company users should access the database.
- The relational database model will be used.
- An automated design tool will be used.
- There is no legacy database on which to base the new database.
- The database should be a single database that resides in one location, but it will be used by many stores.
- The users (cashiers and managers) will need a form interface to query and make changes to data.
- Management should be able to use the database to manage inventory, sales, and cash flow.
- Management should be able to make good business decisions based on product information stored over a given period of time.
- The database should be capable of providing reports to the accountant for tax-preparation purposes.
- The database should be capable of managing payroll.

Defining Organizational Units

Based on the information in the interview, as well as the information extracted from the interview as related to the different individuals associated with the business, the following list of organizational units can be derived:

- Store management
- Department management
- Cashiers
- Grocery
- Produce
- Deli
- Meat
- Flower
- Video
- Garden
- Accounting
- Payroll
- Stock

Defining Data

Based on interview information, basic data elements can be categorized as follows:

- Business ownership
- Product
- Product inventory
- Product sales
- Employee
- Employee work schedule
- Employee pay information
- Payroll
- Account receivable
- Account payable
- Department
- Video rental

14

APPLYING DATABASE DESIGN CONCEPTS

- Advertising
- Product vendor
- Advertising vendor
- Expendable supply
- Expense

Defining Processes

The following root processes have been defined:

Number	Process Name
1.0	Human resources
2.0	Product management
3.0	Sales
4.0	Purchasing
5.0	Accounting
6.0	Work scheduling
7.0	Advertising
8.0	Video sales

After additional interviews with the owner and the individuals responsible for managing these processes, the following preliminary decomposition of the root processes is performed:

1.0 Human Resource Management

    1.1 Hire Employee

        1.1.1 Process Resume

        1.1.2 Interview

        1.1.3 Hiring

    1.2 Change Employee Status

        1.2.1 Rate Employee

        1.2.2 Transfer Employee

        1.2.3 Promote Employee

        1.2.4 Change Personal Information

            1.2.4.1 Deductions

            1.2.4.2 Contact Information

    1.3 Dismiss Employee

        1.3.1 Interview Employee

        1.3.2 Alter Database Status

1.4 Manage Payroll

    1.4.1 Account for All Employees

    1.4.2 Return Report to Managers

    1.4.3 Forward Report to Account Payable

1.5 Advertise Job Opening

    1.5.1 Receive Position Request

    1.5.2 Request Budget

    1.5.3 Purchase Advertising Space

2.0 Product Management

    2.1 Review Product for Spoilage/Damage

        2.1.1 Generate Spoilage Totals

        2.1.2 Repackage/Discard Product

        2.1.3 Forward Spoilage Totals

    2.2 Conduct Inventory Accountability

    2.3 Conduct Expendable Supply Accountability

    2.4 Request Next Work Schedule

        2.4.1 Request Total Hours per Position

        2.4.2 Collect Employee Requests

        2.4.3 Request Actual Work Schedule

        2.4.4 Report Compliance with Work Schedule

    2.5 Conduct Repair/Maintenance

        2.5.1 Get Estimate of Expense

        2.5.2 Receive Approval of Expense

        2.5.3 Submit Request to Accounts Payable

3.0 Sales Processing

    3.1 Input Sales

    3.2 Reconcile Drawer

    3.3 Reconcile Head Cashier

    3.4 Forward Daily Report

    3.5 Generate Daily/Monthly Reports

        3.5.1 Coupons Used Report

        3.5.2 Sales of Items on Sale

        3.5.3 Sales of All Items

    3.6 Compile Daily Deposit to Accounts Receivable

        3.6.1 Leave Out Beginning Drawer Amounts

4.0 Purchasing

    4.1 Receive Inventory Totals

        4.1.1 Compute Loss

        4.1.2 Decrement Inventory

        4.1.3 Generate Reports

    4.2 Review Sales

        4.2.1 Alter Full Inventory Levels

        4.2.2 Generate Surplus Inventory Report

    4.3 Generate Needed Inventory Report

    4.4 Review Vendor Price List

    4.5 Submit Inventory Requests to Management

    4.6 Purchase Approved Inventory Requests

    4.7 Receive New Inventory

        4.7.1 Conduct Invoice Check

        4.7.2 Submit Invoice to Database

    4.8 Request Expendable Supplies

        4.8.1 Receive Expendable Supply Report

        4.8.2 Adjust Expendable Supply Levels

        4.8.3 Reorder Expendable Supplies

5.0 Accounting

    5.1 Reconcile Monthly Bank Statement

        5.1.1 Checks Written Cleared

        5.1.2 Checks Received Cleared

        5.1.3 Credit Card Amounts Received

        5.1.4 Daily Deposits Totaled

    5.2 Review Accounts Payable Requests

    5.3 Forward Accounts Payable Requests

    5.4 Forward Daily Checks/Cash Inflow

    5.5 Compile Profit/Loss Statement

        5.5.1 Pay Owner Profit

        5.5.2 Request Working Capital

6.0 Work Scheduling

    6.1 Receive Staffing Request from Departments

    6.2 Approve Staffing Requests

    6.3 Receive Personnel Preference

6.4 Generate Schedule

6.5 Publish Schedule

6.6 Alter Schedule

7.0 Advertising

7.1 Review Reports to Find Sales Needs

7.1.1 Move Spoil Reductions

7.1.2 Satisfy Consumer Need

7.1.2.1 Holiday Pricing

7.1.2.2 Item Popularity

7.1.2.3 Reaction to Competition

7.1.3 Pass Along Good Vendor Price

7.2 Confirm Advertising Budget

7.3 Review Advertising Efficiency

7.3.1 Compare Sale Items to Sale of Non-sale Items

7.3.2 Compare Increased Sales to Costs

7.4 Order Advertising

7.5 Order Market Research

8.0 Video Sales

8.1 Order New Movies

8.2 Get Sales Report

8.3 Reconcile Inventory

8.3.1 Deduct Lost Movies

8.3.2 Bill for Lost/Overdue Movies

8.3.3 Order More Popular Movies

8.3.4 Sell Unpopular Movies

Further decomposition may occur as the design process progresses. Additional interviews will assist in the further decomposition of both data and processes.

Proceeding with Database Design

At this point, most of the initial footwork has been achieved. The following tasks have been achieved:

- Initial interviews
- Analysis of interviews
- Formulation of mission statement and design objectives

14

APPLYING
DATABASE DESIGN
CONCEPTS

- Designation of organizational units
- Definition of the data
- Definition of business processes

Keep in mind that during analysis of the business, interviews and user-feedback sessions should be considered ongoing processes. Keep the customer as involved as possible initially to ensure that all requirements have been gathered. In this case, the firm had to go back to the owner and other key individuals to clarify information in order to derive what is now considered a complete list of data elements and processes.

It is now time to convert the gathered information into business models. The following subsections cover the listed design processes using the information gathered:

- Constructing an ERD
- Constructing process models
- Designing tables
- Defining constraints
- Designing views

Constructing an ERD

The information from the initial interview (monologue) and the process breakdown can now be used to devise an ERD. Figure 14.1 shows a basic ERD for Ronaldo Foods.

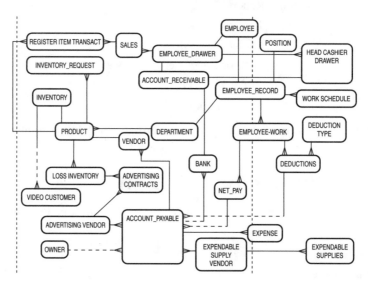

Figure 14.1
Basic ERD for Ronaldo Foods.

The following list shows the entities in the ERD and their attributes. These attributes have been listed, as opposed to shown in a detailed ERD, due to lack of page space. The detailed ERD would span multiple pages and be very difficult to understand in book format.

> **NOTE**
>
> A more detailed ERD is available on Macmillan USA's Web site. The URL for downloading the detailed ERD is www.mcp.com. Search for the book's ISBN, and you will be presented with a page where you can download the Web contents for this book.

ACCOUNT_PAYABLE

ACT_PAY_NO	(PRIMARY KEY)
ACT_PAY_AMT	
ADV_VEND_NO	
BANK_NO	
DEDUC_NO	
EXP_NO	
EXP_SUPPLY_VEND_NO	
NET_PAY_NO	
OWNER_NO	
VEND_NO	

ACCOUNT_RECEIVABLE

ACC_RECV_NO	(PRIMARY KEY)
ACC_RECV_AMT	
EMP_DRAWER_NO	
OFF_TRANSACT_NO	

ADVERTISING_CONTRACTS

ADV_CONTRACT_NO	(PRIMARY KEY)
ADV_VEND_NO	
AMOUNT	
DATE	
PROD_NO	
TYPE	

ADVERTISING_VENDOR

ADV_VEND_NO	(PRIMARY KEY)
ADV_COMPANY	
ADV_TYPE	
ADV_POC	
ADV_STREET	
ADV_CITY	
ADV_STATE	
ADV_ZIP	
ADV_PHONE	

BANK

BANK_NO	(PRIMARY KEY)
AMOUNT	
ACC_RECV_NO	
ACT_PAY_NO	

DEDUCTIONS

DEDUC_NO	(PRIMARY KEY)
DEDUC_AMT	
DEDUC_TYPE	
EMP_WORK_NO	

DEDUCTION_TYPE

DEDUC_TYPE_NO	(PRIMARY KEY)
DEDUC_NAME	

DEPARTMENT

DEPT_NO	(PRIMARY KEY)
STORE_NO	
DEPT_NAME	

EMPLOYEE

EMP_NO	(PRIMARY KEY)
LAST_NAME	
FIRST_NAME	
MIDDLE_NAME	

SSN
STREET
CITY
STATE
ZIP
PHONE
EMAIL
DATE_OF_BITH
DATE_STARTED
CONTACT_LAST
CONTACT_FIRST
CONTACT_MIDDLE
CONTACT_PHONE

EMPLOYEE_DRAWER

EMP_DRAWER_NO	(PRIMARY KEY)
DATE	
EMP_NO	
EMP_DRAWER_CARD	
EMP_DRAWER_CASH	
EMP_DRAWER_CHECK	
EMP_DRW_COUPON	
OFF_TRANSACT_AMT	

EMPLOYEE_RECORD

EMPREC_NO	(PRIMARY KEY)
DEPENDENTS	
DEPT_NO	
EMP_NO	
MONTHS_WORKED	
POS_NO	
PRESENT_PAY_RATE	
PAST_DEPT_NO1	
PAST_DEPT_NO2	
PAST_DEPT_NO3	

EMPLOYEE_WORK

EMP_WORK_NO	(PRIMARY KEY)
EMP_HOURS_WORKED	
EMP_WEEK_ENDING	

EXPENDABLE_SUPPLIES

EXPENDABLE_NO	(PRIMARY KEY)
EXP_VEND_NO	
ITEM_NAME	

EXPENDABLE_SUPPLY_VENDOR

EXP_SUPPLY_VEND_NO	(PRIMARY KEY)
EXP_VEND_COMPANY	
EXP_VEND_FIRST	
EXP_VEND_LAST	
EXP_VEND_MIDDLE	
EXP_VEND_STREET	
EXP_VEND_CITY	
EXP_VEND_STATE	
EXP_VEND_ZIP	
EXP_VEND_PHONE	

EXPENSE

EXP_NO	(PRIMARY KEY)
EXP_AMOUNT	
EXP_DATE	
EXP_NAME	
EXP_PURPOSE	
EXP_POC	
EXP_STREET	
EXP_CITY	
EXP_STATE	
EXP_ZIP	
EXP_PHONE	
EXP_COMMENT	

HEAD_CASHIER_DRAWER

OFF_TRANSACT_NO	(PRIMARY KEY)
AMOUNT	
EMP_DRAWER_NO	
OFF_TRANSACT_DATE	

INVENTORY

INV_NO	(PRIMARY KEY)
AMOUNT	
INVOICE_NO	
PROD_NO	
PURCHASE_PRICE_PER_ITEM	
RENTAL_ITEM	

INVENTORY_REQUEST

INVREQ_NO	(PRIMARY KEY)
AMOUNT	
PROD_NO	

LOSS_INVENTORY

LOSS_NO	(PRIMARY KEY)
PROD_NO	
PROD_AMOUNT	
PURCHASE_AMT	
REDUCTION	
RETAIL_AMT	
SPOIL	
THEFT	

NET_PAY

NET_PAY_NO	(PRIMARY KEY)
EMP_WHEN_PAID	
EMP_WORK_NO	
NET_PAY_AMT	

14

APPLYING
DATABASE DESIGN
CONCEPTS

OWNER

OWN_TRANS_NO	(PRIMARY KEY)
OWN_PROFIT_PAY	
OWN_PROF_PAY_DT	

POSITION

POS_NO	(PRIMARY KEY)
POSITION_NAME	

PRODUCT

PROD_NO	(PRIMARY KEY)
PRODUCT_NAME	
AMOUNT	
DEPT_NO	
VEND_NO	
WHOLESALE_PRICE	
RETAIL_PRICE	
ON_SALE	

REGISTER_ITEM_TRANSACT

REG_ITEM_TRANS_NO	(PRIMARY KEY)
AMOUNT	
PROD_NO	
SALE_NO	

SALES

SALE_NO	(PRIMARY KEY)
EMP_DRAWER_NO	
SALE_AMT	
SALE_TYPE	

VENDOR

VEND_NO	(PRIMARY KEY)
VEND_COMPANY	
VEND_POC	
VEND_LAST	
VEND_FIRST	

VEND_MIDDLE
VEND_STREET
VEND_CITY
VEND_STATE
VEND_ZIP
VEND_PHONE

VIDEO_CUSTOMER

VIDEO_NO	(PRIMARY KEY)
VIDEO_LAST	
VIDEO_FIRST	
VIDEO_MIDDLE	
VIDEO_STREET	
VIDEO_CITY	
VIDEO_STATE	
VIDEO_ZIP	
VIDEO_PHONE	
RENT1	
RENT2	
RENT3	
VIDEO_AMOUNT	
VIDEO_TOTAL	

WORK_SCHEDULE

WORK_SCH_NO	(PRIMARY KEY)
DATE_SUBMITTED	
EMPREC_NO	
WORK_DAY	
WORK_END	
WORK_MONTH	
WORK_START	
WORK_WEEKDAY	

Constructing Process Models

Because of space constraints in the book, not all the processes defined are modeled. Keep in mind that a detailed decomposition and discussion of business processes are out of the scope of this book. As stated before, it is important to define and model processes while modeling data to best ensure that the data model is complete.

Figure 14.2 shows a process model of the root processes that have been defined. Figure 14.3 shows a child process of Human Resource Management.

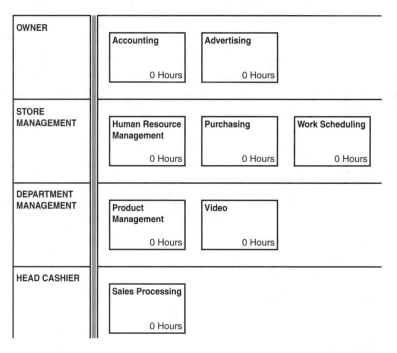

FIGURE 14.2

Sample process model for Ronaldo Foods.

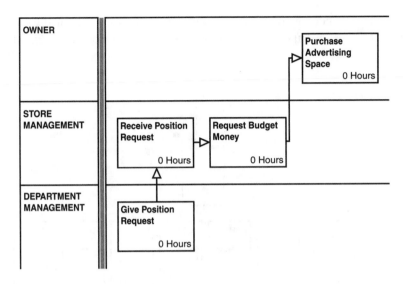

FIGURE 14.3

A sample child process.

Figure 14.4 is a data flow diagram, illustrating the flow of data based on the process modeled in Figure 14.3.

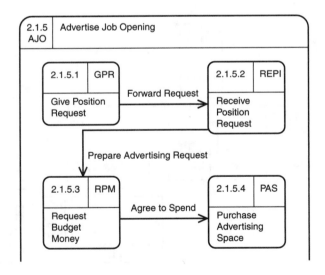

FIGURE 14.4

Sample data flow diagram for Ronaldo Foods.

Figure 14.5 shows a function hierarchy diagram of the root processes defined for Ronaldo Foods. Figure 14.6 illustrates the expansion of the child function modeled in Figure 14.3.

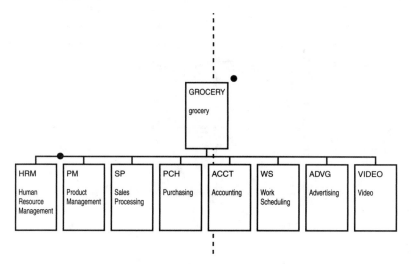

FIGURE 14.5

Sample function hierarchy diagram for Ronaldo Foods.

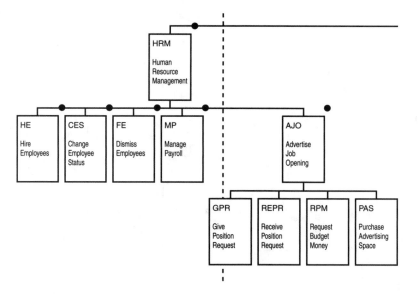

FIGURE 14.6

Partially expanded function hierarchy diagram for Ronaldo Foods.

This is just a minute portion of the process modeling that needs to take place for Ronaldo Foods. Once all processes have been modeled, they should be associated with entities, where appropriate, so that data usage can be checked for completeness. Remember that every entity should be accessed by a process and that processes, with few exceptions, should affect data.

Designing Tables

Based on the ERD, entities have been converted into tables and attributes into columns. Table 14.1 contains a list of tables, columns, data types, column nullability, and primary key (PK) and foreign key (FK) constraints.

TABLE 14.1   Table and Column List for Ronaldo Foods

Table/Columns	Data Type	Nullable	Constraint
ACCOUNTS_PAYABLE			
ACT_PAY_NO	NUMBER(10)	NOT NULL	PK
ACT_PAY_AMT	NUMBER(10,2)	NOT NULL	
ADV_VEND_NO	NUMBER(10)	NULL	FK
BANK_NO	NUMBER(10)	NOT NULL	FK
DEDUC_NO	NUMBER(10)	NOT NULL	FK
EXP_NO	NUMBER(10)	NOT NULL	FK
EXP_SUPPLY_VEND_NO	NUMBER(10)	NULL	FK
NET_PAY_NO	NUMBER(10)	NULL	FK
OWNER_NO	NUMBER(10)	NULL	FK
VEND_NO	NUMBER(10)	NULL	FK
ACCOUNTS_RECEIVABLE			
ACC_RECV_NO	NUMBER(10)	NOT NULL	PK
ACC_RECV_AMT	NUMBER(10,2)	NOT NULL	
EMP_DRAWER_NO	NUMBER(10)	NULL	FK
OFF_TRANSACT_NO	NUMBER(10)	NULL	FK
ADVERTISING_CONTRACTS			
ADV_CONTRACT_NO	NUMBER(10)	NOT NULL	PK
ADV_VEND_NO	NUMBER(10)	NOT NULL	FK
AMOUNT	NUMBER(10,2)	NOT NULL	
ADV_DATE	DATE	NOT NULL	
PROD_NO	NUMBER(10)	NOT NULL	FK
TYPE	VARCHAR2(30)	NULL	

TABLE 14.1 Continued

Table/Columns	Data Type	Nullable	Constraint
ADVERTISING_VENDORS			
ADV_VEND_NO	NUMBER(10)	NOT NULL	PK
ADV_COMPANY	VARCHAR2(30)	NOT NULL	
ADV_TYPE	VARCHAR2(30)	NOT NULL	
ADV_POC	VARCHAR2(30)	NULL	
ADV_STREET	VARCHAR2(30)	NOT NULL	
ADV_CITY	VARCHAR2(30)	NOT NULL	
ADV_STATE	VARCHAR2(2)	NOT NULL	
ADV_ZIP	VARCHAR2(5)	NOT NULL	
ADV_PHONE	VARCHAR2(10)	NOT NULL	
BANKS			
BANK_NO	NUMBER(10)	NOT NULL	PK
AMOUNT	NUMBER(10,2)	NOT NULL	
ACC_RECV_NO	NUMBER(10)	NOT NULL	FK
ACT_PAY_NO	NUMBER(10)	NOT NULL	FK
DEDUCTIONS			
DEDUC_NO	NUMBER(10)	NOT NULL	PK
DEDUC_AMT	NUMBER(10,2)	NOT NULL	
DEDUC_TYPE_NO	NUMBER(10)	NOT NULL	FK
EMP_WORK_NO	NUMBER(10)	NOT NULL	FK
DEDUCTION_TYPES			
DEDUC_TYPE_NO	NUMBER(10)	NOT NULL	PK
DEDUC_NAME	VARCHAR2(30)	NOT NULL	
DEPARTMENTS			
DEPT_NO	NUMBER(10)	NOT NULL	PK
STORE_NO	NUMBER(10)	NOT NULL	
DEPT_NAME	VARCHAR2(30)	NOT NULL	
EMPLOYEES			
EMP_NO	NUMBER(10)	NOT NULL	PK
LAST_NAME	VARCHAR2(30)	NOT NULL	
FIRST_NAME	VARCHAR2(30)	NOT NULL	
MIDDLE_NAME	VARCHAR2(30)	NULL	

TABLE 14.1   Continued

Table/Columns	Data Type	Nullable	Constraint
SSN	VARCHAR2(9)	NOT NULL	
STREET	VARCHAR2(30)	NOT NULL	
CITY	VARCHAR2(30)	NOT NULL	
STATE	VARCHAR2(2)	NOT NULL	
ZIP	VARCHAR2(5)	NOT NULL	
PHONE	VARCHAR2(10)	NOT NULL	
EMAIL	VARCHAR2(50)	NULL	
DATE_OF_BITH	DATE	NOT NULL	
DATE_STARTED	DATE	NOT NULL	
CONTACT_LAST	VARCHAR2(30)	NULL	
CONTACT_FIRST	VARCHAR2(30)	NULL	
CONTACT_MIDDLE	VARCHAR2(30)	NULL	
CONTACT_PHONE	VARCHAR2(10)	NULL	
EMPLOYEE_DRAWERS			
EMP_DRAWER_NO	NUMBER(10)	NOT NULL	PK
WORK_DATE	DATE	NOT NULL	
EMP_NO	NUMBER(10)	NOT NULL	FK
EMP_DRAWER_CARD	NUMBER(10,2)	NULL	
EMP_DRAWER_CASH	NUMBER(10,2)	NULL	
EMP_DRAWER_CHECK	NUMBER(10,2)	NULL	
EMP_DRW_COUPON	NUMBER(10,2)	NULL	
OFF_TRANSACT_AMT	NUMBER(10,2)	NULL	
EMPLOYEE_RECORDS			
EMPREC_NO	NUMBER(10)	NOT NULL	PK
DEPENDENTS	NUMBER(2)	NULL	
DEPT_NO	NUMBER(10)	NOT NULL	FK
EMP_NO	NUMBER(10)	NOT NULL	FK
MONTHS_WORKED	NUMBER(4)	NULL	
POS_NO	NUMBER(10)	NOT NULL	FK
PRESENT_PAY_RATE	NUMBER(4,2)	NOT NULL	
PAST_DEPT_NO1	NUMBER(10)	NULL	FK
PAST_DEPT_NO2	NUMBER(10)	NULL	FK
PAST_DEPT_NO3	NUMBER(10)	NULL	FK

14

APPLYING DATABASE DESIGN CONCEPTS

TABLE 14.1   Continued

Table/Columns	Data Type	Nullable	Constraint
EMPLOYEE_WORK			
EMP_WORK_NO	NUMBER(10)	NOT NULL	PK
EMP_HOURS_WORKED	NUMBER(2)	NOT NULL	
EMP_WEEK_ENDING	DATE	NOT NULL	
EXPENDABLE_SUPPLIES			
EXPENDABLE_NO	NUMBER(10)	NOT NULL	PK
EXP_VEND_NO	NUMBER(10)	NOT NULL	FK
ITEM_NAME	VARCHAR2(30)	NOT NULL	
EXPENDABLE_SUPPLY_VENDORS			
EXP_SUPPLY_VEND_NO	NUMBER(10)	NOT NULL	PK
EXP_VEND_COMPANY	VARCHAR2(30)	NOT NULL	
EXP_VEND_POC	VARCHAR2(30)	NOT NULL	
EXP_VEND_STREET	VARCHAR2(30)	NOT NULL	
EXP_VEND_CITY	VARCHAR2(30)	NOT NULL	
EXP_VEND_STATE	VARCHAR2(2)	NOT NULL	
EXP_VEND_ZIP	VARCHAR2(5)	NOT NULL	
EXP_VEND_PHONE	VARCHAR2(10)	NOT NULL	
EXPENSES			
EXP_NO	NUMBER(10)	NOT NULL	PK
EXP_AMOUNT	NUMBER(10,2)	NOT NULL	
EXP_DATE	DATE	NOT NULL	
EXP_NAME	VARCHAR2(30)	NOT NULL	
EXP_PURPOSE	VARCHAR2(200)	NOT NULL	
EXP_POC	VARCHAR2(30)	NULL	
EXP_STREET	VARCHAR2(30)	NOT NULL	
EXP_CITY	VARCHAR2(30)	NOT NULL	
EXP_STATE	VARCHAR2(2)	NOT NULL	
EXP_ZIP	VARCHAR2(5)	NOT NULL	
EXP_PHONE	VARCHAR2(10)	NOT NULL	
EXP_COMMENT	VARCHAR2(200)	NULL	

TABLE 14.1 Continued

Table/Columns	Data Type	Nullable	Constraint
HEAD_CASHIER_DRAWERS			
OFF_TRANSACT_NO	NUMBER(10)	NOT NULL	PK
AMOUNT	NUMBER(10,2)	NOT NULL	
EMP_DRAWER_NO	NUMBER(10)	NOT NULL	FK
OFF_TRANSACT_DATE	DATE	NOT NULL	
INVENTORY			
INV_NO	NUMBER(10)	NOT NULL	PK
AMOUNT	NUMBER(10)	NOT NULL	
INVOICE_NO	NUMBER(10)	NOT NULL	
PROD_NO	NUMBER(10)	NOT NULL	FK
PURC_PRC_PER_ITEM	NUMBER(10,2)	NOT NULL	
RENTAL_ITEM	VARCHAR2(1)	NULL	
INVENTORY_REQUEST			
INVREQ_NO	NUMBER(10)	NOT NULL	PK
AMOUNT	NUMBER(10,2)	NOT NULL	
PROD_NO	NUMBER(10)	NOT NULL	FK
LOSS_INVENTORY			
LOSS_NO	NUMBER(10)	NOT NULL	PK
PROD_NO	NUMBER(10)	NOT NULL	FK
PROD_AMOUNT	NUMBER(10,2)	NOT NULL	
PURCHASE_AMT	NUMBER(10,2)	NOT NULL	
REDUCTION	NUMBER(10,2)	NOT NULL	
RETAIL_AMT	NUMBER(10,2)	NOT NULL	
SPOIL	VARCHAR2(1)	NULL	
THEFT	VARCHAR2(1)	NULL	
NET_PAY			
NET_PAY_NO	NUMBER(10)	NOT NULL	PK
EMP_WHEN_PAID	DATE	NOT NULL	
EMP_WORK_NO	NUMBER(10)	NOT NULL	FK
NET_PAY_AMT	NUMBER(10,2)	NOT NULL	
OWNER			
OWN_TRANS_NO	NUMBER(10)	NOT NULL	PK
OWN_PROFIT_PAY	NUMBER(10,2)	NOT NULL	
OWN_PROF_PAY_DT	DATE	NOT NULL	

TABLE 14.1   Continued

Table/Columns	Data Type	Nullable	Constraint
		POSITIONS	
POS_NO	NUMBER(10)	NOT NULL	PK
POSITION_NAME	VARCHAR2(30)	NOT NULL	
		PRODUCTS	
PROD_NO	NUMBER(10)	NOT NULL	PK
PRODUCT_NAME	VARCHAR2(30)	NOT NULL	
AMOUNT	NUMBER(10,2)	NOT NULL	
DEPT_NO	NUMBER(10)	NOT NULL	FK
VEND_NO	NUMBER(10)	NOT NULL	FK
WHOLESALE_PRICE	NUMBER(10,2)	NOT NULL	
RETAIL_PRICE	NUMBER(10,2)	NOT NULL	
ON_SALE	VARCHAR2(10)	NULL	
		REGISTER_ITEM_TRANSACT	
REG_ITEM_TRANS_NO	NUMBER(10)	NOT NULL	PK
AMOUNT	NUMBER(10,2)	NOT NULL	
PROD_NO	NUMBER(10)	NOT NULL	FK
SALE_NO	NUMBER(10)	NOT NULL	FK
		SALES	
SALE_NO	NUMBER(10)	NOT NULL	PK
EMP_DRAWER_NO	NUMBER(10)	NOT NULL	FK
SALE_AMT	NUMBER(10,2)	NOT NULL	
SALE_TYPE	VARCHAR2(30)	NOT NULL	
		VENDORS	
VEND_NO	NUMBER(10)	NOT NULL	PK
VEND_COMPANY	VARCHAR2(30)	NOT NULL	
VEND_POC	VARCHAR2(30)	NULL	
VEND_STREET	VARCHAR2(30)	NOT NULL	
VEND_CITY	VARCHAR2(30)	NOT NULL	
VEND_STATE	VARCHAR2(2)	NOT NULL	
VEND_ZIP	VARCHAR2(5)	NOT NULL	
VEND_PHONE	VARCHAR2(10)	NOT NULL	

TABLE 14.1   Continued

Table/Columns	Data Type	Nullable	Constraint
	VIDEO_CUSTOMERS		
VIDEO_NO	NUMBER(10)	NOT NULL	PK
VIDEO_LAST	VARCHAR2(30)	NOT NULL	
VIDEO_FIRST	VARCHAR2(30)	NOT NULL	
VIDEO_MIDDLE	VARCHAR2(30)	NULL	
VIDEO_STREET	VARCHAR2(30)	NOT NULL	
VIDEO_CITY	VARCHAR2(30)	NOT NULL	
VIDEO_STATE	VARCHAR2(2)	NOT NULL	
VIDEO_ZIP	VARCHAR2(5)	NOT NULL	
VIDEO_PHONE	VARCHAR2(10)	NOT NULL	
RENT1	VARCHAR2(30)	NULL	
RENT2	VARCHAR2(30)	NULL	
RENT3	VARCHAR2(30)	NULL	
VIDEO_AMOUNT	NUMBER(10,2)	NOT NULL	
VIDEO_TOTAL	NUMBER(10,2)	NOT NULL	
	WORK_SCHEDULES		
WORK_SCH_NO	NUMBER(10)	NOT NULL	PK
DATE_SUBMITTED	DATE	NOT NULL	
EMPREC_NO	NUMBER(10)	NOT NULL	FK
WORK_DAY	DATE	NOT NULL	
WORK_END	DATE	NOT NULL	
WORK_MONTH	VARCHAR2(15)	NOT NULL	
WORK_START	VARCHAR2(15)	NOT NULL	
WORK_WEEKDAY	VARCHAR2(15)	NOT NULL	

After a close look at the VIDEO_CUSTOMER table, it has been decide that ample normalization has not occurred. This table needs normalized because redundant information will be stored for customers (such as name and address) every time a video is rented. Study the following table structure:

VIDEO_CUSTOMERS	
VIDEO_NO	(PRIMARY KEY)
VIDEO_LAST	
VIDEO_FIRST	

VIDEO_MIDDLE

VIDEO_STREET

VIDEO_CITY

VIDEO_STATE

VIDEO_ZIP

VIDEO_PHONE

RENT_VIDEO

VIDEO_AMOUNT

VIDEO_TOTAL

After further interview with the owner, it has been determined that a customer can rent up to three videos. A customer can rent videos many times, so VIDEO_CUSTOMER was normalized into three tables, as follows:

VIDEO_CUSTOMERS	*VIDEOS*	*VIDEO_RENTALS*
VIDEO_CUST_NO	VIDEO_NO	VID_RENT_NO
VIDEO_LAST	VIDEO_NAME	VID_RENT_DT
VIDEO_FIRST	VIDEO_CATEGORY	VID_RENT1
VIDEO_MIDDLE	VIDEO_RATING	VID_RENT2
VIDEO_STREET		VID_RENT3
VIDEO_CITY		VID_AMOUNT
VIDEO_STATE		VID_DUE_DT
VIDEO_ZIP		OVERDUE
VIDEO_PHONE		

In doing this, it was realized that a table to track the videos themselves didn't exist. Although it is best to normalize as much as possible when creating the ERD, there will be times during table design, such as this, that require further normalization.

The EMPLOYEE_RECORD table should also be normalized because employees might not have previous departments. Additionally, an employee might have more previous departments than the three allocated by the following table. After all, before this grocery store was started, the owner started out as a bag boy and worked his way up to store manager through several departments in another grocery store chain.

EMPLOYEE_RECORDS
EMPREC_NO
DEPENDENTS
DEPT_NO

EMP_NO
MONTHS_WORKED
POS_NO
PRESENT_PAY_RATE
PAST_DEPT_NO1
PAST_DEPT_NO2
PAST_DEPT_NO3

The normalization of this table produces the following tables:

EMPLOYEE_RECORDS	*EMPLOYEE_HISTORY*
EMPREC_NO	EMPREC_NO
DEPENDENTS	PREVIOUS_PAY
DEPT_NO	PREVIOUS_POS_NO
EMP_NO	PREVIOUS_DEPT_NO
POS_NO	
PAY_RATE	

Defining Constraints

In review, the following constraints should be defined as a part of table design:

- Primary key constraints
- Foreign key constraints
- Unique constraints
- Check constraints

Primary key and foreign key constraints, also referred to as *referential integrity* (RI) *constraints*, were designated in the previous section. However, there are several unique constraint and check constraint candidates that should be defined.

Here's a list of some possible unique constraint candidates:

Table	Column
EMPLOYEES	SSN
EMPLOYEES	EMAIL
ADVERTISING_VENDORS	ADV_COMPANY
EXPENDABLE_SUPPLY_VENDORS	EXP_VEND_COMPANY
DEDUCTION_TYPES	DEDUC_NAME
DEPARTMENTS	DEPT_NAME

POSITIONS	POSITION_NAME
VENDORS	VEND_COMPANY

The following is a list of some possible check constraint candidates:

Table	Sample Constraint Definition
INVENTORY	CHECK (RENTAL_ITEM IN ('Y',NULL))
LOSS_INVENTORY	CHECK (SPOIL IN ('Y',NULL))
LOSS_INVENTORY	CHECK (THEFT IN ('Y',NULL))
PRODUCTS	CHECK (ON_SALE IN ('Y',NULL))
DEPARTMENTS	CHECK (STORE IN (1, 2, 3, 4, 5))
EMPLOYEES	CHECK (STATE = 'IN')
WORK_SCHEDULES	CHECK (WORK_WEEKDAY IN ('MONDAY', 'TUESDAY','WEDNESDAY', 'THURSDAY','FRIDAY', 'SATURDAY','SUNDAY'))

And the list goes on. Keep in mind that these are just a few of the possible candidates.

Designing Views

As you'll recall from Chapter 13, "Designing Views," there are several purposes for designing views. In this scenario, some of the most appropriate views might be designed to filter and summarize data. It may be important to filter data so that certain individuals do not see data that they should not. For example, it might not be a good idea for the department managers to see what the other department managers get paid. Table 14.2 provides an example of the different levels of user access that might exist in a database used by a grocery store.

TABLE 14.2   Levels of User Access

Level	Type of Access	Users
1	Full access	Store management
2	Full access within dept	Department management
3	Sell/refund	Cashiers
4	Manage dept inventory	Department workers
5	Manage payroll data	Payroll clerk

> **NOTE**
>
> Database roles can be created for each level of access in Table 14.2 to enforce security between the users with different levels of access. A role contains a group of privileges that may be assigned to individual database users. Refer to Chapter 15, "Implementing Database Security," for a discussion of database security, which occurs after the initial design of the database.

In addition to the use of database features such as roles, views can be created to filter the data that users see. For instance, the following view can be created to restrict department managers to viewing only the employee records in their respective departments:

```
CREATE VIEW VIDEO_DEPT_EMP_VIEW AS
SELECT E.EMP_NO, E.LAST_NAME, E.FIRST_NAME, E.MIDDLE_NAME,
       E.SSN, E.STREET, E.CITY, E.STATE, E.ZIP, E.PHONE,
       E.EMAIL, E.DATE_OF_BIRTH, E.DATE_STARTED,
       E.CONTACT_LAST, E.CONTACT_FIRST, E.CONTACT_MIDDLE,
       E.CONTACT_PHONE, ER.DEPENDENTS, P.POSITION_NAME,
       ER.PRESENT_PAY_RATE
FROM EMPLOYEES E,
     EMPLOYEE_RECORD ER,
     POSITIONS P,
     DEPARTMENTS D
WHERE E.EMP_NO = ER.EMP_NO
  AND ER.POS_NO = P.POS_NO
  AND ER.DEPT_NO = D.DEPT_NO
  AND D.DEPT_NAME = 'VIDEO';
```

The following views could be created to summarize data to help the owner and managers make intelligent business decisions:

View Name	Brief Description
PRODUCT_VIEW	Information about product cost, sales, inventory, and season of best sales
VENDOR_VIEW	Information about products vendors provide, total costs, average costs, comparison to other vendors for similar products, quantity sold per vendor, and cost sold per vendor

14

APPLYING DATABASE DESIGN CONCEPTS

EMPLOYEE_VIEW	Information about hire date, position, pay rate, total income since hire data, average income per month, number of positions held, number of departments worked, and age (computed from date of birth)
EMPLOYEE_SCHEDULE_VIEW	Information about total hours worked, average hours worked per week, holidays worked, and weekends worked

Summary

The most fundamental concepts discussed so far in this book have been exemplified in this chapter using a practical case study. You can see how much information can be obtained from a seemingly simple situation. This case study started with an initial interview that triggered a monologue from the owner of the business. If you listen carefully, a lot information can be obtained—enough information to develop a plan to ask further interview questions and to begin modeling the business. Once the business was modeled, the process of physical design became more straightforward. Consider the examples in this chapter as just examples—every situation is different. Likewise, one designer's approach may vary widely from another's. Regardless of differing thought processes, the basic steps for designing a database are the same, and the end products should function the same, as prescribed by the business rules of the organization.

The following chapters discuss concepts that are integral to any database design. The concepts covered generally occur after the majority or all of the physical design is complete.

Life After Design

IN THIS PART

Chapter 15, "Implementing Database Security," covers the consideration of database security. Database security should be integrated into the database before it is released to production. This chapter covers the use of RDBMS security features and the management of security after design and implementation.

Chapter 16, "Change Control," discusses changes that might occur to a database after implementation. This chapter discusses standard practices for change management, also referred to as configuration management. It is very unlikely that a database will never require changes to provide fixes, or to provide the end user with additionally requested functionality in the database and database application.

Chapter 17, "Analyzing Legacy Databases for Redesign," covers the consideration of redesigning a legacy database. The redesign of a legacy database must adhere to the same principles of design as discussed in this book, but several considerations are used to justify the effort involved in redesigning an existing database. This chapter discusses the pros and cons of redesign. How to assist an organization in making the right decisions as well as how to be more prepared for a redesign effort—which will inevitably occur at some point in the future—are also discussed.

Implementing Database Security

IN THIS CHAPTER

In order for the databases we design to support our enterprise in achieving its business goals, the database has to be accessed and updated by users. This is where the proverbial rubber meets the road. Murphy's Law—whatever can go wrong, will go wrong and at the worst possible time—is as directly applicable to your database under the onslaught of your users and the network/Web environment as it is to a military operation, an auto race, or an attempt to climb Mt. Everest. The DBA and application developers must give users or customers access to the database resources they require to do their work or make their purchases, while minimizing damage they can do to the system and keeping data—which they shouldn't or have no need to see—secure from them at the same time.

How Is Security Important to Database Design?

For users to access the system, it must be accessible on the local (LAN) or wide area network (WAN) and these days most often via the World Wide Web as well. Applications using Web browsers as the primary user interface are so common as to be the norm for new development. When we put the database on the Web, it becomes vulnerable to hackers and other criminals from outside your organization who will damage your system or steal your data just because they can. Imagine that everyone's salary, personnel files, or your company's trade secrets are posted for public view on a Web site. Spies from your competitors who are after your company's trade secrets, or other unpleasant people who are after your employee's personal information are an ever present threat. Even from within your company, you can have disgruntled employees who will do whatever damage they can on their way out the door when they're fired, and internal nuts, traitors, or just generally evil people who will do whatever harm their access privileges will let them do.

The vast majority of databases these days will include WWW access. Part of your design must include the database objects (users, code, tables, roles) that support Web access and the vital security provisions such as certificates and SSL that must be included with that access.

The capacity for deliberate harm from people both inside and outside your organization must be defended against. However, an even larger problem could be that your people have to cope daily with the myriad chances for honest mistakes to occur and exposure to data they shouldn't see. Deleting or overwriting a data file, dropping a table or updating a column incorrectly by accident, can wreak havoc just as much as a hacker can. People can't help it if the application puts data they shouldn't see on the screen in the course of their normal work. You can't really fault people for curiosity, either. If the application allows them to see interesting things such as other people's salaries, they're going to look. Therefore, security should be well planned and integrated into the design of a database. A database should not only provide the end user with the data needed to function, but also it should provide protection for the data.

> **NOTE**
>
> Given Murphy's Law, the threats from malicious people both from within and without your organization and the daily potential for accidents and normal human curiosity for our good people, we have to include security in our database design from the very beginning. Security is a fundamental part of database design.

Who Needs Access to the Database?

Most information required throughout design and for implementation will be gathered from interviews during analysis. In order to plan for database security during database design and enforce the security after implementation, all users of the database must first be established. There are potentially different categories of users for any information system, ranging from end users to administrators of the information system. Some of the most common users, or individuals who might have access to any information system, include

- End users
- Customers
- Management
- Network administrator
- System administrator
- Database administrator
- Schema owner

Each of these users should have different levels of access. Granted, the easiest way to implement security is to provide all users with maximum access, but the obvious cost is the potential loss or misuse of data. What is the minimum access needed to perform the job? A database user should have adequate access to perform required job functions, and no more. In other words, as little access as possible should be allowed to avoid potential problems, although malicious intent never occurs to most users. Some users might take it personally that they do not have access to all data, but remember the point—to protect the data.

Be conservative when granting privileges; people tend to play. Users like to look around, especially when they find out that they have special privileges.

Some information might be sensitive or classified. Is a security clearance required to access certain data? Certain users typically have access to certain sensitive data. Sensitive data might include social security numbers, pay information, or classified government and military information. If sensitive data exists, consider isolating data by breaking it out into separate tables that can be related to nonsensitive tables, or by creating views that exclude sensitive data. The users who need to see all data will be granted access to the tables, and the users who do not have security clearance will be granted access to the views only.

When user access to data is determined, types of access must then be determined. Generally speaking, data can be created, retrieved, updated, and deleted from the database. Some users might need to perform all operations against data in the database. Other users might only need to query the database, or update data from certain tables in the database. Deletion of data might be restricted to certain users. User access must be established relating to the possible combinations of data access that a user requires. These concepts will be discussed in more detail throughout the chapter.

Levels of Access

Database users are given a database user ID with a password and the ability to connect to the database. Modern databases require several decisions about security design pertaining to user IDs and passwords. Do you force regular password changes and enforce password complexity rules requiring a certain length password that includes some alphabetical, some numeric, and some special characters? Do you prevent reuse of the same password and lock accounts after a number of failed login attempts? Do you limit a users' resources such as number of concurrent logins, central processing unit utilization per session, connect time, idle time, number of disk reads, or server memory use? If so, what are the limits per user session for each of these resources? These limits will be defined by functional requirements and are thus design issues. Security is used to control access. Users have access to both data and resources, both of which can be controlled at the database level.

Given a user ID, the users can log directly into the database over a network via a client/server application. They can also log in to a middle tier application to access the database. For instance, the user can log in to a Web application server that has many Web users log into it. The Web application server then communicates with the database by logging in with a user account(s) that has the minimum access required to accomplish whatever work the Web application is undertaking. Client server applications generally will have a single user ID for each user. Web applications using a middle tier Web application server can use one or a few generic database users. In either case, part of database design is determining what combination of Create, Retrieve, Update, Delete (CRUD—or INSERT, SELECT, UPDATE, DELETE in SQL) privileges on what combination of database tables are required to accomplish each of the particular work functions that the database is designed to support. Each combination of privileges required to accomplish a particular work function has to be defined and then analyzed to ensure that no more access than what is required to accomplish the work is provided to the functional privilege set.

In some databases, users can log in to a database based on external authorization. In external authorization, the user has an operating system (OS) user account created on the UNIX, NOVELL or NT host machine for the database. That host account OS user has a corresponding database user that is set up for external authorization. Using external authorization, an OS user logged into the database host can automatically log into the database without a password. OS and database users who are set up for external authorization are generally DBA accounts or database accounts that are running external programs such as a C++ executable program that accesses the database. These external authorization accounts are generally powerful accounts and access to them needs to be closely controlled.

The OS system administrator (SA) (root in UNIX, Admin in NOVELL, and so on) can control these OS accounts and thus the database account. Both SAs and DBAs have a huge potential for mischief. Part of your process should be a system of checks and balances to ensure that these powerful accounts aren't misused. The best system, however, is vulnerable to abuse if a DBA or SA wants to do so. Choose these people with care.

Starting with the most powerful account, the following list shows the typical levels of access to any information system:

- The super user (root on UNIX systems, Admin in NOVELL)
- The database owner
- The schema owner
- The end user

The super user is the account on an operating system that has the most privileges. In fact, the super user has access to any file stored on the system. The database owner has access to all files associated with database software and data files on a system. Although the database owner is restricted to database related files, remember that most files on most systems are in fact database related. The schema owner is the creator and owner of database objects that are used for a user application. The schema owner has unlimited access to all schema objects and is responsible for controlling that access to other user accounts. The end user has the least amount of actual access, although the database exists for the end user. All accounts are equally dangerous as far as jeopardizing the integrity of the database if care is not taken.

Figure 15.1 shows the end user's relation to the database. Database objects are owned by the schema owner, who grants appropriate access on objects to end users. If and only if end users have adequate privileges, they can access tables, views, and other applicable objects in the target schema.

15

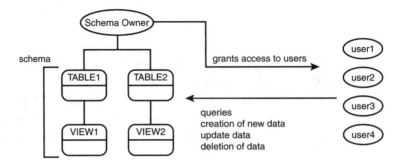

FIGURE 15.1

Accessing schema objects.

Users in one database can also access another database by way of database links between the two databases. The link will connect the user in the first database to a user in the second, and the user in the first database can then access the second database with the privilege set of the user in the second. Database links are powerful tools, but must be closely managed to ensure that they are not abused. It is extremely easy to overlook a user from some other database with link access to a database. Links can be made by DBA accounts.

Privileges

Privileges are used to control user access. Privileges exist at the operating system level, database level, and application level. Database privileges control user access in the database environment, such as manipulation of the actual database structure and access to schema objects. Two basic types of privileges in a relational database are as follows:

- System privileges
- Object privileges

System privileges consist of those that allow the user to perform tasks within the scope of the database, whereas object privileges allow a user to perform tasks within the scope of a schema. Common system privileges include the ability to create a table, drop a table, alter the structure of a table, create indexes and views, and manipulate user accounts. Common object privileges include the ability to retrieve data from a table and manipulate table data. System privileges vary widely between different relational database software. Object privileges are more standardized.

Following are standard object privileges for a relational database:

- SELECT—Allows data to be retrieved from a table
- INSERT—Allows the creation of a new row of data in a table

- UPDATE—Allows existing data in a table to be modified
- DELETE—Allows existing table data to be deleted
- REFERENCES—Allows columns in a table to be referenced by other columns (such as through a foreign key)
- USAGE—Allows authorized usage of a specific domain

> **NOTE**
>
> As a general rule, system privileges must be granted by a DBA, and object privileges must be granted by the owner of the object.

Privileges are granted to users with the GRANT command and revoked from users with the REVOKE command. Sometimes the task for a DBA or schema owner to manage privileges is overwhelming. Two options can be used with the GRANT command to allow another user the ability of granting assigned privileges to other users. If a user is granted an object privilege with the WITH GRANT OPTION, he is allowed specific access to the database object, but can also grant specific access on the database object to another user, even though the original user does not own the object. Likewise, the WITH ADMIN OPTION can be attached to a GRANT command associated with system privileges, and also allows the target user to grant the system privilege to other users.

Figure 15.2 illustrates the process of managing end-user access through database privileges. Two types of privileges are shown in the figure: object and system privileges. The schema owner is responsible for granting object privileges to users, and the DBA grants system (database-wide) privileges to users. Sometimes, a security administrator might be designated to assist the DBA and schema owner in the management of privileges. When a security manager is designated, it is common to grant DBA authority to the user, or grant the appropriate system and object privileges with the WITH GRANT OPTION and WITH ADMIN OPTION options, the latter being the best choice by far.

> **NOTE**
>
> Keep in mind that although security is fundamentally the same for all relational databases, it might be implemented in a different fashion by different RDBMS vendors.

15

IMPLEMENTING DATABASE SECURITY

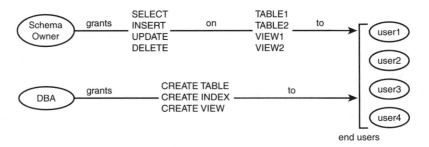

FIGURE 15.2

Managing database privileges.

CAUTION

Be careful not to use the WITH ADMIN OPTION and WITH GRANT OPTION options too liberally because privilege management can quickly turn into an uncontrollable nightmare.

Roles

The combination of database and table CRUD privileges needed to accomplish a particular work function can be assigned to users individually. However, when you consider that potentially hundreds of users exist for a single database with hundreds, or even thousands, of individual privileges—each based on their work requirements—managing privileges on an individual basis would be a daunting undertaking. Instead, as part of design, we determine what the job functions are within our application and what privileges on the database, its tables, and other database objects each work function requires. We then create a database object called a role, which includes all the privileges required to accomplish that function.

Users are then granted one or more of a relatively small number of roles as opposed to hundreds or thousands of individual privileges. The user ID is granted the roles that it needs to accomplish all the functions a particular user is authorized to do. In addition to SELECT, INSERT, UPDATE, or DELETE in various combinations on whatever tables are required, the role might also include the privileges to alter an object, create an index on it, reference it via a foreign key, or execute it, if it is a program built into the database.

Using roles greatly simplifies management of database access and of database object privileges. Definition of roles to allow users to meet all the application functional requirements is a key part of design.

Figure 15.3 illustrates the application of database roles. First, the DBA creates a role. When a role is first created, it is an empty object with no apparent significance other than the fact that it has a name. The role can be granted to users any time after it has been created, although privileges are usually granted to the role first. Object privileges can be granted to the role by the schema owner and system privileges can be granted by the DBA. A role becomes a so-called group of privileges that can easily be granted to or revoked from a database user. A user can be granted one or many roles, based on the division of privileges for the application and the level of access of the individual user. When logging in to the database, the user has all privileges contained in the roles that have been granted.

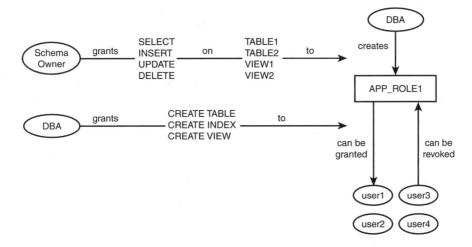

FIGURE 15.3

Using roles to manage privileges.

> **NOTE**
>
> In some relational database implementations, users cannot perform certain operations such as create object based on role privileges. In some cases, the user must be granted explicit privileges to accomplish certain tasks.

Who Is in Charge of Security?

No single individual is responsible for security, unless you are speaking of a one-person organization. All users must be held accountable to some degree for the implementation, adherence, and enforcement of security. System administrators, DBAs, and schema owners are responsible for implementation and enforcement. All users must adhere to security. Users must be trusted to use the data to which they have access appropriately. Administrators must carefully distribute data access and ensure that policies are followed by all users, including fellow administrators.

> **NOTE**
>
> Although the end user is solely responsible for making use of the database as intended, the implication is that the user must adhere to security policies and use the database in a professional manner, only as intended. The data that users access might be sensitive, and a security clearance might be required. Security can only be implemented to a certain degree, and then it is the user's responsibility to protect the data.

Security policies are established by management and technical staff. These policies should be used as guidelines during design and implementation of information systems. Technical staff involved in the creation of security policies should include network administrators, system administrators, and database administrators. It is important to get input and viewpoints from information system management in order to establish the best policies for the organization.

Three basic levels of management of security associated with an information system are as follows:

- System level management
- Database level management
- Application level management

The levels of user access are controlled by the administrators of the operating system, the database, and the application. Traditionally, end users would have to login to the operating system in order to access the application, which in turn, accessed the database. Both the application and the database resided in the operating system environment. Now, most users bypass operating system authentication, navigating directly to the database from a front-end application installed on the PC or via the Web browser on the PC.

Based on the needs of the end user, different levels of access can be granted. Most users must deal with a combination of database and application authentication. Suppose that a user is accessing the database via a Visual Basic application installed on the PC. The user can be given database access, granted by the schema owner. The application relies on the privileges that have been assigned to the user in the database. If user authentication is handled at the application level, suppose that a shared database account is used for all users connecting to the database through the application. Sole reliance on the security of an application is weak, and generally bad design. If the shared account is known (there is always a risk of the password for the shared account becoming public knowledge), any user can connect to the database with unlimited access by bypassing the application. With a shared account, it is also difficult to monitor individual users, which somewhat defeats the purpose of users having their own database accounts. User authentication should be handled at the database level as much as possible, using privileges and built-in features such as roles. Application security is a bonus, and should be used only to enhance the security built into the database.

> **NOTE**
>
> The most common individuals in an organization associated with the integration and enforcement of security include system administrators and database administrators. The following sections discuss the levels of security associated with these technical users. Remember that the responsibilities of these individuals will vary between organizations, as there are variations in size of staff, business priorities, and potentially different degrees of sensitive data.

The following subsections discuss security implementation from the viewpoints of the operating system, database, and application.

System Level Management

The system administrators mentioned previously control the host computer for the database and thus the physical files on which the database is based. They have the capacity to damage or misappropriate those physical data files at will; either by accident or deliberately. Deleting or overwriting database data files will crash the database until they can be restored.

An operating system owned account will be created for the database files. That owning account can do the same harm that the system administrator can do by deleting or overwriting database files or misappropriating copies of the data. The OS owning account will correspond to a powerful database DBA account.

In a UNIX environment, for example, host OS database file privileges (read, write, execute) are a key security issue and need to be closely monitored. In UNIX, the database owner OS user account should be able to read, write, and execute all the database files. In a Windows NT environment, the administrator account would have "Full Control" while local users would require "Read" access to execute database-executable programs such as SQL.

Users other than the database owner should have limited privileges to eliminate the possibility of inadvertent changes or deletions of files. Ensure that OS file level access privileges are set up correctly, with no more privileges provided to users than are necessary.

15

> **NOTE**
>
> Normally, file access and permissions are controlled by a system or database adminis-
> trator. Certain database products and designs require different file permissions. The
> core programs and executables should be owned and controlled by one administrator
> account. Other local access users could require access to the executables to interact
> with the database. Generally with today's network computing, users bypass the oper-
> ating system and log directly into the database.

Physical security of the database host is a vital issue. Computer rooms with restricted access
and good locks are a necessity for key enterprise databases. Depending on the level of importance of the data, such as with certain government agencies, armed guards and security systems
can be included as well. The same is true of Web or application servers and key network components such as hubs and routers. The information as to what database is on which host in
which location should be protected as much as possible as well. System backups with off-site
storage of tapes are also necessary in the event that physical security should fail.

Copies of the database data files either to other drives or to tape can be taken to other host systems and installed. The copied database on the new host can then be accessed by the SAs and
DBAs of the new host. Your data is theirs once it is copied to the new machine. Your tape
backups and database export files need to be thoroughly secured to prevent this. Procedures
need to be put in place to control disk/tape backups and database export files. If the data is
confidential or proprietary, you must secure the tapes and files you use to back it up.

Other vulnerabilities exist on the operating systems that can put database files at risk. Hackers
who are filtering network packets for passwords, filtering network packets for classified data,
corrupting data, or deleting data can pose a tremendous threat to an organization. Depending
on the level of your data's privacy, every measure should be taken to secure your data.

Database-level Management

The DBA controls and manages the database. In the final analysis, he can do and undo most
anything he wants to. He is responsible for ensuring that the database has adequate memory
and disk space resources and is properly configured in terms of a wide variety of technical
parameters. He really controls database security, although he might delegate large pieces of
security to others, and the owners of tables and other database objects have direct control on
who can access those objects.

Most of what the DBA does on the detail level with application database objects is based on database object creation scripts he gets from application developers. The DBA is similar to a mayor or a policeman. He has a lot of power and does a lot in terms of providing infrastructure and a secure environment, but he doesn't try to control the details of what's happening in the environment after he has it set up unless there's a problem. His job is first to prevent problems by providing resources and enforcing good security procedures, and second to fix problems quickly when they arise.

It is important to establish database level security, not just tool or application level security. Creating powerful user roles within the database and then paring down their capabilities via application security might work just for that application, but many applications can access those database objects. Application or tool-based security will often be inconsistent across multiple tools and applications running against the same tables. Tool- and application-based security also runs the risk of re-inventing the security wheel from application to application.

CAUTION

Probably the greatest risk inherent in application based security, however, is the potential for users accessing your database using their powerful user accounts with ad-hoc query tools other than your application using open database connectivity (ODBC). In most cases, they can have access to your data without the control of your application. If the power user can access the data using his favorite desktop tool over ODBC, he will. The skill and sophistication required to set up and use ODBC is not exceptional. Build your security into the database. It will always be there, in whatever manner your users choose to access it. Also, as part of the design, look at the potential harm users using ODBC-based applications such as Access might do to your database given their privilege set. If they could do harm, you must design in defense against such access.

NOTE

It is important in data warehousing—where you take data from many sources in operational systems—that you extend the same security access controls to the warehouse presentation of the data as those included in the operational system data sources from which the warehouse data is derived. At the least, you must be able to justify the exceptions to those controls and have the concurrence of the production data's owner with the exceptions.

Management of Database User Accounts

One of the issues that application designers will have to resolve is who will create and manage users in the database. Should it be the DBA team or a trusted group of users from the applications that run against it? This is a major security issue. Making users, granting them privileges, and controlling their passwords is a large and important job. Abused or badly managed user creation can be a disastrous hole in your database security. Slow reaction to requirements to create or alter users can lead to unhappy users and unhappy user management.

The key issue is which users are allowed access to the special user accounts created to manage users? If they can manage DBA accounts—which is possible if set up incorrectly—these user managers can get complete access to the database by changing a DBA's password. However, the DBA can overcome this problem by programming procedures that let them manage most users but not DBA or other powerful accounts.

Managing users is generally a big job, but it doesn't require exceptional technical skills. Setting up special users from the application groups to manage users, while limiting vulnerability to their mistakes or their misdeeds, is standard practice. This is particularly the case when the application has its own security built in. Managing application and database security in tandem is cost effective in terms of time. In those cases where DBAs actually do manage users, it is generally the job of the junior person on the team or a trainee. In cases where there is a single DBA or a small DBA team, the DBAs simply won't have time to do the user management job and, by necessity, must delegate it.

Whether to grant privileges or roles to users along with the ability to grant those same privileges or roles to other users is another issue that will need to be addressed. It is generally not done other than on an exception basis. The users who manage users previously discussed would certainly need this ability with roles. Other users in some cases might need the ability as well. This is, however, an exception granted only rarely based on specific application functional requirements.

As a DBA, ensure that the default passwords for built-in database utility user accounts (for utilities such as backups) get changed after the install is complete. This is a gaping hole in security that is left open a surprising number of times. This is especially true with some of the lesser known standard database utility users.

Many databases come with auditing features. The DBA can audit and record user implementation of database definition language (create, alter, drop) on database objects such as links, tables, roles, and users. You can record logon attempts. You can audit INSERT, UPDATE, and DELETE database manipulation language (DML) on tables. You can even audit SELECTs on particular tables if you want. Pick your audit events and manage the resultant audit tables closely. Auditing can effect database performance, and the audit tables can quickly become unmanageably large depending on what you audit. This again is a design issue. What do we need to audit, if anything, for this application? How much of a performance hit are you willing to take, and how much work are you willing to do to manage auditing in order to get the auditing information?

Rather than providing users with standard roles and all the capabilities that come with them, the DBA can program procedures that give users ability to do specific database tasks—such as create or drop users or change user passwords—but limit potential dangers by excluding the dangerous items from the capability provided in the code. This is an extremely flexible tool in terms of providing specific capabilities to a user.

In development, environments application developers want all the privileges that they can get. Some developers still grouse because they can't have DBA after years of being told no. Obviously, the DBA must draw the line somewhere short of DBA privilege for developers. Still, the developer users will undoubtedly have more privileges both on a host OS and database level in a development environment than in production. In development, they'll usually have the application schema owner password. In production they probably won't, although they might if they have application DBAs who handle the data administration tasks such as creation or modification of tables.

NOTE

Only minimum privileges should be granted to end users and developers. Databases and applications should never be developed by a user with DBA privileges. The reliance on DBA privileges can (1) cause the database and application not to work if DBA authority is removed, or (2) cause interference with unrelated database structures that reside in the same database environment.

Security in the Development Environment

Generally, security controls on developers will be looser in a development environment than in production. The additional capability or privileges granted developers on the development machine let them work faster because they can do things for themselves without having to hunt up a DBA or an SA for every little thing. In production, however, a small change can break a whole production system and prevent hundreds of users from working or thousands of customers from purchasing. Therefore, production systems are locked down tight in terms of security.

It's a good idea to have development and production on separate host machines. This prevents accidents on production systems from powerful development users while still allowing more freedom for the developer to do his job faster in development. There should be no development OS accounts on a production system.

Development or test data is often a copy of production data. Test data must be good relational data with referential integrity to support testing, and this is not easy to produce. There is a great temptation to use production data for testing, but if your data is confidential or proprietary, you need either to clean it up before using it for test or development or to incorporate production level security in development.

Where possible, specific user accounts rather than generic user accounts should be used. The intent here is to establish responsibility for actions taken in the database. Database auditing and application security can tie a particular user ID to a database action. Generic user accounts such as temporaryuser_12, are not tied to a particular person, and their passwords tend to be common knowledge.

Generic user accounts are often created because the application user managers hire short-term employees who regularly cycle through every few weeks. The user managers don't want to go through the administrative process to request the creation of new users and the deletion of old ones for that class of user that frequently. If these users are modifying the database, they should not be generic. If you think about it, these short term people are probably the ones you want to track most closely, nuisance or not.

Users who are selecting from tables such as those using one of the online analytical processing (OLAP) ad hoc query/reporting tools such as COGNOS or Oracle Discoverer probably can be generic without harm. Some Web applications will also use a generic user to save bandwidth utilization between the Web and database servers. This again is a design issue.

DBMS standard roles (for example, DBA) are powerful. They might be more powerful than you might expect. Standard roles and privileges should be inspected before being granted to users. A user should have no more privileges than necessary to perform his job.

> **NOTE**
>
> Close review of the standard roles that come with the database before granting them to your users is a good idea. Do not change the standard roles, but where applicable create new ones with the necessary functions that omit potentially harmful system privileges. When you must use a potentially dangerous role or privilege, monitor its use closely and revoke it when it's no longer necessary.

Application-level Management

Application developers define the table structures, write the programs that run against them, and define the privilege set roles that allow users to do CRUD actions on the tables and execute the programs. Almost all the grunt work on tables and code is done at the application development level.

Applications can include their own security as an augmentation to database security. Tables can be created within the application owning schema to store information on a particular user and application roles can be defined and then configured based upon that table or tables. Perhaps a particular user might have several menu options grayed out in his GUI program interface based on his application role whereas another doesn't, based on her application role. Basically the application limits options for a particular user based on values in application tables or the value of some variable set within the application.

Application developers decide what privileges (CRUD) on what tables are to be included in each functional role or privilege set placed in the database. If a particular user lacks the privilege to access a table or execute a program, he can't do it. Correct definition of roles is one of the most important aspects of security. Too few privileges for a role, and a user can't do his job. Too many privileges, and the user sees too much information or can actually damage data he shouldn't even be able to see. Privilege sets, particularly when it comes to privileges on user objects like tables, can be enormously complicated. Defining roles and testing them after you define them is a very big job.

Modern database and application software now includes facilities for biometric authentication of users at login time via fingerprints, retinal scans, or voice verification. Security cards or other physical keys are also included in database login authentication capabilities. Authentication to central services—which then allow login to numerous hosts or databases managed by that service based on a single authentication—is also an option. All or some of these new authentication capabilities can be applied to your design as appropriate for your application.

Using Views and Procedures to Enhance Security

Views and stored procedures are excellent mechanisms associated with a relational database that help improve the flexibility of security integration. These objects are most useful for restricting access to data and filtering subsets of data to which the user is authorized access.

> **NOTE**
>
> These can also be implemented via Data Access Projects in Access 2000.

The use of views is a common application level security tool. A view is a logical table. What this means is a view is a query on a physical table or tables that has been named and stored in the database as a separate database object. Privileges can then be granted to users on the view rather than on the base tables behind it. The view can then be selected by those users with privileges as if it were a table.

A view allows the application developer to create logical tables with only the columns a particular user must see to do his work at that point in time. It allows the developer to exclude from the view and thereby protect table columns, which the user shouldn't see, from the user's access altogether. The user has access just to the view, not the table or tables behind it. To the user, only the view columns that he has privileges on exist. The table columns, which he does not have privileges on, do not exist for him.

The user can see the data in just about any format the developer desires with column names of the developer's choice. Views can also include grouped or presummarized data. Under some conditions, the data in the tables behind the view can be updated through the view.

NOTE

Views can be used to hide sensitive data found in database tables. For example, a view can be created based on nonsensitive columns in a table. When the view has been created, it is stored in the database and can be accessed by authorized users as if it were a table. Users not authorized to see sensitive data are granted access on the view, not the base table itself.

The creation of stored procedures are also a popular method used to enhance overall security. A procedure can be created that allows operations to be performed against one or more database tables. Logic is coded into the stored procedure so that the user executing the procedure is restricted. The user executing the procedure can only perform the actions as coded into the logic. For instance, suppose a procedure is created to manage employee data. The procedure allows new employees to be entered, as well as employee personal modifications such as address. The procedure does not allow employees to be removed from the database. As with a view, access is granted to the procedure and not the base table.

The user can only perform activities allowed by procedure, which is executed under the privileges of its owner. A procedure such as this might stop a user from erroneously deleting all records in the table. Perhaps records are somehow marked for deletion and later verified by another user who actually has access to authorize the removal.

Designing a Security Management System

Although built-in security features such as roles exist, some developers insist on the development of a security management system. A security management system usually involves the design and creation of database tables that are used by an application to determine a particular user's access to data. In-house security management systems are necessary only if the built-in features of the database software used do not completely meet the security needs of the organization. Regardless, a security system should never be devised to replace, or re-invent, the features of the database—but rather, augment those features.

Some in-house security systems that we have seen involve a table stored with the other objects in the schema that tracks the database user account and object level access for each user account. Gee, doesn't this sound similar to the basic object privileges that can be granted to users? If there are different groups of database users who have different levels of access, roles can be created, privileges granted to the roles, and the roles granted to the users. This would alleviate the need for an in-house security system in nearly every case.

> **NOTE**
>
> When possible, rely on built-in database features such as roles and privileges instead of security tables. Database security features are more stable and easier to manage. Avoid designing complicated security systems if possible. Roles are quite robust, yet very easy to manage.

Taking Additional Precautionary Measures

Databases and networks are intimately joined these days. With the proliferation of Web-based applications, this trend will only grow. Security on the Web is primary for many, and perhaps most, new applications. Database Internet communication is almost always based on the Internet's TCP/IP protocol. TCP/IP is the standard data communication protocol for the Web. Unfortunately TCP/IP in itself has no security. Your data and people's credit card numbers are wide open for interception using TCP/IP. Security has to be added to TCP/IP from other sources to make the modern Web database secure.

- Network security
- Network firewall
- Secure sockets layer

Network Security

Your first line of defense is network security. If you can keep the bad guys from getting your database's IP address, you will have accomplished a lot toward keeping them out of your database. This is called hiding. Network Address Translation (NAT) will translate the real IP address your system uses and hide it from users on the Web. NAT is included in most firewall products and will help keep the less sophisticated hackers out of your system. Hiding, unfortunately, won't stop the skilled hacker, it will only prolong the process.

Having different versions of work station network configuration files based on the needs of particular groups is also a good idea. At least you don't put the IP addresses for your whole enterprise into a single file ready for theft and misuse both from your internal problem people and the outside world.

Network Firewall

The network firewall is your real defense from outside hackers. It comes with a price, however. You have to acquire it, install it, and maintain it; and skilled people and ongoing work are required. Properly setting up the firewall will protect your network, but it can also slow down network performance to sites outside the firewall to the point in which your application runs too slowly. Improperly configuring the firewall can grind your Web-based operations to a halt. It therefore requires people who know what they're doing to maintain it. Hackers tend to prey on organizations with the assumption that skilled network administrators are sparsely available.

Network firewalls are a combination of hardware and software that is intended to keep the hackers out of your network while letting those in who are allowed access. A firewall filters incoming and outgoing TCP/IP data packets based on source and destination IP address and of the function contained in the packet data payload. The network router has a list of allowable source and destination IP addresses. Packets with addresses not on the list don't get in. Your main enterprise network, on which your database host will generally reside, will be behind a firewall with a very restrictive list of allowable addresses. In a subnet with a less restrictive set of filters, often referred to as a demilitarized zone (DMZ), will be the Web and application servers that talk to the outside world. The DMZ network has a secure port through the firewall into the main network. The Web or application servers then talk from the DMZ to the database on the internal enterprise network through that port.

Secure Sockets Layer

Additional capabilities like Secure Sockets Layer (SSL) or Internet Engineering Task Force Transport Layer Security (IETF TLS) are necessary to make TCP/IP secure.

SSL provides data encryption so that data is not vulnerable as it moves through internet routers, two-way authentication—certificate security both on user end and on server end to avoid spoofing on either side and data validation services. Encryption systems have often used a secret key system—a single large number that is used to scramble data for transmission and then unscramble the data on the other end. Unfortunately the secret key is vulnerable to capture and misuse.

SSL uses a public key encryption method. The SSL system generates pairs of keys—one public and one private—that together can be used to encrypt or unencrypt data. You make your public key available to those you want to communicate with over the Web, and they use it to encrypt the data they send to you and unencrypt data you send to them. You use your private key to encrypt the data you send and to unencrypt data sent to you that was encrypted by your customer or associate using your public key. Public key encryption is relatively slow, so SSL uses it during the initial creation of a session and then generates and exchanges, with the remote communication session, a secret key called a session key that is used by both sides for the rest of the session. Secret key encryption is relatively fast compared to public key encryption.

SSL also authenticates, showing that we're both who we say we are throughout the communication. Part of setting up a secure Web site is obtaining an electronic site credential called a certificate from a trusted third-party company called a certifying authority. A certifying authority will validate that you are a legitimate organization before providing you with a certificate. Your users' communication sessions then access your certificate as an initial authentication step as they contact your database over the Web. SSL also validates data integrity at both ends of the communication.

Breaches in Security

Breaches in security are usually recognized through regular database monitoring (proactive), or during problem resolution (reactive). Breaches are either intentional or unintentional.

- Intentional breaches are typically spawned by malicious intent, or the need to look around and see what can be gotten into.

- Unintentional breaches can be as simple as mistakenly entering a screen in the application to which the user is not supposed to have accessed (sometimes administrators make mistakes when assigning privileges).

Breaches can originate externally from the organization, or can take place in-house. Suppose that a user has access to certain data (authorized access), and purposely makes unauthorized changes to data (not approved through corporate procedures). This is an example of a breach. Another obvious example is a hack attempt into an unauthorized database.

The following proactive measures can be taken to help prevent security breaches:

- Change administrator passwords regularly
- Force users to change passwords frequently
- Discourage the sharing of passwords
- Remove inactive user accounts
- Remove nonemployee user accounts
- Perform random monitoring of all activities
- Perform database auditing

15

IMPLEMENTING
DATABASE
SECURITY

- Educate the end user
- Conduct brief security training sessions

Security mechanisms should be established at the following levels as much as possible without interfering with daily business operations (remember how important it is to protect the data):

- Internet security (Web, WAN)
- Internal network security (intranet, LAN)
- Operating system security
- Database security
- Schema object security
- User application security
- PC security (Windows NT login)

Security breaches should be taken seriously and handled accordingly. A breach can lead to the termination of an employee—and rightfully so if the employee does not have the organization's best interests in mind. As stated earlier, all users are responsible for ensuring that security policies are followed. Security policies should provide guidelines to users if security breaches are suspected. Any known breaches should be directed to management for further action.

Summary

The application of security to database design is imperative before the finished product is offered to the end user for utilization. Database security is not normally very complex, but must be taken seriously in order to protect the data. An excellent database design will inevitably be tarnished by the lack of thought towards security management. First of all, identify the users that need access to the data. Then, determine the appropriate levels of access to allow the users to perform, while restricting unauthorized activity that can jeopardize the data. Keep in mind that different users take part in security implementation and adherence, such as network administrators, system administrators, database administrators, schema owners, developers, and end users.

Use built-in privileges and roles to implement and enforce security. Within the scope of the database, system and object privileges exist. System privileges allow the user to perform database-wide operations, such as creating tables. Object privileges allow users to create, retrieve, update, and delete (CRUD) data in schema objects. The DBA typically grants system privileges, whereas the schema owner must grant object privileges. Roles simplify security management, but are not used to their full extent in many databases—to the dismay of many database administrators.

Application security can be used to enhance database security, but should not be used in place of database security. A well-designed system integrates both database and application security, using all the built-in features of the database software before application functions are considered. The use of views and stored procedures are powerful enhancements to database and application security. Views can be used to filter sensitive data, and stored procedures can be used to restrict tasks performed by a user. When views and procedures are used, the user is granted access to the view or procedure, not the base table. By doing this, the user can only see the subset of data in the view, or perform only those actions coded into the logic of the stored procedure.

Other precautionary measures—such as network security, firewalls, and the secure socket layer—can be taken to ensure that a secure system exists. By now, you should understand the importance of security management. It would be a shame to have a well-designed database, one with which the customer is pleased, until the walls come crashing down because of an unexpected security breach. Although not all problems can be foreseen, proactive measures such as regular monitoring should take place to minimize future problems that might be encountered. If a security breach is encountered, it should be reported to the appropriate technical administrators and management for immediate action.

15

IMPLEMENTING
DATABASE
SECURITY

Change Control

IN THIS CHAPTER

The need to avoid random changes to any complex system should be obvious, and a database is no exception. A change control process helps you understand when it is acceptable to make changes and when it is not. Although bugs or new requirements certainly appear after a database system is in use, it might not be wise to modify a database product without careful contemplation. This conclusion might stem from factors beyond cost and performance considerations, such as the effects that a change might have on daily business operations.

It is said that it is easy to start a business, but difficult to keep it open. Likewise, database design is the first step in bringing a database to life, but much more work is involved in its life to ensure that it continues to function as originally intended and designed. Change control is the process used to manage the inevitable changes that will occur to a database after implementation. This process takes all components of the database into consideration, as well as possible effects on business operations, before database changes are allowed.

This chapter begins with a summary of motivations for change control. These include data integrity, information security, and requirements traceability. It is certainly unnecessary to build up new approaches for change control because many formal methods exist. This chapter offers a list of such methods, which can be selected and modified to meet an organization's specific needs. The final topics of this chapter include a basic set of guidelines for change propagation and considerations of automated tools for change management.

Necessity of Change Control in Database Design

As basic laws suggest, nature, itself, seems to abhor change. Newton's laws of motion state that an object in motion tends to remain as such with inertia being a measure of its capacity to change its motion. Humans are equally resistant to change, especially those involved in complex situations. Predictability is much more comfortable.

A database system must evolve over in order for errors to be corrected and new features to be added. It is usually most cost effective to make such modifications in an evolutionary manner. New designs are often cost prohibitive. However, there is no counterpart for natural selection. Either the database works and is efficient or it does not. Consequently, some mechanism for achieving a smooth transition between database versions is essential to avoid disrupting the work of users. Change control, also called *change management*, is this method.

Change management is applicable to a database system, referring to a back-end database and a user front-end application implemented to access the data. It is important to discuss change management from the viewpoints of both the database and the user application because they are both used together by the end user. Changes that are requested typically have an impact on both the database and the application, so these issues must be addressed together.

There are two basic origination points for changes that are required to improve a system, or more specifically, a database:

- Changes in business needs
- Changes in system needs

Changes in Business Needs

There are many events associated with a business that require changes to a database system. Because business requirements drive the design of a database, it is these same requirements that often drive the need for changes in the current database. Business requirements are constantly changing throughout the life of a business, for a variety of reasons.

For instance, the following are examples of business events that invoke system changes:

- The expansion of the business (new services or products).
- The business merges with another business.
- The business elects to integrate new technology.
- The business is prospering better than originally expected.
- Budget dollars are restricted.

Here are some of the implications of the aforementioned business events:

- The need to store new data
- The need to accommodate growing data
- The need to purge old data
- The need to make better use of online storage
- The need to integrate new technologies with the current system
- The need to partition data

As a business grows, new products or services may be added to the business portfolio. New products or services may mean growth in the customer base or increased activity with current customers. One of the main implications of business growth is the need to store more data and increase the efficiency of data access. As more data is added to the database, management may have to consider archiving historic data so that current data can be accessed more efficiently. The addition of new data, or dimensions of data, means that the structure of the database will be affected.

Changes in System Needs

Ever-changing system needs invoke the need for changes. For example, suppose an existing system includes a back-end relational database and an end-user application consisting of forms. After using the application for some time, the end user may find it beneficial to add a button or menu selection to the form to automate some task. Business needs have not changed, but a change must still be considered based on the use of the current system. Suppose that every time an end user queries a customer record, the response time ranges from 5 to 10 seconds, which is determined unacceptable (an acceptable response time is 2 to 5 seconds). The end user complains and requests that performance be improved for this particular query. To facilitate the user's request, indexes may need to be added to the base table or tables of the query, and the query itself may need to be redesigned or streamlined to improve performance.

The following motivations drive changes and are addressed in the following subsections.

- Improving data integrity
- Implementing security features for sensitive data
- Requirements-based testing
- Improving consistency of documentation
- Improving system performance

Improving Data Integrity

The observations of the need for change control relate to a more formal concept called *data integrity*. Although details depend on implementations, data integrity is a formal process that documents access to and changes of information within a database system. Many processes also restrict access to some areas to achieve data integrity. Denial of access always keeps data safe but may not be useful in some user environments. The balancing point between access and risk is a judgment call that the project manager must make.

Implementing Security Features for Sensitive Data

Information security might be another reason for establishing formal change control. A database system might have embedded within it very sensitive information that is proprietary, sensitive, or even classified. The ordinary user would not have access to such data but could execute programs in the same environment as the sensitive information. A system manager might rely on a change-control process to document access to this information or any modifications to the execution environment that might jeopardize it.

Requirements-Based Testing

In formal developments, some projects rely on a method of verification called *requirements-based testing*. The essence of this method involves identifying a specific test (or portion) for each system requirement. This is also an important aspect of requirements verification because any requirements that can't be tested should be deleted. Because the test suite is the benchmark for product verification, any changes that circumvent the requirements process are very dangerous. For example, suppose a developer decides to add a new record to the database but does not formally submit the change. A user may accidentally write a query involving the same variable names as the new feature. The consequence is likely to be erratic system behavior. As another example, suppose a user finds an error but does not report it. Instead, the user actually designs a query around the erroneous behavior because it is more efficient than the intended design. If someone else submits the error later and it is fixed in a later version, the custom query will no longer work.

Improving Consistency of Documentation

Consistency of documentation is another consideration. This includes user manuals, test procedures, and requirements documents. Some managers do not appreciate the fact that documentation is as important as the database itself. When documentation and the database do not match, the database testing will be inadequate, and users are likely to encounter more errors.

Improving System Performance

Performance tuning is a major concern when discussing change control. When a database has been designed, it must meet the customer's storage needs and must perform well enough to enhance the end user's productivity. Performance problems are normally due to hardware problems, database design, and application design. Regardless of a performance complaint, the actual cause of the problem must be pinpointed. It is important to distinguish the cause of the performance issue so that it can be addressed appropriately. Often, the end user may have misperceptions concerning the underlying cause of a performance problem, which is why the technical team should be involved as quickly as possible. Database performance is related to response time and throughput. Response time is the elapsed time involved for data to be retrieved or confirmation of a transaction to be passed back to the end user. Throughput deals with larger amounts of data associated with large queries of batch transactional processing. For the most part, acceptable response time is the primary concern for the end user, although unacceptable throughput may slow batch processing, thus potentially overlapping with transactional activity and slowing response time.

Formal Change-Control Methods

Change control is important at least for data integrity, information security, requirements-based verification, and documentation consistency. Once a project manager understands the importance of change control, the natural impulse is to simply select an automated tool, train the team members, and demand its usage. This approach can work in some cases but can lead to disaster in others. In order to understand when it is acceptable to simply rely on a tool, you need to understand the change process relative to other aspects of database maintenance, development, and testing. On the same note, you would not want to begin using an AD tool to design a database without first understanding basic database design concepts.

Formal methods rely on industry-accepted best practices described in standards. Industry consortia, in conjunction with government and academic agencies, formulate documents that provide guidelines for change management, which is applied in the management of a database throughout its life. Organizations of this type include the American National Standards Institute (ANSI), the Department of Defense (DoD), the Electronic Industries Association (EIA), and the Institute of Electrical and Electronic Engineers (IEEE). Table 16.1 provides a listing of some standards related to configuration management.

TABLE 16.1 Sample Configuration Management Standards

Standard Reference	Topics
ANSI T1.250-1996	Telecommunications—Operations, Administration, Maintenance, and Provisioning (OAM&P)—Extension to Generic Network Information Model for Interfaces Between Operations Systems and Network Elements to Support Configuration Management
ANSI T1.246-1998	Telecommunications—Operations, Administration, Maintenance, and Provisioning (OAM&P)—Information Model and Services for Interfaces Between Operations Systems Across Jurisdictional Boundaries to Support Configuration Management
ANSI/EIA-649-98	National Consensus Standard for Configuration Management • Computer Software Libraries • Configuration Status Accounting • Configuration Management Requirements for Subcontractors/Vendors • Configuration and Data Management References • Reviews and Configuration Audits • Configuration Change Control for Digital Computer Programs • Education in Configuration and Data Management

Standard Reference	Topics
	• Configuration Control
	• Configuration Identification for Digital Computer Programs
MIL-STD-973 (DoD)	Military Standard for Configuration Management
IEEE-828-1998	IEEE Standard for Software Configuration Management Plans
IEEE-1042-1987	IEEE Guide to Software Configuration Management
IEEE-1074-1997	Standard for Developing Software Life Cycle Processes
IEEE-1219-1998	Standard for Software Maintenance
ISO/IEC TR 15846:1998	Information Technology—Software Life Cycle Processes—Configuration Management
ISO 10007:1995	Quality Management—Guidelines for Configuration Management

The following list identifies acronyms for common standards organizations:

- *ANSI*. American National Standards Institute (www.ansi.org)
- *DoD*. Department of Defense (www.dtic.mil)
- *EIA*. Electronic Industries Association (www.eia.org)
- *IEEE*. Institute of Electrical and Electronic Engineers (www.ieee.org)
- *ISO*. International Standards Organization

NOTE

EIA, IEEE, and ISO standards are also available through ANSI.

The selection of a particular standard for guidance depends on several factors related to processes. An in-house process might be the basis of the decision. On the other hand, an engineering services company might encounter any of the listed change management standards because of differing quality processes among customers. It is important that you find a standard that works for your organization, and modify the guidelines in the standard if necessary. Management should approve a standard to be used. Dictating the use of a standard and enforcing the use of one are two different things. Some companies might be prone to adopt the ANSI or ISO standard; for example, most relational database vendors have adopted the latest SQL3 ANSI standard.

Although the detailed requirements and terminology vary among these standards listed, there are many common features. These include version numbering, change priorities, and change-request tracking. In addition, these documents present change control as a subset of configuration management (CM). CM covers all product phases as well as management and technical coordination tasks.

The next subsections cover the following concepts:

- Version control
- Prioritizing changes
- Tracking change requests

Version Control

One of the most essential features of any product-management system is the capability to define a product baseline with a designated a configuration. A software configuration includes a list of all source listings, documents, data files, or other components. It also must include a version-numbering system. The convention for the numbering system often involves a major and minor number. Changes in the major number suggest large numbers of modifications, whereas the minor number tracks smaller variations. It is also conventional to reset the minor number to zero each time the major number increments. Therefore, version 6.0 suggests that an important update is released. However, version 6.15 implies that the baseline is quite stable and is undergoing periodic maintenance.

Here are some sample versions for a database system:

- *Version 1.0.* First release of database/application
- *Version 1.1.* Indexes added to database for improved performance
- *Version 1.2.* Views created to enhance security
- *Version 1.3.* Minor features added to the application
- *Version 2.0.* Major database/application redesign

Disaster recovery of the database environment must also be considered. For instance, the DBA should be able to rollback to previous database versions if a modification ends up having a negative impact on the database or application after testing and implementation. Version control allows manageability of database system rollbacks. In addition to version control, a backup plan must also be developed so that a copy of each version can be maintained and retrieved if the original copy is lost. It would be silly, and defeat the purpose, to have multiple versions that were not backed up.

NOTE

The importance of documenting change requests, changes to the system, and change test results is paramount, especially when dealing with multiple versions of a project. Documentation should provide descriptions of each version, known bugs, fixes to bugs, and enhancements to previous versions of database systems.

Prioritizing Changes

A priority system is an important characteristic of change control. There must be a formal definition of criteria serving as a basis for the priorities. Safety issues are a common, high-priority area, whereas cleanup of user messages might be a low-priority task. As an example of the former, consider a database system used to automate air traffic control operations. A data or logic flaw might result in an accident. On the other hand, the misspelling of a table or heading within a report are probably low-priority changes.

Tracking Change Requests

Submitters should be able to track change requests. Most large projects maintain a change-request database for this purpose. When a user submits a request, the tracking system responds simply with a tracking number. The submitter can then check the tracking number periodically using the online database. Status indications for a particular tracking number usually involve categories such as the following:

- Pending
- Approved
- Rejected
- Assigned

Pending status indicates that the control board has not yet ruled on the change request. The final ruling from this board will either be an acceptance or rejection. If the board accepts the change request, it will usually identify that the request has been assigned to a technical person for resolution. It also indicates the version of the baseline that will contain the change. On the other hand, if the board rejects the change request, there will usually be some sort of explanatory message sent to the submitter. This message also becomes part of the change log so as to avoid considering the same proposed change many times.

Once a change has been approved and made, the team must log changes for the sake of configuration management. A version description document (VDD) often contains the product history. The VDD becomes part of the baseline for the product.

Change-Control Participants

On the basis of these general concepts, the roles of key participants in change control should be a bit clearer. End users of the baseline are one class of participants in the change process. When the software is very complex and there are many users, a program team might establish a user group (UG). A representation of the UG might also be a member of the Change Control Board (CCB). Product management must also have a representative to the CCB because its decisions usually have an impact on the cost and schedule. Engineering must participate in the CCB because this organization contains the developers who will analyze and perform changes. Finally, a Quality Assurance representative should participate because change decisions often affect test procedures. Details become more apparent as an adjunct of considering the steps necessary for an implementation.

> **NOTE**
>
> A particular project must staff the slots implied by the process model and assemble other resources. For change control, staffing the Change Control Board (CCB) must be an early priority. It is also important to establish area leads for domains, such as Quality Assurance, Test, and Development. Depending on the size of an organization, the size of the CCB could range from one to several individuals.

Change-Process Implementation

The technical team must accomplish several important tasks as part of starting up a change-control system. Some of these are project specific, whereas others apply to all projects within the organization. Such tasks include process definition, staffing, and tool selection. Staffing has already been introduced and tool selection will be covered later. It is most important to define and understand the change process. This section focuses on the selection and implementation of a particular change control process for your organization's database system.

Process definition involves the selection of a particular model for the enterprise. More concretely, the management must select a process model based on careful examination of the types of development and maintenance projects. There are several process descriptions that are broken into classes, depending on the database architecture and mechanisms planned for updates.

The database system architecture defines relationships among constituents (tables, views, queries, end-user forms). Identification of such constituents is a key step in a divide-and-conquer development strategy, which is the classic problem-solving method for dealing with very complex issues. However, this same approach is valuable for both database testing and maintenance.

Change methods rely directly on the update plans—typically either a waterfall method or iterative. In the former, the architecture involves large blocks that the team builds and tests completely before moving to another. The iterative method involves co-development of such blocks. It's becoming more popular because of a method called *rapid prototyping*. One pitfall to avoid with the rapid prototyping method is that the prototype can become the product baseline as an attempt to save time. The prototype can be valuable for requirements analysis, validating the database architecture, and verifying performance needs.

NOTE

It is important for an organization to have an enterprise-wide model upon which to build a development project. This is the most efficient way for an organization to address process improvement, code reuse, and a number of other efficiency tactics. It is even more crucial to avoid selecting an automated tool and molding a project around it. Some process managers view this also as a time-saving measure, but it often leads to dead ends in terms of process improvement because the methods are so interwoven with a particular technology.

The change review process ordinarily begins when a product user submits a change request. The CCB acknowledges receipt by posting the status of the request as pending, as described earlier. The technical point of contact is usually responsible for duplicating the problem (if identified), validating the change priority based on severity, and estimating the time and cost for the change. The response time must be much smaller than the length between periodic updates. For commercial software, periodic updates might occur several times per year, with response to a change request within a week. The scale for military software is usually much greater because of the longer budget cycles and more complex safety issues. The configuration managers must show the change, once completed, in the VDD. Figure 16.1 provides a general overview of the change control process.

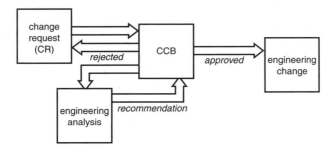

FIGURE 16.1
Overview of the change process.

In Figure 16.1, you can see that change requests are submitted to the CCB. Keep in mind that depending on the size of the organization, the CCB might consist of several individuals, or it could be a single DBA for smaller organizations. Assuming that multiple members comprise the CCB, a technical point of contact is assigned the request, analyzes the request, and reports his recommendation for approval or denial back to the CCB. If approved, the CCB directs the request to the appropriate developers to make the change.

Change request forms should be used to submit change requests to the CCB. The change-request form itself could be the subject of debate. In fact, the number and types of forms are the real starting points of such considerations. Some projects are large enough that change requests and trouble reports require separate forms. However, the goal should be to include sufficient information for problem resolution and status tracking without making the forms too complicated. Figure 16.2 depicts a composite from a variety of projects.

```
        PRODUCT CHANGE REQUEST/PROBLEM REPORT

    DATE:                              _____

    SUBMITTED BY:                      _____

    PRODUCT:                           _____

    ENVIRONMENT:
         Operating system:            _____

         Standalone of network:       _____

    CHANGE DESCRIPTION:
         (include source code or data for problem reports)
         _____


                  STATUS (indicate date of action)
                      FOR USE BY CCB ONLY


    RECEIVED:                          _____

    ASSIGNED:                          _____

    APPROVED:
         (include new version number) _____

    REJECTED:
         (include issue number)        _____
```

FIGURE 16.2

Sample change control form.

The change description in Figure 16.2 covers a wide variety of project types. The following example should help to clarify the application of these ideas. Consider a large database project, such as a payroll system. A key point of contact is responsible for verifying the accuracy of calculations and issuing checks. This point of contact functions as the chairman of the CCB. Rapid problem isolation is crucial, so it is important for the CCB to have programming support as well as data-entry clerks. Payroll clerks might originate problem reports based on their own usage of the system or complaints from other employees. The payroll manager must assign these as change items. With all this in mind, remember that the database must continue to operate while developers address the change requests.

NOTE

Implementing a change control process relates directly to succession planning. Yes, people hop around in this industry like a bunch of Mexican jumping beans. These days, IT professionals move between employers quite often and may leave a mess behind them if there is no change control process in place. For instance, stored procedures may exist with no source or documentation. Compiled programs may not have a source, or even worse, a source much older than the source used to build the current program.

Problem isolation is often closely related to the emergence of new requirements. In this example, suppose employees report that the calculations for Medicare and Social Security are not always correct. At tax time, they owe. Is it simply a data-entry problem or is it a logic error? Once the problem is solved, the program manager vows never to suffer such torment again. Embedded accuracy checking becomes a new requirement for the programmers.

One approach to this requirement is to incorporate subtotals into the design to offer an immediate check of both data entry and programming. For example, it is possible to subtotal all the withholding done on a percentage basis and compare this to the sum of the individual elements:

GROSS		$4,000
Medicare	1.45%	$58
Social Security	6.2%	$248
State withholding	3.5%	$140
TOTAL	11.15%	$446
CHECK		$446

Auditors can provide many other examples related to payroll. The example is interesting, though, because it illustrates how software can improve over time as a result of practical experience.

> **NOTE**
>
> When isolating problems, the key is to find the root of the problem because a domino effect often occurs. Consider the previous example. What is really the cause of the problem with miscalculated payroll figures? Maybe it is data entry, which may require additional edits in the front-end application or additional constraints at the database level. Maybe the data is correct, but a view is reporting the wrong information. Perhaps the query that creates the pay stubs is incorrectly retrieving the data. All approaches must be considered when resolving problem reports.

The change process can become quite complex to manage, especially for large projects. There are many automated tools to make this management more efficient (see the section titled "Considerations for Using Automated Configuration Management Tools"). However, it is crucial to project success that any change process be requirements based. A manager should never select an automated tool and build up a process around it. Instead, the wise manager will carefully define the process and then opt for the tool that best matches the team needs. This approach offers technology independence for configuration management so that the team will not be forever tied to a particular vendor and tool.

> **NOTE**
>
> A change control process should always be established before a configuration-management tool is selected or developed. Because there are many configuration management tools to chose from, it is important (and should not be overly challenging) to find a tool that meets a project's needs.

Basic Guidelines for Change Propagation

By now, you should understand the importance of establishing a change control process. The intent of this section is to provide some basic guidelines for propagating changes into a production environment for the back-end database and the front-end user application. Figure 16.3 illustrates some basic concepts that can be used when propagating changes, whether a formal method has been selected or an in-house method has been devised. Regardless of the method utilized, this is a standard process for any changes made to a database system.

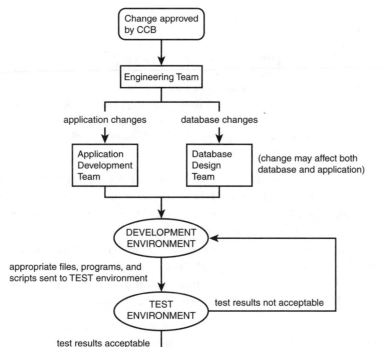

FIGURE 16.3

Basic change control process.

As discussed earlier, all changes should be approved by the Change Control Board (CCB). Once a change has been approved, the change request is sent to the engineering team, which may consist of one or more groups of technical individuals. Suppose that this engineering team consists of an application-development team and a database-design team. Any change requests that affect the design of the application are sent to the application-development team, and any changes that affect the structure of the database are forwarded to the database-design team. Some changes may require work from both teams. For example, if a table is added to the database to store new information, the application must also be changed to allow user access to the new data.

> **NOTE**
>
> All changes made to the database and application must be carefully tracked. No two developers should be allowed to sign out the same piece of code at the same time. At the database level, no two developers should attempt to make changes to a database object at the same time. Management of change request assignments and communication is key.

All changes must be made in the established development environment. The database-development environment is established by the database administrator. It is important for the database-development environment to mimic the production environment. In development, real data is not important. The structure of the database is what's important. The development environment for the application developers is usually a personal computer with installed application-development tools, such as Visual Basic. The application-development environment is usually connected to the database-development environment. Again, the focus is on making necessary changes to the structure of the database and application features.

Once work has been accomplished in the development environment, the appropriate files, compiled programs, and scripts to build database structures are applied to the test environment. The database test environment should mimic the latest development environment. Real data is created in the test environment so that users can test the application against the database. Changes should never be tested in a production environment. Sometimes it is difficult to foresee all the effects of a small change before testing. The latest version of the application is installed on test computers, where assigned end users try to make the database and application break.

After changes have been tested, two conclusions may be drawn: Either the test was successful because all changes were made and the system works as expected, or the test was not successful because changes were not completely made or the system does not function properly. If the end users are not satisfied with the test results, the engineering team must redirect its efforts back to the development environment with the new data that was gathered during testing. It is important that the project manager and test users sign off (approve changes) when testing is successfully completed. If the users are satisfied with test results, the changes made may be propagated to the production environment—but never any sooner!

> **NOTE**
>
> The development, test, and production environments must always be in synchronization with one another, which is simply part of the change-management process. There is simply no other way to effectively manage changes to the database.

Considerations for Using Automated Configuration Management Tools

Once a process model is in place, the time for automated tool selection is at hand. Evaluators should not be intimidated by tool demonstrations that focus on a particular software language. A tool should support any file type valid for the development environment. This allows developers to baseline not just source code but also data files, batch files, test results, and product documentation.

The tool-selection criteria should be requirements based. This topic describes some common requirements and tool examples. The requirements are both technical and nontechnical. The examples of tools are a sampling of an ocean of possibilities.

The following paragraphs explain the considerations in this list for selecting an automated configuration management tool.

- Access control
- Automatic change notification
- Rollback capability
- Remote capability
- Compatibility with the development environment
- Cost and ease of use

Access control is a paramount requirement of any automated configuration management tool selected. This is a locking mechanism for restricting file access to selected users. An author of a file checks it into the system. Later, the author might check out the file to make modifications. The version system tracks and reconciles differences among files. Others within the project can check the file out of the system, but access control prevents anyone but the author from making modifications. Some systems allow multiple authors for a given file.

Automatic change notification is another useful feature for a selected automated configuration management tool. Once again, the typical scenario involves an author checking out a file and then checking it back in with modifications. In this case, the notification feature will send an email message alerting all project members to the change.

Rollback is another important feature. It allows a team member to retrieve all the files associated with a particular version of the product. This can be crucial for efficiency in a development environment. During development, it's common for new files to break the entire product. That is, some changes are so fundamental that if the new file has an error, nothing works. Rollback allows users to retrieve an earlier, working version while the author debugs.

The remote capabilities can be important for a project, especially large ones. Accessibility might span the spectrum from local networks to the Internet. The wider the access capability, the more important an automated tool with sophisticated security features is.

The requirements for tool features relate to the file system of the development environment. That is, the operating system is an important consideration. Microsoft Windows and UNIX are very common choices. Because the UNIX file system already involves a multiple-user environment with some built-in security features, it may be more compatible with some automated change-tracking tools. Therefore, UNIX is a common choice for large programs. Nonetheless, some large projects operate using networked Windows machines for each team member. There are also mixed environments in which individuals use a Windows machine to access a UNIX server (apologies to Macintosh users, for whom many of the UNIX tools are available).

Other, nontechnical aspects are also likely to play a role in tool selection. Cost is an obvious consideration. Ease of use is often as crucial because it is inefficient to spend large amounts of project time simply learning to use the management system. Furthermore, a tool that is difficult to learn discourages its use. In such cases, developers, maintainers, and testers are likely to "cheat" by simply copying files, not checking them out.

> **NOTE**
>
> There are a variety of automated tools for Windows-based systems from which to choose for a database project. There are literally too many to list. Use a search engine to find the various Web sites. The product descriptions of this section are not intended as an endorsement.

One example of an automated configuration management tool is Microsoft Visual SourceSafe. This product offers the capabilities mentioned earlier, and it has a familiar user interface, similar to Windows Explorer. Consequently, this tool can offer good capability with a minimal learning curve. The Professional PVCS product from Merant is quite similar in core capabilities. However, PVCS offers more automation, including change notification, project status tracking, and process metrics formulation. Once again, there are many other possibilities for the Windows environment. The complexity of the project, automation needs, and tool cost are usually the key factors.

The UNIX environment is equally rich in support. The two classic programs are Source Code Control System (SCCS) and Revision Control System (RCS). These are available for download, and a user group supports each. In addition, full C source code and make files are available for those who wish to customize the product. There are some philosophical differences between the two, but it is relatively easy to build (or download) preprocessors to fill the gaps. Once again, many other options are available.

> **NOTE**
>
> A process to manage changes should be in place before picking an automated tool. Many, very general tools are available. The selected tool need not be specifically for a particular database management system.

Summary

Change control is the process of managing changes that occur during the life of a database system. This book refers to the database and the end-user application as a database system. When discussing changes, it is important to discuss both the database and end-user application because changes to one often affect the other. You have learned that changes are necessary for a variety of reasons, due to changes in business requirements and changes in system requirements. Business requirements deal with the way the business is conducted, the products and services offered, the customer base, and changes in business data. System requirements may change once a database system is already in place. For example, indexes may be added to the database, and buttons may be added to the front-end user application. When a change is made, other areas may be affected. For example, if a table is normalized, the application will need to be changed to recognize the fact that one table has been divided into two.

The only way to effectively manage changes is to implement a change-control process. Many change-control methods were discussed, including those outlined by organizations such as the American National Standards Institution (ANSI) and the Department of Defense (DoD). This chapter provided some basic guidelines for managing changes and propagating changes to a production environment. Considerations for selecting automated configuration-management tools were also discussed. These tools greatly assist in the management of changes but should not be used as a crutch (as is the case with any other tool).

Analyzing Legacy Databases for Redesign

The term *legacy*, as defined by Webster's Dictionary, is something that is handed down from an ancestor or from the past. This definition commonly describes old databases that were once developed using third-generation languages and early RDBMS versions. The term *legacy* implies that a database has been around for some time. In information technology, generally anything that is old is out-of-date or obsolete.

When something is out-of-date, it might still function as originally intended, but might lack some of the bells and whistles as something more up-to-date. Even if something, particularly a database, functions as intended, it might not fully optimize the use of the end user's time in order to effectively perform on the job. If a database is obsolete, it might no longer be of use, or its original purpose might have been modified to the point that the database no longer meets the current needs of an organization.

We will begin this chapter with an overview of the legacy database, reviewing examples of such legacies. This chapter discusses the process of redesigning legacy databases, including deciding whether or not a redesign effort is justified and cost-effective. If so, the existing database must be analyzed as part of the design process.

We will cover business process re-engineering (BPR), which is a possible triggering event to the redesign of a database. Then, we'll discuss the design of the database, which corresponds to the concepts already discussed in this book. Documentation and the future of the database are also discussed. Finally, we'll consider how legacy data will be converted and stored in the new database.

Overview of the Legacy Database

This book has focused on properly designing a relational database according to standards and methodologies that are accepted in today's IT world. Developers are constantly looking for new and better ways to store data. When these ways are found, software must be developed that is compatible with new technology. New software features and methods of data usage might demand improvements to data storage. As you can see, there is no end to the frequent changes to anything related to computers or information technology. Therefore, every database designed eventually becomes a legacy database—it eventually is out-of-date, and often obsolete.

Legacy databases usually share common functional issues such as the following:

- Unnecessary manual operation and maintenance administration
- Multiple inappropriate interfaces (stovepipes)
- Performance degradation over time with data growth
- Difficult and costly upgrades or migrations

- Unsupported or discontinued software
- Undesirable interface appearance
- Incompatibilities with new hardware and software
- Inadequate and deficient business processes

These are just a few of the issues that can trigger a proposal to redesign a legacy database. Other scenarios prompting redesign might include these:

- An organization changes the way it does business, which changes processes, data storage, and data access.
- An organization that is successful usually grows, which means more customers and more data. As an organization grows, new business processes might surface, along with requirements for new data.
- New ways are discovered to use data to streamline business functionality.

Table 17.1 shows examples of legacy database conversions into newer, and perhaps more useful, technology. The first column lists the legacy database, either referring to a database model used, or a specific RDMBS. The second column lists either the new database model or RDMBS used. The third column lists the justification for redesigning the legacy database.

TABLE 17.1 Sample Legacy Database Conversions and Justifications

Legacy Database	New Database	Comments
Flat-file	Relational	Flat-file database is obsolete.
Spreadsheet	Relational	With the growth of data and processes, a company needs to automate management of its business processes.
Hierarchical	Relational	Company can take advantage of relational features over hierarchical.
Relational	Relational	Redesign of current RDBMS should improve database design, business process re-engineering.
Relational	Object-relational (OR)	Company can integrate OR features into current relational database.
Microsoft Access	MS SQL Server	Company can use same vendor, but handle greater volumes of data.
Oracle v6	Oracle v8	Version 6 is no longer supported by a vendor; company can take advantage of new features.

Is It Worth the Effort?

"Is it worth it?" is the big question when considering redesign of a legacy database. This is a question that can only be answered with careful contemplation. Is it worth the time, money, effort, and sacrifice?

Consider the analogy to a couple who have lived in a starter home for the past few years, plenty big enough for two adults—maybe even a child. As the couple begin to plan for a family, they begin to wonder whether their home will be big enough—and for how long? They begin to harbor thoughts of investing in a new home, or perhaps, adding on to their existing home. How would either of the two choices affect their lifestyle? They like their current neighborhood, but will they like a new one, if they move? If they add on to their existing home, will they get a return on their investment? For the money spent, will they be happy with an add-on? These are just a few of the initial questions that are probably going through the homeowners' minds before they settle on a decision.

A proposal to redesign a legacy database involves some of the very same questions and the same need for common sense, but involving more technically inclined issues, of course.

There are many considerations that must be weighed before concluding whether to invest in a legacy redesign effort, or to continue working with the current database. Some of these include

- How important is it to stay current with technology?
- What are the hardware and software requirements?
- What costs are involved?
- What business interruptions might be encountered?
- Will training be required?
- How heavily do politics affect the decision to redesign?
- Must the database be synchronized with another database, perhaps as a result of an acquisition or merger?
- What are the performance implications?

Staying Current with Technology

How important is it to the organization to stay current with technology? Why spend money in a seemingly vain effort to keep up with ever-changing technology? To some companies, staying current is more important than to others. For instance, a company providing a catalog for ordering products might want to provide its customers with a more effective ordering tool, by designing a database with a Web-based front-end. The convenience to the customer of Internet shopping means higher sales potential.

A computer training company is another example of a business that holds high the importance of current technology. Who wants to pay dearly for hardware and software training that is outdated or obsolete? Take a computer consulting firm, for example. If consultants do not stay trained in recent technologies, the consulting firm will lose its edge in the market; the consultants will be unable to provide support for newer technologies. It is important for such a consulting firm to stay current.

An organization that might not find it so important to stay current with technology could be a product manufacturing company. Suppose the company has an internally used database to manage the production and inventory of thousands of different products. Let's say the company's legacy system works fine. The database stores the required information, and performs reasonably well even though the data has grown tremendously over the past few years. Performance has degraded, but management feels that users can live with it because it does not affect production and distribution of products to customers. The customers do not care about an attractive database interface—they just want the shipment of products to come in so they can satisfy their customers. Management has considered a redesign of the current database, but the fear remains that too much time will be spent on development and data conversion to justify the effort spent and the potential kinks that might arise in production. Management does not want to jeopardize customer service, especially because the current database still meets the organization's needs.

In summation, it is probably important for an organization to stay current with technology if the customers' demands dictate that the organization do so. There are risks involved in redesign. If the desire to stay current with technology is one of the only considerations for redesigning a database, the effort is probably not justified.

Hardware and Software Requirements

With any proposal to redesign a legacy database comes the possible need to upgrade hardware and software. Besides, if you are spending the effort to redesign the database, why not invest a little bit more to improve the hardware components and software that let you use that database? Keep in mind though, that investment in new hardware and software will yield only temporary improvements as compared to a quality database design. Many organizations are becoming more willing to rely on new hardware and software to solve their design and performance problems because of the plummeting costs of hardware and the increasing costs of consulting and training. Too much focus on hardware, software, and tools, and too little focus on effort to improve design, will diminish the value of the overall investment made by an organization. More hardware is often a very temporary fix and might not at all solve the issues at hand. Yet many companies choose this path and then when no other choice remains will redesign anyway, and of course balk at even more cost.

Database redesign might prompt you to consider these modifications of hardware components:

- Replace the host server
- Replace end-user workstations
- Increase host server disk space for growing data
- Increase host server memory
- Increase the number of CPUs on the host server
- Upgrade network components
- Upgrade network cards in end-user workstations

Software to consider replacing with upgraded models includes

- Operating system software
- Database software
- Database design tools
- Database administration software
- Application development software

NOTE

Although some of the previous bullets in the previous lists referred to application, keep in mind that purchases of both application- and database-related hardware and software might be funded with the same budget dollars within the organization.

Is newer equipment and software really necessary? Maybe the old equipment is obsolete, or of very little use? Or maybe the current configuration meets the needs of the current information system, and will suffice for any near-future redesigns. Does the old equipment meet the organization's needs performance-wise? Will the organization actually use the new features in the latest version of the desired software? What benefits will really be gained by investing in hardware and software upgrades? The benefits could be monumental, or a waste of budget dollars could result.

Costs

Redesign considerations relate to the database's business function. The decision to redesign a database is a simple yes or no answer when analysis facts are available. The most prevalent question to consider is this: "Are the potential improvements to business functions associated with the database worth the monetary cost to redesign them?"

There are several monetary costs to contemplate when a database has been selected for possible redesign. Potential costs would fall into one of the following categories:

- Hardware purchases
- Software licensing for the RDBMS
- Software licensing for development and testing tools
- Employee and contracting manpower resources

The scope of the financial obligation depends on the size of the database redesign, the expected release date, unexpected bottlenecks, and continued future enhancements and releases. Explanations for each of the previous considerations follow.

Business Interruptions

Anytime a database is being redesigned, business interruptions can occur. Interruptions in daily business can inconvenience the customer and users of the existing system. Interruptions are generally caused during the conversion of the old system to the new system (also called the *implementation*). Some organizations are considered 24×7 shops, meaning the database must be available 24 hours per day, 7 days per week. There is typically no scheduled downtime. Obviously, there will be a degree of downtime during implementation of a new system. An organization is considered a 24×7 shop because of the requirements its customers have placed on data availability and service. In a situation such as this, some downtime must be expected, accepted by the customer, and carefully scheduled. The rollover must be perfect to not affect the business.

If an online product-ordering system experiences a business interruption during the attempted implementation of a new database, the business could experience the following:

1. An old database is taken offline.
2. Customers cannot place product orders.
3. Company attempts to place new database online.
4. Problems arise with implementation.
5. Customers still cannot place orders.
6. Customers become frustrated.
7. Customers shop elsewhere.
8. Implementation problems are resolved.
9. The new database is brought online.
10. Customers can now order products.

The end results for this sample business interruption might include

- Loss of customers, which leads to
- Loss of potential revenue, which leads to
- Loss of repeat sales to customers lost, which leads to
- Loss of customer referrals, which leads to
- Loss of more revenue

The chance of business interruptions should not be a factor in deciding whether or not to redesign a database. Interruptions in production are always a risk, although they do not have to occur more than necessary. Any database, application, or changes to a database system should be thoroughly tested before attempting an implementation. Between testing and careful scheduling, downtime during implementation should be minimized in every situation.

Training Considerations

Training is always a major consideration in today's age of evolving technology. The amount of money spent on training often leaves a bad taste in an employer's mouth because of many factors. For example, a company might have invested thousands of dollars in training an employee, who after the training, pursues new employment. A loss of investment has occurred. Training money might be invested, only to find that, months later, the technology has changed again. Maybe an organization feels that training expertise sometimes seems inadequate. There are many reasons an organization might try to avoid training, but there is really no way of getting around it if productivity is a concern. Even in-house training can be performed if sufficient expertise exists within the organization.

Training might adversely affect an organization in the following ways:

- Budget dollars are spent quickly.
- Users must spend time away from the job.
- Training can result in temporary decreases in productivity.

On the upside, training is beneficial because

- Developers can learn to use automated design tools, speeding the design process, and saving the organization money.
- A knowledge transfer can occur between individuals in the organization.
- The technical team can become more proactive, heading off problems before they occur.

When considering a legacy database redesign, keep in mind that training primarily affects the following groups of individuals:

- End users of the database application
- The technical team trained to use automated design tools
- The technical team that will manage the new database, and make required changes to it
- The technical team that will manage new hardware or software components, if applicable to the redesign

Performance Issues

Poor performance is an excellent reason to consider redesigning the current system, or developing an entirely new system. Most non-design–related performance issues can be handled by tuning at the following levels:

- Operating system
- Database (RDBMS)
- Application SQL
- Database denormalization

A poorly designed database is a fundamental cause of poor performance. Even tuning at the previously mentioned levels cannot fully optimize database performance if the database structure itself is not sound. Modifying the database structure through denormalization should be the last resort when attempting to tune a database. However, there is really no substitute for redesigning a poorly designed database.

How does the current performance measure up to user expectations? Answering this question will determine if performance is currently a factor. If performance is acceptable, then a redesign effort is not justified using this consideration. If performance is not acceptable, then a redesign might be considered. If a redesign effort is proposed, how is performance expected to improve with the new database? The implication of anything new or refined is that it is supposed to be better—and perform better—than the method it replaces.

Assessment of the Existing Database

Legacy database redesign can be compared to rebuilding or remodeling an older home. The design and condition of the home's interior and exterior structure will determine how much work is necessary to make it livable. Any good assessment of the legacy database will provide much information regarding its strengths and weaknesses. A legacy database can be assessed by interviewing the end users, and by the development team mining for information in the database. Assessment questions to consider are

- **What is the type of database—OLAP or OLTP?** An *online analytical processing (OLAP) database* is one that stores massive volumes of data, such as a data warehouse or decision support system (DSS). Data can be stored, summarized, and mined from the OLAP to assist in business decision-making. An *online transactional processing (OLTP) database* is used to manage data. The focus is on storing and manipulating data, such as for an online bookstore. The design objectives differ dramatically between these two database types. An OLAP database is designed for queries, whereas an OLTP database is designed for transactions.

- **What types of objects are used in the database?** Does the database consist only of tables and indexes, or are views, snapshots, and other objects used as well? Perhaps the creation of new object types can add value to the database.

- **Are data storage needs being met?** Does the database provide capability for storing all types of data needed by the organization? Do the current version of the RDBMS, the operating system of the host server, and the hardware used all still support data requirements? The current equipment and software might now be inadequate.

- **Is the database secure?** Are there any known security violations that have occurred recently? How are security breaches handled? Does the current database take advantage of the RDBMS built-in security features, such as database roles? Are views used to enhance the control of internal security?

- **Is database performance acceptable to the end user?** Is query performance acceptable? Is transactional performance acceptable? Have indexes been created where appropriate to improve performance? Has the database been denormalized? Has tuning been performed at the back-end database level, as well as at the application level?

- **From an overall perspective, is the data relatively easy to manage?** What limitations seem to exist? How can the user interface to the database be improved?

- **What is the current size of the database?** How is space allocation being managed? How has the data grown since implementation? How is data growth being handled? Does historic data exist? If so, how is historic data handled?

- **Has a change management procedure been established?** Are change management policies being followed? (If a change management procedure is not in place, one should be established for the new database.)

The Effects of Business Process Re-engineering

Re-engineering a legacy database can fundamentally alter the database structure. New SQL features such as Object Relation Models and PLSQL give developers more flexibility within the database. 3GL programs will no longer be required to handle common procedures, integrity rules, and other mundane tasks. The structures within the new database will be more organized and defined. Distribution and replication to other databases will also affect database structure. Database warehouses, which use distribution or replication, are now common for archival and history data.

Analyzing Legacy Databases for Redesign

CHAPTER 17

437

17

ANALYZING
LEGACY
DATABASES FOR
REDESIGN

Picture the normal legacy databases. Usually they have been given every aid in the first-aid kit. They are patched up so often that a true release version no longer exists. At this stage, fixes are made directly to production, instead of being properly tested first in a test environment. The structure of the database and its external functions have grown completely out of control.

Re-engineering allows the implementation of module-based programming. Each portion of the BPR can be isolated into separate modules or units. They can operate independently for design and test phases. After testing, they can then be integrated into the final database design. It would then be possible to quickly remedy bugs by dissecting and patching the appropriate module or unit.

> **NOTE**
>
> As processes are refined, data storage requirements might also change, even if the data itself stays the same. Refined processes might require data to be accessed differently than it was before, affecting database design in the areas of normalization, view definitions, and other data replication methods.

During the redesign of a legacy database, it is generally necessary to re-engineer the existing business processes. Technology advancements are major factors in BPR. Legacy databases with older RDBMS versions are not always compatible with newer versions and tools. New technology concepts can offer new and more efficient business process development that was previously not available.

Cost is another factor in BPR. Generally, it is more affordable to redesign and re-engineer a legacy database within the same strategy plan rather than use a different methodology. Though cost effective, the combined redesign and reengineering phase will add more time and congestion to the project.

Designing for the New System

Assuming that a legacy redesign effort has been proposed and accepted by an organization's decision makers, design should proceed. Whether designing a new database, or redesigning a legacy database, the basic steps as outlined in this book remain constant.

The life cycle of a legacy database, even throughout redesign, should follow the basic life cycle phases as defined earlier in this book. Table 17.2 reviews the database life cycle.

TABLE 17.2   Adherence of the Legacy Database to the Standard Life Cycle

Step	Database Environment	Description of Work Involved
1	Development	Information gathered. Legacy database analyzed. Database designed. Application designed. Changes made to database. Change propagation starts.
2	Test	Database and application tested. Changes tested before released. Quality assurance testing occurs. User accepts new database/changes. DBA converts development to test.
3	Production	DBA converts test to production. Database implemented. Application implemented. End user is able to work. DBA maintains database. Performance tuning occurs. User change requests made.

The following legacy redesign concepts are discussed in the subsequent sections:

- Selection of a database design method
- Selection of database software
- Redesign of data structures
- Migration of legacy data

Database Design Method to Be Used

The database design methodology used to redesign a legacy might not differ from that used to design the original database. Database, software, and hardware technology will always change, but the basic thought process to model an organization's data storage needs, and then convert the model into a working database, will never change. Although, during a redesign would be a good time to start using a different methodology, if consideration to do so was already in motion. If the design team is comfortable with the previously used methodology, then it might be easier to avoid a change. Why change something that is not broken? The problem with a legacy database probably doesn't lie in the methodology, but in how the methodology was applied.

Database Software to Be Used

New software might be used with a newly designed database. New software and later versions of software are almost always a consideration in redesigning a legacy database. Why not use newly developed features to automate the process of design and improve management of data?

There are different types of software that are affected during a redesign. This software includes the following:

- RDBMS software
- Database management software
- Configuration management (change management) software
- Database design software
- Application development software

RDBMS software might be changed or upgraded to improve data management and take advantage of new RDBMS features. For example, a Microsoft Access database might be transformed into a Microsoft SQL Server database for a growing company. Microsoft SQL Server is designed to handle larger amounts of data than Access. An example of version upgrade might be represented by the installation of Oracle8i, whereas the previous version of Oracle used might have been Oracle 7.3.4. Software can be used, from the DBA's perspective, to manage the database once it is implemented. Configuration management software can be purchased to manage changes to the database, especially if a change management procedure is not currently in place. Software can also be changed or upgraded to design both the database and the user application. If the organization has never used a CASE or AD tool, now might be a good time to try a highly rated AD tool, or begin using a more current version with fixes to bugs that might have existed in previous versions.

Redesigning Data Structures

Once again, the processes of designing and redesigning a relational database involve the same basic steps, as discussed throughout this book. If the legacy database is a relational database, then tables will still be tables. These tables, however, will be redesigned. Some tables might look the same; others might be normalized or denormalized where appropriate. Views can also be defined or refined during redesign. Depending on the RDBMS software used, new features and object types can be integrated into the design.

If the legacy database differs from the relational model, such as a flat-file system, then flat files will have to be converted into relational tables. For example, a file containing customer contact information can be thought of as a table. Fields in the file can be thought of as columns. Keep in mind though, that normalization might be required to optimally transform the flat-file database into a relational database. Denormalization might also occur at a later date.

A legacy database can be used to feed the new database with data. For example, the legacy database might be a combination of transactional (OLTP) and analytical processing (OLAP). The database might be redesigned so that it is split into two separate databases, in which the OLAP feeds from the OLTP for historic and summarized data. Or, the OLTP portion of the legacy database might stay intact, and the new database might consist only of the OLAP portion of the legacy database. In any case, the basic design of data structures is the same during legacy redesign.

Migrating Legacy Data

Migrating legacy data is a major issue when redesigning a legacy database. Sometimes, developers forget during database redesign that data exists. When redesigning a legacy database, it is just as important to care for the existing data as it is to design the new database structures. The appearance of the data might change, thereby requiring conversions. Legacy data must then be loaded, once converted, into the new data structures. The migration of data is a major part of legacy redesign. Adequate time and resources must be allocated for data migration. Individuals can be assigned the responsibility to begin planning data migration from the beginning of the redesign effort.

The migration of legacy data consists of these three steps:

1. Back up the legacy data.
2. Convert the legacy data to the new format.
3. Load the data into the new database.

As implied, the conversion of legacy data might involve combining or splitting data because of normalization and denormalization steps taken during design. The following section provides an example of a legacy data conversion.

A Sample Conversion of Legacy Data

There are some tools available that offer simple solutions to converting a legacy database to a new RDBMS. There are also other approaches besides using a conversion tool. The amount of data can determine the approach used. The most common tool used is a flat-file–loading utility that can parse through a delimited flat file. Data can be pulled from the legacy database by using a SELECT statement and writing the output to a formatted file. The file data is then loaded into the new database one table at a time. Referential integrity constraints can be applied after the data is loaded. The following simple example references Oracle's SQL Loader. It is ideal for loading data from a flat file into an Oracle database.

The flat-file data appears as follows:

```
"533","4506 PARK AVENUE","OSHKOSH","WI",40166"
"534","112 OAK LANE","SAN ANTONIO","TX","49120"
"535","3419 GREEN LANE","BRECKENRIDGE","CO","61224"
"536","44 EAST WHITESBURG ROAD","OAKLAND CITY","CA","41986"
"537","551 WEST VISTA STREET","LAS VEGAS","NV","81121"
```

Field data is enclosed by quotation marks. Each field is *delimited*, or separated, by a comma.

The SQL*Loader control file appears as follows:

```
load data
infile 'address.dat'
into table PERS_ADDRESS_TBL
insert
fields terminated by ',' optionally enclosed by '"'
(EMP_ID, STREET, CITY, ST, ZIP)
```

This control file is used by the SQL*Loader utility to read data in the flat file, matching delimited fields with database columns for a given table. The concept here is much more important than the syntax. If using an RDBMS other than Oracle, check for a utility used to load flat-file data.

The following statement is used to execute SQL*Loader:

```
sqlload userid=datconvert/mypasswd control=address.ctl
```

This statement requires a database login and password, as well as a reference to a control file. The database login is the owner of the PERS_ADDRESS_TBL table.

The following SQL query can be used to query the PERS_ADDRESS_TBL table for the newly inserted data:

```
SELECT EMP_ID, STREET, CITY, ST, ZIP
FROM PERS_ADDRESS_TBL;
```

Following is the query output:

EMP_ID	STREET	CITY	STATE	ZIP
533	4506 PARK AVENUE	OSHKOSH	WI	40166
534	112 OAK LANE	SAN ANTONIO	TX	49120
535	3419 GREEN LANE	BRECKENRIDGE	CO	61224
536	44 EAST WHITESBURG ROAD	OAKLAND CITY	CA	41986
537	551 WEST VISTA STREET	LAS VEGAS	NV	81121

NOTE

We have seen a lot of flat-file conversions. The conversion of flat-file data to a relational database is pretty much a standard procedure. A database utility can be used, if available, to read fields in the flat file, and load data in the fields into database columns. If file I/O is supported by the RDBMS, programs can be written to read flat-file data and load it into the database. Database programs can also be written to convert data.

Documentation

Because documentation provides an overall picture of the database as a whole, it must be updated as well. Redesigning brings new business rules and architecture that should be thoroughly documented. It might be relevant to re-document the entire database design if previous documentation is inaccurate or incomplete. End-user processing and troubleshooting should also be included. Generally, a thoroughly documented database is a well designed database.

Thorough documentation is always a complement to a database. It is an essential part of the initial analysis and redesign strategy. It is necessary to review the existing documentation to analyze existing business processes. Documentation can help reveal deficiencies and bottlenecks with the legacy system.

The two most important types of documentation are

- System documentation
- End-user documentation

System documentation contains information about the system itself. System documentation contains design plans, diagrams, and other information associated with the structure of the system. The system is made up of both the back-end database and the user application. System documentation should include information about the interaction between the database and the application, as well as proposed hardware and software configurations. System documentation is used mainly by the technical team in understanding the system. This documentation also helps in the event that the system is redesigned in the future, or used as a reference to design a similar system.

End-user documentation should be brought up-to-date as well. End-user documentation contains information about the application interface to the database. This documentation describes the features and uses of the application, as related to the database. End-user documentation is a good source for end-user training. This documentation is also useful in gathering information about an existing system during redesign, and understanding the end users' daily functions.

Future of the New Database

What is the future of the new database? You might begin to wonder whether any database has a real future because of all the changes that the information technology world is experiencing. However, if a database is well designed, it always has a future in an organization. In the event that a database is redesigned, the legacy database gives life to the new database just as a mother gives life to a child. The structure of the database might change, but the data lives.

The following catalysts affect the future of any database:

- Projection of new features
- Future releases of database

- Future releases of RDBMS software

- Future releases of other software

- The growth of the database

Redesigning a database will enable developers to use new RDBMS features. Concepts such as partitioning, object relational types, and more enhanced PL/SQL are excellent considerations for new features. Front-end interfaces also have opportunities for a facelift.

"Web, Web, Web" is now the word of choice. Most front-end and some back-end development is designed for database access through a Web browser interface, otherwise known as a *thin client*. This gives developers a central location for client-type files that would normally reside on the client PC. Some of the latest breakthroughs in RDBMS versions are their capabilities to communicate well with Java and the Internet. Redesigning for the Web is an excellent choice.

After implementation, users will inevitably find deficiencies with the new database, and demand changes. Changes are good if they enable the database to progress. A database might experience many versions throughout its life, all the time increasing in quality and value to the end user. If a database works, it might be more beneficial to upgrade to a newer version periodically as opposed to completely overhauling the design.

Computer technology is moving so fast that by the time a new database is designed and implemented into production, newer RDBMS features have since been introduced. We previously discussed how newer RDBMS versions can simplify or relieve the need for mundane business processes used in legacy databases.

17

ANALYZING LEGACY DATABASES FOR REDESIGN

Tip

Try to stay close enough to the technology so that the newly redesigned database does not become a legacy database before its release. The incurred cost burden for new feature concepts today will save expenses for redesign in the future.

The growth of the database, as mentioned many times in this book, also affects the future of the database. As a database grows, more storage is required. This means that it might be necessary to invest in additional hardware devices. As an alternative to additional hardware, you could get rid of the old data to make room for the new. This involves archiving or purging data, or a combination of both. If a particular database (that is, the way a database is designed) or an RDBMS cannot handle the amount of data being generated, then the future of the database might be looking somewhat grim. Luckily, data growth can usually be accommodated by increased physical disk space (which is much less expensive than it used to be), or by archiving to tape (which can be read back to disk and accessed when necessary).

Summary

A legacy database is the current database used by an organization, which has typically been around for many years. The term *legacy* implies that the database has been passed down by an organization, in many cases outliving the employment of managers and end users. You might have developers and users who are loyal to the database, having been by its side from the beginning. However loyal, these users tend to have another software, besides RDBMS, that might become available that blows away the features of current software used with a database. For example, data mining software is being improved constantly. Software such as this might be used in conjunction with the database and the application interface, as a supplement that allows alternative access to data. Using new versions of software such as this does not mandate changes to the database. However, software might evolve that requires compatibility with a particular RDBMS that is not in use in the organization. In a case such as this, either the database or the software must be modified.

There are a few attributes that legacy databases usually have in common with one another, such as a tendency for unnecessary manual intervention, an unfriendly user interface, performance degradation, incompatibilities with new hardware and software, and an inability to accommodate current business requirements. An organization might determine the need to redesign a legacy database based on various requirements, such as the need to store more and new data as the organization grows, the need to accommodate different types of data and business processes, and the discovery of new data uses.

Much effort is involved in redesigning a legacy database; potentially more effort than with designing a new database. If the legacy database was well designed, information about its structure should prove to be very helpful in its redesign. The big question is, "Is it worth the effort?" There are several considerations involved in justifying a legacy redesign, such as the importance of staying current with technology, changing hardware and software requirements, the time and manpower costs involved, the possibility for business interruptions, and the need for training.

If your organization decides to redesign a legacy database, the basic steps taken should correspond with those outlined in the database-design methodology selected. During redesign, as much information can be gathered from the legacy database (and application interface) as from the end user. The legacy database must be carefully assessed, determining the deficiencies and outlining the possible improvements. A major concern in redesigning a database is the care that must be taken to preserve the existing data. The data might need to be converted before it is migrated to the new database, based on structural changes to the database. Time and resources must be allocated for data migration, as it is an integral part of legacy redesign.

Appendixes

Sample Physical Database Implementation

This appendix provides a sample physical database implementation for a resume-tracking system. The ERD in Figure A.1 shows the relationships between entities representing information found on a person's resume. It just so happens that the code generated for this appendix is for an Oracle database, although the concepts here apply to any relational database. The point is to show the reader what occurs, from a general standpoint, after the database has been designed and before actual release of the database to production. The code is generated to build the database based on the design that took place. The code can be manually typed, or generated using an automated design tool, such as Irwin or Oracle Designer.

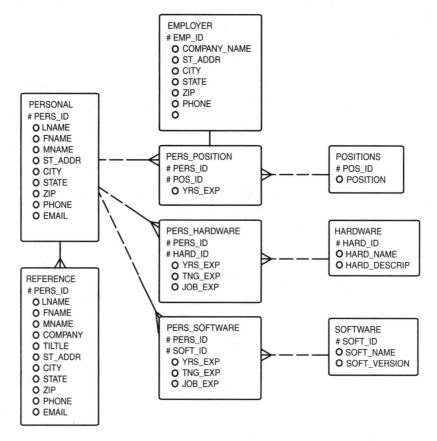

FIGURE A.1

Sample ERD for resume database.

Figure A.2 illustrates a server model diagram that was generated by the automated design tool, Oracle Designer, when the conversion occurred from entities to tables. Notice the similarity between the server model diagram and the ERD. Different symbols exist, though, between the two diagrams. For instance, the pound sign (#) represents primary keys, the asterisk (*)

represents required columns, and the "o" represents optional columns. Additionally, the "789" icon represents a numeric data type, the "A" represents a character data type, and the "31" (which looks like a calendar page) represents a date data type.

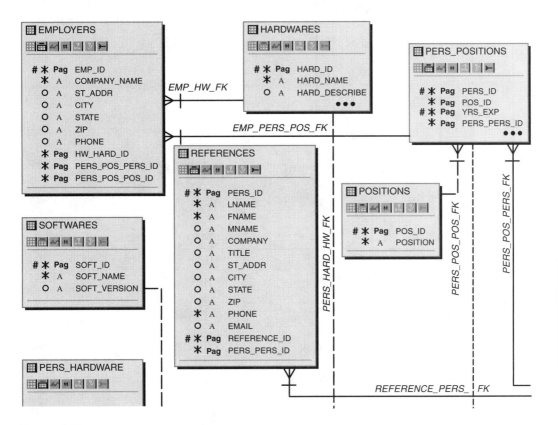

FIGURE A.2

Sample server model diagram for resume database.

The tables, as shown in the ERD in the Figure A.1, were designed using the following structures. The following table descriptions represent more detail than what is shown in the ERD. Study the data types, primary key, foreign key, and unique constraint definitions.

PERSONALS:

COLUMN NAME	DATA TYPE	NULLABLE	CONSTRAINT
PERS_ID	NUMBER(10)	NOT NULL	PK
L_NAME	VARCHAR2(30)	NOT NULL	
F_NAME	VARCHAR2(30)	NOT NULL	

PERSONALS: Continued

COLUMN NAME	DATA TYPE	NULLABLE	CONSTRAINT
M_NAME	VARCHAR2(30)	NULL	
ST_ADDR	VARCHAR2(30)	NOT NULL	
CITY	VARCHAR2(30)	NOT NULL	
STATE	VARCHAR2(2)	NOT NULL	
ZIP	VARCHAR2(5)	NOT NULL	
PHONE	VARCHAR2(10)	NOT NULL	
EMAIL	VARCHAR2(50)	NULL	UNIQUE

REFERENCES:

COLUMN NAME	DATA TYPE	NULLABLE	CONSTRAINT
PERS_ID	NUMBER(10)	NOT NULL	FK
L_NAME	VARCHAR2(30)	NOT NULL	
F_NAME	VARCHAR2(30)	NOT NULL	
M_NAME	VARCHAR2(30)	NULL	
COMPANY	VARCHAR2(30)	NULL	
TITLE	VARCHAR2(30)	NULL	
ST_ADDR	VARCHAR2(30)	NULL	
CITY	VARCHAR2(30)	NULL	
STATE	VARCHAR2(2)	NULL	
ZIP	VARCHAR2(5)	NULL	
PHONE	VARCHAR2(10)	NOT NULL	UNIQUE
EMAIL	VARCHAR2(50)	NULL	UNIQUE

EMPLOYERS:

COLUMN NAME	DATA TYPE	NULLABLE	CONSTRAINT
EMP_ID	NUMBER(10)	NOT NULL	PK
COMPANY_NAME	VARCHAR2(30)	NOT NULL	UNIQUE
ST_ADDR	VARCHAR2(30)	NULL	
CITY	VARCHAR2(30)	NULL	
STATE	VARCHAR2(30)	NULL	
ZIP	VARCHAR2(5)	NULL	
PHONE	VARCHAR2(10)	NULL	

PERS_POSITIONS:

COLUMN NAME	DATA TYPE	NULLABLE	CONSTRAINT
PERS_ID	NUMBER(10)	NOT NULL	PK, FK
POS_ID	NUMBER(10)	NOT NULL	PK
YRS_EXP	NUMBER(2)	NOT NULL	

PERS_HARDWARE:

COLUMN NAME	DATA TYPE	NULLABLE	CONSTRAINT
PERS_ID	NUMBER(10)	NOT NULL	PK, FK
HARD_ID	NUMBER(10)	NOT NULL	PK
YRS_EXP	NUMBER(2)	NULL	
TNG_EXP	VARCHAR2(1)	NULL	
JOB_EXP	VARCHAR2(1)	NULL	

PERS_SOFTWARE:

COLUMN NAME	DATA TYPE	NULLABLE	CONSTRAINT
PERS_ID	NUMBER(10)	NOT NULL	PK, FK
SOFT_ID	NUMBER(10)	NOT NULL	PK
YRS_EXP	NUMBER(2)	NULL	
TNG_EXP	VARCHAR2(1)	NULL	
JOB_EXP	VARCHAR2(1)	NULL	

POSITIONS:

COLUMN NAME	DATA TYPE	NULLABLE	CONSTRAINT
POS_ID	NUMBER(10)	NOT NULL	PK
POSITION	VARCHAR2(30)	NOT NULL	UNIQUE

HARDWARE:

COLUMN NAME	DATA TYPE	NULLABLE	CONSTRAINT
HARD_ID	NUMBER(10)	NOT NULL	PK
HARD_NAME	VARCHAR2(30)	NOT NULL	UNIQUE
HARD_DESCRIP	VARCHAR2(100)	NULL	

SOFTWARE:

COLUMN NAME	DATA TYPE	NULLABLE	CONSTRAINT
SOFT_ID	NUMBER(10)	NOT NULL	PK
SOFT_NAME	VARCHAR2(30)	NOT NULL	UNIQUE
SOFT_VERSION	VARCHAR2(10)	NULL	

The DDL (table creation scripts) was generated using the automated design (AD) tool Oracle Designer.

A user account was created in the database by the DBA to act as the schema owner for the resume tables, as follows. Notice that the user is assigned a tablespace called "resume_ts". A *tablespace* is an area reserved in the database in which tables can be created. Also notice that the user is granted two Oracle roles: connect and resource. These are roles that allow a user to create all types of objects in the database, such as tables, indexes, and views.

```
SQL> create user resume_own
  2  identified by manager
  3  default tablespace resume_ts;

User created.

SQL> grant connect, resource to resume_own;

Grant succeeded.
```

The data definition language (DDL) must be generated from the design so that the database can be built under the schema that was created in the previous step. The generated DDL was executed by the schema owner, as follows. Notice in the following list of SQL code that tables, constraints, and indexes are generated by Designer, based on information supplied during design. After each individual SQL statement (individual table creation, for example) is executed, the database reports feedback stating that the object was created. Again, keep in mind that this example uses Oracle SQL, but the concepts are the same for all relational databases. The exact syntax of DDL varies among relational database vendors.

```
SQL> @c:\projects\resume\resume.sql
SQL> -- c:\projects\resume\resume.sql
SQL> --
SQL> -- Generated for Oracle 8 on Fri Jul 14  12:21:43 2000 by
➥Server Generator 2.1.24.3.0
SQL>
SQL>
SQL>
SQL> PROMPT Creating Table 'PERS_HARDWARE'
Creating Table 'PERS_HARDWARE'
SQL> CREATE TABLE PERS_HARDWARE
  2  (PERS_ID NUMBER(10) NOT NULL
  3  ,HARD_ID NUMBER(10) NOT NULL
  4  ,YRS_EXP NUMBER(2)
  5  ,TNG_EXP VARCHAR2(1)
  6  ,JOB_EXP VARCHAR2(1)
  7  ,PERS__PERS_ID NUMBER(10) NOT NULL
  8  ,HW_HARD_ID NUMBER(10)
  9  )
 10  /
```

A

```
Table created.

SQL>
SQL> PROMPT Creating Table 'PERSONALS'
Creating Table 'PERSONALS'
SQL> CREATE TABLE PERSONALS
  2    (PERS_ID NUMBER(10) NOT NULL
  3    ,L_NAME VARCHAR2(30) NOT NULL
  4    ,F_NAME VARCHAR2(30) NOT NULL
  5    ,M_NAME VARCHAR2(30)
  6    ,ST_ADDR VARCHAR2(30) NOT NULL
  7    ,CITY VARCHAR2(30) NOT NULL
  8    ,STATE VARCHAR2(2) NOT NULL
  9    ,ZIP VARCHAR2(5) NOT NULL
 10    ,PHONE VARCHAR2(10) NOT NULL
 11    ,EMAIL VARCHAR2(50)
 12    )
 13    /

Table created.

SQL>
SQL> PROMPT Creating Table 'SOFTWARES'
Creating Table 'SOFTWARES'
SQL> CREATE TABLE SOFTWARES
  2    (SOFT_ID NUMBER(10) NOT NULL
  3    ,SOFT_NAME VARCHAR2(30) NOT NULL
  4    ,SOFT_VERSION VARCHAR2(10)
  5    )
  6    /

Table created.

SQL>
SQL> PROMPT Creating Table 'REFERENCES'
Creating Table 'REFERENCES'
SQL> CREATE TABLE REFERENCES
  2    (PERS_ID NUMBER(10) NOT NULL
  3    ,LNAME VARCHAR2(30) NOT NULL
  4    ,FNAME VARCHAR2(30) NOT NULL
  5    ,MNAME VARCHAR2(30)
  6    ,COMPANY VARCHAR2(30)
  7    ,TITLE VARCHAR2(30)
  8    ,ST_ADDR VARCHAR2(30)
  9    ,CITY VARCHAR2(30)
```

```
10      ,STATE VARCHAR2(2)
11      ,ZIP VARCHAR2(5)
12      ,PHONE VARCHAR2(10) NOT NULL
13      ,EMAIL VARCHAR2(50)
14      ,REFERENCE_ID NUMBER(10,0) NOT NULL
15      ,PERS__PERS_ID NUMBER(10) NOT NULL
16      )
17  /

Table created.

SQL>
SQL> PROMPT Creating Table 'POSITIONS'
Creating Table 'POSITIONS'
SQL> CREATE TABLE POSITIONS
 2      (POS_ID NUMBER(10) NOT NULL
 3      ,POSITION VARCHAR2(30) NOT NULL
 4      )
 5  /

Table created.

SQL>
SQL> PROMPT Creating Table 'PERS_SOFTWARE'
Creating Table 'PERS_SOFTWARE'
SQL> CREATE TABLE PERS_SOFTWARE
 2      (PERS_ID NUMBER(10) NOT NULL
 3      ,SOFT_ID NUMBER(10) NOT NULL
 4      ,YRS_EXP NUMBER(2)
 5      ,TNG_EXP VARCHAR2(1)
 6      ,JOB_EXP VARCHAR2(1)
 7      ,PERS__PERS_ID NUMBER(10) NOT NULL
 8      ,SW_SOFT_ID NUMBER(10)
 9      )
10  /

Table created.

SQL>
SQL> PROMPT Creating Table 'PERS_POSITIONS'
Creating Table 'PERS_POSITIONS'
SQL> CREATE TABLE PERS_POSITIONS
 2      (PERS_ID NUMBER(10) NOT NULL
 3      ,POS_ID NUMBER(10) NOT NULL
 4      ,YRS_EXP NUMBER(2) NOT NULL
 5      ,PERS__PERS_ID NUMBER(10) NOT NULL
```

```
  6    ,POS_POS_ID NUMBER(10)
  7    )
  8    /

Table created.

SQL>
SQL> PROMPT Creating Table 'EMPLOYERS'
Creating Table 'EMPLOYERS'
SQL> CREATE TABLE EMPLOYERS
  2    (EMP_ID NUMBER(10) NOT NULL
  3    ,COMPANY_NAME VARCHAR2(30) NOT NULL
  4    ,ST_ADDR VARCHAR2(30)
  5    ,CITY VARCHAR2(30)
  6    ,STATE VARCHAR2(30)
  7    ,ZIP VARCHAR2(5)
  8    ,PHONE VARCHAR2(10)
  9    ,HW_HARD_ID NUMBER(10) NOT NULL
 10    ,PERS_POS_PERS_ID NUMBER(10) NOT NULL
 11    ,PERS_POS_POS_ID NUMBER(10) NOT NULL
 12    )
 13    /

Table created.

SQL>
SQL> PROMPT Creating Table 'HARDWARES'
Creating Table 'HARDWARES'
SQL> CREATE TABLE HARDWARES
  2    (HARD_ID NUMBER(10) NOT NULL
  3    ,HARD_NAME VARCHAR2(30) NOT NULL
  4    ,HARD_DESCRIP VARCHAR2(100)
  5    )
  6    /

Table created.

SQL>
SQL> @c:\mcp\db_des\appendixes\resume.con
SQL> -- c:\mcp\db_des\appendixes\resume.con
SQL>
SQL> PROMPT Creating Primary Key on 'PERS_HARDWARE'
Creating Primary Key on 'PERS_HARDWARE'
SQL> ALTER TABLE PERS_HARDWARE
  2    ADD CONSTRAINT PERS_HARD_PK PRIMARY KEY
  3      (PERS_ID
```

```
   4    ,HARD_ID)
   5  /

Table altered.

SQL>
SQL> PROMPT Creating Primary Key on 'PERSONALS'
Creating Primary Key on 'PERSONALS'
SQL> ALTER TABLE PERSONALS
   2    ADD CONSTRAINT PERS__PK PRIMARY KEY
   3     (PERS_ID)
   4  /

Table altered.

SQL>
SQL> PROMPT Creating Primary Key on 'SOFTWARES'
Creating Primary Key on 'SOFTWARES'
SQL> ALTER TABLE SOFTWARES
   2    ADD CONSTRAINT SW_PK PRIMARY KEY
   3     (SOFT_ID)
   4  /

Table altered.

SQL>
SQL> PROMPT Creating Primary Key on 'REFERENCES'
Creating Primary Key on 'REFERENCES'
SQL> ALTER TABLE REFERENCES
   2    ADD CONSTRAINT REFERENCE_PK PRIMARY KEY
   3     (REFERENCE_ID)
   4  /

Table altered.

SQL>
SQL> PROMPT Creating Primary Key on 'POSITIONS'
Creating Primary Key on 'POSITIONS'
SQL> ALTER TABLE POSITIONS
   2    ADD CONSTRAINT POS_PK PRIMARY KEY
   3     (POS_ID)
   4  /

Table altered.

SQL>
```

```
SQL> PROMPT Creating Primary Key on 'PERS_SOFTWARE'
Creating Primary Key on 'PERS_SOFTWARE'
SQL> ALTER TABLE PERS_SOFTWARE
  2    ADD CONSTRAINT PERS_SOFT_PK PRIMARY KEY
  3    (PERS_ID
  4    ,SOFT_ID)
  5  /

Table altered.

SQL>
SQL> PROMPT Creating Primary Key on 'PERS_POSITIONS'
Creating Primary Key on 'PERS_POSITIONS'
SQL> ALTER TABLE PERS_POSITIONS
  2    ADD CONSTRAINT PERS_POS_PK PRIMARY KEY
  3    (PERS_ID
  4    ,POS_ID)
  5  /

Table altered.

SQL>
SQL> PROMPT Creating Primary Key on 'EMPLOYERS'
Creating Primary Key on 'EMPLOYERS'
SQL> ALTER TABLE EMPLOYERS
  2    ADD CONSTRAINT EMP__PK PRIMARY KEY
  3    (EMP_ID)
  4  /

Table altered.

SQL>
SQL> PROMPT Creating Primary Key on 'HARDWARES'
Creating Primary Key on 'HARDWARES'
SQL> ALTER TABLE HARDWARES
  2    ADD CONSTRAINT HW_PK PRIMARY KEY
  3    (HARD_ID)
  4  /

Table altered.

SQL>
SQL> PROMPT Creating Foreign Keys on 'PERS_HARDWARE'
Creating Foreign Keys on 'PERS_HARDWARE'
SQL> ALTER TABLE PERS_HARDWARE ADD CONSTRAINT
  2    PERS_HARD_HW_FK FOREIGN KEY
```

```
   3    (HW_HARD_ID) REFERENCES HARDWARES
   4    (HARD_ID) ADD CONSTRAINT
   5   PERS_HARD_PERS__FK FOREIGN KEY
   6    (PERS__PERS_ID) REFERENCES PERSONALS
   7    (PERS_ID)
   8   /

Table altered.

SQL>
SQL> PROMPT Creating Foreign Keys on 'REFERENCES'
Creating Foreign Keys on 'REFERENCES'
SQL> ALTER TABLE REFERENCES ADD CONSTRAINT
   2    REFERENCE_PERS__FK FOREIGN KEY
   3    (PERS__PERS_ID) REFERENCES PERSONALS
   4    (PERS_ID)
   5   /

Table altered.

SQL>
SQL> PROMPT Creating Foreign Keys on 'PERS_SOFTWARE'
Creating Foreign Keys on 'PERS_SOFTWARE'
SQL> ALTER TABLE PERS_SOFTWARE ADD CONSTRAINT
   2    PERS_SOFT_PERS__FK FOREIGN KEY
   3    (PERS__PERS_ID) REFERENCES PERSONALS
   4    (PERS_ID) ADD CONSTRAINT
   5   PERS_SOFT_SW_FK FOREIGN KEY
   6    (SW_SOFT_ID) REFERENCES SOFTWARES
   7    (SOFT_ID)
   8   /

Table altered.

SQL>
SQL> PROMPT Creating Foreign Keys on 'PERS_POSITIONS'
Creating Foreign Keys on 'PERS_POSITIONS'
SQL> ALTER TABLE PERS_POSITIONS ADD CONSTRAINT
   2    PERS_POS_PERS__FK FOREIGN KEY
   3    (PERS__PERS_ID) REFERENCES PERSONALS
   4    (PERS_ID) ADD CONSTRAINT
   5   PERS_POS_POS_FK FOREIGN KEY
   6    (POS_POS_ID) REFERENCES POSITIONS
   7    (POS_ID)
   8   /

Table altered.
```

```
SQL>
SQL> PROMPT Creating Foreign Keys on 'EMPLOYERS'
Creating Foreign Keys on 'EMPLOYERS'
SQL> ALTER TABLE EMPLOYERS ADD CONSTRAINT
  2   EMP__HW_FK FOREIGN KEY
  3    (HW_HARD_ID) REFERENCES HARDWARES
  4    (HARD_ID) ADD CONSTRAINT
  5   EMP__PERS_POS_FK FOREIGN KEY
  6    (PERS_POS_PERS_ID
  7    ,PERS_POS_POS_ID) REFERENCES PERS_POSITIONS
  8    (PERS_ID
  9    ,POS_ID)
 10   /

Table altered.

SQL>
SQL> PROMPT Creating Index 'PERS_HARD_HW_FK_I'
Creating Index 'PERS_HARD_HW_FK_I'
SQL> CREATE INDEX PERS_HARD_HW_FK_I ON PERS_HARDWARE
  2    (HW_HARD_ID)
  3   /

Index created.

SQL>
SQL> PROMPT Creating Index 'PERS_HARD_PERS__FK_I'
Creating Index 'PERS_HARD_PERS__FK_I'
SQL> CREATE INDEX PERS_HARD_PERS__FK_I ON PERS_HARDWARE
  2    (PERS__PERS_ID)
  3   /

Index created.

SQL>
SQL> PROMPT Creating Index 'REFERENCE_PERS__FK_I'
Creating Index 'REFERENCE_PERS__FK_I'
SQL> CREATE INDEX REFERENCE_PERS__FK_I ON REFERENCES
  2    (PERS__PERS_ID)
  3   /

Index created.

SQL>
SQL> PROMPT Creating Index 'PERS_SOFT_PERS__FK_I'
```

```
Creating Index 'PERS_SOFT_PERS__FK_I'
SQL> CREATE INDEX PERS_SOFT_PERS__FK_I ON PERS_SOFTWARE
  2   (PERS__PERS_ID)
  3   /

Index created.

SQL>
SQL> PROMPT Creating Index 'PERS_SOFT_SW_FK_I'
Creating Index 'PERS_SOFT_SW_FK_I'
SQL> CREATE INDEX PERS_SOFT_SW_FK_I ON PERS_SOFTWARE
  2   (SW_SOFT_ID)
  3   /

Index created.

SQL>
SQL> PROMPT Creating Index 'PERS_POS_PERS__FK_I'
Creating Index 'PERS_POS_PERS__FK_I'
SQL> CREATE INDEX PERS_POS_PERS__FK_I ON PERS_POSITIONS
  2   (PERS__PERS_ID)
  3   /

Index created.

SQL>
SQL> PROMPT Creating Index 'PERS_POS_POS_FK_I'
Creating Index 'PERS_POS_POS_FK_I'
SQL> CREATE INDEX PERS_POS_POS_FK_I ON PERS_POSITIONS
  2   (POS_POS_ID)
  3   /

Index created.

SQL>
SQL> PROMPT Creating Index 'EMP__HW_FK_I'
Creating Index 'EMP__HW_FK_I'
SQL> CREATE INDEX EMP__HW_FK_I ON EMPLOYERS
  2   (HW_HARD_ID)
  3   /

Index created.

SQL>
SQL> PROMPT Creating Index 'EMP__PERS_POS_FK_I'
Creating Index 'EMP__PERS_POS_FK_I'
```

A

SAMPLE PHYSICAL
DATABASE
IMPLEMENTATION

```
SQL> CREATE INDEX EMP__PERS_POS_FK_I ON EMPLOYERS
  2   (PERS_POS_PERS_ID
  3   ,PERS_POS_POS_ID)
  4  /
```

Index created.

This resume database will most likely be associated with other data, such as personnel data managed by the Human Resources department. Suppose that an HR database already exists. Until now, resumes were processed manually and stored in a file cabinet. If looking for certain skills to fill a position, one would have to review all resumes in the cabinet. With this database, a simple query will return specific individuals based on criteria. For example, you might query for all individuals who have technical management experience of more than three years. This database might be related to the HR database, in that employee records will be associated with resume records. Remember that all individuals who submit resumes are prospective employees.

Popular Database Design Tools

The following is a list of some popular automated design (AD) tools, arranged by product name, vendor, and Web site.

Product:	Oracle Designer and Developer
Vendor:	Oracle Corporation
Web Site:	www.oracle.com

Oracle Designer is currently the leading automated design tool available on the market. The Oracle Designer Repository records design versioning, ERDs, Process Models, and many other database design elements. Oracle Developer offers interface design tools such as forms and reports. Oracle Designer and Developer support RDBMS types other than Oracle.

Product:	Platinum Erwin
Vendor:	Computer Associates
Web Site:	www.cai.com/products/alm/ erwin.htm

Erwin is a transactional and data warehouse database design tool used for database generation and maintenance. It supports logical and physical database design and enterprise modeling.

Product:	EasyCASE
Vendor:	Aeronaut Industries
Web Site:	www.aeronaut.com.au

EasyCASE is a comprehensive AD tool supporting more than 12 CASE methodologies and 6 symbol sets to generate schema, data dictionaries, and reports for nearly all SQL platforms. Reverse-engineering of schema is also supported.

Product:	Starteam Enterprise Edition
Vendor:	StarBase Corporation
Web Site:	www.starbase.com

Starteam offers defect tracking, change management, version control, threaded conversation, Internet transparency, and repository access via a Web browser. Features include Task Management, MS Project Integration, and Repository Customization.

Product:	Data Junction
Vendor:	Data Junction Corporation
Web Site:	www.datajunction.com

Data Junction is a visual design tool for rapidly integrating and transforming data between hundreds of applications and structured data formats.

Database Design Checklists

IN THIS APPENDIX

This appendix was devised to provide you with a collection of checklists to use as a reference for relational database design. Each checklist is covered and explained throughout the book. This appendix can also serve as a refresher or study guide in addition to providing a reference.

Planning Database Design

Questions to help define database design objectives:

- What is the purpose of the database?
- Who will use the database?
- What type of database will this be?
- What model and methodologies will be used?
- Is this a new system?
- Will this system be modeled after a legacy system?
- Will the database need modified in the near future?
- Will there be multiple databases?
- What are the user expectations?
- What means will the customer use to access the database?

Database design work plan checklist:

- Define the location of the work to be done
- Establish a design team
- Define business rules
- Define hardware to be used
- Define software to be used
- Designate tools for development
- Designate tools for the end users
- Establish a backup plan for development work done
- Determine database environments used for development
- Determine basic standards and naming conventions
- Determine database environment for production
- Establish a change control system

Trademarks of a good database design:

- A functional database model is generated.
- The database accurately represents the business' data.

- The database will be easy to use and maintain.
- Good performance for the end users.
- Modifications are easily made to the structure.
- Data can be retrieved and modified easily.
- Down time because of bad design is kept to a minimum.
- Very little maintenance is needed.
- Data is kept safe by good security.
- Redundant data is minimized or non-existent.
- Data can be easily backed up or recovered.
- The actual structure of the database will be virtually transparent to the end user.

Gathering Information to Design the Database

Questions to help determine data structures:

- What type of data must be stored in the database?
- Is all data internal to this organization?
- What data is external to this organization?
- Who is the primary user of the data?
- Will there be different levels of users?
- How long must the data be kept?
- What methods will be used to retrieve and modify the data?
- What manual processes exist?
- What are the current responsibilities of the users?
- With whom do the users currently interact?
- What service or product is provided to the customer?

Questions to help determine business rules associated with data:

- Will the data be modified?
- How long will the data be stored before being archived or purged?
- What means will be used to modify the data?
- When must the data be modified?
- How can the data be modified?
- Why must the data not be modified by what users, and under what circumstances?
- Is data character, numeric, or date?

- Must this information be unique? If so, when?
- Does this data depend on the existence of other data?
- Is this data referenced by other data?

Sample management interview questions:

- From your perspective, what are the goals of the business?
- From your perspective, what are the goals of the proposed database?
- Why is the database important from your standpoint?
- How will the database affect management?
- How will the database affect the customer?
- What is the expected life of the database?
- Have upgrades been forecasted for the near future?
- How do different departments interact?
- How is data transmitted between departments?
- What are the different user groups of the database?
- What are management's expectations of the system?
- What promises have been made to the customer?
- What are the plans for user training?
- Are sufficient resources available for the database?
- When is the drop-dead date for the database?

Sample customer interview questions:

- What are the primary goals of your business?
- Who are your customers?
- What services or products do you provide?
- How do you interact with other individuals in the organization?
- From your perspective, what are the goals of the proposed database?
- What are the different activities that take place on a daily basis?
- Who performs these activities?
- How are these activities related to the data?
- Are activities manual or automated processes?
- Can processes be refined?
- What manual processes can be automated?

- What problems exist with current automated processes?
- What is the triggering event for each business process?
- What is the expected outcome of each business process?
- What is the data?
- How is the data used to support the business?
- Who uses the data?
- What business processes require what data?
- How long must the data be kept?
- When can data be purged or archived?
- How timely should archived data be accessible?
- How often will archived data be accessed?
- Is the data static, or will it change often?
- How will the data grow over a period of time?
- How do you expect data needs to change over a period of time?
- How much data do you have?
- From where does the data originate?
- Are there any existing data sources?
- Who should have access to the data?
- How is data currently protected?

Sample end-user interview questions:

- What is your primary job function?
- What else do you do?
- How do you do it?
- What tools are currently used to perform your job?
- Is a database currently used?
- What improvements could be made to the functions you perform?
- What improvements can be made to current tools or databases?
- How do you interact with other individuals in the organization?
- From your perspective, what are the goals of the business?
- From your perspective, what are the goals of the proposed database?
- What is the data?
- Who uses the data?

- Why is the data accessed?
- How is the data used?
- How often is the data accessed?
- When does the data change?
- What is the approximate growth rate of the data?

Checklist for evaluating existing business processes:

- Has a walk-through with the customer and end user been performed for each process?
- How are business transactions currently handled?
- What is the goal of each process?
- Are the goals currently being met?
- How will the goals change based on the need for a new database?
- What unnecessary process steps currently exist?
- Which process steps are mandatory for the framework of the new database?
- Do the processes defined imply the use of data that has not yet been defined?
- Can processes be streamlined so that users can make better use of their time?
- What processes can be automated that are not already?

Sample major milestones for a database design effort:

1. Design team is formed.
2. Project kick-off meeting is conducted.
3. Strategy plan is devised.
4. Interview plan is devised.
5. Interviews are conducted.
6. Lists of fields are established.
7. Initial ERD.
8. Process models, data flow models, function hierarchies.
9. User feedback session.
10. Detailed ERD.
11. User feedback session.
12. Cross check ERD with processes.
13. User feedback session.
14. Design physical model.

15. Normalize physical model.

16. Design views.

17. Generate database.

18. Test database with user application.

19. Production implementation.

Modeling Entity Relationships

Checklist for defining entity relationships:

1. Does a relationship exist?

2. If a relationship exists, identify a verb for each direction of the relationship.

3. Identify an optionality for each direction of the relationship.

4. Identify a degree for each direction of the relationship.

5. Validate the relationship by reading it.

Physical Design Considerations

Column definition checklist:

- What is the name of the column?
- What is the data type?
- Are NULL values allowed?
- What are the key values?
- Are there any applicable constraints?
- What are the allowed data values?
- Are duplicate values allowed?

Denormalization avoidance checklist:

- Did you design the database badly? Is the join you need between two tables going through four intermediate tables to get the connection? Perhaps an additional foreign key to create a direct connection between the two tables will solve the problem.

- Are the host hardware and OS set up optimally? Could you add RAM or processors to the host? Adding RAM to databases is the single most common solution to any performance problem. Databases love RAM.

- Could you add more or faster processors to the host? Parallel processing with multiple host processors can greatly speed performance, as well.

- Is your database operating on a host that is already overworked by other applications? Could you move elsewhere?

- Is the RDBMS set up optimally? Is there additional host RAM that could be allocated to the database? Is the RDBMS block size large enough?

- Can the application be tuned? Are there indexes on the columns being used for the joins or searches and is the RDBMS using them? Indexes greatly speed join performance.

- Is the network saturated or are there just too many router hops between the user and the host? Either improve the network, move the database to a host nearer the user, or rewrite the application to a thinner client with more processing happening on the server.

Security Considerations

Checklist of proactive measure to improve database security:

- Change administrator passwords regularly.
- Force users to change passwords frequently.
- Discourage the sharing of passwords.
- Remove inactive user accounts.
- Remove non-employee user accounts.
- Perform random monitoring of all activities.
- Perform database auditing.
- Educate the end user.
- Conduct brief security training sessions.

Checklist of security integration at various levels:

- Internet security (Web, WAN)
- Internal network security (intranet, LAN)
- Operating system security
- Database security
- Schema object security
- User application security
- PC security (Windows NT login)

Legacy Database Redesign Considerations

Checklist of hardware and software components to consider replacing or upgrading during legacy database redesign:

- Replace host server
- Replace end-user workstation
- Increase host server disk space for growing data
- Increase host server memory
- Increase number of CPUs on host server
- Upgrade network components
- Upgrade network cards in end-user workstations
- Upgrade operating system software
- Upgrade database software
- Upgrade database design tools
- Upgrade database administration software
- Upgrade application development software

Evaluating the Completeness of Stages in the Database Life Cycle

Checklist to prepare for database testing:

- Are all processes reflected in the application?
- Are all business entities accounted for in the database?
- Do all data units allow new records to be entered?
- Do all data units allow existing records to be modified?
- Do all data units allow existing records to be deleted?
- Do all data units allow existing records to be queried?
- Are all table relationships accurate?
- Has referential integrity been applied?
- Have obvious indexes been created?
- Have views been created where needed?
- Does the database need to be normalized?
- Have all errors been accounted for and corrected during object creation?

Sample test evaluation checklist/implementation preparation:

- How much time has been allocated to test the system?
- When is the system expected in production?
- Do any data relationships need to be modified?
- Are business rules being followed?
- How did the database application interface perform?
- Was the system tested with real data?
- Was the system tested with a realistic volume of data?
- Was data integrity compromised during testing?
- Were all changes tested thoroughly?
- Was the database queried after changes were made to data using the application interface? You should use a combination of the application and manual transactions and queries to ensure that the application is working properly.
- Have all requirements for the system been double-checked for completeness?

Sample production evaluation checklist:

- Were there any errors during implementation?
- Does the end user have any complaints?
- How does the system seem to perform?
- Does the perceived performance meet user expectations?
- Was all live data loaded or converted successfully?
- What is the average number of concurrent users?
- Are any areas for immediate improvement in database functionality or performance recognized?
- Has a backup plan been established?
- Has regular database maintenance been planned?
- Are any areas for immediate improvement in application functionality or performance recognized?

Sample Database Designs

IN THIS APPENDIX

This appendix supplies you with a variety of sample database designs in the form of entity relationship diagrams (ERDs) along with a brief description of each and its purpose.

> **NOTE**
>
> These are basic ERDs, showing only prospective entities and their relationships. Keep in mind that there might be different viewpoints on designing databases such as these. These samples exist for guidance and comparison purposes.

In the sample designs that follow, business processes are used to justify the design of each model. These processes must be understood in order to better design the database. A database exists because of the need to not only store the data, but also to access and use the data, which is accomplished through processes. We have not included every possible process in the description of the models. These processes help to understand the relationships between entities shown in the ERDs. When studying these samples, consider the explanations of the major processes, and pay attention to the relationships between entities. How can these relationship differ based on business processes and rules? Can any entities be added to make each model complete? These are the questions that can be raised to increase your understanding of database design.

ERDs are included for the following types of situations:

- BILLING
- CLASS SCHEDULING
- CLIENT CONTACTS
- GROCERY STORE MANAGEMENT
- HUMAN RESOURCES
- PRODUCT INVENTORY
- PRODUCT ORDERS
- RESUME MANAGEMENT
- SYSTEM MANAGEMENT
- USER MANAGEMENT

BILLING

Figure D.1 illustrates the BILLING ERD.

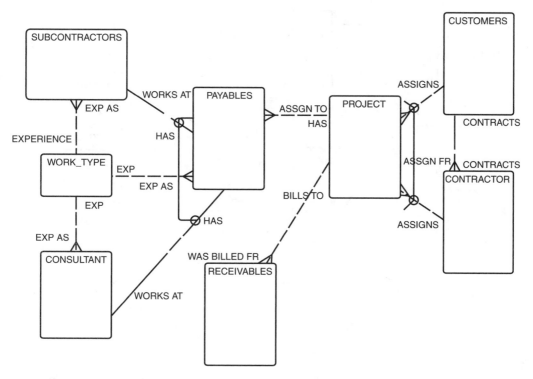

This diagram shows billing a client for services performed. An entry into PROJECT represents the work to be performed. The contractor works on all or part of this project, and is entered in CONTRACTOR. This breaks the project down into parts entered into SUBCONTRACTORS with a pairing of the project and the contractor.

Different types of work required by the project are listed in WORK_TYPE. The rate of compensation is based on work type as well as who the subcontractor is. Both of these are entered in the WORK_TYPE table.

CLASS SCHEDULING

Figure D.2 illustrates the CLASS SCHEDULING ERD.

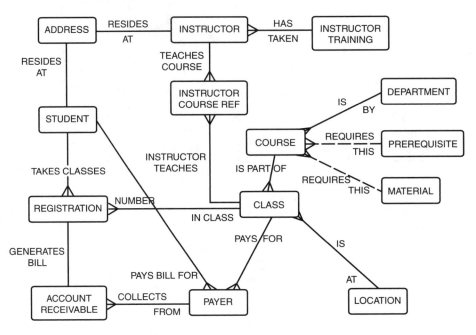

FIGURE D.2
CLASS SCHEDULING ERD.

This diagram shows each part of the class registration process. Class scheduling requires matching the course, student, instructor, and location with each other. (There are entities for each one). The student selects the class, provided a room is available, and then pays for it. A student can register for many courses, which can be offered and taught many times by many different instructors. Both the student and instructor have addresses entered into ADDRESS.

The course must exist and have a place in a degree program or be an approved elective. The course is matched to an entry in DEPARTMENT. A specific location must exist in order for the class to be taught. Class locations are associated with classes based on location availability. When both the course and the location are matched, an entry is generated in CLASS. A location can host many different classes taught at different times.

An instructor must be available by not being previously assigned in that time slot, although an instructor is capable of teaching multiple classes, just not simultaneously. This would be shown in INSTRUCTOR_COURSE_REF. The instructor also needs to meet the standards in INSTRUCTOR TRAINING.

Sample Database Designs

APPENDIX D

479

D

SAMPLE
DATABASE
DESIGNS

For the student to register, there must be enough seats filled to enable the class to be held but fewer seats filled than the class limit. This would allow the student to be entered in REGISTRATION. The student also needs to have taken any course listed in PREREQUISITE, and be willing to purchase course materials listed in MATERIAL.

A sponsor (or student) pays for the class by grants or loans. This is entered into PAYER, and the transaction is entered into ACCOUNT_RECEIVABLE upon completion.

CLIENT CONTACTS

Figure D.3 illustrates the CLIENT CONTACTS ERD.

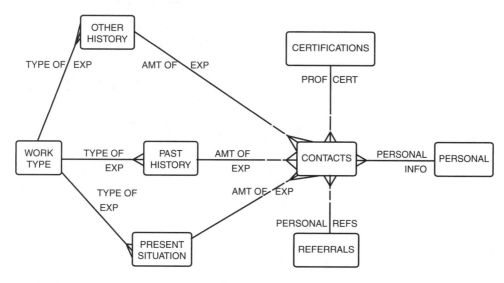

FIGURE D.3
CLIENT CONTACTS ERD.

This diagram categorizes clients and their work type in order to efficiently match them with this company's employees or subcontractors. A client might be a source of revenue for the company, provided the client is now contracting, has a stable financial status, and if contracting with this client would provide a solid reference to give to other clients. The three history entities provide this information.

The OTHER_HISTORY entity lists projects the client has had outside of contracting with this company. These would show competence and trustworthiness in a particular field. In PAST_HISTORY, an entry shows a client's past experience with this company. PRESENT_HISTORY shows work in progress or projected to be started. All history entities can be compared because they reference common work types as shown in WORK_TYPES.

CERTIFICATIONS can show what type of work a client might be able to furnish this company in the future. A client might have knowledge of other clients and might be a good reference in dealing with the others. This information would be provided in REFERRALS. All of the schema's information is brought together as an entry in CONTACTS.

GROCERY STORE MANAGEMENT

Figure D.4 illustrates the GROCERY STORE MANAGEMENT ERD.

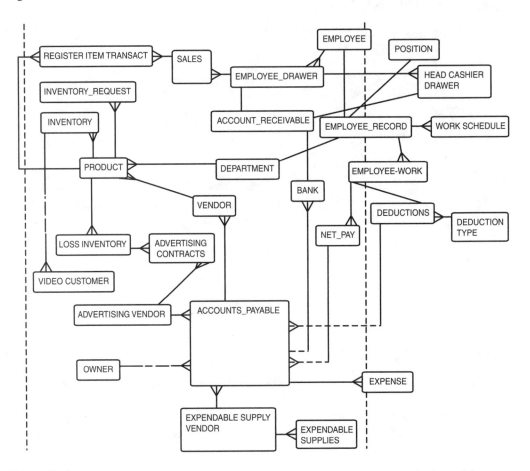

FIGURE D.4
GROCERY STORE MANAGEMENT ERD.

Each product is entered into PRODUCT and listed as coming from a vendor in VENDOR. There is a entity that reflects how much product is on hand (INVENTORY) and another (INVENTORY_REQUEST) that shows how much product has been ordered.

EMPLOYEE lists employees along with contact information. Each employee holds down a position that is specified in POSITION, with a department that is specified in DEPARTMENT. EMPLOYEE_RECORD has this and other information showing company position and pay rate. This information is referred to in EMPLOYEE_WORK along with the history of how much an employee worked. This information generates a request for pay and is listed in ACCOUNT PAYABLE.

At the cash register, each product is listed as having being sold in REGISTER_ITEM_ TRANSACT. The product is later deducted from INVENTORY and/or requested by manual procedure. The total amount an individual purchased is listed in SALES. Each employee is accountable for a drawer at the cash register at any point in time. This information is entered or referred to in EMPLOYEE_DRAWER. When the employee reconciles a drawer, that amount is entered in ACCOUNT_RECEIVABLE.

BANK lists funds received from the owner or from cash register receipts listed in ACCOUNT_ RECEIVABLE. BANK also lists requests for payment from VENDOR, EXPENSE, EMPLOYEE, or OWNER (as profit). These requests come through ACCOUNT_PAYABLE. Individual entries are received and then later updated as they are paid in BANK.

HUMAN RESOURCES

Figure D.5 illustrates the HUMAN RESOURCES ERD.

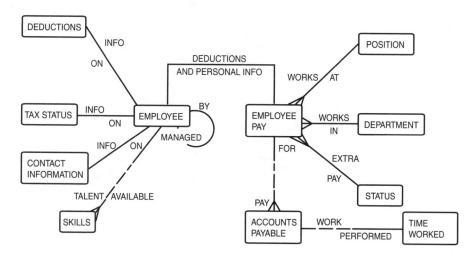

FIGURE D.5
HUMAN RESOURCES ERD.

This diagram tracks how employees are paid, their positions in the company, and the skills in their fields. The employee is an unique individual with many possible skills; these are listed in SKILLS. Payroll deductions for every employee are shown in DEDUCTIONS. Personal contacts such as addresses and phone numbers are given in CONTACT_INFORMATION. There is also TAX STATUS, which lists the number of deductions.

The employees work in a position given in DEPARTMENT. This table provides information about base pay rates, whom the employer manages, and who is managed by the employee. STATUS could show a different management setup, whether the employee is available for work, and other things such as the level of experience.

Everything needed to determine the employee rate of pay can be determined by EMPLOYEE_PAY or the entities that it refers to. The employee's recent work history is shown in TIME_WORKED. Both of these tables provide adequate information for an entry into ACCOUNTS_PAYABLE to enable the employee to receive pay.

PRODUCT INVENTORY

Figure D.6 illustrates the PRODUCT INVENTORY ERD.

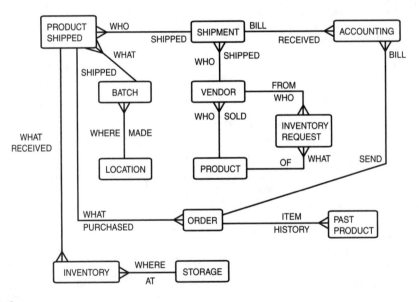

FIGURE D.6
PRODUCT INVENTORY ERD.

Sample Database Designs

APPENDIX D

483

D

SAMPLE
DATABASE
DESIGNS

Vendors are listed in VENDOR as well as the products they sell which are referenced from PRODUCT. Products requested but not yet shipped are listed in INVENTORY_REQUEST. Any shipment comes from just one vendor as listed in SHIPMENT. Shipments are billed as is listed in ACCOUNTING.

PRODUCT SHIPPED matches the shipment number with one of the product batches that was shipped to form a one-line entry. A product is made in a batch as stated in BATCH. The batch is made at a specific location as stated LOCATION.

INVENTORY records the product shipped as well as where the product is now stored as stated in STORAGE. When a product is ordered, the product shipped number, which can refer to the batch number, is recorded in ORDER. The order amount and price determined from the PRODUCT_SHIPPED table then composes a price, which is recorded in ACCOUNTING. Listing past products in PAST_PRODUCT allows product and customer research.

PRODUCT ORDERS

Figure D.7 illustrates the PRODUCT ORDERS ERD.

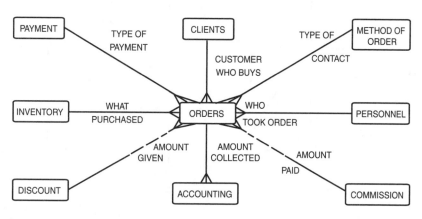

FIGURE D.7
PRODUCT ORDERS ERD.

The diagram illustrates taking customer orders. An order is placed by a client by phone call, letter, fax, or email. This is the entry's METHOD_OF_ORDER. One order taker is responsible for accepting the order and is found in PERSONNEL. Only one client is recorded per order and is listed in CLIENTS. Only one payment type is also recorded per order and is listed in PAYMENT. (This could be check, VISA, MasterCard, and so on.)

Possibly the order is recorded as being eligible for a commission in COMMISSION. If the order qualified for a discount, that fact is entered in DISCOUNT.

According to the order, the level of product is reduced in INVENTORY. The actual order itself is entered into ORDERS. When the proper information is compiled, it is then sent to accounting for the proper billing or handling, and is entered into ACCOUNTING.

RESUME MANAGEMENT

Figure D.8 illustrates the RESUME MANAGEMENT ERD.

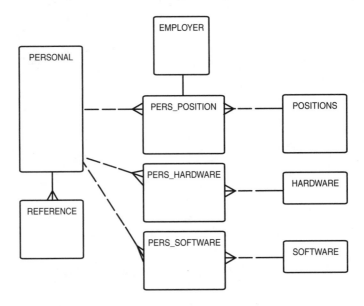

FIGURE D.8
RESUME MANAGEMENT ERD.

This diagram categorizes the information found on a resume in order to match a qualified candidate with a job. Every applicant supplies personal information, such as contact information. This is entered into PERSONAL. Any references listed for an individual would be entered into REFERENCE.

Matching up applicants with jobs can be most efficiently done by quantifying the applicants' experience. Both Software and Hardware are specifically defined attributes and can be entered into tables for reference. An applicant might be associated with particular positions, hardware platforms, and software through the following cross-reference entities: PERS_POSITION, PERS_HARDWARE, and PERS_SOFTWARE. Where possible, positions held also might be

Sample Database Designs

APPENDIX D

485

D

SAMPLE
DATABASE
DESIGNS

quantifiable and known to the employer as well as the applicant. This would define an entry in POSITIONS. An applicant is associated with a previous employer through a previously held position. Individual qualifications can now be measured by any combination of the following: position held, hardware experience, and software experience.

SYSTEM MANAGEMENT

Figure D.9 illustrates the SYSTEM MANAGEMENT ERD.

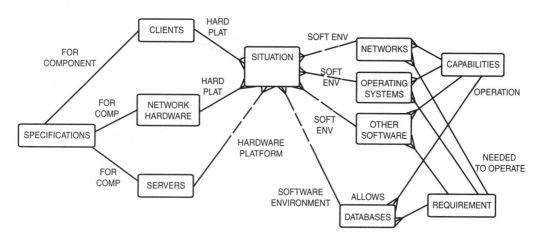

FIGURE D.9
SYSTEM MANAGEMENT ERD.

This diagram helps match software with hardware, both for use today and to help plan for future purchases. (This information could also help schedule computer training.) System management involves keeping track of four types of software items—networks, operating systems, software (programming languages), and databases. System managers must also deal with three categories of hardware: client machines (PCs), server computers, and network hardware. All these types have tables for entries.

The characteristics of each type of hardware will be listed in SPECIFICATIONS. The software needs for both hardware capacity and software compatibility will be listed in REQUIREMENT. Also, what the software offers both in software compatibility and application capability will be entered in CAPABILITIES.

The real world setup for each client machine (more than one is possible) will be given in SITUATION. This portrays an actual software usage of the system resources to accomplish a given task by the computer user.

USER MANAGEMENT

Figure D.10 illustrates the USER MANAGEMENT ERD.

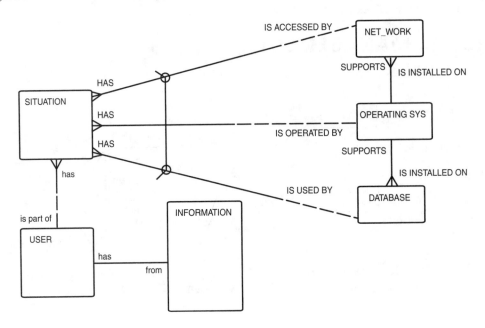

FIGURE D.10

USER MANAGEMENT ERD.

Relational database management systems do not typically come installed with software to manage user accounts. An organization's system environment might consist of multiple servers on a network, providing residence to many databases. As the number of database environments and user accounts increase, user access might be very difficult to manage. For example, if a user leaves the organization, the user's account should be removed from all databases and systems. This sample USER MANAGEMENT ERD can manage this.

USER identifies the user account, which should match with the network, operating system, or database account appropriately. Every user might have different levels of access. Each instance of access is entered into SITUATION. A user could have many different accounts on many platforms over a period of time.

Sample Table Sizing Worksheet

Table sizing is integral to the implementation of a database to optimize storage allocation and usage, as well as database performance. Table E.1 provides a generic guide for estimating the size of tables. A worksheet such as Table E.1 is most effectively implemented as a spreadsheet, or even a database table.

TABLE E.1 Sample Table Sizing Worksheet

Table Name	Max Row Length	Avg Row Length	Est # Rows	Est Size (Bytes)	Size in Megabytes
EMP	100	UNKNOWN	100	10,000	0.010
PROD	100	85	100	8,500	0.008
CUST	137	121	9,562	1157002	1.103
ORDERS	45	37	4500000	166500000	158.787
TOTAL					159.908

The maximum row length can be figured by adding the maximum size of all columns that comprise a row of data in the table. Estimate each stored character as one byte. The average row length is an estimate, based on existing data. If a legacy system does not exist, it may be difficult to estimate the average row length. Once again, the estimated number of rows relies on knowledge of the data. If a legacy database exists, it will be very easy to estimate the number of rows stored in each table. The estimated number of rows should include present data, as well as near-future data (allowance for growth). Multiply either the maximum or average row length by the number of estimated rows for an estimated byte size for the table.

Bytes can by converted as shown in Table E.2. There are 8 bits in a byte, 1024 bytes in a kilobyte, 1024 kilobytes in a megabyte, and so on.

TABLE E.2 Conversion of Bytes

Bytes	To Kilobytes	To Megabytes	To Gigabytes
Value *n*	/ 1024	/ 1024	/ 1024

Although there are many different RDBMS versions, there are common principles and practices that can be applied to calculating storage for tables and indexes. In addition to the actual data stored in a table, there is row overhead for every RDBMS and overhead in the allocation of data pages that varies from system to system. Refer to the storage documentation for the RDBMS implemented at your location to further customize the sizing worksheet provided here. Most vendors provide a row calculation formula to accurately estimate space usage. If a row calculation formula is not provided, row overhead can be derived from the vendor documentation and plugged into the basic equation that we have provided.

In addition to estimating sizes for tables, index sizing is also a significant factor, since index data sometimes consumes nearly as much space as table data. Properly estimating the sizes of table and indexes reduces fragmentation and leads to improved database performance. Proper sizing also eases the task of managing space allocation.

Indexes should only be created on tables when needed to optimize performance. As a generality, OLTP implementations should have as few indexes as possible while still providing needed performance. The reason for this is that more write operations are occurring to the database. Every time data is modified, the index on the data must also be modified. If an index does not exist, the write operation to change the data can occur faster than if an index exists. In production, for example, one user update to one table with three indexes will result in at least four physical writes; one write for the table, and one for each index on the table. Heavy online entry systems pay a heavy price for every index. Conversely, OLAP databases will have many indexes based on the analysis needs of the end user. The purpose of an OLAP database is to return data to the end user as fast as possible based on queries submitted. Write operations rarely occur in OLAP databases, therefore the overhead of maintaining indexes on tables is minimized.

Operating systems and platforms have numerous file system approaches to physically storing data. Some approaches ease administration, and others increase proficiency.

Glossary

This glossary covers most of the common terms and concepts that are important to understand the task of database design, implementation, and management. All the terms found here are covered in detail throughout the book.

ANSI—American National Standards Institute. An organization that provides standards for various industries, such as that of the computer and relational databases.

Atomic Value—a value that occurs only one time per row in a table.

Attribute—The smallest structure in an RDBMS. The data stored represents a characteristic of the subject of the table. An attribute is also known as a *field*.

Boolean Value—A value consisting of one of the following values: TRUE, FALSE, or NULL. Boolean values are typically used as switches, and are common in database programs.

Boyce-Codd NORMAL FORM —In effect when an entity is in THIRD NORMAL FORM, and when every attribute or combination of attributes (a determinant) upon which another attribute is functionally dependent is a candidate key (that is, unique).

BPR—Business process re-engineering, also known as BPR, is the process of revising existing business processes and data model features in order to improve the daily operations of a business through the use of the current information system.

Business Function—A process or related block of work that a business needs to accomplish in the course of meeting its business goals. Functions can be studied and manipulated to support different and better ways to accomplish these tasks.

Business Modeling—Deals with capturing the needs of a business from a business perspective.

Business Process—Deals with the daily activities that take place in a commercial venture.

Business Process Re-engineering—The task of redesigning an existing system in order to improve business processes and methods for storing and accessing the data.

Business Requirement—A mandate for how the business should operate in order to function on a daily basis.

Business Rule—Places restrictions and limitations on a database, based on how the company uses the data.

Business System Life Cycle—Seven stages that make up the development of a business system. The stages are strategy, analysis, design, build, documentation, transition, and production. Also known as the *development life cycle*.

Cardinality—Refers to the multiplicity of possible relationships between entities, such as one-to-one, one-to-many, and many-to-many. For instance, an instance in one entity may have multiple matching instances in a second entity.

Cartesian Product—The resultset of a multi-table query with no join operation, matching every row in the first table with every row in the second table. Shows all possible combinations of data between tables, and should be avoided in most cases.

CASE—Computer Aided Systems Engineering. Usually a combination of software tools used to assist developers in developing and maintaining systems for the end user.

Catalog—Usually refers to the database objects to which a user has access.

Change Control—A mechanism for achieving a smooth transition between software versions and is essential to avoid disrupting the work of users. Change control is this method.

Client/Server—Involves a main computer, called a *server*, and one or more personal computers (*clients*) that are networked to the server.

Column—Also known as a *field*, it is a subdivision of a table. Assigned a specific data type.

Composite or Concatenated Key—The combination of two or more column values used to define a key in a table.

Constraint—Rules or restrictions to control data integrity.

Cursor—A pointer to a row in a table. Created automatically by the RDBMS when SQL commands are issued to access data.

Data Dictionary—Also called system catalog. Stores metadata about the database such as users, objects, space allocation and consumption, and privileges.

Data Integrity—The assurance of accurate data in the database.

Data Integrity—Includes the maintenance of accurate, valid, and consist data, and is a major concern for the design of any database.

Data Modeling—The process of visually representing data for a business, and then eventually converting the business model into a data model.

Data Type—Defines the particular type of data that is stored. Common data types are number, varchar2, and date.

Database—A collection of either files or tables owned by a database management system.

Dataflow—A named flow of data among datastores, functions, and any external entities.

DBMS—Database Management System. A software product that allows the storage and access of data.

Denormalization—The process of taking a normalized database and modifying table structures to allow controlled redundancy for increased database performance.

DFD—Data Flow Diagram. Shows processes and data flows like the process modeler, but it also assigns an ID number to each process.

Domain—A set of business data validation rules, data range limits, and data type and data format standards that will be applied to attributes of common types.

Entities—Classes of things of importance about which data must be stored or manipulated in the course of business processes. Entities are the nouns of your information system and represent one occurrence of an object. An entity can have only one value for any attribute at any one time. See **Subtype Entity** and **Super-type Entity.**

Equi Join—The type of join operation that merges data from two tables based on equality of compared key values.

ERD—Entity Relationship Diagram. A tool used in the Analysis phase of development to model the initial design of your data structures in an unconstrained, logical environment.

ERD Process—Models logical data structures during the Analysis phase of system development.

FHD—Functional Hierarchy Diagram. Best for displaying the process hierarchy. An FHD can show processes in various levels of decomposition (parent and child processes) depending on the point of interest at the time.

Field—See **Column.**

Firewall—A combination of hardware and software intended to keep hackers out of your network while letting in those who are allowed access.

Flat-File Database—A database comprised of readable text files. It stores records as lines in a file with columns that are fixed length or separated by some delimiter.

Foreign Key—The combination of one or more column values in a table that references a primary key in another table. In other words, a child key that references a parent key.

GUI—Graphical User Interface. A presentable, visual display that allows the use of the keyboard and the mouse. An example is a user input form.

Hierarchical Database—Its structure uses a single table as the root of an inverted tree. The other tables act as branches going down from the root table.

Index—An object in a relational database that is used to increase performance of data retrieval. An index can also be used to enforce uniqueness of values.

Inner Join—Tests for equality between key values in two tables. See **Equi Join.**

ISO—International Standards Organization. Works in conjunction with ANSI to provide standards for various industries, such as the SQL3 (SQL-99) standard for relational databases.

Join—A method of combining two or more tables, and in some cases a table with itself, to retrieve necessary data.

Legacy Database—A database that is currently in use by a company.

Locks—Mechanisms used to restrict user access to a row of data while that same row is being modified by another user, to maintain consistency.

Logical Database—Related data that is stored in one or more schemas.

Logical Modeling—Deals with gathering business requirements and converting those requirements into a model.

Mainframe—A large central server that can be accessed directly or over a network with "dumb terminals" (a monitor and keyboard).

Metadata—Data about other data.

Mission Objective—Lists the tasks that will be performed against the data in a database.

Mission Statement—A summation of the overall purpose of a proposed database system.

Network—A connection between computers in order to exchange information or data.

Network Database—Structured as an inverted tree. Several inverted trees can share branches and still be considered in the same database structure. Tables in a network database are related by one table as an owner and the other table(s) as members.

NORMAL FORM—A degree of Normalization, such as FIRST NORMAL FORM, SECOND NORMAL FORM, and THIRD NORMAL FORM. The THIRD NORMAL FORM is typically the highest degree of normalization applied in real-world production environments. However, additional NORMAL FORMS such as Boyce-Codd, FOURTH, and FIFTH exist—these forms are used more in theory, but not realistically practiced.

Normalization—The process of reducing the redundancy of data in a relational database.

Not NULL—A form of constraint on a column in a table. If a column is labeled as Not NULL, the column must contain data.

NULL—A form of constraint on a column in a table. If a column is labeled as NULL, the column might or might not contain data.

Object—In an RDBMS, also known as an *element*, and is used to represent or access data. Common types of objects are tables and indexes.

Object-Oriented Database (OO)—Based on object-oriented analysis and design. An OO database combines database capabilities with an OO programming language, such as Java or C++. Object orientation views programming and database elements as objects with properties that can be distributed to or inherited from other objects.

Object-Relational Database (OR)—Supports not only the RDBMS features, but also object-oriented features such as inheritance and encapsulation.

ODBC—Open Database Connectivity. Driver that allows the connection of a client to a remote relational database.

Optionality—Either "must be" or "may be." Optionality is used to specify whether a relationship between two or more entities is optional or required.

Outer Join—Shows all data from the first table even if a matching key value does not exist in the second table.

Physical Database—Consists of the data files.

Physical Modeling—Involves the actual design of a database according to the requirements that were established during logical modeling.

Primary Key—Combination of one or more column values in a table that make a row of data unique within the table.

Procedure—An object that allows an operation to be performed against one or more database tables.

Privilege—Can be a system-level or object-level permission to perform a specific action in the database.

Query—A database request, written in SQL, for data that meets given criteria.

RAID—Redundant Arrays of Inexpensive Disks. The use of multiple storage devices to stripe data to increase performance, and to store redundant data in case of hardware failure.

RDBMS—Relational Database Management System. A program used to store and retrieve data that is organized into tables.

Record—A set of fields in a table. It is also known as a *row*.

Record Type—A predetermined set of fields within a file.

Redundant Data—Refers to the same data that is stored in more than one location in the database.

Referential Integrity—Guarantees that values of one column will depend on the values from another column. Enforcement is through integrity constraints.

Relation—A table. See **Table.**

Relationship—A two-directional connection between two entities. In some cases, an entity will have a relationship with itself. This is called a recursive relationship.

Requirements Analysis—The process of analyzing the needs of a business and gathering system requirements from the end user, which will eventually become the building blocks for the new database.

Requirements Gathering—The process of conducting meetings and/or interviews with customers, end users, and other individuals in the company to establish the requirements for the proposed system.

Role—A privilege or a set of privileges that can be granted to users of a database. Roles provide security by restricting what actions users can perform in a database.

Row—A primary key value and columnar data associated with a particular instance of a table.

Schema—An owner of objects in a relational database.

Security Table—Stores user data such as name, phone number, systems assigned to, and so forth.

Self Join—A join that merges data from a table with data in the same table, based on columns in a table that are related to one another.

SQL—Structured Query Language. The standard language of relational databases.

Subset Table—Contain columns that describe specific versions of the subject in the main table. Columns that would represent the same characteristics in the subset table as in the main table should only be in the main table.

Sub-type Entity—An entity that has common attributes and relationships. A sub-type entity can have lower levels.

Super-type Entity—An entity that has a sub-type entity.

Table—A grouping of columns of data that pertains to a single, particular class of people, things, events, or ideas in an enterprise, about which information needs to be stored or calculations made.

TCP/IP—The standard data communication protocol for the Web.

Trigger—A stored procedure that is associated with a specific table and will automatically fire or execute when a specified event occurs such as a delete, update, or insert.

Tuple—A record. See **Record.**

Validation Table—Stores data used to validate values that end users enter into a data table for data integrity. The data in the validation table rarely changes.

View—A virtual table that takes no physical storage space in the database. A view is accessed as if it were a table.

INDEX

SYMBOLS

K-L-M

Other Titles

Software Testing
Ron Patton
ISBN: 0-672-31983-7
$39.99 US/$59.95 CAN

Foundations of Service Level Management
Rick Strumm, Wayne Morris, and Mary Jander
ISBN: 0-672-31743-5
$12.95 US/$18.95 CAN

Writing Stored Procedures for Microsoft SQL Server
Matthew Shepker
ISBN: 0-672-31886-5
$39.99 US/$59.95 CAN

Applied XML Solutions
Benoit Marchal
ISBN: 0-672-32054-1
$44.99 US/$67.95 CAN

Integration Models: Templates for Business Transformation
Laura Brown
ISBN: 0-672-32055-X
$49.99 US/$74.95 CAN

Realizing e-Business with Application Service Providers
Louis Columbus
ISBN: 0-672-32053-3
$44.99 US/$67.95 CAN

Sams Teach Yourself UML in 24 Hours
Joseph Schmuller
ISBN: 0-672-31636-6
$24.99 US/$37.95 CAN

Sams Teach Yourself Data Structures and Algorithms in 24 Hours
Robert LaFore
ISBN: 0-672-31633-1
$24.99 US/$37.95 CAN

Sams Teach Yourself SQL in 21 Days, Third Edition
Ryan Stephens
ISBN: 0-672-31674-9
$34.99 US/$52.95 CAN

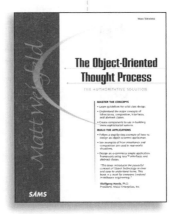

The Object-Oriented Thought Process
Matt Weisfeld
ISBN: 0-672-31853-9
$29.99 US/$44.95 CAN

SAMS

www.samspublishing.com

All prices are subject to change.

Solutions from experts you know and trust.

Home | Articles | Free Library | eBooks | Books | Expert Q & A | Training | Career Center | Downloads | MyInformIT
Login | Register | About InformIT

Topics
Operating Systems
Web Development
Programming
Networking
Certification
and more...

Expert
Access

Free
Content

www.informit.com

✓ Free, in-depth articles and supplements

✓ Master the skills you need, when you need them

✓ Choose from industry leading books, ebooks, and training products

✓ Get answers when you need them - from live experts or InformIT's comprehensive library

✓ Achieve industry certification and advance your career

Visit *InformIT* today
and get great content
from **SAMS**

Sams and InformIT are trademarks of Pearson plc / Copyright © 2000 Pearson